The Management of Intellectual Property

NEW HORIZONS IN INTELLECTUAL PROPERTY

Series Editors: Christine Greenhalgh, Robert Pitkethly and Michael Spence, *Senior Research Associates, Oxford Intellectual Property Research Centre, St Peter's College, Oxford, UK*

In an increasingly virtual world, where information is more freely accessible, protection of intellectual property rights is facing a new set of challenges and raising new issues. This exciting new series is designed to provide a unique interdisciplinary forum for high quality works of scholarship on all aspects of intellectual property, drawing from the fields of economics, management and law.

The focus of the series is on the development of original thinking in intellectual property, with topics ranging from copyright to patents, from trademarks to confidentiality and from trade-related intellectual property agreements to competition policy and antitrust. Innovative theoretical and empirical work will be encouraged from both established authors and the new generation of scholars.

Titles in this series include:

The Management of Intellectual Property

Edited by

Derek Bosworth

Emeritus Professor, University of Manchester and Senior Research Associate, Oxford Intellectual Property Research Centre, St Peter's College, Oxford, UK

Elizabeth Webster

Principal Research Fellow, Intellectual Property Research Institute of Australia and Melbourne Institute of Applied Economic and Social Research, University of Melbourne, Australia

NEW HORIZONS IN INTELLECTUAL PROPERTY

Edward Elgar

Cheltenham, UK • Northampton, MA, USA

Published by
Edward Elgar Publishing Limited
Glensanda House
Montpellier Parade
Cheltenham
Glos GL50 1UA
UK

Edward Elgar Publishing, Inc.
136 West Street
Suite 202
Northampton
Massachusetts 01060
USA

A catalogue record for this book
is available from the British Library

ISBN-13:   978 1 84542 112 0
ISBN-10:   1 84542 112 4

Printed and bound in Great Britain by MPG Books Ltd, Bodmin, Cornwall

Contents

Contributors

Derek Bosworth Emeritus Professor, University of Manchester and Senior Research Associate, Oxford Intellectual Property Research Centre, St Peter's College, Oxford, UK.

Andrew F. Christie Davies Collison Cave Professor of Intellectual Property, Faculty of Law, University of Melbourne and Director, Intellectual Property Research Institute of Australia, University of Melbourne.

Dirk Czarnitzki KU Leuven and ZEW Mannheim, Department of Applied Economics and Steunpunt O&O Statistieken.

Christine Greenhalgh Oxford Intellectual Property Research Centre, St Peter's College, Oxford University.

William Griffiths Department of Economics, Melbourne University.

Bronwyn H. Hall Professor of the Graduate School, University of California, Berkeley and Professor of Technology and the Economy, University of Maastricht.

Laurie Hunter Emeritus Professor, School of Business and Management, University of Glasgow.

Eric J. Iversen NIFU STEP Norwegian Institute for Studies in Innovation, Research and Education and the Australian Innovation Research Centre (AIRC), Faculty of Business, University of Tasmania.

Paul H. Jensen Intellectual Property Research Institute of Australia and the Melbourne Institute of Applied Economic and Social Research, University of Melbourne.

Aris Kaloudis NIFU STEP Norwegian Institute for Studies in Innovation, Research and Education.

Raffaele Oriani Department of Management, University of Bologna.

Alfons Palangkaraya Intellectual Property Research Institute of Australia and the Melbourne Institute of Applied Economic and Social Research, University of Melbourne.

Carine Peeters Belgian American Educational Foundation Fellow Researcher, Visiting Scholar at the Fuqua School of Business, Duke University and Visiting Professor, Solvay Business School.

Robert Pitkethly Said Business School and Oxford Intellectual Property Research Centre, Oxford University.

Markus Reitzig Associate Professor for Intellectual Property Strategy, Department of Industrial Economics and Strategy, The Copenhagen Business School, Denmark.

Mark Rogers Oxford Intellectual Property Research Centre, Harris Manchester College, Oxford University.

Bruno van Pottelsberghe de la Potterie Chief Economist of the European Patent Office and Associate Professor, Solvay Business School, Universite Libre de Bruxelles, Solvay SA Chair of Innovation.

Elizabeth Webster Intellectual Property Research Institute of Australia and the Melbourne Institute of Applied Economic and Social Research, University of Melbourne.

Anne Wyatt School of Commerce, University of Adelaide and Department of Accounting and Business Information Systems, University of Melbourne.

PART I

Introduction

1. The management of intellectual property: introduction

Derek Bosworth

1 IMPORTANCE OF IP AND IPRS

The present book brings together 15 chapters by economists, managerial scientists, accountants and lawyers on different dimensions of the management of intellectual property (IP) and, by implication, intellectual property rights (IPRs). Management could, in principle, imply management by government as well as by companies. In practice, the focus of the present contributions is on private sector issues such as the private costs and benefits of alternative strategies, rather than on how the government or international bodies manage (or should manage) IPRs. Almost without exception, the discussion considers company and organizational issues within the context of the existing IPR framework. Thus, the optimal design of the framework of IP laws lies well outside the bounds of the present book.

In principle, IP covers the creative activities of literary, artistic and scientific works; performances of performing artists, phonograms and broadcasts; inventions in all fields of human endeavour; scientific discoveries; industrial designs; trademarks, service marks, and commercial names and designations; protection against unfair competition; and all other rights resulting from intellectual activity in the industrial, scientific, literary or artistic fields (WIPO, 1967, Article 2(viii)).

The present book, in principle at least, has a somewhat broader focus than some of the earlier attempts to explore the management of IP, which have tended to focus on patents and patent-related IPRs (for example, Granstrand, 1999). Patenting remains an important dimension of the present discussion, but there is some coverage of the trade and service marks, as well as an attempt to place them in the broader context of other forms of IP and IPRs. The discussion in this chapter does not dwell on the different forms of IPRs; these are made clear in Chapter 2 (although not every form of IPR is considered) as well as when they are discussed in various other chapters (for example, Chapter 7). In addition, the present discussion does not outline the distinction between IP, intellectual capital (IC) or intangible assets (IAs), but detailed consideration is given to the differences between them in Chapters 3 to 5.

2 THE CHANGING ECONOMIC LANDSCAPE

The world in which firms operate today is very different to that of the past. While IP and, more broadly, intangible assets have always been important to firms, there is no doubt that the shift towards a knowledge-based economy has given them even greater prominence as a focus for company behaviour and decision-making. This can be illustrated by the growing importance of investment in computers and software vis-à-vis the net capital stock in Australia. The growth in the net information technology (IT) capital stock relative to the overall net capital stock was 4.4 per cent per annum, while the corresponding relative growth in the net stock of software was 6.4 per cent per annum over the period 1991 to 2002 (Figure 1.1). More broadly, Webster (1999, p. 58) shows that the ratio of intangible to tangible capital among Australian publicly listed companies approximately doubled over the period 1947 to 1997 (from about 15 to 30 per cent).

By 1997 over half of the value added of the UK was attributed to knowledge-based services and industries (DTI 2001, p. 78). In Germany the

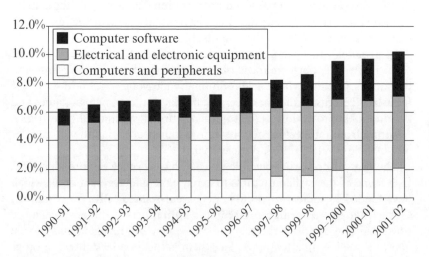

Source: ABS (2004) Cat. No. 5204.0, tables 98 and 86.

Figure 1.1   Share of selected equipment in the net capital stock, Australia, 1991–2002, per cent

figure was closer to 60 per cent. By late 2004, statistics show that about 11.25 per cent of private sector business investment was on computer software and hardware – about 4.5 per cent on software and 6.75 per cent on hardware. The results of a number of mainly US studies show how such investments have impacted on company organization and performance (see Chapter 5 in this volume; Bosworth, 2005). Estimates of intangibles for particular companies, such as Gillette and Coca-Cola, suggest that they represent significantly higher values than the tangible assets and, even though the ratio of intangible to tangible assets is lower in Proctor and Gamble and Pepsicola, it is still high (Buchan and Davies 1997, p. 116). In the mid-1990s GrandMet (now Diageo) reported their brand value to be £3.8 billion compared with other assets of £7.3 billion (Corbett 1997); by the year 2000, that value was reported at £5 billion (Bartram 2000, p. 1).

One reflection of the growing importance of IP and the associated IPRs is the growth in licensing revenues. Ganguli (2000, p. 167) argues that the USA's annual licensing revenue grew from $200 million in 1980 to $20 billion 1997. IBM moved from 1724 registered patents in 1997 to 2658 in 1998 and the company made over $1 billion through licensing arrangements. Samsung Electronics, which earned about $400 000 from its IP in 1998, is reported to be expecting to generate more than $1 billion from its Moving Picture Expert Group 2 (MPEG2) technology. High-technology exports are also highly dependent on protection from IPRs. According to the World Development Indicators compiled by the World Bank, high-technology exports formed about 18 per cent of all manufacturing exports in 2003. However, this overall average hides a huge variation across countries, with the UK having 26 per cent, the USA 31 per cent and East Asia 33 per cent. The percentage for China grew from 17 per cent in 1999 to 27 per cent by 2003.

In this increasingly global economy, many of the changes are linked to IP and IPRs. Foreign direct investment (FDI), for example, often involves various forms of technology transfer, as well as the transfer of management skills, organizational forms, and so on. The World Bank's World Development Indicators database highlights the massive growth in FDI. In the case of China, for example, prior to the open-door policy FDI was largely non-existent, but this has changed enormously over the subsequent 30 years or so, and by 1999 net inflows of FDI[1] had reached US$38 billion, and by 2003 this had further risen to $53 billion. This investment would not have been made without the introduction of a whole raft of IPRs (Bosworth and Yang 2000).

There is considerable evidence that the gestation time between invention and innovation has been falling. Gomulka (1990, p. 37) shows how the average time lag between invention and innovation fell from around 90 years in 1725 to about 20 years in 1925. He also demonstrates that the same patterns of reduction can be found in different areas of technology (for example, basic chemical inventions, basic electronic inventions, other early basic inventions and other modern basic inventions – ibid., p. 36). The finding is not surprising; while there are costs of reducing the applied research cycle time, the benefits can be even larger. In a study of participants in the US Advanced Technology Program (ATP), Laidlaw (2003) asked them to give the economic benefit associated with just a *one-year* reduction. The estimates ranged from $1 million to 'billions' for a one-year reduction (the median was $5–6 million). These estimates not only exclude the potential broader social benefits, but also the fact that some participants on the ATP believed they had saved up to ten years of research time, saving on expenditure, getting to market early and bringing forward in time the stream of revenues associated with the new product or process.

Products also appear to have moved closer to the science base. In an analysis of the UK Community Innovation Survey 3, Tether and Swann (2003) report that, while a relatively small percentage of all firms utilize the science base as a source of information (19 per cent of production and 14 per cent of service firms), the proportions were significantly higher amongst those that made the greatest commitments to innovation. Half of production and 45 per cent of service firms in the highest quintile of innovators indicated they had used the science base as a source of information for innovation. The result is further confirmed by relating a measure of dynamism among firms undertaking at least some innovation activity and the use of the science base. They report that, while less than one in ten of the firms that scored only one dynamism point used the public science base as a source of information for innovation, more than half those that scored seven or more points used the science base. A similar relationship can be found between innovation expenditures and collaboration with universities and between dynamism and collaboration with universities.

Of course, as the authors point out, there are also indirect ways in which the science base can impact on firms. A simple example is that, while an interaction may lead one firm to be the first to innovate, other firms may imitate this innovation. A further example is that universities supply graduates and there is a link between the employment of graduates and enterprise performance (Bosworth 2005; Bosworth et al. 1992). Tether and Swann (2003) again use the UK Community Innovation Survey to demonstrate this linkage. They report that, within the same industrial sub-sectors, firms that employ graduates tended to have higher dynamism scores than those that did not employ graduates and, in addition, firms that employ more than the median value of graduates for their sector tended to have even higher dynamism scores.

Innovation is important in the generation of profit because, even in the presence of patents, firms eventually invent around or invent a superior product or process (Gort and Klepper 1982; Mansfield et al. 1981; Pavitt 1999) or the patent eventually expires. When that occurs, abnormal profits created by the innovation are competed away, although some firms may reduce the effects of new competition through their trademarks and brand names. There seems to be a view that product life cycles have become shorter, reducing the period in which monopoly profits are made (Powell 1997; Zirulia 2004, p. 2), although not all authors adhere to this (Bayus 1992; Golder and Tellis 2003). Shorter product life cycles would be consistent with increased innovation activity, the pressure to reduce the applied research cycle time and increased speed to market.

This form of dynamic competition, in which innovation and quality are an integral part, increases the importance of appropriation of the results of discretionary investments of the firm. Discretionary investments refer to expenditures on research and development (R&D), advertising and marketing, training, management information systems (MIS), and so on. As Laursen and Salter (2005, p. 18) argue, 'Obviously, the ability of innovative firms to control the imitation strategies of other firms in their market will always remain limited. However, the choices managers make about how best to protect their intellectual capital can be a matter of life and death for their firm'.

Laursen and Salter (2005, pp. 19–20) outline the two major contrasting strategies for appropriation: a 'legal strategy' and a 'fast mover strategy'. They conclude that,

> Both legal and fast mover appropriability strategies, associated with increased managerial attention to appropriability, helps innovative performance. This finding indicates that managerial researchers are right to point to the need for managers to greater attention to appropriation in the development of their corporate and innovation strategies. However, we also found that an overemphasis on either legal or fast mover appropriability can have detrimental consequences for innovation performance – this is especially the case with respect to the legal appropriability strategy.

One other feature is that these forms of investment, which have become increasingly important with the passage of time, are inherently risky – a factor which management (and shareholders) have to take into account. New forms of decision-making focusing on the inherent risk or uncertainty need to be introduced.

As IP and other intangibles have taken centre stage, IPRs have become a strategic policy issue both at the company level and nationally. The USA has been at the forefront of changing the IPR landscape, initially at least through

what became known as 'Special 301', introduced under the Omnibus Trade
and Competitiveness Act, signed by President Reagan in 1988. Section
301 authorizes the US Trade Representatives (USTR) to retaliate against
countries that take unjustifiable, unreasonable or discriminatory trade
practices. The USA was also actively involved in the Uruguay Round
of the General Agreement on Tariffs and Trade (GATT), which set out
the agreement on Trade-Related Aspects of Intellectual Property Rights
(TRIPS) in December 1993 and established the World Trade Organization
(WTO), both of which became effective in 1994. This was an attempt to
overcome the wholly inadequate protection for IP in many developing
countries. TRIPS is binding on all WTO signatories and, hence, formed
a further source of pressure for countries such as China, who wanted to
become a WTO member, to introduce the necessary IP legislation. Under
TRIPS, any countries intent on accessing world markets must introduce
and enforce IP protection of the same standard as developed countries
within five years. At the same time a range of parallel negotiations at the
international, regional and bilateral levels has been taking place, which has
already begun to reshape the existing IPR regime – the so-called 'TRIPS-
plus' agreements (Vivas-Eugui, 2003). These agreements often involve
commitments well beyond the minimum standards set by TRIPS.

3   THE FOCUS AND CONTENTS OF THE PRESENT
   BOOK

The developments outlined above have major implications for the
management of companies. The present book focuses on information
and analytical tools used for the management of IP and intangible assets.
These assets are driven by investments in R&D, advertising and marketing,
education and training, management information systems, organizational
structure, and so on. The development of such assets can involve invention
or some other creative step, as well as innovation. The investments and
the activities involved are all inherently risky. Thus, understanding the
management of IP and intangible assets requires inputs from a variety of
disciplines, including economics, law, accounting and finance, management,
and so on.

   Part II of the book contains four chapters drawn from four different
disciplines, providing legal, accounting, management and economic
perspectives. These chapters describe how the different disciplines define and
view intellectual property and other intangible assets, as well as describing
the evolution of the literature in their area.

Chapter 2, by Andrew Christie, gives a legal perspective. It indicates how the importance of and interest in IP and IPRs has grown over time, and how a knowledge gap has emerged among certain sections of the community as the range of rights has increased and the overall framework of protection has become more complex. The discussion suggests that this area is made complicated by the fact that IP laws create rights between individuals that are vested in intangible 'objects'. The chapter begins with an outline of four somewhat different interpretations of what the law means by intellectual property. It points out that the subject matter of IP is generally derived from various forms of human intellectual – generally creative – activities. Property is taken to mean the legal rights to the subject matter, rather than the subject matter per se and the subsequent discussion outlines a particular case which illustrates this point. Intangible assets, such as IP have the problem that they cannot be physically secured to prevent their use by third parties. While IPRs offer a certain degree of exclusivity of rights over certain creative outputs, the chapter argues that these are not absolute in nature for a variety of reasons. The chapter then goes on to outline the principle regimes governing IP law – copyright, designs, patents and trademarks – as well as other statutory regimes, such as integrated circuits and plant breeders rights, and briefly touches on non-statutory regimes such as trade secrets.

In Chapter 3, Anne Wyatt sets out the issues surrounding IP and IPRs from an accounting perspective. Although intangible assets have no physical form, they are nevertheless viewed as potential sources of long-term future economic benefit. As in the case of the legal perspective, the 'asset' is formed by the *right* that the owner – the firm – has to control access to and use of the asset. For any item to appear in the accounts, it has to meet both the recognition and definition rules, which are set out in detail. The asset can only be recognized and appear on the balance sheet if it gives rise to probable future economic benefits and if it has a cost or some other value that can be reliably measured. Given that there is considerable uncertainty over both the future value of many of these assets, as well has how to place a value upon them, this provides a major restriction over what accountants can or are allowed to do in their accounts.

Despite the obvious evidence of the increasing importance of intangible assets within companies, advances in accounting standards to reflect them are reported to be scant. Practices such as expensing internal investments in R&D appear to be the norm. Wyatt reports that, if anything, the trends in accounting standards have been away from the recognition of intangible assets, while economists and most management scientists have been arguing for just the opposite. This does not mean that companies are not recording intangibles outside the formal financial and accounting activities – for use by managers in the effective management of the company. However, Wyatt argues that, to the extent the externally reported data drives the internal data collection, internal (management) and external users of accounting information will not have accurate data for their investment decisions.

In Chapter 4, Laurie Hunter provides a management perspective on IP and, indeed, the broader range of intangible capital within which IP is embedded. Intangible capital comprises human capital, organizational capital, relational capital and IP. Again the discussion outlines the various trends that have enhanced the importance of intangible assets and placed them centre stage as a vital factor in competitive rivalry in many sectors of business. It is the ownership of the rights over such assets that provide a potential form of competitive advantage, for example, the ability to preclude other companies from producing a particular product or using a particular technology. The management view is that IP is complex, as it involves elements of the firm's know-how and competencies, as well as the products of other creative activities, such as R&D, carried out by the company.

As such activities are core to competitiveness, it is argued that there is a real concern over the current failure of the accounting profession to address the measurement issues, although an understanding of the problems they face. It is crucial for managers taking strategic decisions of the firm to understand what intangible investments will pay off in the future and how well they will pay off. This requires at least internal measurement and accounting, even if this is not externally reported. However, Hunter suggests that all too often internal reporting systems are developed simply to supply the formal financial and accounting activities. The final part of the chapter is devoted to the idea of developing some system or framework of internal metrics and indicators that will be of use to management decision-making.

Derek Bosworth and Beth Webster, in Chapter 5, provide an economic perspective of a number of the issues surrounding the management of IP. While Chapter 4 outlined the main components of intangible capital including IP, Chapter 5 begins with a discussion of the nature of intellectual capital and how this can be distinguished from the broader concept of intangible assets. It not only reconsiders the question of ownership rights, but introduces the concept of appropriability – the ability to appropriate the rewards from the ownership of the IP that allow the creator to recoup the investment expenditures made in developing the creation. In addition, the chapter outlines the special nature and properties of intangible assets from an economic perspective – not just that intangibles do not have a physical form, but that their contribution to the profitability of the firm is often associated with uncertainty or, at best, a high degree of risk. There are many sources of risk and uncertainty, for example, they attach to investments in R&D and the ability to appropriate the rewards from such investments (for example, obtaining a defensible patent). Certain types of intangible assets such as knowledge, have other special properties, such as indivisibility.

The chapter then turns to the internal discretionary investments of the enterprise in IAs from an economic perspective (that is, expenditures on R&D, advertising, training, and so on). In particular, it considers the economic evidence about the degree to which the *ex ante* investment decisions focus on the likely effects on the profitability of the enterprise. In doing so, the discussion outlines the role played by both science- and technology-push factors vis-à-vis demand-pull factors. While historically these were seen as alternative explanations of the rate and direction of technological change, today they are generally integrated in an eclectic empirical model. Having dealt with the internal investments, the chapter then explores the sources of IAs that lie external to the firm and how the enterprise might efficiently access such sources. It is argued that efficient access to external sources generally require internal discretionary investments of the type outlined above. Finally, Chapter 5 looks at studies of the value of IAs to enterprises. In doing so, it extends the discussion beyond the traditional focus on R&D and explores other investments, such as high-performance work practices (HPWPs) and IT.

Part III considers the issue of the linkages between IP and company performance, and the issue of using IP-based measures to monitor and benchmark performance. All of these in some way draw upon the market valuation approach developed by Griliches (1981). In this approach, market valuation represents the expected discounted sum of future dividends, which, if the retention ratio – the proportion of profits paid as dividend – remains reasonably constant, will be directly related to the expected sum of discounted future profits (see Chapter 5). All the studies in this part use 'panel data', which combines cross-sectional and time-series data about individual companies. Panel estimation techniques allow the researcher to control for unmeasured company characteristics that do not vary over time. As Griffiths and Webster (Chapter 8) point out, 'This may include that part of the expertise of a specific manager, a particular customer market advantage a firm possesses which is constant over the data period'. Or, as Jensen and Palangkaraya suggest (Chapter 9), it may be able to capture unobserved influences on performance, such as the possession of trade secrets.

Dirk Czarnitzki, Bronwyn Hall and Raffaele Oriani, in Chapter 6, outline their preference for market valuation as the performance measure rather than current profits, which fail to represent the stream of benefits than an innovation is likely to bring. The authors present an outline of what they term a 'hedonic regression approach to measuring the market value of the knowledge assets'. By this they mean that they specify a relationship in which various tangible and intangible assets influence the performance and, hence, the market value of the company. The term 'hedonic' refers to a literature linking product prices with their characteristics or attributes – in the present case the 'product' is the company. With one or two variations, this approach is widely adopted in the literature and underpins all the chapters in this part of the book.

Given that the chapter draws upon a wide range of estimates, including those undertaken by the authors themselves, the discussion outlines the way in which the generally used measures are constructed. For example, the study outlines the construction of an 'R&D stock of knowledge', using the perpetual inventory method (for example, the depreciated sum of past R&D expenditures, where the depreciation rate is assumed to be 15 per cent), as well as the relationship between the R&D stock and flow measures. Problems with the R&D measures as a proxy for knowledge capital are also discussed. As the authors point out, many studies also use patent data in an attempt to partially overcome any measurement problems associated with R&D. The patent data take the form of either simple patent application counts or citation-weighted patent counts. The rationale for the citation weights is that patents which are more heavily cited by subsequent patents are likely to be technologically and commercially more important. Past results from applying the method to firm data on market value, capital, R&D and patents are summarized, along with a more detailed presentation of some recent results for US and European firms. The conclusion is that measures based on R&D, patents and citation-weighted patents are each highly significant in a market value regression, although patent-based measures tend to be somewhat less significant in the presence of R&D measures.

Chapter 7 by Christine Greenhalgh and Mark Rogers makes an important contribution in two respects: first, it extends the IP data from just patents to include trademarks; second, it provides an analysis of the financial services sector, the transport, communications and utilities service sector, and manufacturing. They use firm-level data on the intellectual property activity of around 1300 UK companies, to analyse the importance of trademarking and patenting over the period 1996 to 2000. The authors note that patenting activity is minimal in the two service sectors, but trademark activity is substantial across all three sectors. All sectors experienced an increase in IP activity over the period, although the most rapid growth is in trademarking by financial service sector firms. In addition, the database contains financial information, allowing the construction of a measure of market value.

The authors present some descriptive statistics that compare four different performance measures for trademark active and inactive firms. In virtually all cases trademark active firms outperform inactive firms. They also report results which show a very similar pattern emerges for patent active and inactive. The authors then set out a fairly standard economic model for the analysis of the relationship between the net present value of the firm, as reflected in its market value, and the tangible and intangible assets of the firm, including within the latter its IP. Their results show important differences across sectors. For manufacturing firms, UK and European Patent Office (EPO) patent activity is associated with higher stock market values, with trademarking having little impact. In contrast, for financial sector firms, higher trademark intensity is associated with higher market values. Furthermore, for financial sector firms, the market's valuation of trademarking increased in the late 1990s.

Chapter 8, by Bill Griffiths and Beth Webster, also uses a market value framework to examine the relationship between the effort Australian companies make creating assets and future anticipated profits. The focus of their study is not so much the value of innovative activities, but the extent to which the value has been rising or falling over time. In doing so, the study adopts a long panel data set, comprising over 300 Australian companies from 1989 to 2002. While they adopt similar measures to the previous authors, there are a number of differences. The Australia data provided by IP Australia include design information as well as patents and trademarks. In addition, there is information about whether the patents, trademarks and designs are still in force, which provides accurate figures about the stocks of IP, rather than having to estimate them with assumed depreciation rates.

In their initial model, they obtain estimates of the value of each type of IP, where on average: the value of an additional patent (with other unmeasured and correlated investments) adds A$933 000 to the value of the company; an additional trademark adds A$141 000; and an additional design adds A$803 000. The authors then allowed the values of each form of IP to vary linearly over time. Their main findings were that: the average present value of a patent fell from 1989 to 2002, which they tentatively suggest might be attributed to the lower intrinsic value of invention over time or more competitive markets; the average present value of a registered trademark rose, which they suggest may be due to strong macroeconomic growth over that period, the rising importance of branded goods and services and/or the benefits to firms of using brands as barriers between themselves and rivals.

In Chapter 9, Paul Jensen and Alfons Palangkaraya report on the construction of an index of innovative activity at the company level for Australian companies. The innovation index is based on the same market valuation approach described in the earlier chapters and reflects many of the recent developments in the academic literature. The authors reject the use of a single indicator of innovation, such as R&D expenditure, patent counts or the number of new products introduced over any given period of time. They argue that multiple indicators give the researcher a much better chance of establishing the true extent of company innovativeness and adopt a market valuation function that includes R&D, patents, trademarks and designs. Each of the indicators relates to a different stage of the innovation pathway, as, for example, R&D relates to a measure of inputs to the innovation process, patents reflect that an invention has been made and trademarks are often taken out at the stage that a modified or new product has been launched.

The market valuation equation is estimated to provide weights for the various indices of innovation. The weighted sum of the indicators then forms an index, which is then used to compile an 'innovation scoreboard'. The data, provided by IBISWorld and IP Australia, are restricted to those companies for which both R&D and market value information are available. The weighted sum of the R&D and IP indicators gives each firm's indexed 'score' in a given year, which forms the basis of the authors' comparison of the innovative performance of Australian companies and sectors over the period 1998–2003. Matching their data to a survey of Australian companies, the authors are able to explore what factors distinguish the most innovative companies from the rest. They report that the most innovative companies are more likely to pursue information gathering from primary sources (for example, their clients) and do so in a more systematic way. The innovative firms more readily adapt their strategic plans to meet the challenge of external changes and are more likely to develop new products and react to early signs of opportunity in the market.

Part IV considers a number of strategic management issues, including the decision to take out formal IP protection and the more general management of intangible assets. Chapter 10 focuses on an overview of the benefits of a company focus on IPRs; Chapter 11 looks at the propensity to trademark, as well as the links between trademarking and company performance; and Chapter 12 examines the propensity to patent and the determinants of the size of the patent portfolio.

While chapters in the previous part of the book were based on the analysis of large-scale statistical databases, showing the link between IP and company performance, in Chapter 10, Derek Bosworth draws upon information built up during case studies of IP and IPRs by the author and illustrates them with examples drawn from other sources, such as the World Intellectual Property Organization (WIPO) small and medium-size enterprises (SME) case study website. This allows a richer picture to emerge as to how IP and IPRs are managed in order to lever value to the companies that own them. In particular, the chapter discusses the value of the technical information reported in patent specifications as a source of technical information that firms can use in their own creative activities. It demonstrates how patenting can be used as strategic activity to hinder other companies' inventive activities. Finally, it reports on examples of where companies use their patents as a 'shop window' to attract potential clients. The discussion then turns to the use of patent (and other IPR) watching and search mechanisms for discovering what rivals, potential takeover targets and potential collaborators are doing.

Chapter 10 then looks at the use of patenting as a mechanism for triggering rewards to motivate and incentivize employees. It considers the role that IPRs play not only in attracting investors, but also as collateral for raising funding. Issues concerning the raising of finance may be particularly important in increasingly knowledge-based firms with few tangible assets that can be used as surety. The discussion then turns to the role of IPRs in allowing various forms of licensing and franchising, for example, the role of patents in allowing the licensing of a firm's technology. The author then moves on to consider the use of cross-licensing and patent pooling to improve the firm's freedom to operate and to increase access to technologies owned by other companies. At this stage it is possible to show how IP and IPRs can act as a key strategic focus of the enterprise, as well as how different IP and IPR strategies become increasingly woven into the business strategy of the firm. Finally, the chapter concludes with a discussion of the more traditional role of IPRs in protecting the firm against infringement, thereby enabling it to recoup its R&D and marketing outlays and improve its dynamic performance.

In Chapter 11 Christine Greenhalgh and Mark Rogers document the extent of intellectual property assets held by financial services firms, which they then compare with corresponding intangible assets held by manufacturing firms and utilities providers. In practice, financial services is a very important sector in the UK, for example, in terms of employment; it accounts for about 16 per cent of total employment, compared with 14 per cent in manufacturing. They argue that the financial services sector now plays a role that was previously carried out by manufacturing, both as an engine of productivity growth and a transmitter of innovation. Growth through innovation was associated with service product differentiation and a rapid increase in product range, which is likely to be reflected in trade- and service mark activity. Thus, the authors focus on the extent and determinants of trademark activity and whether this activity is linked to firm performance.

Greenhalgh and Rogers demonstrate that the strong growth and development of the financial services sector in the UK has been accompanied by a significant rise in the acquisition of intangible assets in the form of intellectual property rights held by firms in this sector. The main type of IP asset acquired was trademarks, with only a few venture capital companies reporting R&D expenditure or acquiring patents. This pattern is consistent with the development of new varieties of financial services products, using new process technology bought-in from the manufacturing sector. Even so, the incidence of new trademarks during 1996–2000 for financial service firms was still zero in over half these firms; this is well below the rates in the manufacturing and utilities sectors. Although large firms account for much of the observed trademark activity, smaller firms make more trademark applications per employee. They found no role for stock market listed status or the extent of product diversification of the firm in the propensity to acquire trademarks. Across all firms a variety of measures of firm performance were positively correlated with being active in acquiring trademarks; within the financial services sector, trademark active firms showed higher rates of investment and faster growth of employment.

In Chapter 12, Carine Peeters and Bruno van Pottelsberghe de la Potterie attempt to gain a better understanding of large firms' patenting behaviour. The conceptual framework suggests that this behaviour can be influenced by three types of factors: (1) the innovation strategy and the general attitude of firms towards IPRs; (2) the barriers firms perceive as hindering their innovation activities and as preventing them from patenting; and (3) firm- and sector-specific factors like size, age and the level of competition. The authors undertake a quantitative analysis of the effect of these factors on the propensity to patent and the number of patents held. Two econometric models are estimated using an original survey of 148 large Belgian firms in 2001. Firms are categorized by size (small, medium and large) and by sector (high, medium and low technology, plus services). The rich database contains a variety of new measures, distinguishing, for example, basic and applied R&D from development activities.

Both the probability of having a patent portfolio and the size of this portfolio correlate with four dimensions of an innovation strategy: a focus on basic and applied research (as opposed to development); the effective collaboration with knowledge-based institutions (university and public labs) or with competitors; a product-orientated strategy (as opposed to process); and the importance given to a formal management of intellectual property. The firms that perceive more barriers to their innovation process (internal organizational barriers, risk- and cost-related barriers, and external barriers coming from customers' rigidities and inappropriate regulations) patent less than other firms. The perception of barriers to the use of the patent system is not correlated with the actual patenting behaviour.

Part V turns attention to the specific decision rules to be used when taking decisions under risk. All stages of the innovation processes generally associated with IP are inherently risky, from the investment in basic research, applied research, development, seeking patent or trademark protection, product launch and competitor response, to patent renewal or lapse. While these stages should not be conceived as wholly linear, there are key times at which decisions have to be made and each choice has a degree of risk or uncertainty. These choices depend upon the adoption of appropriate valuation techniques.

Chapter 13, by Eric Iversen and Aris Kaloudis, argues that more reliable valuation techniques can lay the basis for better management of innovation processes within the firm, as well as allowing better co-ordination mechanisms between innovating firms and the wider economy (for example, collaborators, funding agencies, users, and so on). The authors describe three basic scenarios that help substantiate the increasing relevance of valuation techniques, and the challenges they pose. The first involves the changing way innovation activities are organized, such as collaborative research, which requires an agreed way to value IAs prior to, during and after the collaboration. This second scenario is where there are high R&D costs and long gestation periods, where valuation techniques are needed in order to obtain investment. A third scenario emerges at the firm-level, in cases where the challenge of proactively organizing company activities substantially involves IAs. Thus, the authors argue that, to be successful, a firm must know the value of its IAs, have a strategy for monetizing them, and be effective in generating a return on them. They go on to outline how improved valuation techniques would also improve the macroeconomy.

Iversen and Kaloudis reiterate the importance of distinguishing between the value of the invention and the value of the patent protection. They then introduce a variety of different cost-based and value-based approaches to the valuation of intangible assets, including real option methods which they view as the potentially most promising way forward. In addition, they outline the use of balanced scorecards and citation analyses. From an empirical perspective, the authors present interesting evidence about Norwegian companies' patenting activities. This shows significant differences in the completion of the patenting process: individual inventors and small firms are much more likely to withdraw their application before it is granted. Higher withdrawal rates may be an indication of the lower quality of the invention, poor framing of the application, fear of litigation, and so on. However, it may also reflect an inability to value the invention and demonstrate this value to potential funding agencies and other organizations that might help in the development and commercialization of the invention. The authors argue for the need to improve firm-internal processes, including knowledge of valuation techniques.

In Chapter 14, Robert Pitkethly makes the case for the objective valuation of patents. He argues that the inventor, the patent agent and marketing

managers are likely to be the individuals with the information and knowledge
to allow this to take place. The author notes that companies all too often do
not consider carrying out an objective valuation of patents, which are then
applied for or renewed because no one can or wants to prove that they are
not valuable. In addition, it is important to distinguish between the patent,
the underlying invention and commercialization of the patented invention
in decisions such as whether to apply for a patent or to renew a patent.

The discussion then turns to a description of the various methods of
valuation. These include: (1) cost- and market-based methods – accounting
for historical costs and market conditions; (2) income-based methods –
accounting for future value; (3) discounted cash flow methods – accounting
for time and uncertainty; (4) decision tree analysis methods – accounting
for flexibility; (5) options pricing theory methods – accounting for changing
risk. All these methods are discussed, although Pitkethly concentrates on
those that he feels are more accurate and useful. The author argues that
option-based valuation approaches are a useful framework within which to
consider management decisions about company IPRs even if the method
is not applied in detail. He suggests that valuation methods for assets
involving choices and varied outcomes can seriously understate their true
value if they do not take account of any options involved. In addition, an
important part of the discussion of a number of the above techniques is
that investments are often multi-stage in nature and the degree of risk differs
considerably across these stages. In order to operationalize the options
pricing approach, information is needed about the distribution of returns.
Here Pitkethly points to the emerging, mainly econometric literature on the
skewed distribution of returns, which suggests that a search for meaningful
distributions is worthwhile.

In Chapter 15, Markus Reitzig seeks to complement Pitkethly's (1999)
survey of patent valuation methods (see Chapter 14, which contains much
of the earlier paper). The identification of spanning traded assets, used to
provide estimates of the present value of the cash flows and their volatility
for the options pricing calculation, are difficult to identify in the case of
patents and, more particularly, patent portfolios. For this reason, the author
attempts to assess patent value without market benchmarking, by searching
for patent-based indicators that are likely to be strongly correlated with
patent value and can act as proxies for the cash flows and their volatility.
The author argues that, in addition to their correlation with 'value drivers',
such indicators should be both publicly available and able to provide low-
cost valuations.

The types of value drivers that Reitzig has in mind are (1) the patent's
duration (or remaining life time), which corresponds to the maximum
time to invest in the project; (2) the present value of cash flows, which

will be related to its novelty, inventive step (non-obviousness), disclosure, breadth, difficulty in inventing around, its position within a portfolio of other patents and the complementary assets of the patent holder; (3) the standard deviation of the patent's value (volatility) is likely to be determined by technical, legal and market uncertainty. The author then undertakes a review of the empirical literature linking the potential indicators with the value of patents. The chapter also discusses the shortcomings of current practice, including the problem of assigning weights to indicators and assigning indicators to the input parameters of a real option valuation. While the latter would be ideal, if done correctly, Reitzig argues that we are still some way from being able to do so. Nevertheless, he argues that more simplistic valuations using indicators are still worthwhile, particularly where large portfolios of patents need to be evaluated quickly and on a regular basis.

NOTE

1. The World Bank defines this as net inflows of investment to acquire a lasting management interest (10 per cent or more of voting stock) in an enterprise operating in an economy other than that of the investor. It is the sum of equity capital, reinvestment of earnings, other long-term capital and short-term capital as shown in the balance of payments. This series shows net inflows in the reporting economy. Data are in current US dollars.

REFERENCES

Bartram, P. (2000), 'Brand power', *Management Accounting*, June, 17–18.
Bayus, B.L. (1992), 'Have diffusion rates been accelerating over time?', *Marketing Letters*, **3**, 215–26.
Bosworth, D.L. (2005), *Determinants of Enterprise Performance*, Manchester and New York: Manchester University Press.
Bosworth, D.L. and D. Yang (2000), 'Intellectual property law, technology flow and licensing opportunities in the People's Republic of China', *International Business Review*, **9** (4), 453–77.
Bosworth, D.L., R. Wilson and P. Taylor (1992), *Technological Change: The Role of Scientists and Engineers*, Aldershot: Avebury Press.
Buchan, E. and N. Davies (1997), 'Mergers and acquisitions', in R. Perrier (ed.), *Brand Valuation*, London: Premier Books, pp. 109–16.
Convention Establishing the World Intellectual Property Organisation (1967), article 2 (viii), http://www.wipo.int/treaties/en/convention/trtdocs_wo029.html.
Corbett, G. (1997), 'The benefits of valuing brands', in R. Perrier (ed.), *Brand Valuation*, London: Premier Books, pp. 11–18.
Department of Trade and Industry (DTI) (2001), *UK Productivity Competitiveness Indicators*, London: Department of Trade and Industry.
Ganguli, P. (2000), *World Patent Information*, **22**, 167–75.

Golder, P.N. and G.J. Tellis (2003), 'Growing, growing, gone: cascades, diffusion, and turning points in the product life cycle', report no. 03–120, Marketing Science Institute, Cambridge, MA.

Gomulka, S. (1990), *The Theory of Technological Change and Economic Growth*, London: Routledge.

Gort, M. and S. Klepper (1982), 'Time paths in the diffusion of product innovations', *Economic Journal*, **92** (367), 630–53.

Granstrand, O. (1999), *The Economics and Management of Intellectual Property*, Cheltenham, UK and Northampton, MA, USA: Edward Elgar.

Griliches, Z. (1981), 'Market value, R & D, and patents', *Economic Letters*, **7**, 183–7.

Laidlaw, F.J. (2003), 'Acceleration of technology development by the Advanced Technology Program: the experience of 28 projects funded in 1991', US Office of Economic Assessment, National Institute of Standards and Technology, Technology Administration, US Department of Commerce, www.atp.nist.gov/eao/ir-6047.htm#Chapter%201.

Laursen, K. and A. Salter (2005), 'My precious: the role of appropriability strategies in shaping innovative performance', Danish Research Unit for Industrial Dynamics, working paper no. 05-02, Copenhagen Business School. Frederiksberg, Denmark.

Mansfield, E., M. Schwartz and S. Wagner (1981), 'Imitation costs and patents: an empirical study', *Economic Journal*, **91**, December, 907–18.

Pavitt, K. (1999), *Technology, Management and Systems of Innovation*, Cheltenham, UK and Northampton, MA, USA: Edward Elgar.

Pithelky, R. (1999), 'The valuation of patents: a review of patent valuation methods with consideration of option based methods and the potential for further research', Judge Institute working paper WP 21/97, Cambridge.

Powell, J. (1997), 'Development, commercialization, and diffusion of enabling technologies: progress report for projects funded 1993–1995', Office of Economic Assessment, Advanced Technology Program, National Institute of Standards and Technology, report NISTIR-6098, US Department of Commerce Gaithersburg, www.atp.nist.gov/eao/ir-6098/contents.htm.

Tether, B.S. and G.M.P. Swann (2003), 'Sourcing science: the use by industry of the science base for innovation; evidence from the UK's Innovation Survey', discussion paper, Centre for Research into Innovation and Competitiveness (CRIC), University of Manchester and UMIST.

Vivas-Eugui, D. (2003), *Regional and Bilateral Agreements and a TRIPS-plus World: The Free Trade Area of the Americas (FTAA)*, Quaker United Nations Office (QUNO), Geneva; Quaker International Affairs Programme (QIAP), Ottawa; International Centre for Trade and Sustainable Development (ICTSD), Geneva.

Webster, E. (1999), *The Economics of Intangible Assets*, Cheltenham, UK and Northampton, MA, USA: Edward Elgar.

WIPO (1967), *Convention Establishing the World Intellectual Property Organization*.

Zirulia, L. (2004), 'The evolution of R&D networks', MERIT-Infonomics Research Memorandum series, working paper 2004-007, Merit, Maastricht.

PART II

Perspectives on intellectual property and intangible assets

2. A legal perspective

Andrew F. Christie

1 INTRODUCTION

> Intellectual property could be called the Cinderella of the new economy. A drab
> but useful servant, consigned to the dusty and uneventful offices of corporate
> legal departments until the princes of globalisation and technological innovation
> – revealing her true value – swept her to prominence and gave her an enticing
> new allure.[1]

This quote, taken from a World Intellectual Property Organization (WIPO)
publication, says much about the state of intellectual property today. After all,
it has only been a couple of decades since intellectual property was generally
regarded as a rather obscure, but necessary, field of legal regulation. In the
last few years, however, intellectual property has become recognized as the
driving force of economic growth and cultural development. As a result, the
law of intellectual property has entered the consciousness of an ever-widening
part of the public, and is increasingly seen as a matter for public policy as
well as for private exploitation.

Despite its growing importance, intellectual property remains a challenging
area of law. This is because, unlike the laws of real property, the laws of
intellectual property create rights between individuals that are vested
in abstract objects – being objects that, inherently, are difficult to define.
Furthermore, intellectual property is an ever-expanding field, and its role in
society has become increasingly significant and complex. This is due in part
at least to its cultural specificity, as a regime that is founded on the notion of
both knowledge and art as commodities.[2] In that sense at least, 'intellectual
property' can be considered to be just another, albeit very special, type of
intangible asset.

There is an unfortunate tension regarding modern intellectual property. On
the one hand, intellectual property has never been of more importance to a
wide range of actors, both public and private, within society. On the other
hand, intellectual property has become more, not less, complex in its substance
and regulation by the law. As a result, there is a non-trivial 'knowledge gap'
in significant sections of the community about intellectual property.

This chapter seeks to help bridge that gap, by explaining how intellectual property is seen by the law and by lawyers. To do so, the chapter focuses on the way in which the law defines these special types of intangible asset to which protection is given, and on the way in which the law allocates rights to them. The chapter begins by considering the different meanings given by lawyers to the term 'intellectual property'. Then follows a discussion of the fundamental concepts of intellectual property and intellectual property rights. The chapter ends by comparing and contrasting the basic features of the different types of intellectual property laws.

2   THE DIFFERENT MEANINGS OF 'INTELLECTUAL PROPERTY'

The term 'intellectual property' can be, and is, used to mean a number of different things. The different senses in which the term is used are not always explained, and indeed are not always recognized, by those using it. Perhaps surprisingly, given that they pride themselves on accurate usage of language, lawyers are often the worse offenders in this respect. The very fact that lawyers are prone to using the term in multiple ways is a reflection of the complexity of the legal concepts concerning intellectual property.

As a general rule, lawyers use the term 'intellectual property' to mean three different, but related, things. First, they use it to mean a particular sub-group of a particular type of subject matter. The type of subject matter is intangible subject matter – that is, things which exist but which cannot be touched. The sub-group called 'intellectual property' consists of a number of intangible subject matters that the law recognizes as sharing certain features that warrant particular treatment under the law. In this sense, 'intellectual property' is used to refer to a particular type of 'stuff'. This is the sense in which the term 'intellectual property', or the abbreviation 'IP', is used in this chapter.

The second way in which the term 'intellectual property' is used by lawyers is to refer to certain legal entitlements that exist in relation to this stuff. These entitlements are 'rights' – that is, entitlements held by legal entities (individuals or companies) that are enforceable under law against other legal entities. In this chapter, the term 'intellectual property rights', or the abbreviation 'IPRs', is used to refer to these entitlements.

The third way in which lawyers use the term 'intellectual property' is to refer to the particular laws that give rise to intellectual property rights in respect of particular intangible stuff. These laws are grouped under particular titles – for example, 'patent', 'copyright', and so on – resulting in 'patent law', 'copyright law', and so on. In this chapter, the laws that give rise to rights over intellectual property are referred to as 'intellectual property laws' or 'IP laws'.

There is, of course, a fourth way in which the term 'intellectual property' can be used. This is to refer to the entire field of discourse concerning all of the above. Put another way, it is valid to say that this chapter is about 'intellectual property' because it is about the subject matter that is known as IP, it is about the rights granted in relation to that subject matter, and it is about the legal regimes that grant and regulate rights in relation to that subject matter.

3 INTELLECTUAL PROPERTY

If a tangible asset is something that can be touched then an intangible asset is, by definition, a thing that cannot be touched. What are the characteristics that make some types of intangible assets 'intellectual property' in the eyes of the law? A way to answer that question is to consider the concepts behind the two words included in the phrase 'intellectual property'.

3.1 'Intellectual'

A common way of classifying those intangible assets that constitute IP is as 'all those things which emanate from the exercise of the human brain, such as ideas, inventions, poems, designs, microcomputers and Mickey Mouse'.[3] This classification is consistent with the notion that the subject matters constituting IP are primarily derived from human intellectual activity – hence the word 'intellectual' in the title. The particular human intellectual activities that commonly result in most IP are innovation and creativity.

Innovation and creativity result in doing something new or bringing into existence something new. An idea about how to do a thing differently is a subject matter that may be protected by patent law. A new piece of art or music is a subject matter that may be protected by copyright law. A new way of naming a product or service is a subject matter that may be protected by trademark law. Thus, it can be seen that many of the assets that are considered to be IP can be identified by the fact that they are an innovative or a creative product of the human intellect.

3.2 'Property'

To lawyers, the concept of 'property' is more one of *rights to* subject matter than of subject matter per se. That is to say, a lawyer is more likely to see 'property' as the entitlements to something exercisable against third parties, than as the thing in respect of which those entitlements exist. Put another way, land is property only if someone has rights exercisable against others in relation to that land. Absent such rights, there is no property in the land and hence it may be said that the land is not property.

The key entitlement one may have in relation to something is the right to possess it exclusively – the corollary of which is the right to exclude others from accessing it. This right of exclusivity is a hallmark of property.

3.3 'Intellectual Property'

The above descriptions of 'intellectual' and 'property' provide a basis for describing IP as an intangible subject matter emanating from the human intellect in respect of which a legal right of exclusivity may be granted.

The legal case of *Re Dickens*[4] presents a useful example when attempting to convey this concept of intellectual property. When the British author Charles Dickens died, he left an unpublished manuscript. Ownership of this manuscript passed to person X, as part of a bequest of Dickens 'private papers whatsoever and wheresoever' under his will. Dickens's will also provided for a bequest to Y of his residuary estate (that is, those assets not otherwise transferred under the will). When X sought to publish the manuscript some years later, the question arose as to whether he could do so. It was clear that X owned the manuscript (the tangible asset), but did he also own the literary work embodied in the manuscript (the intangible asset in which copyright subsisted)? To resolve that question it was necessary for the court to determine whether the copyright in the literary work formed an integral part of the manuscript itself and thus passed automatically to X under the will, or rather whether it was a separate asset forming part of the residuary of the estate which had passed to Y?

The court ruled that, because Dickens's will had not referred to the copyright when bequeathing the manuscript, the copyright fell into the residue of the estate. As a result, the ownership of the copyright in the literary work embodied in the manuscript had become separated from the ownership of the manuscript itself. The practical significance of this ruling was that X could not publish the manuscript without the consent of Y. This was because publication of the manuscript would amount to a reproduction of the literary work embodied in the manuscript, and the right to reproduce the literary work was held exclusively by the owner of copyright, Y.

Although this ruling and its outcome was probably contrary to what Dickens had intended when making his will, it is a good illustration of the fundamental characteristics of IP. Intellectual property is an intangible subject matter (in this case, a literary work) emanating from the human intellect (in this case, the creative mind of Charles Dickens) in respect of which a legal right of exclusivity (in this case, copyright) may be granted. The case also illustrates the way in which the law treats an intangible asset (in this case, a literary work in copyright subsists) as separate from any tangible asset (in this case, a manuscript) to which the intangible asset may relate.

4 INTELLECTUAL PROPERTY RIGHTS

Intellectual property rights are rights to IP – that is, legal entitlements granted in respect of intangible subject matter emanating from the human intellect. This section considers the primary nature of these entitlements, and some of their common characteristics.

4.1 The Right of Exclusivity

Most tangible assets can be possessed exclusively by virtue of the fact that they are tangible – and hence can be physically secured against access by third parties. Thus, a movable tangible asset (such as a television) can be possessed exclusively by locking it within a house; and an immovable tangible asset (such as land) can be possessed exclusively by fencing it. It is, of course, the case that most, if not all, means of physical security can be overcome – that is, most tangible assets can be stolen. To counter this, the law imposes legal prohibitions on the overriding physical means of securitization – for example, the law makes theft of another's goods a crime.

Exclusive possession of intangible assets is problematic, precisely because they are intangible. This means they usually cannot be *physically* secured against access by third parties; as an economist would put it, they are non-excludable. To remedy this defect, the law provides the means by which intangible assets can be legally secured against access by third parties. The particular means provided by the law is the grant of (intellectual) property rights, enforceable by the owner of the rights, with the backing of the state, against third parties by way of legal action in the courts.

In the case of Charles Dickens and the unpublished manuscript, the means by which the beneficiary of the residuary of the estate, Y, obtained exclusivity to the literary work embodied in the manuscript was through the IPR of copyright. Under copyright law, the owner of copyright is granted, amongst other things, the exclusive right to reproduce the work. In the absence of such a right, X would in practice have had the exclusive entitlement to publish the manuscript by virtue of his physical (and legal) possession of it.

4.2 Common Characteristics of IPRs

In general terms, intellectual property rights have certain common characteristics. First, the rights apply only in relation to a sub-set of all innovative/creative emanations from the human intellect – this sub-set being specific types of IP subject matter defined in the IPR laws. Second, the rights apply only to those defined subject matters that satisfy a specific innovation/ creativity threshold. Third, the rights are not absolute; third parties remain free to engage in certain types of activity with the IP, even without the consent of the IP owner. Fourth, the rights are generally of limited duration. Fifth, the rights are generally freely transferable to other parties. Sixth, the rights are usually, but not always, created under statute. Each of these characteristics of IPRs is considered in some detail below.

Specific subject matters

Just as not all intangible assets are IP,[5] not all IP is protected by IPRs. Rather, only those IP subject matters for which there is a specific legal regime obtain the benefit of the grant of exclusive rights. The various IPR regimes specify the sub-set of IP to which they are applicable. For example, only 'inventions' may be granted a patent, and only 'signs' may be registered as trademarks.

Innovation/creation thresholds

The laws that create IPRs generally specify a threshold of innovativeness or creativity that must be satisfied for the subject matter to gain the benefit of the rights. Thus, it is only inventions that are both 'new' and 'non-obvious' which may be granted protection by a patent. Likewise, it is only a literary work that is 'original' which will be protected by copyright law.

Limitations on exclusivity of rights

The exclusivity provided by IPRs is not, as a rule, absolute. Rather, certain activities in relation to the IP remain free for all to undertake, even though the IPR owner does not consent. In patent law, for example, it is generally recognized that uses of an invention for 'experimental purposes' are not within the exclusive entitlements of the patent owner. Likewise, in copyright law, certain uses of a work are considered 'fair uses' or 'fair dealings' and thus permitted without the consent of the copyright owner.

Limitations on duration of rights

Most IPRs do not subsist indefinitely; rather, they last for set period of time. In the case of patents, for example, the duration of the patentee's exclusive rights is 20 years from the date of filing the application for the patent. Some IPRs, however, may last indefinitely. A good example is provided by trademark registration, where the exclusivity continues so long as the registration is maintained – and there is no limit on how long that may be.

Transferability of rights

Intellectual property rights are assets like other property rights. Accordingly, they may be transferred to other parties at the will of the owner. The rights may assigned – that is, transferred absolutely from one person to another (the equivalent of selling title to land). Alternatively, the rights may be licensed – that is, granted for a limited duration but not absolutely transferred (the equivalent of leasing land).

Statutory basis of rights

The majority of IPRs are created by statute – that is, by legislation enacted by Parliament. The statutes usually are titled by the name of the IPR – hence, the Copyright Act, the Patents Act, and so on. In some cases, however, the IPRs arise not by statute but by the 'common law' or by 'equity'; that is, by the unwritten law recognized by judges. Examples of common law and equity IPRs are the entitlements protected by the actions for 'breach of confidence' and for 'passing off'.

5 INTELLECTUAL PROPERTY LAWS

Intellectual property laws derive from various sources: international treaties, legislation, and the common law and equity. In many cases, there is an international treaty for a particular IPR, which mandates the minimum degree of protection that a country must afford to that IP subject matter. Each country then implements that mandated protection through national legislation. In some cases, there is no international treaty on the IPR. In those cases, protection is often provided within a country by non-statutory means.

Below is an outline of the principal regimes that govern IP law. Copyright, designs, patents and trademarks represent the main statutory regimes, while the actions to restrain a breach of confidence and a passing off are the main regimes derived from the common law and equity. For each regime, there are several key features that are described – namely, the subject matter protected; the requirements for protection to arise (including the innovation/creation threshold and the formalities, if any, which must be complied with); and the rights that attach to the protected subject matter, and the limitations to those rights. Where there is an international treaty mandating protection for an IPR, the provisions of that treaty are used to describe the key features of the regime.

5.1   Main Statutory Regimes

5.1.1   Copyright

Subject matter   The relevant international treaty, the *Berne Convention*,[6] mandates copyright protection for 'literary and artistic works'. This phrase is interpreted widely. According to Article 2 of the *Berne Convention*:

> The expression 'literary and artistic works' shall include every production in the literary, scientific and artistic domain, whatever may be the mode or form of its expression, such as books, pamphlets and other writings; lectures, addresses, sermons and other works of the same nature; dramatic or dramatico-musical works; choreographic works and entertainments in dumb show; musical compositions with or without words; cinematographic works to which are assimilated works expressed by a process analogous to cinematography; works of drawing, painting, architecture, sculpture, engraving and lithography; photographic works to which are assimilated works expressed by a process analogous to photography; works of applied art; illustrations, maps, plans, sketches and three-dimensional works relative to geography, topography, architecture or science.

A later international treaty, the *TRIPS Agreement*,[7] has mandated that computer programs and compilations of data must be protected under copyright as literary and artistic works.

Literary and artistic works, widely defined, are considered to be the traditional subject matter of copyright. There are, however, other, non-traditional, subject matters (sometimes called 'neighbouring rights' subject matters) that many countries protect under copyright law. The most prominent of these are performances, sound recordings, and sound and television broadcasts.[8]

Requirements for protection   The *Berne Convention* mandates protection for literary and artistic works that are 'original'. The concept of originality varies considerably from country to country. Some countries, notably continental European countries, adopt the concept of 'the author's intellectual creation' as the test for originality. Other countries, notably the UK and Australia, adopt a somewhat lower standard. In these other countries, intellectual creativity is not required; it will usually be sufficient that the subject matter resulted from some 'independent effort' by the author – that is, it was not merely copied from someone else.

As a general rule, copyright arises automatically upon the creation of the work. Unlike patents and trademarks, therefore, it is not necessary for the work to be registered (indeed, it is usually not possible for the work to be registered) with a state authority for protection to arise. Further, it is not necessary for any notice to be affixed to a work for protection to arise.

Exclusive rights The primary right granted by copyright is the exclusive right to 'reproduce' the work. The right includes both literal reproduction (copying of the exact words, images, sounds, and so on) and non-literal reproduction (reproducing the essence of the work even though different words, images, sounds, and so on are used). Other exclusive rights often provided by copyright law are the rights to adapt (for example, translate) the work, to perform the work in public, to distribute (such as by sale or rental) tangible copies of the work to the public, and to communicate intangible copies of the work to the public (such as by broadcasting or internet transmission).

In addition to these 'economic' rights, copyright laws usually provide the subject matter creator (who may or may not be the copyright owner) with non-economic, or 'moral', rights. These rights include the right to be identified as the author of a work, and the right to prevent an alteration to the work that is prejudicial to the honour of the author.

Most copyright laws provide limitations on the exclusive economic rights of the copyright owner. These limitations vary from country to country, but they usually include exceptions for acts done that are considered to be a 'fair use' or 'fair dealing' with the work – such as copying for research, study, criticism, review or news reporting. Other limitations commonly found are exceptions for private copying of works, and exceptions for copying by libraries and archive.

The exclusive rights of copyright are limited temporally. The *Berne Convention* mandates that copyright last for a *minimum* period of 50 years after the death of the author ('life plus 50'). The USA, the countries of the European Union, and Australia, amongst others, in fact provide for a longer period of protection: life plus 70 years. Once copyright has expired, the work is said to have passed into the 'public domain', and may be reproduced, performed, and so on, without the copyright owner's consent.

5.1.2 Designs

Subject matter Most countries have legislation providing IPRs for the visual appearance of products – including for their shape, configuration, pattern or ornamentation. The products for which design protection may be sought include almost all consumer items, both handmade and manufactured – including cars, furniture, toys and clothing. Some countries limit the protection to those aspects of appearance that have no impact on the functionality of the product.

Requirements for protection In general terms, for a design to be protected it must be new. This means that it must not already exist – that is, there must not already be the same product that has the same or very similar design.

Design protection usually arises upon registration. To obtain registration, an application is made to a state registration authority, specifying the design and the product to which the design applies. The application is examined by the authority, to determine if the design is new. Details of registered designs are published by the state registration authority.

Some countries provide, in addition to design registration, a system of protection for designs that does not involve registration. Such unregistered design protection usually arises by virtue of the copyright legislation. It is possible, for example, for a designed product to be protected under copyright as a 'work of artistic craftsmanship'. It is also possible, in certain circumstances, for design drawings of a product to be protected under copyright as an 'artistic work'.

Exclusive rights   Upon registration, the owner of a design registration is granted the exclusive right to make, use and sell a product in respect of which the design has been registered and to which the design has been applied. Excepted from infringement are acts done for private and non-commercial purposes, acts done for experimental purposes and acts done for teaching purposes.

The maximum duration of registered design protection varies from country to country, but is commonly shorter than the maximum period of protection provided by copyright law. In Australia, for example, protection lasts for a maximum of ten years from application for registration; whereas in the UK it lasts for a maximum of 25 years from registration.

5.1.3   Patents

Subject matter   The *TRIPS Agreement* mandates that countries provide patent protection for 'inventions ... in all fields of technology'.[9] In general terms, an 'invention' is a new and innovative product or process, and a 'field of technology' is a field concerning the mechanical and industrial arts, as contrasted with the fine arts. Some countries, notably the USA and Australia, apply a very broad definition of 'technology', so as to include all artificially created states of affairs. In those countries, non-technical inventions such as new and innovative ways of doing business are patentable, along with more traditional, technical inventions.

The *TRIPS Agreement* permits, but doesn't require, countries to exclude from patentability inventions the commercial exploitation of which would be contrary to *ordre public* (loosely interpretable as 'public policy') or morality. The *TRIPS Agreement* also permits, but does not require, countries to exclude from patent protection diagnostic, therapeutic and surgical methods for the treatment of humans or animals, and plants and animals and essentially biological processes for their production.

Requirements for protection To be entitled to protection by a patent, an invention must satisfy the three requirements of novelty, inventive step (non-obviousness) and utility (industrial applicability). The characteristics of novelty and inventive step are judged against the 'prior art' – which is all information publicly available anywhere in the world, at the time of filing the application for a patent. An invention is new if it does not exist in the prior art. An invention has an inventive step if it is not obvious to a person skilled in that art. An invention has utility if it has at least one specific, substantial and credible use.

To obtain a patent, an inventor must make application to a state registration authority. The state authority examines the application to determine if the requirements of novelty, inventive step and utility (and others) are satisfied. If the requirements are satisfied, a patent for the invention will be granted. Applications for patents, as well as granted patents, are published by the state registration authority, and thus become part of the prior art against which later applications are examined.

A patent is only valid in the country in which it was granted. Patents are granted by individual countries (or, in limited instances, by groups of individual countries). There is no such thing as a 'world patent'. However, by virtue of international agreements there exist mechanisms by which an applicant for a patent can apply to numerous countries in one application. These applications, if successful, result in individual patents in the countries to which application was deemed to be made.

Exclusive rights Where the patented invention is a product, the exclusive rights of the patentee are to make, use and sell that product. Where the patented invention is a process, the exclusive rights of the patentee are to use the process and to use and sell a product obtained directly by that process. Unlike copyright law, there are few limitations on the exclusive rights of the patentee. A number of countries do, however, recognize that an act done for experimental purposes does not constitute an infringement of the patent. In addition, a number of countries have legislation imposing compulsory licences. These licences entitle third parties (including the state itself), upon payment of compensation to the patentee, to make use of a patented invention in limited circumstances – such as to provide relief in the case of national emergency or to remedy an anti-competitive practice.

Patents are of limited duration. Pursuant to the *TRIPS Agreement*, countries must provide a minimum patent term of 20 years from the date of filing of the patent application. A granted patent will lapse unless periodic renewal fees are paid.

5.1.4 Trademarks

Subject matter   Any 'sign' capable of distinguishing the goods or services of one undertaking from those of other undertakings shall be capable of constituting a trademark.[10] Indicia within the concept of a 'sign' include names, letters, numbers, figurative elements, colours, shapes, sounds and smells, and combinations thereof. Thus trademark registration may be obtained for names such as 'Levis Strauss', letters such as 'IBM', numbers such as '4711', a figurative element such as the Nike 'swoosh', a shape such as the curved Coca-Cola bottle, a colour such as the green used at petrol stations by BP, a sound such as the roar of a Harley-Davidson motorcycle, and a smell such as beer (in respect of non-beer products).

Requirements for protection   To be capable of registration, a trademark must be new. This means it must not be substantially identical or deceptively similar to another trademark that has been registered previously in relation to the same or similar goods or services. In addition, the trademark must be capable of distinguishing the goods or services of the applicant from the goods or services of other traders. This means the trademark must not be a sign which other traders could, in good faith, wish to use. By way of example, a sign that is laudatory (for example, 'perfection') or descriptive (for example, 'British', in relation to goods from Britain) is one which all traders, in good faith, may wish to use – and so is not registrable as a trademark by anyone. Finally, to be registrable a trademark must be capable of being represented graphically, and must not consist of material that is likely to deceive or confuse, is scandalous or is contrary to law.

To obtain registered trademark protection, a trademark owner must apply to a state registration authority, specifying the sign and the goods and/or services in respect of which exclusive entitlement to the sign is sought. The authority will examine the application and, if the requirements are satisfied, will enter the trademark, and the goods/services in respect of which it is registered, on a public register.

Exclusive rights   The owner of a registered trademark has the exclusive right to use in the course of trade an identical or similar sign for goods or services which are identical or similar to those in respect of which the trademark is registered. The justification for the exclusive right of trademark registration is to prevent confusion arising in the marketplace. The right provided by registration is not absolute – there is no infringement if the sign (including an identical sign) is used in respect of goods or services that are unrelated to the goods or services in respect of which the trademark is registered. Further, there is no infringement if the sign is used other than in the course of trade. Thus, use of a sign in a work of parody is not an act of trademark infringement.

The exclusive rights subsist so long as the trademark remains registered. To remain registered, the trademark owner must pay renewal fees, must use the trademark[11] and must ensure that the trademark does not become 'generic'. A trademark is said to have become 'generic' when it has become so well known that it is used by many members of the public as *the* name for the goods (or services) of the type to which the trademark owner has applied the mark. A good example is 'heroin', which was a trademark registered by the German chemical company Bayer in the late nineteenth century, but which is now used generically to describe 'diacetylmorphine'. Other former trademarks that are now generic names are 'pogo stick', 'escalator' and 'zipper'.

There is no set limit on how long a trademark may remain registered. Thus, so long as the registration renewal fees are paid, the trademark is used and the trademark does not become generic, a trademark may be protected in perpetuity.

5.2 Other Statutory Regimes

5.2.1 Integrated circuit layouts
The three-dimensional arrangement of the components of an integrated circuit (IC) is a form of IP protected by the law. The *Washington Treaty on Integrated Circuits*[12] established a regime for the protection of IC layouts. This regime, in slightly modified form, is mandated by the *TRIPS Agreement*.[13]

Protection of an IC design is conditional upon the design being 'original', in the sense that it is the result of the creator's own intellectual effort and is not commonplace among creators of layout designs at the time of creation. A few countries, notably the USA, have a registration system whereby protection is obtained by way of an application that is examined by a state authority. Most countries, however, do not have a registration system. In those countries, protection arises automatically upon creation of an IC design that satisfies the conditions for protection.

The owner of IPRs in an IC design has the exclusive rights to make an IC to the design and to sell an IC made to the design. The regime expressly provides that the act of reverse engineering an IC design is not an infringement. The duration of protection is limited. Most countries provide for a period of protection of ten years.

5.2.2   Plant breeders' rights

A 'plant variety' may be the subject of intellectual property rights, known as plant breeders' rights, by virtue of the regime provided by the *UPOV Convention*.[14] To be capable of receiving plant breeders' rights protection, a variety must be new, distinct, uniform and stable, as judged at the time of filing of an application for protection. A variety is new if propagating or harvested material of the variety has not been sold or otherwise disposed of to others. A variety is distinct if it is clearly distinguishable from any other variety whose existence is a matter of common knowledge. A variety is uniform if, subject to the variation that may be expected from the particular features of its propagation, it is sufficiently uniform in its relevant characteristics. A variety is stable if its relevant characteristics remain unchanged after repeated propagation.

To obtain plant breeders' rights protection, a plant breeder must make application to a state registration authority, describing the variety. The authority may require the carrying out of a test growing of the variety, to determine if the requirements of distinctness, uniformity and stability are satisfied. If the application is accepted, the new variety is entered in a public register.

The registered owner of plant breeders' rights has the exclusive rights to produce, reproduce (multiply) and sell the propagating material of the registered variety. As a general rule, these exclusive rights also extend to a variety that is essentially derived from the registered variety, to a variety that is not clearly distinguishable from the registered variety, and to a variety whose production requires repeated use of the registered variety. These exclusive rights are subject to a number of express limitations, which exempt from infringement acts done privately and for non-commercial purposes, acts done for experimental purposes, and acts done for the purpose of breeding other varieties.

The exclusive rights of the registered plant variety owner are of limited duration. For trees and vines, the rights last for 25 years from the date of grant. For plants other than trees and vines, the rights last for 20 years from the date of grant.

5.3   Non-statutory Regimes

5.3.1   Trade secrets protection: breach of confidence

Confidential information is a form of IP recognized by the law as worthy of protection. Generally, this protection is provided by way of the equitable action to obtain a court order to restrain a breach of confidence. The action allows a holder of confidential information to prevent another person, to whom the information has been disclosed, from making use of the information beyond the purposes for which it was disclosed.

Unlike in other IP regimes, the subject matter concerned does not need to be of any particular type: it need only be confidential, and thus not in the public domain. To succeed in the action, the plaintiff must prove that the information is confidential, that the information was confided in a manner that implied an obligation for the confidee to keep the information secret, and that there has been or will be unauthorized disclosure or use of the information. If these three matters are proved, the court will restrain the confidee from disclosing or using the information beyond the purposes for which it was disclosed to the confidee – that is, the court will restrain the confidee from breaching the confidence.

Although originally developed to restrain unauthorized uses of personal information, the action for breach of confidence has been extended to apply to commercial information such as trade secrets. In the course of employment, an employee may come to know information that is considered as belonging to the employer, such as information about customers or information about innovative ways of operating machinery. So long as this information is confidential, in the sense that it is not in the public domain, courts generally regard the employee as having received the information for the purposes only of their employment. Should an employee subsequently leave that employment and seek to use that information in competition with the employer, a court is likely to restrain that use as being in breach of the confidence owed by the employee to the employer.

The employer's entitlement to prevent a breach of confidence by an employee is subject to the limitation that the action must not constitute an unreasonable restraint of trade. Thus, an employer generally is not able to prevent an employee from subsequently using in competition background knowledge and skill acquired during the employment. Rather, it is only specific information that might be considered to be 'owned' by the employer that an employee should be restrained from using following the cessation of that employment.

The duration of protection provided by the action for breach of confidence is not limited. Thus, an employer is entitled to restrain breaches of confidence regarding trade secret information for so long as the information remains confidential – which might be in perpetuity.

5.3.2 Unfair competition protection: passing off

One form of unfair competition that the law generally prevents is the use in trade of a mark that deceives or confuses customers as to the source of goods or services. The law recognizes a right of a trader who has generated a reputation through the use of a particular mark to prevent another trader from using the same or a similar mark so as to 'pass off' that other trader's goods or services as being those of the first trader.

The equitable action to restrain a passing off provides a form of IP protection to trademarks that is similar to the protection provided by the registration of a trademark under the statutory trademark protection legislation. The main difference is that, unlike with statutory trademark protection, there is no requirement that the trader's mark be registered or even be capable of registration. Thus, a laudatory or descriptive trademark is capable of protection by an action for passing off, even though it is not capable of trademark registration.

It might be thought that the availability of an action preventing passing off would make the statutory trademark registration redundant, since the former does not require registration, which carries with it various transaction costs. This is not, however, the case. In an action for passing off, the plaintiff must prove that its mark has a reputation in the marketplace that will be damaged by virtue of the defendant's mark causing deception or confusion. The need to prove reputation requires evidence that a significant portion of consumers do in fact associate the plaintiff's mark with the plaintiff. While this may not be problematic for large traders, it is likely to be so for small traders. Indeed, it was because of the very difficulty of small traders proving reputation that the statutory trademark regime was introduced. Where a trademark is registered, its reputation is, in effect, assumed; thus an action to prevent an infringement of the trademark is more straightforward.

As with the registered trademark regime, there is no limit on the period of protection provided to a mark by the action to prevent a passing off. So long as the mark is one in which the trader can prove a reputation, the trader may prevent others from using in trade the same or a similar mark in a manner that deceives or confuses customers.

6   CONCLUSION

This chapter has attempted to explain the legal understanding of that special class of intangible asset called 'intellectual property'. It has shown that IP is an innovative or creative emanation of the human intellect, in respect of which legal rights of exclusivity may be granted. Not all such emanations are granted exclusive rights, however. Rather, it is only those intangible subject matters specifically defined in IP laws, and which satisfy specified thresholds of innovation/creativity, that benefit from the grant of exclusive rights.

The exclusive rights granted by IP laws are not absolute. Not all acts done in relation to protected IP are an infringement. Also, most IP rights last only for a limited period of time. Like most other assets recognized by the law, IP rights are generally freely transferable.

The constantly changing nature of the IP landscape, due to various economic, cultural and technological forces, has presented many new opportunities and challenges for creators, owners and users of IP. A good understanding of the fundamentals of IP law, both conceptually and operationally, is critical for those who need to manage this most important of intangible assets.

ACKNOWLEDGEMENT

The valuable assistance of Sally Pryor, Legal Researcher at the Intellectual Property Research Institute of Australia, is gratefully acknowledged.

NOTES

1. Idris, Kamal, 'Intellectual property: a power tool for economic growth' (2004), World Intellectual Property Organization, www.wipo.int/about-wipo/en/dgo/wipo_pub_888/index_wipo_pub_888.html.
2. Van Caenegem, William, *Intellectual Property*, Butterworths, Australia, 2001, p. 4.
3. Phillips, Jeremy and Firth, Alison, *Introduction to Intellectual Property Law* (3rd edn), Butterworths, London, 1995, p. 3.
4. *Re Dickens* [1935] Ch 267.
5. Licences, leases and shares, for example, are intangible assets that are not considered to be IP.
6. *Berne Convention for the Protection of Literary and Artistic Works of September 9, 1886*, Paris Act of 24 July 1971, as amended on 28 September 1979.
7. *Agreement on Trade-Related Aspects of Intellectual Property Rights*, being Annexe 1C to the *Agreement Establishing the World Trade Organization 1994*.
8. See, for example, the *International Convention for the Protection of Performers, Producers of Phonograms and Broadcasting Organizations*, Rome, 26 October 1961.
9. *TRIPS Agreement*, article 27(1).
10. *TRIPS Agreement*, article 15(1).
11. This is because a trademark that is not used is liable to be removed from the register, upon the application of a competitor.
12. *Treaty on the Protection of Intellectual Property in Respect of Integrated Circuits*, Washington, 26 May 1989.
13. *TRIPS Agreement*, article 35.
14. *International Convention for the Protection of New Varieties of Plants* of 2 December 1961, as revised at Geneva on 10 November 1972, on 23 October 1978 and on 19 March 1991.

3. An accounting perspective

Anne Wyatt

1 THE ACCOUNTING DEFINITION

Intangible capital (IC) and intellectual property (IP) are not specifically defined in accounting regulations. Instead, as productive resources (or inputs), the individual components of IC and IP are reported as assets on the balance sheet if the asset *definition* and the asset *recognition* rules in the accounting regulations are satisfied. Definition and recognition rules in the accounting regulations are applied in a two-stage process. We first apply the definition rules and, if these are satisfied, the second stage is to then apply the recognition rules. Satisfying the 'definition' rules means the item has attributes that fit the definition criteria. Satisfying the 'recognition' rules means that this item meets the recognition rules and can therefore be recorded in the financial statements – one or more of the profit and loss statement, balance sheet, and cash flow statement. The alternative to recognition is disclosure. 'Disclosure' means that either quantitative or qualitative information about the item is included in the explanatory notes to the financial statements. However, the item is not recorded in the accounting system or reported in the financial statements.

1.1 Definition

According to the International Accounting Standards Board (IASB),[1] in their *Framework for the Preparation and Presentation of Financial Statements* (the Framework), an asset is defined as 'a resource controlled by the entity as a result of past events and from which future economic benefits are expected to flow to the entity' (IASB 2001, para. 49(a)). Most countries employ a similar asset definition. Further, the international accounting standard IAS 38 Intangible Assets defines an intangible asset as 'an identifiable non-monetary asset without physical substance' (para. 8). These two definitions (assets and intangible asset) imbue intangible assets with three attributes: (1) identifiability;[2] (2) there is the capacity to control access and use of the asset where control is a result of a past event; and (3) future economic benefits are expected to flow in to the firm from these items.

In applying the asset definition rules, paragraph 53 of the IASB Framework specifies what the future economic benefit embodied in an asset comprises: it is 'the potential to contribute, directly or indirectly, to the flow of cash and cash equivalents to the entity'. The benefits can be from production directly, take the form of convertibility into cash or cash equivalents, or the benefit can be 'a capability to reduce cash outflows such as when an alternative manufacturing process lowers the costs of production' (para. 53). Thus, the asset definition is prima facie intended to encompass intangible assets of the type represented by IC and IP.

This intention is made clear in paragraph 56 of the IASB Framework, which states that a physical form is 'not essential to the existence of an asset'. Paragraph 57 points out the importance of property rights as evidence of the 'control' criterion: 'the capacity of an entity to control benefits is usually the result of legal rights'. However, the Framework takes the view that it is not necessary to legally own the item for it to be an asset. Hence, the Framework recognizes that property rights can be obtained using other means, for example, a trade secret, which helps the entity control the inflow of expected benefits. However, there is little likelihood that these other means of obtaining control will lead to an asset as these types of IC are more likely to reside in the intellect of employees where secrecy is the basis of control.

The asset definition also implies that there cannot be an asset unless there is an identifiable, originating past transaction or other past event (para. 58 of the Framework). The effect of this criterion is to make most IC and IP identifiable only by reference to a purchase transaction with a party outside the firm.

Further, there is the issue of using cost (expenditure) versus value to measure the asset. The IASB Framework in paragraph 59 states that a close association exists between incurring expenditure and generating assets but the two may not necessarily coincide. This paragraph goes on to say that, while expenditures are indicative that future economic benefits are sought, they are not conclusive evidence that an item satisfying the definition of an asset has been obtained. Conversely, according to paragraph 59, the absence of a related expenditure does not preclude an item from satisfying the definition of an asset and thus becoming a candidate for recognition in the balance sheet (for example, donated items). Ostensibly, this permits firms to recognize IC and IP items that the firm has developed through ongoing effort, which are not directly attributable to specific expenditures. Some examples are patents, trademarks, designs and brands, which have been developed over time from a range of expenditures and intellectual effort. To achieve this outcome, the internal data collection systems must be sufficiently tuned in to the firm's business processes to ensure there is data to verify the IC, or IP meets the four asset definition criteria outlined above. There is little evidence to suggest this is descriptive of current practices (see EC 2003).

1.2 Recognition

An asset is recognizable in an asset account in the accounting system and hence on the balance sheet when: (1) it is probable that the future economic benefits embodied in the asset will eventuate; and (2) the asset possesses a cost or other value that can be measured reliably (para. 83 of the Framework). IAS 38 Intangible Assets further states that an intangible asset shall be recognized only if 'the *cost* of the asset can be measured reliably' (para. 21, emphasis in the original).

A further constraint on recognizing intangible assets is the asset recognition criteria. The first recognition criterion, it is probable that the future economic benefits embodied in the asset will eventuate, is closely linked to the 'control' criterion in the asset definition. Hence, both the asset definition and recognition criteria bring us back to the concept of control in defining and recognizing assets. The most objective evidence of control is property rights via statute, contract or other legal means. We are therefore more likely to see intellectual property, as defined within the law, rather than intangible capital items, on the balance sheet. The second intangible asset recognition criterion, the asset possesses a cost that can be measured reliably (IAS 38, para. 21), means that there must be documentary evidence of the cost, for example, a purchase contract. Accordingly, this criterion excludes from recognition those IC and IP items that cannot be directly linked to specific verifiable costs. Examples include patents, trademarks, designs and brands that have been internally developed over a long period for which the cost data has not been carefully documented.

Hence, in summary, any economic or behavioural factors that impact on the uncertainty of the expected future earnings flowing from the investment, and the calibre of procedures to document the costs of the investment, will impact on the accounting treatment of the expenditure.

1.3 Identifiability

For inclusion in the charts of accounts as a capital item, it is necessary but not sufficient for assets to be definable and recognizable. In addition, an expenditure must satisfy the identifiability criteria. 'Identifiability' is defined in IAS 38 Intangible Assets (para. 12):

An asset meets the identifiability criterion in the definition of an intangible asset when it:
(a) Is separable, that is, is capable of being separated or divided from the entity and sold, transferred, licensed, rented or exchanged, either individually or together with a related contract, asset or liability; or
(b) Arises from contractual or other legal rights, regardless of whether those rights are transferable or separable from the entity or from other rights and obligations.

The significance of this distinction is that only intangible assets that meet the identifiability criteria can be individually measured and recognized on the balance sheet as an asset. Unidentifiable intangible assets are merely a residual from a takeover transaction (of one company by another) as explained below.

1.3.1   Goodwill
Purchased goodwill, which arises when one company acquires an equity holding in another company and the purchase consideration is greater than the net assets acquired, is identifiable and thus recorded as an asset. Purchased goodwill is the only type of goodwill that is recognizable as an intangible asset on the balance sheet. According to the Australian Accounting Standards Board recognition is restricted to purchased goodwill, and not internally generated goodwill, because '[Of] the difficulty, or impossibility, of identifying the events or transactions which contribute to the overall goodwill of the entity. Even if these were identifiable, the extent to which they generate future benefits and the value of such benefits are not usually capable of being measured reliably' (AASB 1013, para. 4.1.1).

As summarized in Figure 3.1 at Level 3, the accounting standard IFRS 3 Business Combinations requires purchased goodwill arising in an acquisition to be recognized as an asset. Purchased goodwill is not depreciated but is subject to impairment testing. IFRS 3 also requires that the cost of the acquisition is allocated over the assets acquired including any identifiable intangible assets that meet the definition and recognition criteria for intangible assets set out in IAS 38 Intangible Assets (paras 36, 45).

Internally generated goodwill is an unidentifiable intangible asset and is consequently not recorded as capital on the balance sheets.[3] Goodwill that is internally generated cannot be recognized even though it is eventually recognized if the company is taken over. This applies to intangibles more broadly, for example:

In determining the amount of purchased goodwill the purchaser needs to recognise all assets acquired, whether of a tangible or intangible nature. This might involve recognising some intangible assets which, if internally generated by the purchaser, would not normally be recognised as assets because the absence of an exchange transaction usually prevents them from being measured reliably. (AASB 1013, para. 5.6.1).

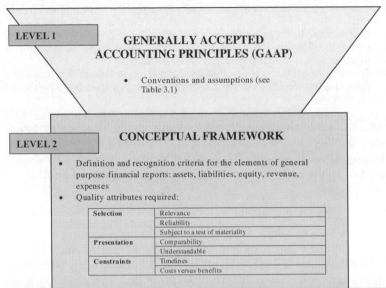

LEVEL 1

GENERALLY ACCEPTED ACCOUNTING PRINCIPLES (GAAP)

- Conventions and assumptions (see Table 3.1)

LEVEL 2

CONCEPTUAL FRAMEWORK

- Definition and recognition criteria for the elements of general purpose financial reports: assets, liabilities, equity, revenue, expenses
- Quality attributes required:

Selection	Relevance
	Reliability
	Subject to a test of materiality
Presentation	Comparability
	Understandable
Constraints	Timelines
	Costs versus benefits

LEVEL 3

ACCOUNTING STANDARDS

Standard Name	Coverage	Accounting method
IFRS 3 Business Combinations	Purchased unidentifiable intangible assets (that is, purchased goodwill)	Recognize goodwill asset if future benefits are probable
	Purchased identifiable intangible assets (for example, patents, trademarks, brands, R&D in-process projects)	Recognize identifiable assets if future benefits are probable
IAS 38 Intangible Assets	Internally generated unidentifiable intangible assets (that is, internally generated goodwill)	Cannot be recognized under any circumstances
	Purchased identifiable intangible assets	Recognize if asset definition and recognition criteria met
	Internally generated intangible assets	Must be evaluated according to whether it is a research or development stage: -research costs must be immediately expensed -development costs can be recognized as assets only if all 6 tests in para. 57 are met
	Internally generated brands, mastheads, publishing titles, customer lists, and 'items similar in substance' (para. 63)	Specifically prohibited from recognition as assets under para. 63 of IAS 38
IFRS 6 Exploration for and Evaluation of Mineral Assets	Exploration and evaluation costs	Choice to recognize as assets on an area of interest (tenement area) basis or expense

Figure 3.1   Accounting regulation – a three-level deductive framework

Examples of the factors accounting regulators consider gives rise to 'unidentifiable' assets that form part of goodwill includes market penetration, effective advertising, good labour relations and a superior operating team.

1.3.2 Other identifiable assets

According to IAS 38 Intangible Assets, examples of identifiable intangible assets that may meet the definition of identifiability above, include brand names, mastheads and publishing titles, computer software, licences and franchises, copyrights, patents, other industrial property rights, service and operating rights, recipes, formulae, models, designs, prototypes and intangible assets under development. If these have been acquired from outside the firm, then the purchase cost is usually taken to be a reliable cost for recognition purposes under IAS 38. Accordingly, as shown in Level 3 of Figure 3.1, purchased identifiable intangible assets can usually be recognized as assets (that is, providing the IAS 38 definition and recognition rules are satisfied).

If the identifiable intangible assets are internally generated, then IAS 38 requires the firm to classify the investment as either research or development phase costs. This rule is motivated by the assumption that the development phase of a project is further advanced than the research phase and therefore the firm may be able to identify an intangible asset and demonstrate that the asset will generate probable future economic benefit (para. 58). Research-related expenditures cannot be treated as assets under any circumstances. If the expenditures relate to the development stage, then six criteria must be satisfied, in addition to the specific asset definition and recognition rules provided in IAS 38, for the items to be recognizable as assets (para. 57). These six criteria include:

> An intangible asset arising from development (or from the development phase of an internal project) shall be recognised if, and only if, an entity can demonstrate all of the following:
>
> (a) The technical feasibility of completing the intangible asset so that it will be available for use or sale;
> (b) Its intention to complete the intangible asset and use or sell it;
> (c) Its ability to use or sell the intangible asset;
> (d) How the intangible asset will generate probable future economic benefits. Among other things, the entity can demonstrate the existence of a market for the output of the intangible asset or the intangible asset itself or, if it is to be used internally, the usefulness of the intangible asset;
> (e) the availability of adequate technical, financial and other resources to complete the development and to use or sell the intangible asset; and

(f) its ability to measure reliably the expenditure attributable to the intangible asset during its development. (IAS 38 Intangible Assets, para. 57)

Examples of development activities provided by the accounting regulators in paragraph 58 include:

(a) The design, construction and testing of pre-production or pre-use prototypes and models;
(b) The design of tools, jigs, moulds, and dies involving new technology;
(c) The design, construction and operation of a pilot plant that is not of a scale economically feasible for commercial production; and
(d) The design, construction and testing of a chosen alternative for new or improved materials, devices, products, processes, systems or services.

Paragraph 63 specifically prohibits the recognition of the following if they are internally generated within the firm: 'brands, mastheads, publishing titles, customer lists and items similar in substance shall not be recognised as intangible assets'.

2 THE REGULATORY FRAMEWORK IMPLICATIONS

Accounting regulates assets from the vantage point of a three-level deductive framework. Figure 3.1 summarizes the three levels of this framework. At the highest level of generality is Level 1 Generally Accepted Accounting Principles (GAAP). Accounting standards are at the other end of the specificity spectrum prescribing accounting rules for particular items and transactions. The asset definition and recognition rules discussed in the previous section are at Level 2 of Figure 3.1. The specific rules for intangible assets in IAS 38 Intangible Assets are at Level 3.

The data collected according to the framework set out in Figure 3.1 is organized using a chart of accounts and the GAAP conventions and assumptions from Level 1 of Figure 3.1 (and illustrated in Table 3.1). The chart of accounts is simply a listing of all the companies' accounts according to an expandable numbering system to allow accounts to be added and deleted as the business evolves. The chart of accounts dictates the classes of data that will be collected and how they will appear in the journals and ledgers.

The classes of data are limited to assets, liabilities, revenues, expenses, and owners' equity under the formal conceptual framework at Level 2 of Figure 3.1. Conceptually, expenditures giving rise to intangible capital and intellectual property are present in each of these classes of data depending on the stage of the firm's investment and operating cycle. However, in practice, financial reporting conventions (such as conservatism) 'anonymously' relegate most of the intangible investment to expenses (as costs of goods sold and sales, general and administrative expenses) and one revenue figure from operations, so that the nature, quantum and returns to intangible investment cannot be determined. This comes about because most charts of accounts are heavily orientated towards traditional plant, property and equipment investments and operations.

Table 3.1   Overview of key GAAP conventions and assumptions

Key GAAP principle	Motivation	Implication for intangible assets
Conservatism	Assets are recognized only if there is a strong probability that future benefits are expected. However, liabilities are recognized if there is any probability of sacrificing future benefits	Accounting conservatism understates the book value of equity. That is, it understates assets minus liabilities, which equals net assets and equals book value of equity. Because the future benefits of intangibles tend to be more uncertain cf. tangibles, this distorts the accounts in favour of tangibles
Historical cost	The historical costs from past transactions are accumulated on the balance sheet. They are allocated over the estimated useful life of the asset, as the asset is consumed in the production of goods and services	Historical cost is misleading if the asset is separable and the prices of the asset are changing due to inflation Historical cost may not be identifiable for intangible assets Historical cost may not indicate the significance of an intangible asset relative to the firm's other assets
Market transaction	To ensure accounting information is objective and verifiable, amounts recorded are determined from past market transactions	Items without an identifiable transaction are excluded from the accounting system. Often intangible assets are not attributable to a specific transaction or even a sequence of transactions and so they are excluded.
Going concern assumption	The motivation for the use of historical cost to record items in the accounting system rather than another measurement system such as liquidation values	Consistent use of one measurement concept across accounting periods to increase user confidence. However, intangible assets may not have an identifiable historical cost. In addition, when intangible assets lose value and cause total (economic) assets to lose value, the going concern is not descriptive. However, going concern is still assumed to apply unless the company has gone into bankruptcy

Table 3.1   continued

Key GAAP principle	Motivation	Implication for intangible assets
Period assumption	It is necessary for accountability and performance measurement purposes to estimate profit for intervals of the life of the firm rather than wait until the firm terminates when profit is known	Requires estimates of accruals, which are adjustments at the close of each accounting period for open (incomplete) transactions The outcome is that the accounting system is a collection of expected future cash flows – where those that are expected will be recorded on the balance sheet, and those that have now been realized appear in the profit and loss statement Even if detailed adjustments were allowed, it is difficult to make these estimates for intangible investment given the current level of understanding of what constitutes an intangible investment and how it is linked to future earnings
Accrual and matching	Profit is a summary performance measure for the period (interval), which is measured by matching revenue earned in the period with expenses incurred to generate those revenues	Estimates are required of the revenues and expenses that belong to the current accounting period (profit and loss items), and those that will belong to future periods (asset and liability accruals on the balance sheet) that have not yet been used up. It provides companies with discretion over the timing of accruals (that is, they are estimates). However, the accrual reverses in the future (for example, an account receivable and associated provision for doubtful debts are reduced, respectively, when a customer pays or defaults on their payment). This reversal process will show up instances when accounting discretion has been used opportunistically. It is more difficult to track these actions for goodwill and other difficult to monitor intangible assets

The GAAP (at Level 1 of Figure 3.1) are, general principles developed through practice over time (that is, in a similar way to common law albeit without the standing of law). These principles are deceptively informal but largely determine accounting practice. For example, the 'going concern' assumption motivates the use of a measurement system (for example, historical cost or market value measurement) other than liquidation value, while the 'period assumption' leads to the provision of accounting information on a regular basis at intervals less than the life of the firm.

Table 3.1 elaborates on Level 1 of Figure 3.1. It provides an overview of the key conventions and assumptions that have been handed down from early times and are fundamental to existing accounting practice. As summarized in Table 3.1, most of the assumptions need specific operational guidelines if they are to be objectively applied to intangible investment.

The principle of conservatism has special implications for the treatment of intangible expenditures. This principle, which requires that the measure of an asset should be verifiable from an actual transaction (preferably with an external party), leads firms to immediately expense (in the current accounting period) most expenditures of an intangible nature. However, immediate expensing of intangible assets is not conservative since it serves to understate book value of equity (assets minus liabilities) and current profits, and overstate future profits. Because intangible investment is relatively unobservable to outsiders, and the rate of investment and depreciation are usually not constant, it is difficult to unravel the direction of distortions to reported profits.

The historical cost basis of measurement is also problematic for many intangible assets because intangible assets are typically developed over time. When this is the case, it can be difficult to identify the stream of expenditures that lead to the development of the asset. This is exacerbated by the classifications of assets included in the chart of accounts, which tend to be the traditional plant, property and equipment classes of assets. This is not implying that historical cost is not appropriate for measuring investments. Instead, the problem lies in the link between historical cost measurement principles and the extent that data collection is linked to business processes. The current approaches tend to aggregate intangible investment into cost of goods sold and operating expenses, rather than intangible investment categories (see Wyatt and Abernethy 2004).

Owing to the small amount of expenditures on intangible investment that are actually accounted for as such, the quantum of expenditures treated as intangible assets can be uninformative about the significance of the asset to the firm (see Wyatt 2005). As a result, a number of alternative measures have been employed using forecasted earnings or cash-flow based measures. Table 3.2 provides some examples of measures that have been used. These types of measurement techniques have been developed as an alternative to historical cost measurement. However, since many countries do not permit companies to capitalize internally generated intangible assets (neither goodwill nor identifiable), these measurement techniques tend to be used for valuations of intangible assets exchanged in mergers and acquisitions.

Table 3.2   Commonly used methods to measure intangible assets

Method	Calculation	Appropriate circumstances for use
Relief from royalty	Capitalized value of after-tax royalties the firm is relieved from paying as a result of ownership of the intangible asset	• Assumes possession of the asset allows the firm to avoid costs of building market share and profitability • Assumes firm capacity to pay a notional royalty • The property right must be sufficiently exclusive
Excess profits or notional maximum royalty payable	Calculate the excess profits over the profit rate required on the firms' net tangible assets and capitalize	• Assumes the entire excess return is derived from the intangible capital estimated. No account for other external regulatory and technical factors that may be relevant to the generation of future profits
Capitalization of earnings	Capitalize earnings according to a multiple, then deduct the current total tangible and monetary assets from this capitalized amount to arrive at total intangibles	• Similar to excess profits method. Usually necessary to analyse the intangibles figure to break down components, for example, mastheads valuation conditional on maintenance of property rights
Net present value of incremental cash flows	Net present value of cash flows generated by the asset over its useful life	• Need to be able to identify the net cash flows for specific intangibles, for example, copyrights for music or programs, film library, licensing royalties • Need to estimate useful life, for example, considering product life cycle, innovation rate, appropriability conditions • Based on cash flows so no accounting distortion
Gross profit differential	Capitalization of the difference between (1) the gross profit contribution (after costs of maintaining) of a branded product; and (2) the gross profit contribution of an unbranded product	• Assumes the entire incremental gross profit is attributable to brand value asset • Need to find a close equivalent product (or service) along with the financial data to make the calculation • Ignores other external sources of uncertainty

Premium sales price	Capitalization of the sales price premium of the branded product over a comparable generic product	• Method ignores costs/external sources of uncertainty • High volume/scale economy products are penalized as having little value (not so with gross profit approach) • It may not be a premium price that is the primary source of benefit – competitive advantage could be market share, quality, marketing (for example, Coca-Cola)
Market valuation	Present value of future benefits obtained from the price in the relevant market	• Need an active market • Need to find a comparable asset • Price information must be available publicly
Cost valuation	Quantification of expenditures outlaid on the assets or replacement expenditures that would be required	• Assumes money unit is constant • Assumes cost and future benefits are identical • Assumes separable but intangibles usually valuable relative to specialized labour and complementary assets (for example, trademark value is greater than cost of publishing the property right for Coca-Cola) • Subject to accounting distortions • Does not differentiate 'costs' from maintenance 'costs' • Replacement cost assumes relevant, active market
Brand strength	Application of a multiple to the brand's estimated profitability	• Assumes a relevant and reliable valuation can be obtained by scoring the brand against a number of selected firm/external competitive/ business conditions • No direct relation from cost to future benefits assumed

Source: Adapted from Ernst & Young (1995).

3 CONSISTENCY OF TREATMENT

Wyatt and Abernethy (2004) analyse the accounting regulation of intangible assets including IC and IP under international and other country rules. They conclude that the rules do not take account of the economics of intangible investment, that the accounting rules are not consistent either internally or relative to economic reality, and as a result lead to ad hoc accounting treatments and outcomes that impact adversely on the interpretability of the information.

Accounting for the intangible expenditures of resource companies has also been particularly controversial due to the uncertainty of unproven projects. The US accounting regulators have entertained either a full cost method that capitalizes all costs and later writes off amounts that were unsuccessful, and the successful efforts approach which only capitalizes assets when a project is expected to be successful. Australian companies account for exploration and evaluation on an area of interest basis.[4] The 'area of interest' method requires immediate expensing of these costs unless the firm holds a tenement over the area and at least one of the following conditions is met:

1. Such costs are expected to be recouped through successful development and exploitation of the area of interest, or alternatively, by its sale; and
2. Exploration and evaluation activities in the area of interest have not at balance date reached a stage which permits a reasonable assessment of the existence or otherwise of economically recoverable reserves, and active and significant operations in, or in relation to, the area of interest are continuing.[5]

In some countries, an additional intangibles category called something like 'Other Deferred Assets' also appears on the balance sheet. It includes items such as employee knowledge, technology under development, software and computer development, advertising and marketing, training and design, manufacturing arrangements, distribution systems, client database development, the costs of forming the company and borrowing costs of establishing loans. However, as we shall discuss below, these practices are not widespread.

Finally, research and development costs have traditionally been treated as an item in their own right and specifically regulated by an accounting standard. While the US Financial Accounting Standard Board (FASB) has continued this practice, the IASB has moved to IAS 38, which classifies all internally generated, identifiable intangibles as in either a research or a development (R&D) stage. The US FASB has historically required the immediate expensing of all R&D expenditures based on a tenuous link from the expenditures to future benefits. The one exception is software development costs, which have been capitalizable as assets since 1985 if technical feasibility tests have been met. The problem with R&D is that it means different things to different industries and firms. For example, when collecting (compulsory) R&D data, Australian Bureau of Statistics staff spend time each year visiting firms to clarify the firm's approach to measuring R&D. As a result of this ambiguity, what is classified as R&D varies and this adversely affects users' ability to interpret R&D numbers. This conjecture is supported in the research discussed ahead.

Table 3.3 illustrates the earnings impact of six different accounting treatments for intangible expenditures, which comprises the combinations available to firms from expensing, capitalizing, amortizing and revaluation.

Table 3.3 shows that the accounting methods employed matter because they affect total assets, profits reported, and ratios such as return on assets, all numbers that are used to evaluate firm performance. This example of the effects of different accounting treatments also shows that the effects of the accounting choices are large and 'lumpy' from year to year. These short-term distortions can lead to misleading spikes in financial measures and adverse effects on the efficiency of capital markets (for example, Lev and Sougiannis 1996).

Possible distortions include treating intangible investments as expenses, amortizing at an incorrect rate, and failing to revalue (in countries where revaluation is permitted) or write down assets when material changes in expected future cash inflows occurs. The total expense recorded and reported in each year varies between $0 and $500 000. The profit varies between $500 000 and $1 000 000 in year 2. The end of year 2 assets on the balance sheet varies between $0 and $1 400 000. The return on asset ratios shows the effect of departing from the economic notion of investment and immediately expensing all the intangibles expenditure. Specifically, there is a $500 000 profit generated in year 2 for an entity that has no assets on the balance sheet at either the beginning or the end of the year. The return on assets in every year for the immediate expensing method, *ceteris paribus*, is zero. Unless the entity has investments with transitory earnings confined only to the current period, full and immediate expensing is unlikely to reflect the underlying economics of the intangible investment. Full capitalization of intangible expenditures and amortization aims to match the costs of generating revenue with the revenue earned in the specific year. Combined with an annual impairment test, this method is more likely to provide profit and ending assets figures that are more probably representative. If intangible investment is not observable, it is difficult to untangle these distortions.[6]

In summary, in almost all countries the GAAP principles of conservativism regarding the certainty of future benefits, and the need for a recorded market transaction, mean that intangible assets fall into the firms' cost of goods sold and/or sales, general and administration expenses.[7] With competition and accompanying business changes, early stage companies or those with very uncertain projects will have few assets on the balance sheet, and negative earnings (negative operating cashflows) reported in the profit and loss

Table 3.3   Profit computed using different accounting method combinations

Year 1 – $500 000 intangibles expenditure and zero revenue:

Immediate expense	Full capitalization	Full capitalization and amortization (over 5 years)	Selective capitalization	Selective capitalization and amortization (over 5 years)	Capitalization and revaluation
Year 1 ($000)	Year 1 ($000)	Year 1 ($000)	Year 1 ($000)	Year 1 ($000)	Year 1 ($000)
Expense 500	Expense 0	Expense 0	Expense 250	Expense 250	.Expense 0
Capitalize 0	Capitalize 500	Capitalize 500	Capitalize 250	Capitalize 250	Capitalize 500
Amortize t_1 0	Amortize t_1 0	Amortize t_1 100	Amortize t_1 0	Amortize t_1 50	Amortize t_1 0
Revalue 0	Revalue 0	Revalue 0	Revalue 0	Revalue 0	Revalue 100
Total revenue $0	Total revenue $0	Total revenue $0	Total revenue $0	Total revenue $0	Total revenue $0
Total expense 500	Total expense 0	Total expense 100	Total expense 250	Total expense 300	Total expense 0
Profit –500	Profit 0	Profit –100	Profit –250	Profit –300	Profit 0
Ending assets 0	Ending assets 500	Ending assets 400	Ending assets 250	Ending assets 200	Ending assets 600
Return on assets 0%	Return on assets 0%	Return on assets –25%	Return on assets –100%	Return on assets –150%	Return on assets 0%

Year 2 – $500 000 intangibles expenditure and $1 000 000 revenue generated:

Immediate expense	Full capitalization	Full capitalization and amortization (over 5 years)	Selective capitalization	Selective capitalization and amortization (over 5 years)	Capitalization and revaluation
Year 2 ($000)	Year 2 ($000)	Year 2 ($000)	Year 2 ($000)	Year 2 ($000)	Year 2 ($000)
Beginning assets 0	Beginning assets 500	Beginning assets 400	Beginning assets 250	Beginning assets 200	Beginning assets 600
Expense 500	Expense 0	Expense 0	Expense 250	Expense 250	Expense 0
Capitalize 0	Capitalize 500	Capitalize 500	Capitalize 250	Capitalize 250	Capitalize 500
Amortize t_2 0	Amortize t_2 0	Amortize t_2 200	Amortize t_2 0	Amortize t_2 100	Amortize t_2 0
Revalue 0	Revalue 0	Revalue 0	Revalue 0	Revalue 0	Revalue 300
Total revenue $1000	Total revenue $1000	Total revenue $1000	Total revenue $1000	Total revenue $1000	Total revenue $1000
Total expense 500	Total expense 0	Total expense 200	Total expense 250	Total expense 350	Total expense 0
Profit 500	Profit 1000	Profit 800	Profit 750	Profit 650	Profit 1000
Ending assets 0	Ending assets 1000	Ending assets 700	Ending assets 500	Ending assets 350	Ending assets 1400
Return on assets 0%	Return on assets 100%	Return on assets 111%	Return on assets 150%	Return on assets 186%	Return on assets 71%

statement (cash flow statement) – even though the company is making significant investments. To the extent the externally reported data defines the structure of internal data collection, both internal users (management) and external users of accounting information will not have the necessary data for investment decisions.

4 CHANGES TO THE TREATMENT OF INTANGIBLE CAPITAL OVER TIME

> Throughout the structure of accounting, I submit, there is far too much emphasis upon the criterion of tangibility in reaching a conclusion on how business costs shall be recorded and reported ... Anyone operating a business nowadays is operating a very speculative undertaking, and the profit-and-loss statement of that business should not be prepared as if it were an abstract situation, entirely independent of the economic setting in which the concern has its being. (Paton 1938, 27–8)

This quotation by an early accounting scholar is one of many in the literature that suggests the longevity of the deliberations and debate concerning the definitions and practices of accounting for intangible investments (see also Yang 1927; Dickerson 1941 in Zeff 1982). This is not surprising given that the costs dominating the production function in early times were current period variable inputs. In early times, accounting practice was not based on concepts of permanent capital and long-term assets.[8] Technical knowledge was embodied in the physical assets, in buildings, machines and transportation, and later in plant and equipment for such industries as water power, textiles, iron, print, steam ships and engines, railways and machine tools. By the turn of the eighteenth century, there was no agreed 'theory of capital' or profit concept and wide diversity in accounting methods. According to Pollard (1963, p. 116)[9]

> the increase in the amount of fixed capital made investments permanent, and the regularity of the income derived from them [made them] ... important. With it, began the 'accountants' problems', 'problems which accountants and bookkeepers had not previously needed to consider, except in a minor way. These problems arose mainly in connection with the large amounts of capital sunk in plant, equipment and transportation facilities.

The accounting emphasis on tangible assets, which has persisted to the present period, arose around the 1600s with the shift away from separately funded, speculative ventures to continuing ventures with a permanent capital.[10] It came about because the ventures were overwhelmed by assets and profits from various trading ventures in different states of completion, and reporting to differing shareholder lists for each venture completed. The significant investment in expensive, long-lived assets increased the economic significance of management practices for assets. As a result of the 'confusion and embarrassment', accounting practice developed to accommodate long-term investment and a permanent capital (Littleton 1981, p. 211). Accounting for depreciation of assets against revenues, renewals, and wear and tear, became increasingly important for economic decisions such as setting prices, calculating period costs, operating efficiency calculations for manufacturing and railroad companies, and differentiating capital and profits (Littleton 1981). The accounting procedures for long-lived assets have changed little from the concepts and methods brought from the earlier, formative periods.

However, growth in technical and science bases underlying economic activity has wrought significant change in the nature and processes of commerce, processes not yet fully accommodated by the accounting system. Changes to the knowledge base, in breadth, complexity, and in the number of specialized areas, are a major component of these new processes (Metcalfe 1997).

There is some good news. In the past decade, accounting academics have found that goodwill assets determined under accounting regulations in each jurisdiction are related to the market value of the firm (Chauvin and Hirschey 1994; McCarthy and Schneider 1996; Jennings et al. 1996; Muller 1994; Vincent 1994; and see Chapters 6–9 in this volume), and this relation holds for purchased goodwill from recent and from past acquisitions. Vincent (1994) found this relation held for up to five years post-acquisition for net goodwill (net of amortization to date). A number of studies have also investigated the association between advertising expenditures and stock market values and other firm performance measures, finding long-lived effects only for non-durable goods industries (Ben Zion 1978; Bublitz and Ettredge 1989; Chauvin and Hirschey 1994; Ettredge and Bublitz 1988; Hirschey 1982; Hirschey and Spencer 1992; Hirschey and Weygandt 1985; Netter 1982).

The usefulness of more detailed reporting of intangible assets is illustrated empirically by Ritter and Wells (2004) and Wyatt (2005) in the Australian setting where reporting of intangible assets comprising IC and IP is more common that in most other countries. Wyatt (2005) finds identifiable intangible assets (comprising acquired and internally generated intangibles) are more highly valued by investors compared with goodwill and R&D. Ritter and Wells (2004) find reported identifiable intangible assets are also correlated with future stock price and accounting earnings, suggesting the forward-looking nature of these items.

However, there is still a large gap in the explanatory power of the models in all these studies. A possible cause, yet to be documented empirically but often invoked, is the apparent increasing relevance of intangible investment to modern commerce. We can draw an analogy between the growth of tangible capital in earlier times and the lag to a framework of relevant accounting concepts and principles.

There have been attempts by accounting regulators to bridge a perceived financial reporting gap in the area of IC and IP. In particular, the Australian accounting regulators, the Australian Accounting Standards Board, earlier took a progressive approach to accounting for intangible assets to accommodate these advances in technology and production. An exposure draft (prelude to an accounting standard), ED 49 Accounting for Identifiable Intangible Assets, which advocated changes to financial reporting practices for intangibles was issued in August 1989. However there was so much opposition to the proposed initiatives that the exposure draft was abruptly withdrawn in March 1992 (Henderson and Peirson 1995, p. 420).

Draft ED 49 defined intangible assets as non-monetary assets without physical substance including but not restricted to brandnames, copyrights, franchises, intellectual property, licences, mastheads, patents and trademarks. It proposed to bring both acquired and internally generated intangibles to account at cost of acquisition or, in the case of internally generated intangibles, either cost or lowest cost at which the assets could be obtained in the normal course of business as determined by independent valuation (para. 21). Any costs recorded in some other asset account could be transferred to the newly recognized asset account. Otherwise, the asset was to be brought onto the balance sheet by offsetting amounts recorded in the new asset account and in a shareholders' equity account (asset revaluation reserve). Amortization was to be mandatory without a maximum period.

The intangibles were to be classified in the financial statements in detail according to classes, with the classes specified in the definition of identifiable intangibles above being the minimum, acceptable level of disaggregation. Most notably, ED 49 paragraph (vi) in the commentary indicates that reliable measurement is important, but not fatal in bringing an identifiable intangible with probable future economic benefits to account:

> it is considered that in most instances a reliable measurement could be obtained through the application of a valuation technique; such technique may involve, for example, the capitalisation of actual or imputed royalty payments due in respect of the asset. However, at this stage, knowledge and understanding the use of such valuation techniques and of the resulting information is not widespread among preparers and users of financial reports. It is expected that as knowledge and use of valuation techniques increases, so may there be an increase in the number of

internally generated identifiable intangible assets to be brought to account. (ED 49 Commentary, para. (vi))

Following the withdrawal of ED 49, Australian accounting regulators and the equivalent bodies in other countries waited for the IASB standard, IAS 38 Intangible Assets that finally emerged in 1998. This standard eschewed the permissive approach in ED 49, and the ED 49 principles have now been rejected in subsequent pronouncements by the Australian regulators (AASB), the UK regulators (Accounting Standards Board – ASB), the international accounting regulators (IASB), and the US accounting regulators (FASB).[11]

As discussed earlier, the ultra conservative IAS 38 Intangible Assets prohibits the recognition of internally generated 'goodwill' assets and takes the view that it is generally difficult to determine the amount and timing of future benefits and a reliable cost for 'internally generated intangible assets' (para. 39). It therefore includes additional measurement and recognition criteria for internally generated intangible assets over and above those set out in the standard for acquired intangible assets. The standard prohibits the recognition as assets of internally generated items of the type or similar in nature to brands, mastheads, publishing titles, customer lists and 'items similar in substance'. The research already shows that these items, which have been included in the financial statements of many Australian companies up until the adoption of an IAS 38 equivalent standard on 1 January 2005, are associated with the underlying economics of the firms and with investors' valuation of the firms' shares (Wyatt 2005). Taken with the consistent evidence from other countries, the justification for this regulatory direction is a mystery.

Following the IAS 38 release, the US FASB, in 2001, went on to issue two accounting standards on intangible assets after lengthy deliberations: SFAS. No. 141 Business Combinations and SFAS No. 142 Goodwill and Other Intangible Assets. SFAS No. 141 requires the purchase method of accounting for mergers and acquisitions and abolishes the amortization of purchased goodwill. The purchase method for mergers and acquisitions recognizes purchased goodwill assets. An alternative, the pooling method, which does not lead to the recognition of purchased goodwill assets and can lead to distorted net assets and earnings figures, is now not allowed in the US. SFAS No. 141 also requires (in mergers and acquisitions) separate recognition of intangible assets from purchased goodwill (1) if the intangible asset has contractual or legal rights, or (2) the assets are capable of being separated or divided from the acquired entity and sold, transferred, licensed, rented or exchanged, either individually or in combination with a related contract, asset or liability (regardless of intent to do so) (para. 39). In

Appendix A, paragraph A11, it states that 'An acquired intangible asset meets the separability criterion if there is evidence of exchange transactions for that type of asset or an asset of a similar type (even if those exchange transactions are infrequent and regardless of whether the acquiring entity is involved in them)'. SFAS No. 142 retains the rule to immediately expense R&D and the prohibition on the recognition of internally generated intangible assets. The IASB has taken the same approach in its business combinations project to the US approach in SFAS No. 141 and SFAS No. 142. The US also allows capitalization of software development R&D under SFAS No. 86 Accounting for the Costs of Computer Software to be Sold, Leased, or Otherwise Marketed (since August 1985). Capitalization is permitted under SFAS No. 86 once technological feasibility has been established with all 'pre-feasibility' research costs being expensed.

Overall, the accounting regulatory trend is in the opposite direction from the extensive evidence provided by accounting researchers, and the directions argued by management and economic analysts. The accounting trend is to permit capitalization of externally acquired intangible assets where the transaction is with an external party and includes a reliable measure of the costs involved, and to generally prohibit capitalization of internally generated intangible assets. This trend appears to be driven by concerns that the assets are too uncertain for future benefits to be predictable.

5 IMPLICATIONS FOR MANAGERS

The main issue in accounting for intangible investments that lead to IC and IP is that people tend to direct their attention towards things that can be seen or measured, regardless of its relative contribution to what is important. Intangible assets, for reasons discussed in this chapter, fulfil neither of these criteria.

There is evidence that unrecognized intangible assets are relevant to investors in their evaluation of the firms' earnings prospects. Barth and Clinch (1996) find that UK firms' unrecognized goodwill asset (UK companies could remove it from the balance sheet by reducing shareholders' equity up until 1996) is positively related to stock prices, when notionally brought to account (this data is from the reconciliation filing required when foreign firms are listed in the US jurisdiction). Consistent with the greater usefulness of more detailed disclosures, the value of goodwill seems to have a weaker association with market value of equity compared to identifiable intangibles, for US and UK firms (Chauvin and Hirschey 1994; Muller 1994). This suggests that measured intangibles have a more direct effect on investors' calculations than unmeasured intangibles.

Similarly, Ittner and Larcker (1998) find data proxying for customer satisfaction assets is value relevant for stock price but is not fully impounded in share price. Since this information is only partially reflected in reported accounting information, their evidence suggests customer satisfaction relates to unrecognized intangible assets and to an associated misvaluation of the firms' stock. Aboody and Lev (1998) examine the software R&D capitalization over the full ten-year record under SFAS No. 86.[12] They find the accounting disclosures under the accounting standard are associated with contemporaneous stock prices, changes in stock prices, and the firms' future profits. This evidence is consistent with the recognition test in this accounting standard providing useful information for evaluating the firm's prospects. This test is to permit capitalization once technological feasibility of the projects have been established.

Further, there is evidence that external investors consistently recognize that reported R&D represents only a portion of the true level of investment by companies into innovation. The (large) literature[13] which uses market values of equity from financial markets to investigate the contribution of R&D to firm performance, suggests that accounting measures of R&D are systematically understated relative to the market's expectations of their value (see Chapters 6–9 in this volume). For example, Hall (1998, p. 10) estimates that R&D expenditures are capitalized by the stock market at a rate between 2.5 and 8 times, while the stock of R&D is valued between 0.5 and 2 times the value of tangible assets. Sougiannis (1994) finds a $1 increase in R&D is associated with a direct $2 gross profit increase over a seven-year amortization period, and a total effect of a $5 increase in market value. Related to this, Lev and Sougiannis (1996) find that the stock of R&D is associated with future changes in share prices, which indicates an undervaluation of R&D expenditures in the past by investors presumably reflecting a risk premium. This highlights the need for a more interpretable classification system for intangibles than R&D, which varies in its composition by industry and firm.

Excluding intangible investments from the chart of accounts implies that managers and investors have little clear idea about the true level of company investments. Expensing these investments, particularly for growing firms (Lev and Sougiannis 1996), leads to distortions in periodic profits. This is also a source of company misinformation. In the USA, where R&D expenditures must be treated as expenses, Lev and Sougiannis (1996) have found average earnings understatements from R&D expensing of approximately 20.6 per cent and a book value of equity (assets minus liabilities equals equity) understatement of 22.2 per cent. The level of distortion depends on the growth rate of R&D.

There is also evidence that giving firms discretion over whether or not to report an intangible expenditure as an investment leads to inconsistencies in the way companies are reporting and thus confusion for stakeholders. For example, in the UK and Australia, some companies appear reluctant to disclose their quantum of annual R&D expenditures (Percy 1997; Stoneman and Toivanen 1997). Abrahams and Sidhu (1998) found 101 firms out of 200 high R&D intensity industry firms did not have any R&D expenditures reported in the income statement (as required under the accounting standard for R&D). Thirteen firms explicitly disclosed an R&D tax benefit but had no R&D asset or expense. Similarly, Griffiths and Webster (2004) find that 12.3 per cent of large Australian companies are patenting but not reporting R&D expenditure in their financial accounts.

6 CONCLUSION

Existing evidence indicates financial reporting on intangible investment is useful information for evaluating the future performance of companies. While we know that the regulated accounting system makes a poor and somewhat capricious choice (from a management and economics perspective) over which intangible expenditures to treat as investments, there is little known evidence on what companies are doing informally to record intangible investment (see Hunter et al. 2005).

In the big picture, the accounting framework gives management of the company the responsibility to record, manage and report the financial effects of the firm's economic transactions. The strategic issues confronting management at the most fundamental level are decisions about '*what to do*' as a function of differences in innovation potential across industries, and decisions about '*how to do it*' given specific, structural characteristics of the firm and industry (Audretsch 1995). From an accounting perspective, managers have a continuing responsibility as stewards, and under the 'decision-usefulness' model of public financial reporting that has been adopted in most countries, to report periodically on the deployment of the firm's resources according to the firm's business plan and strategy. The total of the firm's expenditures in each accounting period will be reflected in the journals and ledger accounts that make up the firms' accounting system. The challenge is to record, analyse, and ultimately report this data in a manner that assists management in (1) implementing the firm's strategy, and (2) concurrently reflecting (a) a true and fair view to external stakeholders by capturing the intentions of management at the time investments decisions were made and (b) also measuring investment outcomes.

The evidence to date looks mainly at investment outcomes, that is, (b). It suggests that the information provided is useful and that its quantum appears to be understated, that information is missing that could be included (of course, accounting is not the only source of information about the firm but the evidence suggests there is room for improvement), and misclassifies some investments as expenses. There is room for research to examine internal reporting issues and whether or not accounting does present a 'true and fair' view of the firm's financial circumstances. One such recent study finds that reported intangible assets by Australian companies are correlated with economic factors underlying the firms' operations (Wyatt 2005).

Aside from claims that there are gaps in the reporting of intangible assets, another characteristic of accounting regulations warrants a mention. This is the focus of long-term asset accounting only on expenditures that are reasonably certain to generate future benefits. This is a problem for the internal management of resources because it does not frame accounting practices from the wider vantage point of the firm's strategy and management intent.

NOTES

1. Given the commitment of accounting regulators around the world to work towards harmonization of accounting standards, and trend to the internationalization of the making of accounting rules, the accounting treatment of intangible assets is discussed by reference to the IASB conceptual framework and accounting standards.
2. IAS 38 Intangible Assets in paragraph 12: an asset is identifiable if (a) it is separable, that is, is capable of being separated or divided from the entity and sold, transferred, licensed, rented or exchanged, either individually or together with a related contract, asset or liability; or (b) it arises from contractual or other legal rights, regardless of whether those rights are transferable or separable from the entity or from other rights and obligations.
3. The Australian accounting standard that has been superceded by an equivalent version of IFRS 3 Business Combinations. The old standard AASB 1013 Accounting for Goodwill, defined goodwill as an 'unidentifiable' asset since it comprises 'future benefits receivable from unidentifiable assets not capable of being both individually identified and specifically recognized' (para. 4.1.1).
4. The Australian accounting standard, ASRB 1022 Accounting for the Extractive Industries, defines these costs as follows: 'exploration' means the search for a mineral deposit or an oil or natural gas field which appears capable of commercial exploitation by an extractive operation and includes topographical, geological, geochemical and geophysical studies and exploratory drilling; 'evaluation' means the determination of the technical feasibility and commercial viability of a particular prospect and includes determination of the volume and grade of the deposit or field, examination and testing of extraction methods and metallurgical or treatment processes, surveys of transportation and infrastructure requirements, and market and finance studies.
5. ASRB 1022 Accounting for the Extractive Industries.
6. For example, consider a firm that has developed telecommunications technology and has not disclosed the estimated measure of $4 million as an asset due to concerns about appropriating the benefits in ensuing periods. In the next period the firm wishes to undertake a secondary equity issue and decides to capitalize the $4 million to signal private information to potential investors. The *economics* of the firm's investment has not materially changed

between successive years but the *accounting* representation changed dramatically from $6 million to $10 million.

7. For example, Amir and Lev (1996) find that the accounting summary numbers, book value of owners' equity (that is, net assets or assets minus liabilities) and earnings (profits) are not informative for the valuation of companies in the wireless telecommunications industry until the 'missing investment' that has been expensed in the form of sales, general and administrative expenses is included in the valuation model.

8. 'Perhaps the outstanding fact to emerge from this brief survey is the enormous variety and range of practices in the counting houses in this [industrial revolution] period, and the variety of assumptions on which they seem to have been based. The differences may be largely derived from the different practical demands which the accounts were designed to meet, but in all the variety found, there was no clear-cut attempt to adapt accounting practice to the notion of capital as generalized, depersonalized property, seeking the highest returns irrespective of its concrete embodiment, as postulated by economic theory' (Pollard 1963, p. 122).

9. 'Even among advanced firms up to the late 1800s, diverse accounting methods were adopted that variously: confused capital, revenue and profit; confused fixed and current expenditure. Fixed capital was treated as working capital; and muddled interest, profit and capital under the apparent assumption that interest is the return on capital while profit was not related to capital but was distinguished as the entrepreneurs' reward (i.e. assuming that capital and profits are not related)' (Pollard 1963, p. 134).

10. In de Roover in Lane and Riemersma 1953, p. 85 and cited in Pollard 1963, p. 116: 'From the standpoint of the theorist the essential difference between industrial and commercial capitalism depends upon the nature of capitalist accumulation under both systems. Under mercantile capitalism, capital is largely a stock in trade or a revolving fund, which is used to buy raw materials and to pay wages and which is replenished by the sale of the finished product. Little is invested in productive equipment, with perhaps two notable exceptions: the shipping and the mining industries. Industrial capitalism, on the contrary, presupposes large investments in equipment before production can really start. Depreciation, maintenance, and overhead thus become important in figuring costs. An example will make this clear: depreciation in one of the sixteenth century Medici partnerships for the manufacture of woollen cloth was less than one per cent of cost. Over head (*sic*) amounted to only ten percent. Direct costs were consequently the determining factor.'

11. The United Kingdom in their FRS 10 Goodwill and Intangible Assets similarly tightened up reporting requirements.

12. SFAS No. 86 Accounting for the Costs of Computer Software to be Sold, Leased, or Otherwise Marketed appeared in August 1985.

13. See the review in the EC study (2003).

REFERENCES

Australian Accounting Review Board (1989), *Accounting for the Extractive Industries*, AASB 1022.

Australian Accounting Research Foundation (1989), *Accounting for Identifiable Intangible Assets*, ED 49, Sydney, Australia.

Australian Accounting Standards Board (1996), *Accounting for Goodwill*, AASB 1013.

Aboody, D. and B. Lev (1998), 'The value relevance of intangibles: the case of software capitalisation', *Journal of Accounting Research*, **36**, supplement, 161–91.

Abrahams, T. and B. Sidhu (1998), 'The role of R&D capitalisation in firm valuation and performance measurement', working paper, Australian Graduate School of Management, University of New South Wales.

Amir, E. and B. Lev (1996), 'Value-relevance of nonfinancial information: the wireless communications industry', *Journal of Accounting and Economics*, **22**, August–December, 3–30.

Audretsch, D. (1995), *Innovation and Industry Evolution*, Cambridge, MA: Massachusetts Institute of Technology.

Barth, M. and G. Clinch (1996), 'International accounting differences and their relation to share prices: evidence from U.K., Australian, and Canadian firms', *Contemporary Accounting Research*, **13**, 135–70.

Ben-Zion, U. (1978), 'The investment aspect of nonproduction expenditures: an empirical test', *Journal of Economics and Business*, Spring–Summer, 224–29.

Bublitz, B. and M. Ettredge (1989), 'The information in discretionary outlays: advertising, research, and development', *The Accounting Review*, **64**, January, 108–25.

Chauvin, K. and M. Hirschey (1994), 'Goodwill, profitability, and the market value of the firm', *Journal of Accounting and Public Policy*, **13**, 159–80.

De Roover in Lane and Riemersma cited in Pollard, S. (1963), 'Capital accounting in the Industrial Revolution', *Yorkshire Bulletin of Economics and Social Research*, **15**, 75–91; reprinted as Pollard, S. (1968), 'Capital accounting in the Industrial Revolution', *Contemporary Studies in the Evolution of Accounting Thought*, M. Chatfield (ed.), Belmont, CA: Dickenson, pp. 113–34.

Dickerson (1941), 'Intangible assets and contingent liabilities' in Zeff, S.A. (1982), *Accounting Principles Through the Years – the Views of Professional and Academic Leaders 1938–1954*, New York and London: Garland Publishing Inc.

Ernst & Young, (1995), *Intangible Asset Valuations*, publication reference EYA 5054, Ernest & Young Australia.

Ettredge, M. and B. Bublitz (1988), 'A reexamination of market-assessed intangible assets: advertising and R&D', unpublished manuscript, June.

European Commission (EC) (2003), *Commission of the European Communities Enterprise Directorate General, Study on the Measurement of Intangible Assets and Associated Reporting Practices*, EU Call for Tender Entr/01/054, Contract N. Fif.20010720, April.

Financial Accounting Standards Board (2001), *Accounting for the Costs of Computer Software to be Sold, Leased, or Otherwise Marketed*, FAS 85.

Financial Accounting Standards Board (2001), *Business Combinations*, FAS 141.

Financial Accounting Standards Board (2001), *Goodwill and Other Intangible Assets*, FAS 142.

Griffiths, W. and E. Webster (2004), 'The determinants of research and development and Intellectual Property usage among Australian companies 1989 to 2002', Working Paper, University of Melbourne.

Hall, B. (1998), 'Innovation and market value', prepared for the NIESR Conference on Productivity and Competitiveness, London, 5–6 February, forthcoming in a Cambridge University Press volume edited by R. Barrell and G. Mason.

Henderson, S. and G. Peirson (1995), *Issues in Financial Accounting*, 7th edn, South Melbourne: Longman Australia .

Hirschey, M. (1982), 'Intangible capital aspects of advertising and R&D expenditures', *Journal of Industrial Economics*, **4**, June, 375–89.

Hirschey, M. and R.S. Spencer (1992), 'Size effects in the market valuation of fundamental factors', *Financial Analysts Journal*, March–April, 91–5.

Hirschey, M. and J.J. Weygandt (1985), 'Amortization policy for advertising and research and development', *Journal of Accounting Research*, **23**, Spring, 326–35.

Hunter, L., E. Webster and A. Wyatt (2005), 'Measuring intangible capital: a review of current practice', *The Australian Accounting Review*, **15** (36), 4–21.

International Accounting Standards Board (2001), *The Framework for the Preparation and Presentation of Financial Statements*, London: IASB.

International Accounting Standards Board (2004), *Intangible Assets* (first issued 1998 and revised 2004), IAS 38.

International Accounting Standards Board (2004), *Business Combinations*, IFRS 3.

Ittner, C.D. and D.F. Larcker (1998), 'Are non-financial measures leading indicators of financial performance? An analysis of customer satisfaction', *Journal of Accounting Research*, **36**, supplement, 1–46.

Jennings, R., J. Robinson, R. Thompson and L. Duvall (1996), 'The relationship between accounting goodwill numbers and equity values', *Journal of Business Finance & Accounting*, **23** (4), 513–33.

Lev, B. and T. Sougiannis (1996), 'The capitalisation, amortisation and value relevance of R&D', *Journal of Accounting and Economics*, **21**, 107–38.

Littleton, A.C. (1981), *Accounting Evolution to 1900*, Accounting History Classics Series, Gary Previts (series ed.), AL: University of Alabama Press.

McCarthy, M. and D. Schneider (1996), 'Evidence from the US market of the association of capitalized non-goodwill intangibles to firm equity value', *Advances in International Accounting*, **9**, 111–27.

Metcalfe, J.S. (1997), 'Evolutionary concepts in relation to evolutionary economics', Department of Economics Discussion Paper, University of Queensland, No. 226, October.

Muller, K. (1994), 'The valuation implications of the accounting measurement of brand names, publishing titles, and goodwill – evidence from the debate in the United Kingdom', unpublished manuscript.

Netter, J. (1982), 'Excessive advertising: an empirical analysis', *Journal of Industrial Economics*, **4**, 360–73.

Paton, W.A. (1938), 'Discussion of "A Statement of Accounting Principles" Principles Related to "Deferred Charges" and 'Prepaid Expenses''', September 29 in Zeff, S.A. (1982), *Accounting Principles Through the Years – the Views of Professional and Academic Leaders 1938–1954*, New York and London: Garland Publishing Inc.

Percy, M. (1997), 'Financial reporting, discretion and voluntary disclosure – corporate research and development expenditures in Australia', PhD thesis, University of Queensland.

Pollard, S. (1963), 'Capital accounting in the Industrial Revolution', *Yorkshire Bulletin of Economics and Social Research*, **15**, 75–91; reprinted as Pollard, S. (1968), 'Capital accounting in the Industrial Revolution', *Contemporary Studies in the Evolution of Accounting Thought*, M. Chatfield (ed.), Belmont, CA: Dickenson, pp. 113–34.

Ritter A. and P. Wells (2004), 'Identifiable intangible assets disclosure, stock prices and future earnings', Working Paper, University of Technology, Sydney.

Sougiannis, T. (1994), 'The accounting based valuation of corporate R&D', *The Accounting Review*, **1**, January, 44–68.

Stoneman, P. and O. Toivanen (1997), 'Innovation and market value in the United Kingdom: some preliminary results', working paper, Warwick Business School.

Vincent, L. (1994), 'The equity valuation implications of accounting acquisition premiums', unpublished manuscript.

Wyatt, A. (2005), 'Accounting recognition of intangible assets: theory and evidence on economic determinants', *The Accounting Review*, **80** (3), 967–1003.

Wyatt, A. and M. Abernethy (2004), 'Accounting for intangible assets: a framework for standard setting', working paper, University of Melbourne.

Yang, J.M. (1927), *Goodwill and Other Intangibles: Their Significance and Treatment in Accounts*, New York: Ronald Press.

Zeff, S.A. (1982), *Accounting Principles Through the Years – the Views of Professional and Academic Leaders 1938–1954*, New York and London: Garland Publishing Inc.

4. A management perspective

Laurie Hunter

1 INTRODUCTION

It is only in the last 20 years or so that the role of intangible assets has begun to be seriously addressed in the business management literature, although some specific forms of intellectual capital such as patents, trademarks and brands have long been recognized as significant contributors to corporate value creation. What has changed is the growing recognition that intellectual capital is a component of a broader range of intangible assets, whose development and management is critical to the competitive capabilities of an increasing proportion of contemporary businesses (Kay 2000). The reason for this new recognition will be examined in more detail later in this chapter, but for the moment it is enough to note that many of the familiar and traditional sources of differentiation among competitors have been neutralized by the emerging globalization of trade and developments in information technology and communication (Quah 2001; Teece 1998). Geographical advantages have been diminished, distinctions between products have been blurred and many new market areas have been created. These trends, in turn, have enhanced the importance of intangible assets as a source of differentiation and competitive advantage because they are much more difficult to imitate and transfer. They have thus moved centre stage as a vital factor in competitive rivalry in many sectors of business.

The relative novelty of systematic analysis of intangibles means that, as with any new area of knowledge, there is some lack of commonly agreed definitions, concepts and taxonomy. Likewise, there are many aspects that have not yet been explored, and problem areas for which new and better solutions have still to be found. Section 2 aims to set out the basic definitions and concepts used here. Section 3 reviews the main formats and structures taken by intangible assets and intellectual capital, and Section 4 discusses the key management issues that have emerged. Section 5 provides a short conclusion.

2 DEFINITION AND CHARACTER OF INTANGIBLE CAPITAL

Investment gives rise to capital assets with the capability of releasing services or income that can be used for production in future time periods. Capital can be embodied either in tangible or intangible form. Tangible assets are typically recognized as land, buildings and physical plant or equipment, and much of economic and accounting practice has evolved with these hard, measurable and tradable assets in mind. Intangible assets comprise 'non-physical sources of future economic benefits' (EC 2003, p. 18). In a business enterprise the most familiar form is registered intellectual property such as patents, trademarks, copyright and product or company brands. These particular devices share a common bond with physical assets, namely, that they assert an ownership right that can be defended against unauthorized use by others, in a court of law if necessary. Possession of such property rights gives their owners a potential form of competitive advantage, which cannot with impunity be used by competitors. In that respect they are similar to tangible assets, for which ownership rights can generally be unequivocally established in law. On the whole, many items are important to the creation of future value to a firm that are not generally reported on the balance sheet. Consider the following preliminary categories of intangible assets:

1. Human capital embodied in the skills, knowledge and experience of the management and workforce.
2. Organizational (or infrastructure) capital in the form of organization-specific structures, procedures and business or operational routines.
3. Relational (or market) capital, the established set of relationships with suppliers, customers, partners and business associates.
4. Intellectual property, comprising assets like patents and trademarks, design titles, copyright and plant and seed breeders' rights, with a legal ownership embodied in the company.

Wherein lie the differences between these and the conventional forms of capital, other than the fact that they are intangible? The answers differ from case to case. *Human capital*, for example, is in no sense 'owned' by the employer, but its services are rented from the employees in return for wages and salaries and other forms of compensation or reward. Even though at least part of the individual employee's human capital may have been developed by investment in education or training paid for by the employer, the ownership remains with the employee, who may transfer to other employment, taking that capital with him or her.[1] In short, the property rights inherent in the employment relationship are contestable, and the employer cannot be sure of appropriating the benefits implicit in the employment contract.

Organizational and relational capital are respectively the product of investment by the company in building up organizational systems, procedures and routines that are believed to be commercially advantageous to the company, and in nurturing relationships with customers and suppliers via development of databases, product and quality certification. In these cases there is no issue about ownership, but they are generally created in-house by the company rather than bought on the market, and therefore fail the test of having a historic market valuation. The exception is when a company is acquired or merged, and a market valuation is agreed as part of the purchase or merger deal, typically summed up in the concept of 'goodwill' in the acquired firm as a going concern.

The final category, *intellectual property*, is complex, containing elements both of competences and know-how embodied in the firm's human capital, and products of research and development (R&D) undertaken within the firm. The human capital element is potentially mobile, and R&D expenditure – though it may well result in patented or licensable outputs with legal or contractual rights – cannot be guaranteed to yield future benefits to the firm. One practical problem here is how to define the stage at which R&D comes sufficiently close to market to be assigned a firm expected value. Different national jurisdictions treat this in different ways, though the trend of international accounting standards appears to be moving against more liberal interpretations of near-market development (see Chapter 3 in this volume).

3   WHY DOES ALL THIS MATTER TO THE FIRM?

And why is it now seen to be more important to many firms than it has in the past? Three sets of reasons can be identified:

3.1   Accounting/Reporting Practices

At least in the context of US and UK business, but less so in Europe, where tax and creditor information tends to be more important, published accounts are essentially seen as providing information for shareholders and potential investors. Accounting procedures are therefore geared to providing reliable information to the investor. There are two views here with respect to the reporting of intangibles. The first is that only verifiable and reliable information should be included in financial statements such as balance sheets and that for the most part intangibles cannot be valued sufficiently accurately to warrant inclusion. This argument has been given extra weight by a series of high-profile financial scandals in the last 20 years, much of it attributable to financial misrepresentation of intangibles, leading to the conclusion that the scope for such malpractice should be minimized. The counter-argument is that only the development of clearer rules, definitions and measurement practices relating to intangibles will tackle the fundamentals of the problem (Hunter et al. 2005; Lev 1999; Wyatt 2006, see Chapter 3, this volume.)

As matters currently stand, the failure to report more than a tiny fraction of the value of intangible assets, combined with the changing structure of business toward firms with a high ratio of intangible to total assets, has led to complaints that the information content of published accounts is becoming increasingly deficient, to the disadvantage of the shareholder and the investor. Webster (2000) and Lev and Zarowin (1999) show that there has been a significant long-term decline in the association between the book value of assets and capital market variables such as share prices or stock market valuation (stock × share price), and hence a loss of information available to the investor. This deficiency is greater, the higher the investment on R&D, typically an important part of intangible investment. The implication is that such distortion conveys imperfect information about future prospects to investors, and hence increases the risk of inefficient allocation of investment resources

A second and related consideration here is the extent to which management's internal accounts at the level of the business unit properly provide a clear picture of intangible assets and intangible investment. This is more conveniently addressed in the following section.

3.2   Value Creation and Intangible Investment

We start from the premise that business enterprises exist to add value to the resources they use, where 'added value' can be defined as 'the difference between the (comprehensively accounted) value of a firm's output and the (comprehensively accounted) cost of the firm's output' (Kay 1993, p. 19). Firms, even in the same industry, show variations in their added value coefficient because of the different ways in which they use their productive resources, which may be more or less efficient and will reflect the set of business arrangements under which they operate – both the *architectural* features (how they are configured in terms of internal organization and how they relate to external partners and networks) and the *process* features, that is, the management systems and procedures that regulate production and investment (such as the exploitation of technology, production and quality control systems, and the presence and deployment of relevant competencies and capabilities). We can define this combination of architectural and process features as the company's *business model*.

At any time, some firms in a given industry will be operating a more efficient business model than others, enabling them to reap the benefits of higher productivity, profitability or growth than their competitors. Maintaining this lead, or in the case of the lagging competitors, catching up, will depend to a large degree on their business strategy and on judicious investment to support the strategic intent. As we argue below, for many contemporary firms this will entail an emphasis on investment in intangible assets (as the source of future streams of added value), whereas in the past the role of tangible assets and tangible investment would have been dominant. But if this is so, it follows that it will be important for managers taking these decisions to be well informed of 'what works' – what kinds of intangible investment will pay off, and how well will they pay off? And that in turn implies that the decision-takers need to have a good understanding of the value to their business of the existing intangible assets, how they might be better exploited or further developed and the risks and expected rate of return on such investments. Unfortunately, internal reporting systems tend to be designed to support external accounting reports, looking back rather than forward, and fail to provide a distinction between items that are 'expensed' (treated as current expenditure for production) and those that are better seen as investments (expenditure to generate future returns, where the future can be defined in terms of periods longer than one year). In this respect, managers face a problem similar to that of investors: the way information is reported runs the risk that significant misallocations of resources may occur.

3.3 Competitive Strategy in a Post-industrial World

As already suggested above, the problems just outlined will increase, the greater the proportion of industry that is intensive in intangible relative to tangible capital. But all the evidence indicates that this is indeed the dominant trend in the post-industrial economy, where strategic development and competitive capability lies increasingly in the possession and leverage of intangible assets (EC 2003; Griliches 1994, 1995; Webster 1999). Thus Teece (2000, p. 3) writes of 'a new fundamental core for wealth creation' in 'the development and astute deployment and utilization of intangible assets, of which knowledge, competence and intellectual property are the most significant'. Many other business strategy experts likewise emphasize the growing importance of intangibles in what is often termed 'the knowledge economy' (Kay 2000; OECD 1999, 2000) The significance of this trend cannot be overstated, for it carries implications that run far beyond the accounting issues discussed above. Some of the main differences in the value creation paradigm of tangible and intangible capital intensive firms are summarily illustrated in Table 4.1.

Table 4.1 Value creation process in the tangible and intangible capital intensive firms

	Tangible capital intensive firm	Intangible capital intensive firm
Value creation factors	Physical capital, labour, management, technology	Technological innovation and associated investment in knowledge and capabilities, human capital; management ability to predict the path of technology paradigms
Property rights	Property rights certain Owner has control	Property rights probabilistic Owner has uncertain control and faces a hold-up problem
Operation of markets and price mechanism	Capital goods purchased through liquid markets at verifiable and reliable prices Owner has control	Markets do not exist for some intangible assets and prices are not verifiable because the assets have been created internally Owner has uncertain control and faces a diffuse entitlements problem (that is, ownership rights to external technology are widely distributed in a market)
Production characteristics	Economies of scale and scope but eventually diminishing returns	High investment (fixed) costs, negligible marginal cost: availability of increasing returns, positive externalities
Organizational boundaries and structure	Hierarchical management exerts control, sets boundaries and structure	Control is dispersed (that is, embodied in individuals, and dispersed through alliances and networks). Hierarchy replaced by distributed or networked management
	Vertical management within: departmental specialization and integration	Management flexible, horizontal as much as vertical, and team based
	Firm boundaries clear, independent entities	Firm boundaries fuzzy and permeable, typically involve shifting networks and alliances
Competitiveness	Predominantly price competition	Predominantly competition through investment in intangibles such as dynamic capabilities, organization's ability to sense and seize new opportunities, learning capabilities, competences
Growth	Technical change exogenous	Technical change may be endogenous through internal and traded R&D and alliances)

Perhaps the most striking points of difference arise in relation to property rights, ownership and control. Whereas in the tangible capital intensive firm property rights (in physical resources) are assured, and ownership permits control to be exercised, the intangible capital intensive firm faces more uncertainty over property rights, so that control is problematic and requires to be exercised in different ways, for example through greater dispersion and more use of networking and alliances. Where the tangible capital element is dominant, transactions are 'most economically governed by a hierarchical form of organization in which management coordinates the gathering and processing of information from lower levels of the organization' which it uses to make decisions (Applebaum and Berg 2000, p. 108). In contrast, the intangible capital intensive firm requires a more flexible and decentralized organization in which new knowledge can come from the bottom (Morris and Empson 1998). Given the other differences in market and production characteristics, and the importance of being able to relate to technology shifts and indeed to inaugurate technical change through in-house research and development, the business model is transformed.

The implications of this discussion are that the significance of intangible capital goes far beyond the issue of how it is treated in the reporting of accounts. It is central to the strategic connection of the business with its market and technological environment, it informs the internal and external architecture of the firm, and it has a powerful influence on the structure and style of management.

4 IMPLICATIONS FOR MANAGEMENT

4.1 Central Role of Intellectual Capital and Intangibles

The managerial perspective on intangibles and intellectual capital has changed significantly in recent years. As shown earlier, a principal determining force has been the emergence of a 'post-industrial' economic structure in which physical capital and tangible investment are less probable routes to sustainable competitive advantage, and the role of intangible assets and investment as a distinctive source of competitive edge has been enhanced. As this is increasingly realized, the management of intangibles is pushed to the forefront of management's strategic concerns, and new thinking and new ways of managing become critical to success.

What then *are* the key issues for management? Of the two major themes identified above – the reporting problem and the management of intellectual capital – the latter is arguably much the more important for the manager. The reporting problem has engaged the various national and international accounting standards bodies; understandably so, due to the proliferation of new financial instruments (for example, hedging and derivatives) and other opaque operations underlying many recent corporate scandals. The way forward has been determined by the new set of international reporting standards devised by the International Accounting Standards Board, implemented from 2005. Rather than moving in the direction recommended by the management literature, however, these standards are more conservative in their recognition of intangible expenditures as capital items (see Wyatt, Chapter 3 in this volume). Businesses will learn to live with the changes and, as before, the standards will determine how firms organize their external and internal financial reporting systems. This will not resolve criticisms about the loss of information to shareholders, nor is it likely to assist internal management's handling of intangible expenditure and asset creation. But, clearly, the accounting standards cannot be ignored.

That being so, there remains much for management to consider both in the running of a business and developing its strategic direction. This is the focus for the remainder of this section, in which we will consider in turn the knowledge base of strategy, the management of R&D and intellectual property, the role of organizational and relational capital, and the metrics and indicators of performance.

4.2 Knowledge and Know-how

Education and training are investments in people that are undertaken in the expectation that the productive capability of the individual will be enhanced, making that individual more attractive to employers and able to command a higher remuneration. That investment, however, resides in the individual and is not owned by the firm; labour services are only rented. Employees are mobile between employers and take with them not only the skills and competences acquired from previous employments, but also accumulated knowledge and experience. An employer therefore has two immediate problems:

- to ensure that the current employees willingly apply their inherent knowledge and skills to the advantage of the employer – the *appropriability* problem.
- to protect its investment in the employee and to prevent an undesired migration of the employee to a competitor – the *retention* problem.

In fact the issues are much more complex than this, in ways that have come to be understood better through research on the nature of knowledge itself. A fundamental distinction is drawn (Nonaka 1990; Nonaka and

Takeuchi 1995) between explicit and tacit knowledge. *Explicit knowledge* is typically codified or articulated knowledge relating to 'knowing about', and is relatively easy to transfer within an organization and between organizations. It may include company manuals and templates, specialized databases and operational rules drawn up to secure consistency of practice. *Tacit knowledge* is 'knowing how', or 'understanding', and is much less readily transferred between individuals and organizations – the traditional and time-intensive training of apprentices by master craftsmen is a good example, where the learning mode is observational and experiential. The contemporary firm needs to attract, develop and retain employees able to integrate external knowledge such as advances in technology available to all firms in an industry, *and* make it work for the specific business in a distinctive, innovative way. Not only that, but the firm will want to ensure such knowledge is diffused and shared by converting tacit knowledge to an explicit form available to all, and achieving effective transfer of 'tacit to tacit' knowledge as security against loss of know-how.[2] The problem lies in the fact that the employee need not release this knowledge, preferring to retain it as a bargaining factor for future employment and earning power. This provides a challenging agenda for all managers, and for human resource management specialists. They need to find a way of managing, and a reward package, that will encourage this sharing mentality, not only among individual employees, but also within and between teams, which are an essential form of work organization in the knowledge-based firm.[3]

The rhetoric of many firms that labour is their key asset ought to be given new emphasis by the importance of knowledge, especially tacit knowledge, as a difficult to imitate source of competitive advantage. Ironically the last two decades have seen many of these firms engage in downsizing and outsourcing (some of it overseas to cheap labour economies), giving rise to workforce concern about job security and sending precisely the wrong signals to employees possessing critical knowledge – though the stock market may see this as a sign of good management, however short term the effect may be (Metcalfe 1998). The conclusion must be that if firms are serious about the value of their employees, they need to send clear signals, backed by consistent action and policy, to secure employee commitment and loyalty. One might add that the stock market analysts should also learn to appreciate the value of such behaviour – but in the absence of standard measures, they may have little to go on.

4.3   Research and Development and Intellectual Property

The relation between R&D investment and corporate value has been subject to more research than any of the other intangibles (see Chapters 6–9 in this volume). This is partly due to the long recognition of intellectual property as a source of corporate value and the greater availability of data for analysis, but partly also to a narrower view of intangible assets than is now the norm. A review of empirical evidence indicates that there is a significant positive relationship between R&D investments and productivity, both for the corporate sector and in social terms; the private sector return may be up to twice the rate of return to tangible investment (Griliches 1995). Nevertheless, the market valuation of R&D is imperfect and varies across enterprises and over time (Hall 1998). This may well be partly due to the crude nature of the reporting of the R&D line in financial statements, which do not provide the detail that would be necessary for a more accurate appraisal.

From the point of view of corporate management, then, the indications are that R&D investment is likely to have a positive outcome, which will at least partly be reflected – usually understated – in the stock market's valuation (EC 2003). But this does not give a real clue to the best approach to determine the scale of such investment, how it relates to strategic development and what organizational and managerial characteristics are required. Nor does the historical evidence necessarily provide a good basis for R&D decisions in what we have termed the post-industrial enterprise.

Technological innovation has long been a prime source of competitive advantage. At some risk of caricature, the tradition was that the independent inventor or an in-house specialist R&D team would produce inventions and innovative production techniques that were patentable or otherwise protected. Even though patents have a limited lifespan, they are capable of yielding monopoly profits for the duration, though this will be less effective where the product life cycle is short and the pace of change rapid. Not surprisingly different industries have different propensities to take out patents,[4] and by no means all of these will actually be turned into products or used in production processes – they simply protect the property rights in the commercial use of that knowledge.

That traditional model still exists, but does so in a very much more complex environment, characterized by rapid developments in science and technology, many of the outputs of which enter the public domain and become available to all potential users. The strategic issue for the firm at this point is to ensure that it is well connected into the relevant streams of emerging technological knowledge and has a well-developed capability of understanding and applying discoveries in its own product range or production processes – or, indeed, into entirely new markets. This capability might also take the form of the ability to reverse engineer competitors' innovations, invent round or otherwise imitate such developments,[5] but the matter does not end there. Once the technical know-how has been developed, there remains the question of its commercialization, which will require the presence of complementary assets such as production and/or distribution systems, or the ability and finance to build them. Failing that, there are options including entering into alliances or networks that can provide the missing complementary assets, or licensing out (for royalties or some agreed compensation). In general, the argument is that for core innovations at the heart of the business, it is better to keep this knowledge in-house, since sharing it will reduce the return, but smaller firms may find this is not possible.

In other respects, however, the smaller firm may have some advantages over the larger incumbent organization with an established staff, facilities and mind-set. A key issue here is the organizational structure of decision-making with respect to technological innovation. Teece (2000) argues that hierarchical organizations tend to have bureaucratic forms of decision-making which are not helpful to innovation; they are risk averse and constrained by past history. Their search for new ideas tends to be close to their known territory and bounded by the possession of established assets and routines they are reluctant to discard. In contrast, the new or smaller firm is more likely to seek ideas wherever they arise, and be less constrained by sunk costs. The point is that, if the larger firms are to capitalize on opportunities, they have to develop more flexible and open-minded searches outside the firm, aspire to organization and decision structures that support and reward creativity, and encourage more entrepreneurial values in decision-taking.

In the contemporary context, the issues are no longer just the rate of expenditure on R&D, the outcome in terms of patents, and their successful commercialization into goods for the product market. Rather the problem has much wider strategic implications affecting the technological search process and the firm's positioning in the (upstream) R&D environment, the ingenuity and creativity required to commercialize innovations and speed the process of decision-taking to get first-mover advantage, and to find ways of protecting that advantage by such combinations of patents, copyright, business secrets, coding and encryption as may be appropriate.

4.4 Organizational and Relational Capital

To complete the coverage of the four main categories of intangible capital, we briefly touch on some main features of organizational and relational capital. Though these are the least well worked out, there is no doubt that both are likely to be significant contributors to value creation in the firm. Organizational capital is the infrastructure on which the business depends, including the administrative structure and management systems, including accounting and finance. But it also encompasses organizational design or architecture, network and strategic alliance linkages and the governance apparatus. Relational capital includes the set of linkages that connect the business to its suppliers and to its markets and customers. It includes market research, data banks relating to customers and suppliers, and forms of certification on standards such as quality of inputs and outputs, which will act as important signals and indicators of reputation to suppliers and customers.

Underlying both these types of intangible capital there is a powerful knowledge factor – partly explicit, as in data banks and specific administrative routines governing how work is done and how the business is managed. But equally, there is a strong element of tacit knowledge at work, embodied in the expertise and experience of the management and workforce. These intangibles will inevitably play a significant role in the competitive success of a firm; the business press daily reports what are, in effect, investment expenditures designed to improve long-run corporate performance. Much more difficult is the problem of assigning values to these expenditures, partly because much of the activity is in-house and hence difficult to match with a market price, and partly because these are complementary assets whose value is only apparent when they are packaged with other assets into goods and services. This is a valuation problem for the shareholder, the financial analyst and the accountant. For management it is a problem in the allocation of investment resources. In the following section we will consider how companies have sought to handle such issues in practice.

4.5   Metrics and Indicators

As we have seen above, decisions affecting investment in intangible assets present formidable problems for management, not least because of the quality of information available to them in making dispositions of resources. Investment in tangible assets is, of course, subject to uncertainty of outcome and riskiness attaching to particular projects, but in the case of intangibles this difficulty is exaggerated by the much greater difficulty of estimating the relation between inputs and outputs, many of which will be 'soft' in the sense that they are difficult to quantify in objective terms. The problem is further aggravated by the time lag that will often occur between the investment itself and the arrival of the flow of expected benefits, plus uncertainty over the duration of that flow – which may be curtailed by innovations by competitors or new technological knowledge.

In addressing the question of how to optimally meet the information gap, managers need to ask how do we want to use this information? And, how should we categorize intangibles to maximize its strategic value to our company?

As discussed previously, the two primary reasons for a business's interest in its intangible capital are:

- external – the provision of information for parties outside the firm, such as shareholders, potential investors and financial analysts, customers and suppliers, and tax authorities[6]
- internal – the assembly and analysis of information that is important for the management of the firm, and particularly its business strategy and strategic implementation.

The information needed for these purposes is not identical. For the external user, the interest is likely to be in the capitalized value of the asset and in the movement of this value through time. Higher capitalized values will be reflected in higher valuations of the stock. The problem here is that many intangible assets are excluded from capitalization by the financial reporting standards and, even where they are includable, there may be some degree of uncertainty or subjectivity in the valuation process.

When we turn to the internal aspect, management may well have an interest in the path of the capital valuation, partly as an indication of how the market views its performance, partly as a benchmark for comparison with competing firms, but also because executive remuneration is often geared to share price performance. However, one would also expect management to be at least as interested in the behaviour of components of intangible capital, not just in terms of valuation but also of the respective contributions they make to corporate value. If it is known that x per cent increase in investment in R&D or human resource development will have a probable rate of return of y per cent, management can use that information to allocate *investment* resources to the areas with the highest expected pay-off in the future. That sort of information is likely to have a strong influence on the strategic direction of investment and also in the implementation of strategic plans (where, for example, improvements in organizational or customer capital can lead to smarter operation, producing additional value from given resources). Thus the measurement of intangible assets is not only a matter of estimating capital values, but goes much more deeply into the value-creation activities of the firm itself, which requires a different kind of information.

In practice, many companies have begun to explore how to overcome these difficulties. Much of this has taken the form of developing a battery of indicators which may include some financial measures but also many non-financial metrics. Such indicators are preponderantly quantitative, measuring some feature of the corporate profile (for example, ratio of basic to applied research) that is seen as important for competitive capability or some index of outcome or performance (such as sales revenue per customer, percentage of repeat customers or a measure of customer satisfaction with a product or service). For some companies these will be limited to a few selected measures relating to what may be termed 'key performance indicators' (KPIs); providing recurrent measures of the performance of the value drivers of the organization and the main areas of risk exposure. This has much to be said for it, since management's awareness of its own business model should highlight the key areas for *its* business, and regular monitoring will provide vital information on progress on different fronts.

Some larger companies have taken this a stage further, producing a set of intellectual capital accounts, as a supplement to financial accounts, which systematically report a wider range of indicators, often grouped into categories such as the four categories of intellectual capital discussed in Section 3 above. Like KPIs, these can be tailored to focus on aspects seen as particularly important to the individual business, providing both a means of comparing achievement over time and a basis for benchmarking against other firms using a similar methodology. There can be no quarrel with companies using these approaches, but these measures do *not* provide a direct and known *causal* relationship between changes in investment expenditure on the range of intellectual capital input variables (for example, R&D or employee development) and outcome in terms of productivity or financial performance. They do not provide a measure of comparative rates of return on the various investment options, and management still suffers a lack of *ex ante* quality information on performance outcomes. Further, there is no evident sign that many of these indicators can be effectively linked into the company's business model, relating them to the real value drivers of the business and reflecting the associated risks.[7]

Despite this criticism, many companies have adopted either some form of intellectual capital accounting or the alternative and much in vogue approach of using a scorecard approach, of which the best known is the Balanced Scorecard developed by Kaplan and Norton (1996, 2001).[8] This is conceived of as a strategic tool, comprising a series of measures of financial, internal business, innovation and learning, and customer perspectives that are linked into an (assumed) chain of cause and effect, leading to impact on the chosen measure of corporate performance. Though not a measure of intellectual capital in itself, it has a number of common features and has the merit of taking a broad view of the organization, bringing together financial and non-financial measures and mapping these onto a strategic vision or plan. The main criticism is that, although intuitively plausible, there is an absence of confirmed causal relationships at the heart of the model. Until this is more fully tested, final judgement must be postponed.

What, then, of the investment limb of the intellectual capital measurement problem, which curiously has been less well considered? Although starting with a different purpose – part of an ongoing Organisation for Economic Co-operation and Development (OECD) programme to develop a *national* accounts framework for intangible investment – Young (1998) begins by setting as a criterion whether they are 'long term outlays by firms aimed at improving their future performance (other than by the acquisition of fixed assets)'; additional criteria relate mainly to the potential for collecting national level data on the components. A slightly modified version of Young's classification with examples is shown in Table 4.2.[9] The adoption of clear criteria for selection of items within each category gives a firmer basis for the grouping of intangible investment activities than many of the other loosely formulated typologies. The classification seems fairly generic, though some categories are likely to be more salient in some industries than others. It puts the emphasis on investment expenditures that seem, in principle, to be capable of being incorporated into the business model that encapsulates the strategic and production decisions of the firm (though this is not attempted here). And it is these investment expenditures that reflect management's expectation that new value will be created and lead to improvements in the firm's distinctive competitive capability – though expectations may not be delivered in practice.

5   CONCLUSIONS

Both investors and managers need good quality information if they are to make efficient decisions. Financial reporting systems and standards, aimed primarily at providing information on tangible assets, need increasingly to take account of intangible assets and investment spending if they are to continue to provide the desired quality of information. The trend of business and economic development has increased the importance of intangibles, typically embedded in the explicit and implicit knowledge of the organization, its management and employees. But there is comparatively little hard evidence on the connection between investments in the components of intellectual capital and the performance outcomes.

The increased attention paid to this area is revealed in debates about appropriate accounting methods for intangible assets, exposing tension between the needs for financial regulation and propriety, and for recognition of the wider asset base of businesses implied by intellectual capital. Academic and consultancy work has begun to develop a better understanding of the anatomy and properties of intellectual capital, but

Table 4.2   Examples of expenditures on resource categories

Classification*	Example of intangible investment expenditures
Information system infrastructure	*Expenditure on*: Information systems planning and development Commercial enterprise systems Software, Databases Other computer services Registered patents, trademarks, designs, licences
Production and technology	*Expenditure on*: Product and process R&D Product design, engineering and development Process design, engineering and development Technology adoption Quality control systems Proprietary technology, patents, trademarks, designs Licences
Human resources	*Expenditure on*: Skill type (for example, scientist, engineer, salesperson) Recruitment and selection Re-engineering incentive systems, Staff development and training Staff goal planning and evaluation Information and knowledge database development Programmes for health and motivation of workforce (for example, labour relations, health care, fitness)
Organization and administration	*Expenditure on*: Organizational design and management technique Corporate governance structures Networks and strategic alliances Administration structure and systems Finance systems Accounting systems
Procurement, distribution, customer linkages	*Expenditure on*: Distribution and market research systems Advertising Trademark Brands Customer lists, subscribers' list, potential customer list Product certification, quality certificates

Note: * There is also some interest in distinguishing process capital from innovation capital (Edvinsson and Malone 1997) and between processes and technologies (Danish Ministry of Science, Technology and Innovation 2003).

Source: This classification is adapted from Young (1998).

much of this remains unsatisfactorily ad hoc and fails to engage with the value and risk drivers of the business. Some progress has been made in developing non-financial indicators that relate to the business model pursued by the individual firm, and provided management itself has a good appreciation of the key sources of value and risk to *its* organization, some useful guidance on the contribution of intangibles can be elicited. If, as argued here, the most valuable (because difficult to imitate or copy) innovations are likely to derive from the embedded knowledge factor, it will become increasingly important for companies to have a more accurate information base on what is working to enhance competitive performance and why. Matters are complicated by the almost certain interactive relationship of complementary factors and the highly variable, and often protracted, period between action and performance outcome. The prediction must be that this is an area that will receive much more attention in the future, both in management practice and in academic research. In the meantime, managers need to maintain a broad perspective on the contribution of intellectual capital to the business and find ways of working towards solutions that are effective in their line of business. Doing nothing is not an option.

NOTES

1. Companies sometimes attempt to restrict such capital transfers through employment contract clauses that seek to prevent ex-employees from passing on sensitive information – or they may use a 'golden handcuff' strategy – providing incentives such as deferred share options to discourage mobility.
2. Nonaka (1990) defines four forms of knowledge creation: socialization (tacit to tacit): externalization (tacit to explicit), combination (explicit to explicit) and internalization (explicit to implicit).
3. For further discussion and references see Hunter (2003).
4. The chemical and pharmaceutical industries, for example, have quite different patterns of patenting, reflecting the way in which their relevant technologies build and use knowledge (see Teece 2000, for a good discussion). See also Granstrand (1999) for variations across countries.
5. Levin et al. (1987) suggest there is often only a marginal time lag between finding an alternative when there is a patent in place and when there is not.
6. We should note in passing that companies may be reluctant to report IC externally. Van der Meer-Koostra and Zijlstra (2001) cite the disadvantages of cost, confidentiality, subjectivity, tax implications and heightened expectations on management performance.
7. For more detailed discussion and illustration, see Hunter et al. (2004).
8. For fuller discussion, see Chapter 13 in this volume. Other partial scorecards, especially for human resources, also exist (Lawson and Hepp 2001).
9. Young's conclusions are that there are variations in the degree to which different types of intangible investment can be clearly defined and some items (like informal training or learning by doing) cannot yet be reliably measured. However, her purpose was the development of national-level accounts, rather than at the level of the individual firm, where some of her reservations may be overcome.

REFERENCES

Applebaum, E. and P. Berg (2000), 'High performance work systems: giving workers a stake', in Margaret M. Blair and Thomas A. Kochan (eds), *The New Relationship – Human Capital in the American Corporation*, Washington, DC: Brookings Institution.

Danish Ministry of Science, Technology and Innovation (2003), 'Intellectual capital statements – the new guideline', www.videnskabsministeriet.dk/fsk/publ/2003/guideline_uk/guideline_uk.pdf.

Edvinsson, L. and M.S. Malone (1997), *Intellectual Capital: Realizing your Company's True Value by Finding its Hidden Brainpower*, New York: HarperCollins.

European Commission (EC) (2003), *Commission of the European Communities Enterprise Directorate General, Study on the Measurement of Intangible Assets and Associated Reporting Practices*, EU Call for tender Entr/01/054, Contract N.Fif20010720, April.

Granstrand, Ove (1999), *The Economics and Management of Intellectual Property: Towards Intellectual Capitalism*, Cheltenham, UK and Northampton, MA, USA: Edward Elgar.

Griliches, Zvi (1994), 'Productivity, R&D and the data constraint', *American Economic Review*, **84** (1), 1–23.

Griliches, Zvi (1995), 'Research and development and productivity: econometric results and measurement issues', in P. Stoneman (ed.), *Handbook of the Economics of Innovation and Technological Change*, Oxford: Blackwell, pp. 52–89.

Hall, Bronwyn M. (1999), 'Innovation and market value', NBER working paper 6984, National Bureau of Economic Research, Cambridge, MA.

Hunter, L.C. (2003), 'Intellectual capital: accumulation and appropriation', Intellectual Property Research Institute of Australia working paper (06/02).

Hunter, L.C., E.M. Webster and A. Wyatt (2004), 'Measuring intangible capital: a review of current practice', Intellectual Property Research Institute of Australia working paper (16/04).

Hunter, L.C., E.M. Webster and A. Wyatt (2005), 'Measuring intangible capital: a review of current practice', *Australian Accounting Review*, **15** (2), 4–21.

Kaplan, R.S. and D.P. Norton (1996), *The Balanced Scorecard: Translating Strategy into Action*, Boston, MA: Harvard Business School Press.

Kaplan, R.S. and D.P. Norton (2000), *The Strategy-Focused Organization*, Boston, MA: Harvard Business School Press.

Kay, John (1993), *Foundations of Corporate Success*, Oxford: Oxford University Press.

Kay, John (2000), 'Knowledge: the 21st century asset', *Journal of the Royal Society of Arts*, **4**, 46–9.

Lawson, T.E. and R.L. Hepp (2001), 'Measuring the performance impact of human resource initiatives', *Human Resource Planning*, **24** (2), 36–44.

Lev, Baruch (1999), 'The inadequate public information of IC and its consequences', OECD International Symposium, Amsterdam.

Lev, Baruch and Zarowin, Paul (1999), 'The boundaries of financial reporting and how to extend them', *Journal of Accounting Research*, **37** (2), 353–85.

Levin, R.C., A.K. Klevorick, R.R. Nelson and S.G. Winter (1987), 'Appropriating the returns from industrial research and development', *Brookings Papers on Economic Activity*, 3.

Metcalfe, J.S. (1998), *Evolutionary Economics and Creative Destruction*, London: Routledge.
Morris, Timothy and Laura Empson (1998), 'Organization and expertise: an exploration of knowledge bases and the management of accounting and consulting firms', *Accounting, Organizations and Society*, **23** (5/6), 609–24.
Nonaka, I. (1991), 'The knowledge-creating company', *Harvard Business Review*, November/December, 96–104.
Nonaka, I. and H. Takeuchi (1995), *The Knowledge Creating Company*, New York: Oxford University Press.
Organisation for Economic Co-operation and Development (OECD) (1999), *The Future of the Global Economy*, Paris: OECD.
Organisation for Economic Co-operation and Development (OECD) (2000), *A New Economy? The Changing Role of Innovation and Information Technology in Growth*, Paris: OECD.
Quah, Danny (2001), 'Technology dissemination and economic growth some lessons for the new economy', CEPR discussion paper 502, London: Centre for Economic Performance.
Teece, David J. (1998), 'Research directions for knowledge management', *California Management Review*, **40** (3).
Teece, David J. (2000), *Managing Intellectual Capital: Organizational, Strategic and Policy Dimensions*, Oxford: Oxford University Press.
Van der Meer-Kooistra, J. and S.M. Zijlstra (2001), 'Reporting on intellectual capital', *Accounting, Auditing and Accountability Journal*, **14** (4), 456–76.
Webster, E.M. (1999), *The Economics of Intangible Investment*, Cheltenham, UK and Northampton, MA, USA: Edward Elgar.
Webster, E.M. (2000), 'The growth of intangible enterprise investment in Australia', *Information Economics and Policy*, **12** (1), 1–25.
Wyatt, A. (2006), 'An accounting perspective', in D. Bosworth and E. Webster (eds), *The Managament of Intellectual Property*, Cheltenham, UK and Northampton, MA, USA: Edward Elgar.
Young, A. (1998), *Towards an Interim Statistical Framework: Selecting the Core Components of Intangible Investment*, Paris: OECD Secretariat.

5. An economic perspective[1]

Derek Bosworth and Elizabeth Webster

1 INTRODUCTION

This chapter reviews theoretical and empirical economic studies that discuss intangible assets (IAs) and intellectual capital (IC), and the associated discretionary investments of the enterprise (that is, R&D, advertising, training, adoption of high-performance work practices – HPWPs – and so on) that generate them (Bosworth 2005). Given that, for a large and an increasing number of companies, intangibles form a considerable proportion of their total assets, an understanding of IAs is not only crucial to the management of IAs themselves, but to the strategic decision-making of the company as a whole.

The bulk of the economic literature, however, is either based on conceptual models or provides empirical estimates based on relatively large-scale, enterprise-level data sets – the results of which managers find difficult to use. By demonstrating what economists have been doing, what has been found, as well as the current limitations to the results, the present chapter may allow managers to press economics and related disciplines to address questions of importance to them. The management orientation of the present chapter restricts the focus of the discussion to the consideration of private issues (that is, those relevant to the commercial sector, as opposed to broader welfare issues).

Section 2 begins by discussing the nature of IC and how this can be distinguished from the broader concept of IAs. It introduces the question of ownership rights and, thereby, appropriability. Section 3 outlines the special nature and properties of IAs from an economic perspective, such as the uncertainty attached to investments in IAs, the ability to appropriate the rewards from such investments and the indivisibility of the products of such investments. Section 4 discusses the concept of the internal discretionary investments of the enterprise in IAs from an economic perspective (that is, expenditures on R&D, advertising, training, and so on). In particular, this section considers the degree to which the *ex ante* investment decisions focus on the likely effects on the profitability of the enterprise. Section 5 explores the sources of IAs that lie external to the firm and how the enterprise might efficiently access such sources. Section 6 looks at studies of the value of IAs to enterprises. In doing so, it extends the discussion beyond the traditional focus on R&D and explores other investments, such as HPWPs and information technology (IT). Section 7 concludes by outlining some of the existing weaknesses of economic approaches to the provision of information likely to be useful to managers.

2   IC, IA AND IPRS: DEFINITIONS AND BOUNDARIES

Economists have generally taken IC to refer to the stored knowledge, cognitive abilities and skills of the workforce. This reflects the historical interests among economists about the results of investments in both the skills and knowledge of a firm's workforce and the invention and development of new products and processes. Lynn (1998) argues that IC includes human capital, relational capital and two types of organizational capital – IPRs and structural capital (similar arguments appear in Brooking 1997; see also Chapter 4 of this book). Economists would perhaps prefer to argue that the broader taxonomies of Lynn and Brooking refer to IAs. Thus, the concept of enterprise-level IAs is broader than IC, as it comprises all forms of capital not embodied in matter. While it includes enterprise-level IC, it also embraces access to distribution networks and markets, systems to optimize the rate of innovation and structures that improve workplace and enterprise efficiency.

While the present chapter adopts the broader definition of IC, it also has a somewhat narrower focus on invention and innovation. Invention – the novel, non-obvious creation of knowledge – and innovation – the introduction of new methods and products into a firm – represent dominant areas in the economics literature and the present discussion is accordingly biased towards them. As demonstrated below, the empirical work of mainstream economics has only made limited inroads into the investigation of the value of investments in other aspects of IAs.

Intellectual property rights (IPRs) enter the economists' approach in two major ways: first, as a proxy for the creative activity associated with the IPR (that is, the invention to which a patent applies – see Chapter 2); second, as a measure of the appropriation of monopoly rights over the intellectual property (that is, a patent gives a firm monopoly rights over an invention). The two values are potentially quite distinct: an invention may have value even if there is no protection from IPRs (that is, from being first to market); however, it may have significantly higher value if it can be protected using a mix of IPRs, such as trade secrets, patents, trademarks, and so on. The former is the value of the invention per se, while the difference between the former and the latter is the value of the IPRs, and the source of the incentive associated with a system of IPRs to 'create' new products, processes, and so on. From an economic perspective, fundamental questions in production concern 'who owns the IPRs?', 'Who benefits from them?' and 'By how much?' This is not only a question that differentiates between one company and another, but between employees and the company they work for. This involves employee inventor rights, and the extent to which employees are paid higher wages by the inventing company, affecting the distribution of returns between profits and wages (Greenhalgh and Longland 2002).

3 NATURE, PROPERTIES AND IMPORTANCE OF IC AND IA

3.1 Knowledge and Performance

What economists view as the basic factors of production depends crucially on the era in which they were writing. Without dwelling on the details, it was the 1950s and following decade or so that saw the emergence of a formal distinction between technology (the relationship between inputs and outputs at a given level of technology) and technological change (the shift in technology, that changes the relationship between inputs and outputs). This important distinction can probably be traced to the seminal work of Solow (1957), who recognized that not all changes in output could be accounted for by changes in physical inputs. Thus, while in the 1970s and 1980s, economists were taught that capital, labour, energy and materials were the basic factors of production, it was intellect (or knowledge) that produced technological improvements that determined what is produced and how (that is, how efficiently) it is produced.

Since the amount of physical matter in the world is fixed, what passes for production, or the creation of goods, is simply a rearrangement of matter. The enterprise actively searches for information and knowledge from outside forms that can be applied directly or recombined in different ways to produce new knowledge. Knowledge that can be applied directly includes the purchase of new plant and machinery that embodies the knowledge of the capital goods producers. While this knowledge may be applied directly, it may take some time, during which learning occurs, for this to be carried out efficiently. The recombination process involving new externally sourced knowledge with existing internal knowledge is most obviously seen in the activities of R&D departments, although it also takes place elsewhere within the company. Some external knowledge is paid for (that is, through takeover or licensing) and part is absorbed through non-market avenues because of the inability of other organizations to fully exclude others from using the knowledge they have produced. One further part of the economic story is that the capacity to assimilate outside knowledge is dependent upon the knowledge and skills of the firm.

Two things are much less clear in the economic story. The first is how these investments become levered into IC and IAs. As demonstrated below, we know that they do, because firm-fixed effects (that is, the relative performance of companies over time) can be shown to be related to investments in R&D and the holding of IPRs (that is, patents, designs and trademarks) over the longer term. Any real story of how this leveraging takes place, however, is largely absent from economic models (see, however, Bosworth 2005). Second, while the allocation of physical labour has been studied extensively in economics, the market for knowledge has been comparatively overlooked. Physical labour has its own characteristics, for example, it can be hired, but not owned; the outputs of the employee, however, are generally owned by the company – including new knowledge. The production and sale of knowledge is further complicated by the three classic forms of market 'failure': uncertainty, inappropriability and indivisibility.

3.2   Uncertainty and Risk

Of the three attributes, uncertainty is arguably the primary distinctive attribute of the production of IC. Uncertainty depends on how often the process has been undertaken before and, thus, how standardized it has become. It also depends on the extent of direct labour involvement, because mechanised activities produce more reliable outcomes than those which are dominated by people. These factors govern the position each investment activity holds on the uncertainty spectrum, an example of which is given in Figure 5.1.

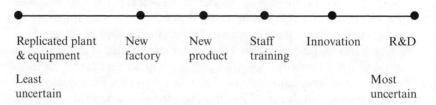

Replicated plant & equipment	New factory	New product	Staff training	Innovation	R&D
Least uncertain					Most uncertain

Figure 5.1   Uncertainty spectrum

Essentially, knowledge creation by R&D is at best risky and can be fundamentally uncertain when it arises from situations which are so singular that it is not possible to provide a meaningful *ex ante* estimate of the outcome of the R&D process. Pooling many projects together may reduce the risk associated with their success rates but cannot entirely eliminate it. This has important implications for the rules adopted to decide upon investments in R&D and other knowledge-creation activities (see Chapters 13 to 15 in this volume).

3.3 Appropriability

Appropriability refers to the extent to which the firm can exert ownership over its creative outputs and, thereby, is crucial to determining its ability to recoup its investment expenditure in the form of profits and/or capital gains. The more able the firm is to prevent duplication and imitation of its IC, the greater the degree of appropriability, *ceteris paribus*. Many analysts regard knowledge capital as highly inappropriable since, in general, 'someone skilled in the art' can reproduce it at relatively low cost and reduce the inventor's ability to extract quasi-rents. Relevant empirical evidence is provided in Mansfield (1995) and Mansfield et al. (1995a). Some of the differences in the degree of appropriability depend on how broadly IC is defined. At one extreme, an idea might be reduced to simple blueprint, while, at the other, IC might lie in the capacity of the workforce to understand and implement new technologies. In the absence of other forms of protection, the latter involves tacit knowledge which is less easily imitated and therefore more appropriable than simple blueprint knowledge. However, there are various means by which firms can increase the appropriation of the returns to their creative outputs, including taking out patent, design and trademark protection, developing brand image, having control over the distribution chain, and having complex and difficult to replicate organizations and production processes.

Increased appropriation has both a cost and benefit to the firm at the margin – so the aim is not to maximize appropriation, but to optimize it. Thus, the enterprise must look at the flow of the costs and benefits over time from different levels of investment in appropriation. In addition to this, there is the question of the appropriate mix of different forms of IP protection. The chosen mix of methods will be influenced by whether the IC is predominantly embodied in labour, in material goods or in written text. If capital is embodied in the incumbent workforce, then it may seek to protect its investment through staff retention, 'golden handcuffs', and so on; IC embodied in goods may require security devices such as locks and theft devices; IC embodied in written text may be protected by patents, copyrights or by trade secrets. Speed to market – 'the ability to keep ahead of the game' – may also form part of its IC, and is a consequence of its human and organizational capital (that is, routines, information systems, and so on). Of course, depending upon the rules regarding the use of IPRs, many of the forms of protection are not mutually exclusive – indeed, they may well be synergistic. Thus, the benefit of patenting *or* trademark protection might be significantly enhanced by undertaking both patenting *and* trademarking.

Finally, this section returns to the issue of uncertainty and risk. When choosing the level and mix of protection, the firm has to consider the costs and benefits of enforcing their rights. A literature is emerging on the treatment of patents as probabilistic property rights (for example, Allison and Lemley 1998; Lemley and Shapiro 2004; Shapiro 2003). Probablistic rights imply that a company which believes its IP is being infringed, may find that its purported 'ownership' of the IPRs is successfully overturned by the 'infringing' company. In addition, firms have to give careful consideration to whether their products and actions infringe other companies' IPRs, although the other companies' IPRs are also probabilistic.

3.4 Indivisibility

Indivisibility means that one must purchase or consume products or services as a complete bundle. A given piece of information is indivisible and, according to Arrow (1962), this poses a problem since people cannot buy only as much as they need. There are similar issues in tangible capital; plant and machinery may have some fixed and large technology efficient size compared with the market. However, there is another important form of indivisibility in terms of IAs, linked to the separability of the intangibles from the company itself. With some companies, for example, it may not be possible to separate the value of the brand from the value of the company. In effect, Coca-Cola cannot sell off its brand without selling the whole company, lock, stock and barrel.

4 THE DETERMINANTS OF INVESTMENTS IN IAS

4.1 Demand-pull versus Technology-push

This section focuses on the discretionary investments that are, in some sense, internal to the enterprise – activities such as R&D, advertising, introduction of new HPWPs, and so on. Section 5 below deals with the corresponding sources of IAs that, in some sense, are external to the firm, although the subsequent discussion shows that this internal/external dichotomy is oversimplistic. In terms of internal discretionary investments, the literature highlights two main explanations of the determinants of inventions. Either inventions are stimulated through exogenous advances in science and technology ('technology-push') or they are demand induced ('demand-pull'). While, in principle, the two may be viewed as alternative explanations, in practice, they are both likely to operate at any one point in time.

4.2 Science- and Technology-push

Perhaps the classic case of 'technology-push' is Galbraith's (1967) 'technocracy' in which company R&D takes place independently from the market, and any new products are 'forced' onto the market using 'persuasive advertising'. An alternative source of 'technology-push' comes from the science base, where, for example, universities develop new technologies that are difficult to commercialize or for which significant parts of the market are reluctant to take them up (for example, genetically modified (GM) foods). The extent to which this can happen is brought into doubt by the high proportions of new products that fail at or soon after launch (for example, Cooper and Kleinschmidt, 1988 and 1990), and examples of product failure (for example, the Ford Edsel – Brooks 1971 – and Corfam – Freeman and Soete 1997). While there are examples of radical new products that consumers had not conceived of, their acceptance might be argued to be the result of a latent demand, rather than as a consequence of persuasive advertising.

Some resonance of the technology-led view can still be found in the evolutionary theories of innovation and technological change. Here, technology-led inventions create diversity, while market forces form a selection mechanism – consistent with the observed degree of new product failure. This selection mechanism is not the same thing as being demand led (that is, at the time the R&D investment is made), only in an *ex post* sense (that is, after the new product is developed). In addition, in evolutionary theories, past technological experience is important in driving the scale and direction of the invention process – invention and innovations are selective and cumulative, forming technology trajectories or 'innovation avenues' (Dosi 1988).

Technological opportunity (that is, areas rich in inventive potential) might be viewed as a supply-side (that is, a technology-push) factor, and there is considerable evidence to support the importance of technological opportunity (proxied by sector, area of technology, and so on) in influencing inventive and innovative activity. Evangelista and Sirilli (1997) interrogated a 1992 Italian innovation survey and reported that technological opportunity appeared to be the most important determinant of innovation. Levin and Reiss (1984) argue that a firm's innovation rate is determined *jointly* by industry differences in market size and technological opportunity.

4.3 Demand-pull

Even if Galbraith's view was true of the 1950s and 1960s, it seems less relevant (though still a worry) today. Over the subsequent period, the innovation, new product launch and technology management literatures have emphasized the need for market-orientated approaches for success in innovation (Freeman and Soete 1997; Ghosh et al. 1994), which seems to have been assimilated into firm decision-making. These market-orientated approaches are effectively a restatement of the importance of 'demand-pull' – they feed into the *ex ante* decision of the scale and direction of R&D – pulling it towards areas where there are profitable markets.

In practice, the demand-led view was emerging at roughly the same time as the technology-push (for example, Nelson 1959). Schmookler (1966, p. 12) examined 14 US manufacturing sectors over the period 1899–1937 and found that capital good patents were largely determined by investment demand (lagged three years) emanating from the industry sector that purchased the patented capital goods. The apparent observation that advances in science stimulate inventions arises from the way the data is classified. If inventions are classified according to their scientific field then, inventions appear to be supply driven. However, if the question is why they are invented, not how they are invented, a demand-side explanation dominates. The rise of the chemical and engineering inventions in the first half of the twentieth century was not solely due the growing science base but also to the needs of large-scale industries for standardized materials.

4.4 Integration of Demand-pull and Supply-push

Technological opportunity, however, can be looked at, not as a supply-side mechanism per se, but as an influence on the profitability of different lines of invention via differences in the efficiency of R&D (that is, inventions per unit of R&D). Thus, Stoneman (1983) takes the original Schmookler (1966) model, where there is a marginal benefit from invention, and extends it to include the marginal costs of invention. One might imagine that at any given level of R&D effort, the productivity of R&D at the margin is higher and diminishing less quickly in areas of high technological opportunity.[2] In the Griliches (1957) diffusion case, the size of the market for growing hybrid corn is tempered by the costs of modification of the hybrid corn to the different climatic regions of the USA.

Symeonidis (1996) reports evidence that more concentrated industries have higher invention rates. Historically, this result was argued to reflect the fact that larger firms in more concentrated sectors have higher profits from which they can invest in inventive and innovative activities. This 'Schumpeterian hypothesis', linking size and concentration with invention, might be viewed as consistent with the 'technology-push' hypothesis, and even consistent with Galbraith's model. Symeonidis (1996), however, argues that this result probably occurs because firms in concentrated sectors are better able to appropriate the benefits; this might be interpreted as a demand-side or demand-pull factor.

4.5 Eclectic Empirical Models

In more recent years, given the recognition of the likely existence of both demand-pull and technology-push forces, the literature has moved on to incorporate an increasingly wide range of influences, mostly tested using large-scale, firm-level databases. This section attempts to provide a flavour of such studies by providing a small number of examples.

Peneder (2002), in a sample of about 100 US manufacturing firms, found that R&D expenditure was primarily correlated with high-skilled white-collar workers, while advertising expenditure was correlated with low-skilled white-collar workers. Bosworth and Rogers (1998) found that R&D intensity was highly correlated with industry and level of enterprise diversification but not ownership (foreign/domestic), firm size or industry concentration. Loundes and Bosworth (2002), in their study of 3569 small and medium Australian companies, found that whether or not a company was an innovator was positively related to lagged R&D, lagged change in training, company size, small market share and HPWPs. There was no correlation with expenditure on tangible capital. In an allied study, Webster (2004) found that factors and generic routines common to all industries, such as the extent of learning, knowledge spillovers, appropriability and the managers' style are more important than industry-specific forces. Rogers (1998a) observed that while small firms are less likely to undertake R&D, those that do have higher R&D intensities, although this pattern may say more about incentives to report R&D than to undertake it.

A limited number of studies have looked at the determinants of other forms of IAs, workplace reorganization and advertising. The paper by Rogers (1998b) considered some characteristics of management, organizational and technological change using a two-wave panel data set of 698 Australian workplaces. Two-thirds of workplaces in 1990 reported at least one type of change, compared with four-fifths in 1995. Types of change were correlated, so firms which have undergone one sort of change are more likely to experience other sorts of change. There is also evidence of persistence: firms that were experiencing change pre-1990 are more likely to experience change five years later. With respect to innovation in new products, work organization and new technologies embodied in tangible equipment, Rogers (1999) found that this was more prevalent in workplaces with better employee–management relations and higher levels of staff training.

5   DIFFUSION OF INTANGIBLE CAPITAL

5.1   External Sources of Knowledge and Technology

Diffusion of IAs to competitor firms is a double-edged sword. Diffusion that flows from the inventing firm to other companies (without payment) is associated with imperfect appropriability, undermining the rewards to invention, but also with improving the performance of the rival firms and the welfare of society. Such flows are referred to as 'spillovers' or 'externalities' and have important welfare consequences and, thereby, implications for government support for investments (such as R&D or education) that give rise to them (Griliches 1992). Of course, diffusion associated with 'proper' compensation for the inventor is associated with greater appropriation of the benefits by the inventor, but lower static welfare of society. The mechanisms for such compensation are broad, including licensing, franchising and the takeover of companies with the knowledge or technology needed. For the same reasons that firms benefit from forming production cartels, it can also be beneficial to firms to promote diffusion via networking within a common group, to develop research consortia and form joint ventures while at the same time limiting external diffusion. Other examples of such relationships include cross-licensing and patent pooling (Teece 2000),

5.2   Types of Technology Transfer

Economists often find it useful to distinguish between: (1) vertical technology transfer – the transfer of knowledge from basic research through to applied research, development and production, as well as from upstream to downstream companies and consumers, and vice versa (that is, the buyer–supplier chain); and (2) horizontal transfer – the transfer of the same technology from one context to another (Mansfield 1995). It is also important to distinguish between technology that is common to the whole industry, system-specific technologies that arise from a specific item of production and firm-specific technologies that are (often) tacit and cannot be transferred to other enterprises. Mansfield also speaks of three types of transfer – material transfer, design transfer (for example, of blueprints) and capacity transfer (that is, the capacity to adapt a new item to local conditions). The last is much more complex than the other two and generally requires the transfer of people who bring tacit information and can adapt to unforeseen contingencies.

Diffusion may occur inadvertently or in a planned way through the interchange of people, though professional meetings, through suppliers and customers, through published patent applications (for example, see Mansfield et al. 1995a) and reverse engineering, via foreign direct investment (FDI), the transmission of written and codified books and manuals, educational services and through international trade. It may be promoted deliberately by governments, industry bodies and firms through subsidies for FDI, networking, personnel exchange, joint ventures and consortia and licensing. However, it may also be deliberately hindered by the same parties through the use of patents, trade secrecy and labour contracts.

Foreign direct investment has long been a major vehicle for the transfer of IAs across national boarders (for example, Buckley 1985; Mansfield and Romeo 1995). Multinationals bring IC, marketing and other business strategies. The IC often includes a critical body of skilled managers and workers to enhance the (usually) tangible asset base in the recipient country, although spillovers in the host country may also raise levels of ICs of other firms. For the large corporation, it allows them to maximize the use of their IAs (in new locations) without spoiling their domestic market. According to Mansfield et al. (1995b), inventing firms are more likely to transfer new technologies via foreign subsidiaries and their older technologies through licensing and joint ventures.

5.3 Economic Evidence on Knowledge and Technology Transfer

A number of studies model the effect of spillovers on firm performance by assuming that the latter depends not only on its own research, but also on a wider pool of knowledge to which the enterprise has access. It is essential to include in the equation to be estimated intangible investment activities by adjacent firms, industries or technologies. Related firms are identified by how closely they lie on the product type, R&D type, location or labour market spectrums. A weighted index to represent a composite spillover is usually calculated and included in the estimating equation. Summaries of studies that have tried to measure spillovers generally find positive effects on adjacent firms (Griliches 1992). However, Klette et al. (2000) warn that these positive findings may reflect other factors that could correlate with firm performance (for example, firms have to perform their own R&D in order to receive others' spillovers) and, furthermore, it is probable that studies that do not report significant effects are less likely to be published.

At present little is known about the costs of learning and trying to absorb spillovers from other firms. They are repeated investments by firms in tapping outside pools of information, and managers may well undertake some form of investment analysis over the extent to which the company should be involved in such activities in much the same way as they decide on market research activities. According to Arora et al. (2001):

> Technological spillovers play an important role in the process of economic growth ... However, the typical description of the mechanism of these spillovers is, in Alfred Marshall's often used phrase, one where 'the secrets ... are in the air'. Important as this ethereal mechanism may be, there are other mechanisms, more material and more amenable to economic analysis, through which technology is transferred across sectors and countries.

Some evidence is provided by the fact that the innovation and diffusion processes are aided by the existence of an R&D department within the company and by the existence of more highly qualified workers in R&D activities (Bosworth et al. 1992; Bosworth 2005). In a regression explaining the extent of innovation activities in UK manufacturing firms, the coefficient on own-R&D is significant positive in the probit equations explaining the adoption of each of the possible technologies; likewise, it is significant and positive in the explanation of the total number of technologies in use (Bosworth 1996). Mansfield and Romeo (1995, p. 83) argue that an increase in a country's R&D expenditure by ten percentage points reduces imitation time by two to three years.

6   MEASURING THE PRIVATE VALUE OF INTANGIBLE CAPITAL

6.1   Scope and Methodology

This section does not attempt to assess the methods of appropriation, but rather looks at studies that have measured private returns given whatever the conditions for appropriability were at the time in the markets under scrutiny.[3] The specific approaches, which are presented below, are intended to measure the private returns to the investment (where the models often allow for the spillover effects outlined above). Three of the current approaches are reviewed: the rate of return approach; the production function approach; the market valuation approach (see Chapters 6, 7 and 8). Most studies have estimated the private return to firms from investment in R&D, while remarkably few have estimated the returns to investment in worker skills, organizational change, marketing, and so on. Accordingly, this section focuses mainly on the former.

6.2 Three Methods of Estimating the Private Rate of Return

Rate of return approach

The typical equation used to estimate the rate of return from an investment (using the formula for an infinite series) is:

$$r = \frac{\Pi}{I}(\delta + x) \qquad (5.1)$$

Where r is the rate of return, D is the perpetual net addition to gross profits (or productivity) that depreciates at the rate of δ over time, I is the cost of the investment and x is the discount factor for the project's uncertainty. Individual firm and time subscripts are not shown. BIE (1994) and Nadiri (1993) summarize the results from over 60 firm and industry level studies from major OECD countries and find that most private rates of return (returns to the business only) range from 20 per cent to 30 per cent and social rates of return vary up to over 100 per cent.[4] However, these estimates are subject to may qualifications such as the ambiguity about defining the counterfactual (for example, in very competitive markets, high R&D may ensure only survival and normal profits). In addition, if market boundaries are not defined properly, or there are very few cases in each market, then it is possible that no apparent relationship between R&D and rates of profit will be obvious.

Production function approach

The typical equation used for the production function approach is:

$$Y = f(KT, KI, L) \qquad (5.2)$$

where Y is output, KT denotes services from the tangible capital stock, KI is the services from the stock of intangible capital (for example, a compound sum of past R&D) and L is labour services. Production function studies generally find that returns to the stock of intangible capital, as proxied by cumulated past R&D or IP stocks, is positive but the size of these effects varies considerably, although this might be partly the result of the risky nature of the investment (for reviews, see Griliches, 1992; 1995; Industry Commission 1995; Mairesse and Mohnen 1995; Mairesse and Sassenou 1991).

Market valuation approach

Several studies have used stock market value (MV) as a measure of performance, although this limits their samples to listed companies. Since market MV is the capitalized value of the future stream of dividends (closely related to the future stream of profits), a positive relationship between MV and discretionary investments of the firm implies that the investments contributed more to expected revenues than actual costs. Since an increase in MV only indicates that profits from that point in time onwards will rise, these studies exclude the effects of any sunk costs arising from prior investment activity, already written off by the stock market. This is a problem where patents are used as an index for intangible capital, since, by the time the firm makes a patent application, it will have already invested considerable resources in R&D. In addition, the interpretation is subject to the same caveats as for profitability studies.

The market valuation studies use the identity:

$$MV \equiv q(KT + KI)^{\sigma} \tag{5.3}$$

where MV is the market value; KT and KI represent the stocks of tangible and intangible capital; q represents the ability of the firm's management to convert the firm's assets into profits and, thereby, MV; σ is an estimated scale parameter. q is generally allowed to vary across firms (estimating firm-specific effects) and over time (estimating general 'macro' changes that affect the market as a whole). The equation uses R&D or patent data to proxy for KI and, by adopting a linear approximation,[5] is estimated as:

$$\log MV = \log q + \sigma \log KT + \sigma \frac{KI}{KT} \tag{5.4}$$

although other explanatory variables are also included. One difficulty with empirically applying these studies is the choice of proxies for the firms' intangible capital. KI in equation (5.4) is the accumulated expenditure by the firm to acquire or create the IAs while the proxies often used are either values of some other variable (for example, a perpetual inventory measure of R&D) or various count measures (number of patents).

If R&D and patents and designs are included in the equation, then double counting may occur as most patents and designs derive from past R&D. Including R&D with recorded IAs is not double counting as normal accounting standards only allow for IAs that have been brought from outside the firm to be recorded in balance sheets (see Chapter 3).[6] Studies that do include R&D with patents not surprisingly appear to run into collinearity problems. An alternative approach using factor analysis to derive a latent variable to represents the firm's intangible investment or capital may yield better results.

6.3 Example Empirical Results: R&D and IP Proxies for IAs

Chauvin and Hirschey (1993) examine 4600 listed US companies in 1988–90 to find that both higher R&D and advertising expenditures are associated with higher MVs. However, the magnitude of these effects varies across industries. Feeny and Rogers (1998, p. 40), using a sample of 118 Australian companies over the period 1996–97, find that patents, tangible assets and trademark applications have a positive effect on the firm's MV. Research and development expenditure was not significant due, perhaps, to the collinearity problem referred to above. This was also found in Bosworth and Rogers (2001) using a slightly different sample of Australian companies. Bosworth and Mahdian (1999) found examples, from their panel data set of pharmaceutical companies, of specifications in which R&D, patents and trademarks had a significant and positive impact on MVs.

Hall (2000), in a review of 16 MV papers, as well as drawing upon her own subsequent work, perhaps offers the best overview of the MV literature to date. The key findings are that:

1. Research and development assets are valued by financial markets. A reasonable fraction of the variance in MV that remains after controlling for ordinary assets is explained by either R&D spending or R&D stock (with the flow coefficient averaging about four to five times the stock coefficient). However, there is still a fair amount of unexplained variance.
2. The R&D coefficient is not stable over time in either the USA or the UK. In the USA, this coefficient reached a recent peak in the early 1980s and has declined since. This result seems to vary across industries, but industry-level findings are somewhat unstable and inconclusive.
3. Patents are informative above and beyond R&D, although the correlation is much weaker. The average R-squared for the MV–R&D relationship is approximately 0.15, while that for the patents–R&D relationship is about 0.08.
4. Citation-weighted patents are slightly more informative than simple patent counts. The average R^2 for citation-weighted patents alone is about 0.10. When both variables are included in a regression, the citation-weighted one clearly wins.
5. The pattern of the patents and citation-weighted patent coefficients in the MV regression over time appears to be identical: they are measuring the same thing, but citation weights improve the precision of the estimates.

6.4   Example Empirical Results: Other Investments in IAs

Training and HPWPs

The literature on the effects of other forms of intangible investment is more meagre, with the exception perhaps of the mainly US literature focusing on the role of HPWPs on enterprise performance. Relatively few studies have been undertaken on enterprise returns to investment in staff training. Several studies have noted that the strongest rises in productivity over the last half century have been concentrated in the highly skilled industries, but these observations are several steps removed from strong evidence about the returns to enterprise training. In addition, a number of studies have linked the capacity to innovate, the success of new ventures and the survival of existing plants to the skills available within the workforce (for a review, see Bosworth 2005).

Perhaps most important, however, is the emergence of a mainly US-based literature linking MV and other measures of firm performance to the adoption of human resources (HR) and other HPWPs, which include training. Indeed, some of these models also include R&D alongside the HPWP variables (Huselid 1995). There are at least two problems with this literature at present. First, the role of training is generally subsumed within some latent variable constructed using factor analysis, and, although the latent variable itself is significant, the precise role of training remains hidden within the composite variable. Second, many of the skills variables that labour economists might view as important are largely absent.

The HPWP literature adds to the understanding of the generation of IAs in at least two further ways to that of the R&D literature (see Bosworth 2005, for discussion). First, it not only supports the view that individual HPWPs can be important in driving firm performance, but that systems of such practices, which exploit complementarities, may be significantly more important. While there may be performance improvements from the introduction of one HR practice or HPWP, the gains from a (consistent) package of such practices seems to be disproportionately larger. However, different systems might be best suited to different sectors (see Laursen and Foss 2000).

The second important contribution concerns the interaction between product market/manufacturing strategies and the HPWP practices adopted. In other words, to what extent and in what way are the effects of particular practices (or systems of practices) moderated by the strategies of the company? Or, which HPWP packages are consistent with the strategies of the company and enhance firm performance? This important issue appears to be entirely absent from the literature in other areas, such as the MV and production function–R&D literatures.

Computers and IT systems

Clearly, computer investment will have contributed to economic growth in the normal manner that arises from the growth in the use of a particular factor (Jorgenson and Stiroh, 1995). This growth in usage has been driven, in part, by the falling quality-constant price of computers. However, other authors have argued that computers act as a facilitating technology, enabling more important organizational changes within firms, not least the introduction of business systems, across a wide range of activities and sectors (Helpman 1998).

There is clear evidence in the literature of a link between computer adoption and productivity growth (Brynjolfsson and Hitt 1993, 1995; Lichtenberg 1995). In a paper linking market valuation and investment in computer capital, Brynjolfsson and Yang (1999) report a significant role for IT investments. In brief, based on a similar, but smaller sample of companies than Hall (1993), they explore the impact of IT on MV and report a large and highly significant coefficient. The empirical specification included a range of other variables, including R&D. When the IT variable was included alongside an R&D variable, the coefficient on IT fell somewhat, but the R&D variable became insignificant, not the IT variable (Brynjolfsson and Yang 1999, p. 25).

The coefficient on IT is likely to be overestimated, in part because neither internally generated nor purchased software can be allowed for in the empirical specifications. In addition, both investments are associated with organizational changes that are potentially performance enhancing, but which generally appear as a non-separable expense that is written off in the firm's accounts. Making a qualitative attempt to allow for the costs of internal and external software, the authors conclude that, 'Our deduction is that the main portion of the computer-related IAs comes from the new business processes, new organizational structure and new market strategies, which each complement the computer technology' (ibid., p. 29). For further discussion, see Bosworth (2005).

7   IMPLICATIONS FOR MANAGEMENT

While the different branches of the economics literature, particularly the market valuation and productivity performance literatures, have made enormous strides in recent years, a number of significant changes in data and methodology are now required to make further advances that will be of use to managers.

1. There is currently an increasing number of papers undertaking (mainly) two-country comparisons of the results of such studies. However, there remain problems of data comparability that need to be resolved to allow them to provide major insights. While this will be a long and tedious process, these comparisons promise advances in our understanding of the performance of companies of different nationalities (as well as the question as to whether particular stock markets, such as the UK, are short-termist).

2. There is a need to not only include the knowledge pool in the performance estimates, but also specific measures of competition in the inventive process. It might be argued, for example, that, while an increase in the pool might have a positive effect on all fishermen at the pool, an increase in a competitor's R&D is likely to have a negative impact on own-performance, other things (that is, size of pool and own-R&D) being equal.

3. There is a clear need for inter-disciplinary approaches to the role played by IAs in driving enterprise performance (and, thereby, in deriving the value of the associated assets). Such studies are beginning to appear; examples include the inclusion of IT investments alongside R&D expenditures and the inclusion of R&D alongside the use of HPWPs. They are, however, still in their infancy.

4. There is an urgent need to explore firms' discretionary investments in R&D, training, advertising, and so on in the context of the company's strategies, as well as in terms of the HR and HPWP activities that best support them. The moderating effects of strategies have been shown to be important in the HPWP literature, but is almost entirely absent from the invention and innovation literature driven by economists.

5. The specification of the MV model needs to move away from the linear approximation (or even direct estimation of the non-linear) accounting tautology to flexible functional forms. The same is true for a move from log-linear productivity functions. The result would enable the interaction of the various influences to be tested to see if they were, for example, substitute or complementary investments that, for example, are synergistic.[7] The work on the role of HPWPs in the human resource management (HRM) literature is much more advanced in this respect than the economists' work on the returns to discretionary investments.

6. The specifications currently allow the estimation of the marginal returns to, say, an additional unit of investment in R&D, averaged across all firms in the sample. Thus, the marginal return to R&D is averaged across companies and does not reflect the degree of risk or uncertainty posed by

the investment (see Bosworth 2005). This raises a number of econometric issues. The first is that uncertainty in the returns is likely to raise the standard error attached to the variable and, given the economists' natural tendency to only select significant results, this will distort the models reported. Second, given that, for example, such a small proportion of patents are valuable, whether the existing use of all firms in the sample is justified and there is a question as to whether existing econometric techniques are suited to looking at the value of patents.

7. There is a need for research on the changing returns to each type of discretionary investment over the life cycle of a product (or portfolio of products of a firm). Once a new product is produced or new technology is installed, if successful, the firm has an interest in exploiting this and the returns to further R&D may be low. On the other hand, as existing product or technology platforms age, the returns to R&D to discover new platforms may rise (Bosworth 2005).

NOTES

1. The present chapter draws upon a number of arguments outlined in Melbourne Institute working paper no. 10/02 (ISSN 1328–4991 and ISBN 0 7340 1534 8), October 2004. Thanks are due to Joanne Loundes, Glenys Harding, Andrew Christie, Mark Rogers and Tim Fry. Views expressed and all remaining errors are the responsibility of the authors.
2. This is quite distinct from the original 'technocracy' model, which implied a certain reckless drive for invention that was not profit motivated – invent what you want and persuade consumers to buy it. It is also distinct from the evolutionary models which would not accept the *ex ante* profit maximization (or even orientation) implied by such a model.
3. Investment decisions such as R&D are probably taken jointly with the decision to invest in the level and mix of appropriation mechanisms (see Section 3).
4. However, BIE (1994) note that, given the serious methodological problems with measuring social returns, these estimates should be treated with caution.
5. This form is appropriate if, and only if, $\frac{K_i}{K_t}$ is small such that $\log\left(1+\frac{K_i}{K_t}\right) \approx \frac{K_i}{K_t}$. In practice, the approximation becomes more suspect, the greater the ratio of intangible to tangible assets.
6. R&D expenditure is conventionally expensed. However, in the UK, purchases of intangibles have historically been written off against the next year's profit or against reserves. In addition, note the earlier argument that in-house R&D and the propensity to purchase intangibles are probably not independent of one another.
7. A recent study of small and medium Australian enterprise by Loundes and Bosworth (2002) has found that R&D was complementary to increases in training expenditure and marketing expenditure but there was no correlation between tangible investment and R&D or marketing expenditure. Chauvin and Hirschey (1993) used data from 1548 US firms over the period 1988–90 also found that advertising and R&D expenditures were not positively correlated between firms, but appeared to be used as alternative means of product differentiation. Other studies paint a more complex picture (Bosworth, 2005).

REFERENCES

Allison, J.R. and M.A. Lemley (1998), 'Empirical evidence on the validity of litigated patents', *American Intellectual Property Law Association Quarterly Journal*, **26**, 185–275.

Arora, A., A. Fosfuri and A. Gambardella (2001), 'Specialised spillovers, international spillovers and investment: evidence from the chemical industry', *Journal of Development Economics*, **65**, 31–54.

Arrow, K.J. (1962), 'Economic welfare and the allocation of resources for invention', *The Rate and Direction of Inventive Activity: Economic and Social Factors*, Princeton, NJ: Princeton University Press, pp. 609–25.

BIE (1993), *R&D, Innovation and Competitiveness: an Evaluation of the Research and Development Tax Concessions*, Canberra: Bureau of Industry Economics.

BIE (1994), *The Economics of Patents*, Canberra: AGPS.

Bosworth, D.L. (1996), 'Determinants of the use of advanced technologies', *International Journal of the Economics of Business*, **3** (3), 269–93.

Bosworth, D.L. (2005), *The Determinants of Enterprise Performance*, Manchester: Manchester University Press.

Bosworth, D.L. and H. Mahdian (1999), 'Returns to intellectual property in the pharmaceuticals sector', *Economie Appliqué*, **52** (2), 69–93.

Bosworth, D. and M. Rogers (1998), 'Research and development, intangible assets and the performance of large Australian companies', *IBIS Collaborative Program in Enterprise Dynamics*, vol. 2/98, University of Melbourne.

Bosworth, D. and M. Rogers (2001), 'Market value, R&D and intellectual property: an empirical analysis of large Australian firms', *Economic Record*, **77**, 323–37.

Bosworth, D.L., R. Wilson and P. Taylor (1992), *Technological Change: the Role of Scientists and Engineers*, Aldershot: Avebury Press.

Brooking, A. (1997), *Intellectual Capital: a Core Asset for the Third Millennium Enterprise*, London: Thompson Press.

Brooks, J. (1971), *Business Adventures*, Harmondsworth: Pelican.

Brynjolfsson, E. and L.M. Hitt (1993), 'Is information systems spending productive? New evidence and new results', in *Proceedings of the 14th International Conference on Information Systems, Orlando, FL*, pp. 47–64.

Brynjolfsson, E. and L.M. Hitt (1995), 'Information technology as a factor of production: the role of differences among firms', *Economics of Innovation and New Technology*, Conference Volume, **3** (4), 183–200.

Brynjolfsson, E. and S. Yang (1999), 'The intangible costs and benefits of computer investments: evidence from financial markets', working paper, Sloan School of Management, Massachusetts Institute of Technology.

Buckley, P.J. (1985), 'A critical view of theories of the multinational enterprise', in P.J. Buckley and M. Casson (eds), *The Economic Theory of the Multinational Enterprise: Selected Papers*, London: Macmillan, pp. 1–19.

Chauvin, K.W. and M. Hirschey (1993), 'Advertising, R&D expenditure and the market value of the firm', *Financial Management*, **22**, 128–40.

Dosi, G. (1988), 'Sources procedures and microeconomic effects of innovation', *Journal of Economic Literature*, **26** (3), 1120–71.

Evangelista, R. and G. Sirilli (1997), 'Innovation in services and manufacturing: results from the Italian surveys', ESRC Centre for Business Research, vol. 73, University of Cambridge.

Feeny, S. and Rogers, M. (1998), 'The use of intellectual property by large Australian enterprises', in a report for IP, University of Melbourne, Melbourne.

Freeman, C. and L. Soete (1997), *The Economics of Industrial Innovation*, Cambridge, MA: MIT Press.

Galbraith, J.K. (1967), *The New Industrial State*, Boston, MA: Houghton Mifflin.

Ghosh, B.C., H.P. Schoch, D.B. Taylor, W.W. Kwan and T.S. Kim (1994), 'Top performing organizations of Australia, New Zealand and Singapore', *Marketing Intelligence and Planning*, **12** (7), 39–48.

Greenhalgh, C. and M. Longland (2002), 'Intellectual property in UK firms: creating intangible assets and distributing the benefits via wages and jobs', *Oxford Bulletin of Economics and Statistics*, **63**, special issue: The Labour Market Consequences of Technical and Structural Change.

Greenhalgh, C. and M. Longland (2002), 'Running to stand still? – intellectual property and value added in innovating firms', in *The Future of Manuacturing in the UK*, mimeo, London School of Economics.

Griliches, Z. (1957), 'Hybrid corn: an exploration in the economics of technological change', *Econometrica*, reprinted in Z. Griliches (ed.) (1988), *Technology, Education, and Productivity*, New York: Basil Blackwell, pp. 27–52.

Griliches, Z. (1992), 'The search for R&D spillovers', *Scandinavian Journal of Economics*, **94**, 29–47.

Griliches, Z. (1995), 'R&D and productivity: econometric results and measurement issues', in P.A. Stoneman (ed.), *Handbook of the Economics of Innovation and Technological Change*, Oxford: Blackwell, pp. 52–89.

Hall, B. (1993), 'The stock market's valuation of R&D investment during the 1980s', *American Economic Review*, **83**, 259–64.

Hall, B.H. (2000), 'Innovation and market value', in R. Barrell, G. Mason and M. O'Mahony (eds), *Productivity, Innovation and Economic Performance*, Cambridge: Cambridge University Press, pp. 177–98.

Helpman, E. (1998), 'Introduction', in E. Helpman (ed.), *General Purpose Technology and Economic Growth*, Cambridge, MA: MIT Press, pp. 1–14.

Huselid, M.A. (1995), 'The impact of human resource management practices on turnover, productivity, and corporate financial performance', *Academy of Management Journal*, **38** (3), 635–72.

Industry Commission (1995), *Research and Development: Vol 3 – Appendices*, report no. 44, Canberra: Australian Government Publishing Service.

Jorgenson, D.W. and K.J. Stiroh (1995), 'Computers and growth', *Journal of Innovation and New Technology*, **3** (3–4), 295–316.

Klette, T.J., J. Moen and Z. Griliches (2000), 'Do subsidies to commercial R&D reduce market failures? Microeconometric evaluation studies', *Research Policy*, **29**, 471–95.

Laursen, K. and N.J. Foss (2000), 'New HRM practices, complementarities, and the impact on innovation performance', paper presented at the Econometrics of Trademarks and Patents Conference, Alicante, Spain.

Lemley, M.A. and C. Shapiro (2004), 'Probabilistic rights', working paper no. CPC04–46, Competition Policy Centre, University of Berkeley, CA, forthcoming in *Journal of Economic Perspectives*.

Levin, R. and P. Reiss (1984), 'Tests of a Schumpeterian model of R&D and market structure', in Z. Griliches (ed.), *R&D, Patents, and Productivity: NBER Conference Report*, Chicago, IL: University of Chicago Press, pp. 175–204.

Lichtenberg, F.R. (1995), 'The output contributions of computer equipment and personnel: a firm-level analysis', *Economics of Innovation and New Technology*, **3**, 201–17.

Loundes, J. and D. Bosworth (2002), 'The dynamic performance of Australian enterprises: a panel analysis of innovation, productivity and profit using the business longitudinal survey', in Melbourne Institute Working Paper Series, Melbourne Institute of Applied Economic and Social Research, University of Melbourne, 3/2002.

Lynn, B.E. (1998), *The Management of Intellectual Capital: the Issues and the Practice*, Hamilton: Society of Management Accountants of Canada.

Mairesse, J. and P. Mohnen (1995), *Research and Development and Productivity – a Survey of the Econometric Literature*, Paris: Insee.

Mairesse, J. and M. Sassenou (1991), 'R&D and productivity: a survey of econometric studies at the firm level', *Science, Technology and Industry Review: OECD*, **7**, 265–9.

Mansfield, E. (1995), 'International technology transfer: forms, resource requirements and policies', in E. Mansfield (ed.), *Innovation, Technology and the Economy: The Selected Essays of Edwin Mansfield*, Aldershot, UK and Brookfield, US: Edward Elgar, pp. 87–91 (first published 1975).

Mansfield, E. and A. Romeo. (1995), 'Technology transfer to overseas subsidiaries by US-based firms', in E. Mansfield (ed.), *Innovation, Technology and the Economy: The Selected Essays of Edwin Mansfield*, Aldershot, UK and Brookfield, US: Edward Elgar, pp. 101–14 (first published 1980).

Mansfield, E., A. Romeo and S. Wagner (1995a), 'Foreign trade and US research and development', in E. Mansfield (ed.), *Innovation, Technology and the Economy: The Selected Essays of Edwin Mansfield*, Aldershot, UK and Brookfield, US: Edward Elgar, pp. 92–100 (first published 1979).

Mansfield, E., M. Schwartz and S. Wagner (1995b), 'Imitation costs and patents: an empirical study', in E. Mansfield (ed.), *Innovation, Technology and the Economy: The Selected Essays of Edwin Mansfield*, Aldershot, UK and Brookfield, US: Edward Elgar, pp. 253–64 (first published 1981).

Nadiri, M.I. (1993), *Innovations and Technological Spillovers*, Cambridge, MA: National Bureau of Economic Research, vol. 4423.

Nelson, R.R. (1959), 'The economics of invention: a survey of the literature', *Journal of Business*, **32**, 101–27.

Peneder, M. (2002), 'Intangible investment and human resources', *Journal of Evolutionary Economics*, **12**, 107–34.

Rogers, M. (1998a), 'Innovation in Australian enterprises: evidence from the GAPS and IBIS Databases', Melbourne Institute Working Paper Series, 19/98, Melbourne Institute of Applied Economic and Social Research, University of Melbourne.

Rogers, M. (1998b), 'Management, organisational and technological change in Australian workplaces: evidence from the AWIRS data sets', Melbourne Institute Working Paper Series, 11/98, Melbourne Institute of Applied Economic and Social Research, University of Melbourne.

Rogers, M. (1999), 'Innovation in Australian workplaces: an empirical analysis using AWIRS 1990 and 1995', Melbourne Institute Working Paper Series, 3/99, Melbourne Institute of Applied Economic and Social Research, University of Melbourne.

Schmookler, J. (1966), *Invention and Economic Growth*, Cambridge, MA: Harvard University Press.

Shapiro, C. (2003), 'Antitrust limits to patent settlements', *Rand Journal of Economics*, **34** (2), 391–411.

Solow, R.M. (1957), 'Technical change and the aggregate production function', *Review of Economics and Statistics*, **39** (3), 312–20.

Stoneman, P.A. (1983), *The Economic Analysis of Technological Change*, Oxford: Oxford University Press.

Symeonidis, G. (1996), 'Innovation, firm size and market structure: Schumpeterian hypotheses and some new themes', Economics Department, OECD, 161.

Teece, D.J. (2000), *Managing Intellectual Capital*, Oxford: Oxford University Press.

Webster, E. (2004), 'Firms' decisions to innovate and innovation routines', *Economics of Innovation and New Technology*, **13** (8), 733–45.

PART III

Intellectual property and company performance

6. Market valuation of US and European intellectual property

Dirk Czarnitzki, Bronwyn H. Hall and Raffaele Oriani

1 INTRODUCTION

Innovation is generally considered to be a major cause of economic growth and is an important source of the wealth of developed countries. A necessary condition for private innovative activity is, however, that innovation has a positive impact on profits of a firm. Because the returns to innovation rarely occur during the period in which investments in innovation occur, and in fact, may be spread over a number of years following such investment, current profits are generally a very partial and incomplete indicator of the returns to innovation. For this reason a number of researchers have turned to stock market value as an indicator of the firm's expected economic results from investing in knowledge capital, following the seminal contribution by Griliches (1981). It has to be noted that this method is intrinsically limited in scope, because it can be used only for private firms and only where these firms are traded on a well-functioning financial market. Nevertheless, using financial market valuation avoids the problems of timing of costs and revenues, and is capable of forward-looking evaluation, something that studies analysing profitability during a given period of time are not able to do. Furthermore, the method is potentially useful for calibrating various innovation measures, in the sense that one can measure their economic impact and possibly enabling one to validate these measures for use elsewhere as proxies for innovation value.

Interest in valuing innovation assets stems from several distinct sources, and as a result there has been more than one strand of literature: first, firms and their accountants have been anxious to develop methods to value intangible assets of the innovative kind, both to help guide decision-making and sometimes for the purpose of transfer pricing or even the settlement of legal cases. This has led to consideration of the problem in the financial accounting literature (see, for example, Hirschey et al. 2001; Lev 2001; Lev and Sougiannis 1996). Second, financial economists and investors often try to construct measures of the 'fundamental' value of publicly traded firms as a guide to investment; a concern with valuing the intangible assets created by R&D and other innovative assets is naturally a part of this endeavour. Finally, policy-makers and economists wish to quantify the private returns to innovative activity in order to increase understanding of its contribution to growth and as a guide for strategies to close any potential gaps between private and social returns.

The remainder of this chapter is as follows: in Section 2 we introduce the basic concept of the market value approach, and we discuss the measurement of knowledge assets in Section 3. Section 4 surveys the results of empirical studies on the market valuation of R&D and patents, and reports in more detail the results of recent comparative studies using US and European firms. The final section concludes.

2 INNOVATION AND MARKET VALUE: REMARKS ON THE ESTIMATION MODELS

Several authors have tested the relationship of different types of innovation investment with firm-level performance measures derived from stock market data. In particular, studies analysing the relationship between knowledge capital and market value implicitly or explicitly assume that the stock market values the firm as a bundle of tangible and intangible assets (Griliches 1981). We outline the model here, using a treatment that follows Hall (2000) and Hall and Oriani (2006).

In equilibrium, the market valuation of any asset results from the interaction between the capitalization of the firm's expected rate of return from investment in that asset and the market supply of capital for that type of asset (Hall 1993a). Using this idea, it is possible to represent the market value V of firm i at time t as a function of its assets:

$$V_{it} = V(A_{it}, K_{it}, I_{it}^{1}, ..., I_{it}^{n}) \qquad (6.1)$$

where A_{it} is the book value of tangible assets, K_{it} is the replacement value of the firm's technological knowledge capital and I_{it}^{j} is the replacement value of the jth other intangible asset. If single assets are purely additive, and ignoring the other intangible assets for the sake of simplicity, it is possible to express the market value of the firm as follows:

$$V_{it} = b(A_{it} + \gamma K_{it})^{\sigma} \qquad (6.2)$$

where b is the market valuation coefficient of firm's total assets, reflecting its differential risk, overall costs of adjusting its capital, and its monopoly position, γ is the relative shadow value of knowledge capital to tangible assets, and the product $b\gamma$ is the absolute shadow value of the knowledge capital. In practice, $b\gamma$ reflects the investors' expectations about the overall effect of K_{it} on the discounted value of present and future earnings of the corporation, while γ expresses the differential valuation of the knowledge capital relative to tangible assets. By definition, when γ is unity, a currency unit spent in knowledge capital has the same stock market valuation of a currency unit spent in tangible assets. Conversely, values of γ higher (lower) than unity suggest that the stock market evaluates knowledge capital more (less) than tangible capital.

The expression (6.2) can be interpreted as a version of the model that is known in the economic literature as the hedonic pricing model, where the good being priced is the firm and the characteristics of the good are its assets, both tangible and intangible. Taking the natural logs of both the sides in (6.2), assuming constant returns to scale ($\sigma = 1$), and subtracting $\log A_{it}$ from both sides, we obtain the following expression:[1]

$$\log(V_{it}/A_{it}) = \log b + \log(1 + \gamma K_{it}/A_{it}) \qquad (6.3)$$

The ratio V/A is a proxy for average Tobin's q, the ratio of the market value of tangible assets to their physical value. The estimation of equation (6.3) allows one to assess the average impact of a euro or dollar invested in knowledge on the market value of a firm at a particular point in time. Bloom and Van Reenen (2002) and Hall et al. (2005) estimate equation (6.3) using non-linear least squares (NLLS). Other authors applying the same model have used the approximation $(1 + x) \approx x$, obtaining the equation below, which can be estimated by ordinary least squares (Cockburn and Griliches 1988; Griliches 1981; Hall 1993a, 1993b; Jaffe 1986):[2]

$$\log(V_{it}/A_{it}) = \log b + \gamma K_{it}/A_{it} \qquad (6.4)$$

3 MEASURING THE KNOWLEDGE CAPITAL

The concept of knowledge capital, measured by the variable K in the previous equations, is very broad and difficult to define empirically. There are in fact so many different types and levels of knowledge that it is practically impossible to aggregate them into one single index (Griliches 1995). Nevertheless, even though the definition of a single comprehensive measure is not possible, one can identify some indicators that correspond to specific dimensions of knowledge capital. Addressing this problem, Pakes and Griliches (1984) presented the path diagram shown in Figure 6.1. This diagram relates the unobservable ΔK, which is the net addition to knowledge capital K during a particular time period, to a set of observables (patents and R&D investments), random disturbances (v, ω), and several indicators of performance (Z), including the stock market value of the firm. Firm performance is also assumed to be influenced by other observable variables such as investment and labour input (X) and unobservables (ε). The disturbance ω reflects the effects of informal R&D activities and the inherent randomness of inventive success, whereas v represents noise in the relationship between the patents a firm is granted and the associated increment to total technological knowledge.

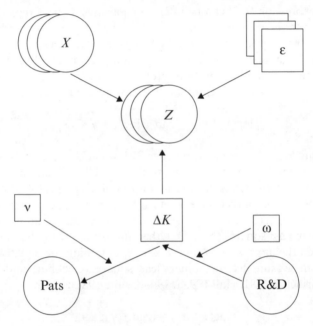

Source: Pakes and Griliches 1984

Figure 6.1   The measurement of knowledge capital

Based on this framework, studies on innovation and market value have used two main proxies for K: R&D- and patent-based. In the absence of patent data, Griliches (1995) defines the following formal relationship between a firm's stock of technological knowledge and R&D investments:

$$K = G\,[W(B)R, \omega] \qquad\qquad (6.5)$$

where K is the current level of technological knowledge, $W(B)R$ is an index of current and past R&D expenditures and ω is the set of unmeasured influences on the accumulated level of knowledge described above. Accordingly, an R&D-based measure of a firm's technological knowledge has been often computed as the capitalization of present and past R&D expenditures using a perpetual inventory formula like that used for tangible capital (Griliches and Mairesse 1984, Hall, 1990):

$$K_{it} = (1 - \delta) K_{i,t-1} + R_{it} \qquad (6.6)$$

where K_{it} is the R&D capital at time t, R_{it} is annual R&D expenditures at time t and δ is the depreciation rate of the R&D capital from year $t-1$ to year t. The use of expression (6.6) to capitalize R&D investments is needed because the Generally Accepted Accounting Principles (GAAP) in the USA and the IAS accounting standards in Europe require R&D costs to be expensed as incurred (with a few exceptions) because of the lack of a clear link between these expenses and subsequent earnings (see Zhao 2002, for details). The use of a depreciation rate is justified by the fact that knowledge tends to decay or become obsolescent over time, losing economic value due to advances in technology.

Most of the studies that have estimated the hedonic model have used a constant annual 15 per cent depreciation rate (Blundell et al. 1999; Cockburn and Griliches 1988; Hall 1993a, 1993b; Hall and Oriani 2006; Jaffe 1986). Other studies have used an estimation procedure that allows one to determine industry- and time-specific economic depreciation rates (for example, Lev and Sougiannis 1996).[3] There also exist analyses using annual R&D expenditures as an alternative measure of R&D capital (Cockburn and Griliches 1988; Hall 1993a, 1993b; Munari and Oriani 2005). Because R&D spending is usually fairly persistent over time at the firm level (Hall et al. 1986), results from specifications using the flow of R&D tend to be quite similar to those using the stock after they are adjusted by the appropriate capitalization rate (the inverse of the growth plus depreciation rates). That is, if R&D capital is constructed using equation (6.6) and real R&D has been growing at a rate g, we have the following relationship between real K and R:

$$K_t = \sum_{s=0}^{\infty} (1-\delta)^{t-s} R_{t-s} = R_t \sum_{s=0}^{\infty} \left(\frac{1-\delta}{1+g} \right)^{t-s} = \frac{1+g}{g+\delta} R_t \qquad (6.7)$$

However, the use of R&D-based measures does not definitively resolve the questions related to the measurement of technological knowledge for several reasons, mostly related to the presence of the disturbance ω

discussed above, which introduces noise into the relationship between R&D and the underlying increment to knowledge capital. The first problem is that the quality of corporate financial reporting on R&D activity and intangibles in general is often inadequate for economic analysis purposes (Lev, 2001). Therefore R&D investments can be a source of greater information asymmetries between ownership and management and may not be properly valued by the market (Aboody and Lev, 2000). Second, national accounting laws often do not require corporations to disclose the amount of their annual R&D expenditures. For example, in the European Union, the UK is one of the few countries where quantitative disclosure of R&D investments is obligatory, while in France, Germany and Italy there exists only an obligation to report qualitative information about R&D (Belcher 1996; KPMG 2001). Because some firms nevertheless do report R&D expenditures, this creates a potential sample selection bias (see the discussion in the next section). Finally, R&D investments are not an output but an input measure of the innovation process. Since the outcome of R&D is highly uncertain (for example, Scherer and Harhoff 2000), in some cases the relationship between R&D investments and a firm's knowledge base may be rather imperfect.

In order to solve these problems, some studies have used patent-based measures of technological knowledge. Recently, the wider availability of patent data in an electronic format and the creation of freely usable databases have spurred the adoption of patent-based measures in the studies on innovation and market value.[4] The first analyses were based on patent counts (for example, Cockburn and Griliches 1988; Griliches 1981), where the number of patents substitutes for R&D investment in expression (6.6). However, such a measure often turns out to be barely significant in the presence of R&D. An explanation of this phenomenon was provided by Griliches et al. (1987), who showed that under reasonable assumptions about the distribution of patent *values*, patent *counts* are an extremely noisy measure of the underlying economic value of the innovations with which they are associated, because the distribution of the value of patented innovations is known to be extremely skew. A few patents are very valuable, and many are worth almost nothing (Harhoff et al. 1999; Scherer et al. 2000).

In an effort to improve the patent measure, more recent studies have weighted the patent counts by the number of citations received by each patent from subsequent patents (Bloom and Van Reenen 2002; Hall et al. 2005). The number of citations a patent receives can be viewed as an indicator of its quality or importance, which should be reflected in its market value. At the individual patent level, the use of citations as a proxy for value has been justified by Trajtenberg (1990) and Harhoff et al. (1999). In this case, the main source of noise is related to the fact that citations can be added for different purposes, so that a citation does not necessarily imply a technological impact of the previous patent (see Jaffe et al. 2002 for a survey on the meaning of patent citations). Moreover, all patent-based measures suffer from the limitation that the propensity to patent significantly differs across industries (Cohen et al. 2000; Levin et al. 1987), which implies that in different industries patents will vary in quality as indicators of technological knowledge.

4 MEASURING THE MARKET VALUE OF KNOWLEDGE ASSETS

In this section we review the empirical results that have been obtained during the past 25 years on the market value of knowledge assets, using the three classes of measures described in Section 3: measures based on R&D, measures based on patent counts and measures based on citation-weighted patent counts.

4.1 The Market Value of R&D

Following the seminal contribution of Griliches (1981), a large number of studies have used a hedonic model like that in equation (6.2) to analyse the relationship between R&D (measured either by R&D capital or R&D expenditures) and market value. The main results are reported in Table 6.1, which reports the value of the estimated coefficient γ for either R&D capital (R&D cap) or R&D expenditures (R&D exp). Previous surveys of the studies on R&D and market value have highlighted two main results (Hall 2000). First, stock markets generally evaluate R&D investments in a positive way (that is, $\gamma > 0$). Second, market valuation of R&D has progressively decreased over time from the 1970s to the present time. The meta-analysis conducted by Oriani and Sobrero (2003) on a sub-sample of these studies has provided support for this finding. It is also worth noticing that these conclusions are based primarily on results using US data from the Compustat Database, whereas only recently has there been a significant amount for work using data on other countries: Australia, Japan, and European.

Looking at a recent example of such studies, Hall and Oriani (2006) analyse the market valuation of R&D investments in the continental European countries, and compare it with the Anglo-Saxon countries (UK and USA). The paper was the first in-depth empirical analysis of the valuation of firms' R&D by the stock market in European countries other than the UK. Extending the analysis to these countries is important for

Table 6.1 Overview of empirical findings on the market valuation of R&D

Study	Dependent variable	R&D coefficient (standard error)	Sample characteristics (country, no. of firms, years, data source)
Griliches (1981)	log Q	Predicted R&D exp: 1.23 (0.54) Surprise R&D exp: 1.58 (0.44)	USA, 157 firms, 1968–74, Compustat
Ben-Zion (1984)	log V	R&D exp: 3.376	USA, 93 firms, 1969–77, Compustat
Jaffe (1986)		R&D cap: 2.95 (1.52) R&D cap * Spillover: 0.526 (0.192)	USA, 432 firms, 1973 and 1979, Compustat
Cockburn and Griliches (1988)	log Q	R&D exp: 11.96 (1.368) R&D exp * Appropr.: 2.788 (1.231) R&D cap: 1.442 (0.174) R&D cap * Appropr.: 0.303 (0.115).	USA, 722 firms, 1980, Compustat
Hall (1993a)	log V	R&D exp: 3.10 (0.08) R&D cap: 0.48 (0.02)	USA, 2400 firms, 1973–91, Compustat
Hall (1993b)	log Q	*By year (1971–90):* R&D exp: from 2.0 to 10.0 R&D cap: from 0.5 to 2.0	USA, 3000 firms, 1959–91, Compustat
Megna and Klock (1993)	Q	R&D cap: 0.488	USA semiconductor, 11 firms, 1972–90, Compustat
Haneda and Odagiri (1998)		R&D cap: ~2.3	Japan, 90 firms, 1981–91, NEEDS database
Blundell et al. (1999)	log Q	R&D cap (1.582) R&D cap * Market share (1.745)	UK, 340 firms, 1972–82, LBS Share Price Database and Datastream

Study	Dep. var.	Coefficient	Data
Bosworth and Rogers (2001)	log V	R&D exp: 2.268	Australia, 60 firms, 1994–96, Australian Stock Exchange and IBIS database
Rogers (2001)	log V	R&D exp: 3.405	Australia, 721 firms, 1995–98, Australian Stock Exchange and IBIS database
Toivanen et al. (2002)	log V	*By year:* R&D exp: from 2.6 to 4.2	UK, 877 firms, 1989–95, Extel financial company analysis
Greenhalgh and Rogers (2005)	log V	R&D exp: 3.703	UK, 347 firms, 1989–99, Extel financial company analysis and Thomson
Munari and Oriani (2005)	log Q	*Privatized* R&D exp: −1.41 (1.26); *Private* R&D exp: 3.059 (1.21)	Finland, France, Germany, UK, Italy, Netherlands, 1982–99, 38 privatized firms and 38 control firms, Datastream and Centrale dei bilanci
Hall et al. (2005)	log Q	R&D cap: 1.736 (0.069)	USA, 4800 firms, 1965–95, Compustat
Hall and Oriani (2006)	log Q	*France* – R&D cap: 0.28 (0.08); *Germany* – R&D cap: 0.33 (0.04); *Italy* – R&D cap: 0.01 (0.12); *UK* – R&D cap: 0.88 (0.10); *USA* – R&D cap: 0.33 (0.02)	France (51 firms), Germany (80 firms), UK (284 firms), Italy (49 firms) 1989–98; Datastream, Global Vantage, Worldscope, Centrale dei bilanci

several reasons: the importance of their economies, the different nature of their corporate governance systems as compared to Anglo-Saxon countries, and the variations in the public incentive schemes for private R&D. However, any analysis for countries like France, Germany and Italy must deal with two difficulties that limit data availability: the fact that R&D disclosure is not compulsory, drastically reducing the number of observations for which R&D is reported; and the small size of the public stock market, when compared to those of the UK and the USA, which restricts the number of publicly traded firms that can be included in the sample.

Starting from the existing models on innovation and market value reviewed in Section 2, the authors tried to correct the potential biases arising from the problems discussed above by applying two estimation methods that have not been widely used in valuation analysis. First, they built a sample selection model in which the probability that a firm discloses R&D investments was modeled as a Probit function of firm size and leverage as well as industry-specific variables (R&D intensity and output growth). Second, they used panel techniques in order to account for left-out unobserved firm-specific effects.

The results obtained exhibited several interesting features. German and French samples show a statistically significant and robust positive evaluation of the R&D capital by the stock market. Moreover, the valuation of R&D capital in the countries is very similar when fixed firm effects are controlled for. However, the estimated coefficients of R&D capital are considerably less than unity in all countries, suggesting either that R&D investments are valued by the stock markets less than investments in tangible assets, or that the depreciation rate we used to construct the R&D capital, 15 per cent, was too low. They are also significantly smaller than the coefficients reported by previous studies on the USA and the UK. Nevertheless, when permanent unobserved differences across firms were controlled for, the results for the Anglo-Saxon countries were consistent with those for the continental European countries, which confirms that the market valuation of R&D expenditures has decreased in all the countries over time, in line with the previous discussion. In addition, the very narrow gap observed between the R&D coefficients across countries is consistent with the anecdotal evidence of a progressive alignment of the European financial markets to the Anglo-Saxon ones within the last two decades (see Rajan and Zingales 2003).

An interesting finding is that the UK sample shows a substantially greater valuation of the R&D investments in the cross section. From the perspective of the financial investors, this means that a currency unit spent on R&D by a company in the UK has on average an impact whose magnitude is nearly three times larger than in France and Germany. The fact that Bond et al. (2003) find much higher marginal productivity of R&D in the UK than in

Germany confirms that this result is probably real. A second interesting finding is that in France and Italy, the market places a significantly positive value on R&D spending only for firms without large controlling shareholders, even though there are quite a few firms controlled by a major shareholder that spend positive amounts on R&D. In some cases, especially in France, this may be because the large shareholder is the government (for example, Bull, which is in their sample). In other cases, it may simply be that majority holders do not respond to market pressures that signal low values for their investment strategies. One avenue for future research could be further exploration of the relationship between the types of large shareholders (governments, families or other firms) and the valuation of firm-level R&D strategy.

4.2 The Market Valuation of Patents in the US and Germany

Since the output of R&D investments is inherently uncertain, some R&D projects will result in the creation of more valuable knowledge capital than others. If this success can be observed by investors, then the associated R&D should impact on market value more than unsuccessful R&D. Empirical testing of this formulation requires an observable proxy for R&D success and the literature suggests using patent indicators for this purpose. Because R&D and patents are highly correlated in the cross-section, it is necessary to be careful about the choice of specification when both variables are entered into the same market value equation. The two possibilities are either to include a measure of the stock of patents held by the firm in place of the stock of R&D, or to include a patents-per-R&D yield variable in addition to the R&D variable:

$$\log(V_{it}/A_{it}) = \log b + \gamma_1 \, K_{it}/A_{it} + \gamma_2 \, P_{it}/K_{it} \qquad (6.8)$$

In the above equation, P_{it} is a measure of the patent stock constructed according to equation (6.6), but with patent grants by date of application rather than R&D spending. The coefficient γ_2 measures the contribution to market value of acquiring an additional patent per unit of R&D stock. Its units therefore depend on the units in which R&D stock is measured, which sometimes makes studies difficult to compare.

When patents are included in the market value equation in addition to R&D, a number of studies have shown that patents add a small amount of information above and beyond that obtained from R&D. Table 6.2 shows results from various studies using US and UK data. In most studies patents contribute positively to firms' market value, although Toivanen et al. (2002) found that in some years they were negative for UK firms.

Table 6.2 Overview of empirical findings on the market valuation of patents

Study	Dependent variable	Patent Coefficient (standard err)	Sample characteristics (country, no. of firms, years, data sources)
Griliches (1981)	log Q	Pat/assets: 10–25	USA, 157 firms, 1968–74, Compustat and USPTO
Ben-Zion (1984)	log V	Pat/assets: 0.065 (0.055)	USA, 93 firms, 1969–77, Compustat and USPTO
Connolly et al. (1986)	Value/sales	Pat/sales: 4.4 (0.6)	USA, 376 firms, 1977, Compustat and Fortune Magazine, USPTO
Shane and Klock (1987)	log Q	Pat/assets: −0.41 (0.25) Cites/assets: 0.012 (0.005)	USA semiconductor, 11 firms, 1977–90, Compustat and CHI Research
Cockburn and Griliches (1988)	log Q	Pat stk/assets: 0.11 (0.09)	USA, 722 firms, 1980, Compustat and USPTO
Connolly and Hirschey (1988)	Value/sales	Pat/sales: 5.7 (0.5)	USA, 390 firms, 1977, Compustat and Fortune Magazine, USPTO
Megna and Klock (1993)	Q	Pat stk: 0.38 (0.2)	USA semiconductor, 11 firms, 1972–90, Compustat and USPTO
Haneda and Odagiri (1998)	log Q	Pat stk elasticity: ~0.3	Japan, 90 firms, 1981–91, NEEDS database
Blundell et al. (1999)	log V	Pat stk/R&D stk: 1.93 (0.93)	UK, 340 firms, 1972–82, LBS Share Price database and Datastream, NBER patent database
Deng et al. (1999)	Q	Pat elasticity: 0.007 Cite elasticity: 0.165	USA, 411 firms, 1985–95, Compustat and CHI Research
Hirschey and Richardson (2001)	V/A	Pat/assets: 2.8 (0.2) US ~0 Japan	USA, 256 firms, 1989–95, Compustat and CHI Research Japan, 184 firms, 1989–95, not given
Bloom and Van Reenen (2002)	log Q	Pat stk elasticity: 0.08 (0.03) Cite stk elasticity: 0.12 (0.03)	UK, 172 firms, 1969–94, Datastream and NBER patent database
Toivanen et al. (2002)	log V	Pat/assets insignificant	UK, 877 firms, 1989–95, Extel financial company analysis
Hall et al. (2005)	log Q	Pat/assets: 0.607 (0.042) Cite stk/assets: 0.108 (0.006)	USA, 4800 firms, 1965–95, Compustat

In a recent study, Czarnitzki and Hall (2005) compare the market valuation of patent stocks in US and German firms. Owing to large differences in the share of publicly traded firms relative to the total number of firms in the USA and continental Europe, the authors employ matched firm samples in the analysis. They first constructed the German sample of publicly traded firms (352 firms), and then drew a matched sample of US firms using industry and size rank, recognizing that, on average, the German firms in the sample are smaller then the US firms. Nevertheless, the resulting samples roughly correspond to the market leading firms in both countries. The firm-level data was then linked to US and German patent data, respectively.[5] The patent stocks are calculated from the annual time series at the individual firm level using the perpetual inventory method and an equation like that in equation (6.6).

In contrast to the US patent data where only granted patents are observed, the German patent database offers two options for the measurement of the knowledge capital to assets ratio using patents (K/A): patents applied for and issued patents. That is, we also observe patents that have not passed the examination process and may never be issued. Given these differences, it is possible to investigate the question of using applied for or granted patents in the market value equations. If the aim of the researcher is to approximate the R&D stock, it would be appropriate to count patent applications. If, however, the results of R&D activities are expected to be inherently different with respect to their value, it might be better to stick to granted patents to reduce the noise created by research with a low inventive step in the market value equation. Hence, a patent may actually reveal its value in two stages: the number of observed applications serves as a proxy for R&D activities and, second, its additional value could uncover with the grant, because the owner of a granted patent may license or sell it, for instance. For this reason, Czarnitzki and Hall explore different specifications for the patent assets in Germany.

The authors estimate pooled cross-sectional regressions (non-linear least squares on equation (6.3) and ordinary least squares on the linearized model of equation (6.4)), fixed and random effects panel data models, instrumental variable panel regressions as well as non-parametric kernel regressions. In both the pooled cross-sectional regressions and panel data estimations the patent stock of firms contributes significantly to their market value. Surprisingly, the results from the German sample are very similar to the USA in terms of the size of the impact. The significant impact in the German sample is quite robust in the panel data estimation that control for fixed effects, while in the cross-section it is important to control for industry differences in average market value.

The patent variables based on applications and grants lead to fairly robust estimation results, with the marginal shadow value of a patent application less than the value of a patent grant. These findings point again to the conclusion that the value of R&D is inherently heterogeneous among projects and firms. Research and development that leads to a patent application represents some value. However, increased value from the R&D programme is revealed when a patent is finally granted and the firm is able to fully exploit its property right to the invention. While the patent application protects the corresponding invention from the date of filing the patent, the actual grant of the patent enables the firm to trade or to license their intellectual property, for instance, which may well yield additional earnings aside from implementing the technology or the product in its own operational business.

4.3   Accounting for Patent Heterogeneity Using Citation-Weighted Patent Stocks

As already pointed out in Section 3, one disadvantage of using patent indicators is the large variance in the significance of value of individual patents, rendering patent counts an extremely noisy indicator of R&D success. One way to account for patent heterogeneity is by means of citation-weighted patent counts, that is, a firm's patent counts are supplemented with the number of subsequent citations to get a better measure of R&D success. A number of researchers have demonstrated that measures of innovation output or profitability are related to the number of times a patent on the relevant invention is cited by other later patents (for example, Deng et al. 1999; Harhoff et al. 1999; Trajtenberg 1990).

Hall et al. (2005) extend the market value equation with respect to the patent yield of R&D (that is, the ratio of patent count stocks to R&D stocks), and the average citations received by these patents (that is, the ratio of citations to patent stocks). Thus equation (6.3) is modified as follows:

$$\log\left(V_{it}/A_{it}\right) = \log b + \log\left(1 + \gamma_1 \frac{R\&D_{it}}{A_{it}} + \gamma_2 \frac{PAT_{it}}{R\&D_{it}} + \gamma_3 \frac{CITES_{it}}{PAT_{it}}\right) \quad (6.9)$$

where *R&D*, *PAT* and *CITES* stand for the stocks of R&D, patent stocks and citations, respectively.

Employing a sample of more than 3000 US firms observed in the period from 1976 to 1992, Hall and her co-authors find that each of the ratios in expression (6.9) has a statistically and economically significant impact on market value. Table 6.3 shows one estimation from the recent Hall et al. study, where they include dummies for six sectors: Drugs and Medical Instrumentation (henceforth just 'Drugs'); Chemicals; Computers and Communications ('Computers'); Electrical; Metals and Machinery; and miscellaneous (low-tech industries), and interact them with the knowledge stock ratios. In column (2) we can see that there is a high premium to being in the Drugs or Computers sector, which comes mostly at the expense of the coefficient of R&D intensity, which drops by a half when the sector dummies are included. The full interactions in column (3) reveal wide differences across sectors in the effects of each knowledge stock ratio. In general, the differential importance of patent yield and of citations per patent rises, at the expense of R&D intensity. Thus, whereas in no sector is the effect of R&D/Assets much larger than the average effect picked up in the base specification displayed in column (1), the impact of patent yield for Drugs is three times the average effect (0.10 versus 0.031), and that of Computers twice as high; similarly but not as pronounced, the impact of Citations/Patents for Drugs is over 50 per cent higher than the average effect, while that for Computers is small, and lower than that for the other sectors except for the low-tech sector. This contrast is consistent with the differing roles played by patents in the two sectors: Drugs is characterized by discrete product technologies where patents serve their traditional role of exclusion, and some of them are therefore valuable on an individual basis, as measured by citations. Computers and Communications is a group of complex product industries where any particular product may rely on various technologies embodied in several patents held by different firms. In this industry patents are largely valued for negotiating cross-licensing agreements, so their individual quality is not as important, although having them is.[6]

In conclusion, not only does the market value R&D inputs and R&D outputs as measured by patent counts, but it also values 'high-quality' R&D output as measured by citation intensity. Hall et al. also report a number of interesting detailed findings about the value of citations. First, the value-citation relationship is highly nonlinear: firms having two or three times the median number of citations per patent display a 35 per cent value premium, and those with 20 citations and more command a staggering 54 per cent market value premium. Second, the market value premia associated with patent citations confirm the forward-looking nature of equity markets: at a given point in time, market value premia are associated with future citations rather than those that have been received in the past, and the portion of total lifetime citations that is unpredictable based on the citation history at a given moment has the largest impact.

Finally, self-citations (that is, those coming from later patents owned by the same firm) are more valuable than citations coming from external

Table 6.3   Market value regression from Hall et al. (2005)

Sample: 1,982 patenting firms, 1979–88 – 12 118 observations Non-linear model with dependent variable: log Tobin's q			
	(1)	(2)	(3)
D (Drugs)		.536 (.028)	.005 (.102)
D (Chemicals)		.026 (.020)	−.231 (.061)
D (Computers)		.311 (.022)	.361 (.050)
D (Electrical)		.166 (.021)	.093 (.061)
D (Metals and Machinery)		.015 (.016)	−.261 (.047)
R&D/Assets			
interacted with,	1.362 (.068)	.686 (.057)	.883 (.198)
Drugs			.561 (.310)
Chemicals			−.017 (.333)
Computers			−.575 (.204)
Electrical			−.343 (.253)
Metals and Machinery			.595 (.241)
Patents/R&D			
interacted with,	.030 (.007)	.025 (.006)	−.020 (.006)
Drugs			.120 (.051)
Chemicals			.059 (.018)
Computers			.078 (.017)
Electrical			.022 (.006)
Metals and Machinery			.070 (.014)
Citations/patents			
interacted with,	.052 (.004)	.036 (.003)	.014 (.004)
Drugs			.065 (.015)
Chemicals			.048 (.012)
Computers			.014 (.006)
Electrical			.022 (.011)
Metals and Machinery			.037 (.009)
D (R&D = 0)	.066 (.019)	.099 (.018)	.123 (.020)
R^2	.254	.292	.308
Standard error	.671	.654	.647
Robust Wald test for added effects *(degrees of freedom)*		503.5 (5)	142.6 (15)

Notes:
Estimation method: non-linear least squares.
Heteroskedastic-consistent standard errors in parentheses.
All equations include year dummies.
The left-out category is miscellaneous (low-tech industries).

patents. This could be explained by cumulative or sequential innovations (see Scotchmer 1991). Firms citing their own patents is a reflection of the cumulative nature of innovation and the increasing returns property of knowledge accumulation. Self-citations indicate that the firm has a strong competitive position and is in a position to internalize some of the knowledge spillovers created by its own developments. This implies both that the firm has lower costs because there is less need to acquire technology from others, and that it may be able to earn higher profits without risking rapid entry since it controls a substantial stretch of the underlying technology. However, the effect of self-citations decreases with the size of the patent portfolio held by the firm simply because the more patents a firm has, the higher the probability that a citation from a new patent it gets will be given to a patent it already has.

5 CONCLUSIONS

The line of research described in this survey is now 25 years old and it has reached a level of maturity that allows us to draw certain conclusions from it, conclusions both about the ability of financial markets to value the intangible assets of firms and about appropriate methodology to apply to the problem. As Tables 6.1–6.3 show, several empirical regularities have emerged from the various studies.

First, in most countries and in most time periods R&D capital is valued somewhere between 0.5 and 1 times ordinary capital. The implication of this finding is that the appropriate private obsolescence rate for R&D investment is probably somewhat greater than 15 per cent, more in the neighbourhood of 20 per cent to 30 per cent. This conclusion is reinforced by the fact that current R&D spending usually has a coefficient of around 3 to 4, rather than the 6 implied by a 15 per cent depreciation rate. In the UK, R&D seems to be valued more highly than in the other countries. An implication is that firms in the UK may be under-investing in R&D.

Second, patent coefficients are more variable than R&D coefficients, partly because the specifications using patents are more variable. Where they can be compared, it appears that patent yield has a much smaller effect on value than R&D, but this is to be expected if patents are a very noisy measure of the underlying inventive success. Using citation-weights improves the patent measure, but it is still a relatively weak predictor of value. The best predictor of value turns out to be citations not yet received by the patents, so the measure is of limited use for forecasting.

Third, although most of the studies are either for the entire manufacturing or for the entire publicly traded firm sector, the impact of knowledge assets on market value varies considerably across technology sector and industry, with pharmaceuticals having higher values and computing and electrical sectors having much lower values.

With respect to methodology, it has become increasingly clear that research in this area would be helped by agreement on a common specification of the market value equation. Using kernel regression methods, Hall and Oriani (2006) have confirmed that the nonlinear version of the model (equation (6.3)) is probably preferred to a linear version, because it dampens the impact of R&D on market value when firms are extremely R&D intensive. When there are multiple indicators (such as patents and R&D) in the same equation, for interpretive reasons it is preferable to include these variables in a roughly orthogonal way (for example, R&D and patents per R&D), especially in the presence of substantial measurement error in the patents variable. There remains the challenge of interpreting the meaning of the patent coefficient when it is normalized by R&D measures which can be in various currency units, and for comparative reasons, it may be preferred to express this coefficient as an elasticity by multiplying it by the patents – R&D ratio.

NOTES

1. The assumption of constant returns to scale (homogeneity of degree one) in the value function has been confirmed repeatedly in the literature, at least for cross sections of firms.
2. In order to investigate the appropriateness of equation (6.3) or (6.4), Hall and Oriani (2006) explored the use of semi-parametric estimation for the simple Tobin's q–R&D capital relationship by means of kernel regression using data for the USA (refer to the NBER working paper n. 10408 for details). They found that the relationship resembles a logistic curve, with zero and very small amounts of R&D capital (less than about 1 per cent of tangible assets) having no effect on Tobin's q, a roughly linear relationship until $K/A = 1$, and a flatter relationship thereafter. Above K/A value of 1 per cent, the relationship is somewhat better described by equation (6.3) than equation (6.4).
3. More precisely, the authors estimate a regression model in which the dependent variable is the annual operating income and the independent variables are the lagged values of total assets and advertising expenditures and a vector of the past R&D investments.
4. See Hall et al. 2002 for a description of the NBER/Case Western patent database.
5. The German patent data contain patent application that have been filed with the German patent office and also those filed with the European Patent Office and where the applicant requested patent protection for Germany.
6. See Arora et al. (2004) for further discussion of this contrast and Hall and Ziedonis (2001) for evidence on semiconductors.

REFERENCES

Aboody, D. and B. Lev (2000), 'Information asymmetry, R&D, and insider gains', *Journal of Finance*, **55**, 2747–66.

Arora, A., M. Ceccagnoli and W.M. Cohen (2004), 'R&D and the patent premium', mimeo, Carnegie-Mellon University.

Belcher, A. (1996), 'R&D disclosure: theory and practice', in A. Belcher, J. Hassard and S. Procter (eds), *R&D Decisions: Strategy, Policy and Disclosure*, London: Routledge.

Ben-Zion, U. (1984), 'The R&D and investment decision and its relationship to the firm's market value: some preliminary results', in Z. Griliches (ed.), *R&D, Patents, and Productivity*, Chicago, IL: University of Chicago Press and NBER.

Bloom, N. and J. Van Reenen (2002), 'Patents, real options and firm performance', *Economic Journal*, **112**, 97–116.

Blundell, R., R. Griffith and J. Van Reenen (1999), 'Market share, market value and innovation in a panel of British manufacturing firms', *Review of Economic Studies*, **66**, 529–54.

Bond, S., D. Harhoff and J. Van Reenen (2003), 'Corporate R&D and productivity in Germany and the United Kingdom', CEP discussion paper 595, London School of Economics, London.

Bosworth, D. and M. Rogers, (2001), 'Market value, R&D and intellectual property: an empirical analysis of large Australian firms', *The Economic Record*, **77**, 323–37.

Cockburn, I. and Z. Griliches (1988), 'Industry effects and appropriability measures in the stock market's valuation of R&D and patents', *American Economic Review*, **78**, 419–23.

Cohen, W.M., R.R. Nelson and J.P. Walsh (2000), 'Protecting their intellectual assets: appropriability conditions and why U.S. manufacturing firms patent (or not)', National Bureau of Economic Research working paper 7552, Cambridge, MA.

Connolly, R.A. and M. Hirschey (1988), 'Market value and patents: a Bayesian approach', *Economics Letters*, **27**, 83–7.

Connolly, R.A., B.T. Hirsch and M. Hirschey (1986), 'Union rent seeking, intangible capital, and market value of the firm', *Review of Economics and Statistics*, **68** (4), 567–77.

Czarnitzki, D. and B.H. Hall (2005), 'Comparing the market valuation of innovative assets in U.S. and German firms', mimeo, University of California Berkeley and KU Leuven.

Deng, Z., B. Lev and F. Narin (1999), 'Science and technology as predictors of stock performance', *Financial Analysts Journal*, May/June, 20–32.

Greenhalgh, C. and M. Rogers (2005), 'The value of innovation: the interaction of competition, R&D and IP', mimeo, Oxford Intellectual Property Research Centre, Oxford University.

Griliches, Z. (1981), 'Market value, R&D and patents', *Economics Letters*, **7**, 183–7.

Griliches, Z. (1995), 'R&D and productivity: econometric results and measurement issues', in P. Stoneman (ed.), *Handbook of the Economics of Innovation and Technological Change*, Oxford: Blackwell.

Griliches, Z. and J. Mairesse (1984), 'Productivity and R&D at the firm level', in Z. Griliches (ed.), *R&D, Patents, and Productivity*, Chicago, IL: University of Chicago Press and NBER.

Griliches Z., A. Pakes and B.H. Hall (1987), 'The value of patents as indicators of inventive activity', in P. Dasgupta and P. Stoneman (eds), *Economic Policy and Technological Performance*, Cambridge: Cambridge University Press.

Hall, B.H. (1990), 'The manufacturing sector masterfile: 1959–1987', National Bureau of Economic Research working paper 3366, Cambridge, MA.

Hall, B.H. (1993a), 'Industrial research during the 1980s: did the rate of return fall?', *Brookings Papers on Economic Activity. Microeconomics*, 289–343.

Hall, B.H. (1993b), 'The stock market's valuation of R&D investment during the 1980's', *American Economic Review*, **83**, 259–64.

Hall, B.H. (2000), 'Innovation and market value', in R. Barrell, G. Mason and M. O'Mahoney (eds), *Productivity, Innovation and Economic Performance*, Cambridge: Cambridge University Press.

Hall, B.H. and R. Oriani (2006), 'Does the Market Value R&D Investment by European Firms? Evidence from a Panel of Manufacturing Firms in France, Germany, and Italy', *International Journal of Industrial Organization*, forthcoming.

Hall B.H. and R.H. Ziedonis (2001), 'The patent paradox revisited: determinants of patenting in the U.S. semiconductor industry 1980–94', *Rand Journal of Economics*, **32**, 101–28.

Hall, B.H., Z. Griliches and J.A. Hausman (1986), 'Patents and R&D: is there a lag?', *International Economic Review*, **27**, 265–83.

Hall, B.H., A.B. Jaffe and M. Trajtenberg (2002), 'The NBER patent citations datafile: lessons, insights and methodological tools', in A.B. Jaffe and M. Trajtenberg (eds), *Patents, Citations and Innovations: A Window on the Knowledge Economy*, Cambridge, MA: MIT Press.

Hall, B.H., A.B. Jaffe and M. Trajtenberg (2005), 'Market value and patent citations', *Rand Journal of Economics*, **36**, 16–38.

Haneda, S., and H. Odagiri, (1998), 'Appropriation of returns from technological assets and the values of patents and R&D in Japanese high-tech firms', *Economics of Innovation and New Technology*, **7**, 303–22.

Harhoff, D., F. Narin, F.M. Scherer and K. Vopel (1999), 'Citation frequency and the value of patented inventions', *Review of Economics and Statistics*, **81** (3), 511–15.

Hirschey, M. and V.J. Richardson (2001), 'Valuation effects of patent quality: a comparison for Japanese and US firms', *Pacific-Basin Finance Journal*, **9**, 65–82.

Hirschey, M., V.J. Richardson and S. Scholtz (2001), 'Value relevance of nonfinancial information: the case of patent data', *Review of Quantitative Finance and Accounting*, **17** (3), 223–35.

Jaffe, A.B. (1986), 'Technological opportunity and spillovers of R&D: evidence from firms' patents, profits, and market value', *American Economic Review*, **76**, 984–1001.

Jaffe, A.B., M. Trajtenberg and M.S. Fogarty (2002), 'The meaning of patent citations: report on the NBER/Case-Western Reserve Survey of Patentees', in A.B. Jaffe and M. Trajtenberg (eds), *Patents, Citations and Innovations: A Window on the Knowledge Economy*, Cambridge, MA: MIT Press.

KPMG (2001), *TRANSACC. Transnational Accounting*, London: Macmillan.

Lev, B. (2001), *Intangibles: Management, Measurement, and Reporting*, Washington, DC: Brookings Institution Press.

Lev, B. and T. Sougiannis (1996), 'The capitalization, amortization, and value-relevance of R&D', *Journal of Business, Accounting & Economics*, **21**, 107–38.

Levin, R.C., A.K. Klevorick, R.R. Nelson and S.G. Winter (1987), 'Appropriating the returns from industrial research and development', *Brookings Papers on Economic Activity*, 3, 783–832.

Megna, P. and M. Klock (1993), 'The impact of intangible capital on Tobin's q in the semiconductor industry', *American Economic Review*, **83** (2), 265–9.

Munari, F. and R. Oriani (2005), 'Privatization and economic returns to R&D investments', *Industrial and Corporate Change*, **14**, 61–91.

Oriani, R. and M. Sobrero (2003), 'A meta-analytic study of the relationship between R&D investments and corporate value', in M. Calderini, P. Garrone and M. Sobrero (eds), *Corporate Governance, Market Structure and Innovation*, Cheltenham, UK and Northampton, MA, USA: Edward Elgar.

Pakes, A. and Z. Griliches (1984), 'Patents and R&D at firm level: a first look', in Z. Griliches (ed.), *R&D, Patents, and Productivity*, Chicago, IL: NBER and University of Chicago Press.

Rajan, R.G. and L. Zingales (2003), 'Banks and markets: the changing character of the European finance', National Bureau of Economic Research working paper 9595, Cambridge, MA.

Rogers, M. (2002), 'Firm performance and investment in R&D and intellectual property', Melbourne Institute working paper No. wp2002n15.

Scherer, F.M. and D. Harhoff (2000), 'Technology policy for a world of skew-distributed outcomes', *Research Policy*, **29**, 559–66.

Scherer, F.M., D. Harhoff and J. Kukies (2000), 'Uncertainty and the size distribution of rewards from technological innovation', *Journal of Evolutionary Economics*, **10**, 175–200.

Scotchmer, S. (1991), 'Standing on the shoulders of giants: cumulative innovation and the patent law', *Journal of Economic Perspectives*, **5**, 29–41.

Shane, H. and M. Klock, (1997), 'The relation between patent citations and Tobin's q in the semiconductor industry', *Review of Quantitative Finance and Accounting*, **9**, 131–46.

Toivanen, O., P. Stoneman and D. Bosworth (2002), 'Innovation and market value of UK firms, 1989–1995', *Oxford Bulletin of Economics and Statistics*, **64**, 39–61.

Trajtenberg, M. (1990), 'A penny for your quotes: patent citation and the value of innovations', *Rand Journal of Economics*, **21**, 172–87.

Zhao, R. (2002), 'Relative value relevance of R&D reporting: an international comparison', *Journal of International Financial Management and Accounting*, **13**, 153–74.

7. Market valuation of UK intellectual property: manufacturing, utility and financial services firms[1]

Christine Greenhalgh and Mark Rogers

1 INTRODUCTION

In the UK, as in many countries, there is an ongoing debate over the extent and value of innovative activities. An understanding of the factors that underpin innovation, which is critical to maintaining competitiveness and productivity growth, provides the information to formulate key targets for both firms and policy-makers. Within this debate there is keen interest in the role of the intellectual property (IP) system. Specifically, in the UK there is a concern that firms do not optimally use the IP system, as historically there has been a good record of scientific discovery but a poor record of commercial innovation (Department of Trade and Industry 2003; HM Treasury and Inland Revenue 2001). This, in turn, results in either a failure to extract full value from the innovation process or a lack of investment in innovation, or both. Related to these issues are concerns over whether the existing IP system, and the institutional framework surrounding innovation in general, is keeping pace with the changing nature of the economy. An important change to the UK and other economies in recent decades has been the growing importance of the service sector and, within this, the financial services sector, yet there is relatively little data and analysis on the role of innovation and IP in the service sector. A contribution of this chapter is to analyse new data on the IP activity of UK financial services sector firms, which tends to be dominated by the use of trademarks.

In the first part of this chapter we briefly document the levels and trends in IP acquisition, comparing the financial services sector with the transport, communications and utilities service sector, and both of these service groups with manufacturing. (Further details of this sample are given in Chapter 11.) Then we set out a standard economic model for the analysis of the relationship between the net present value of the firm, as reflected in its market value, and the tangible and intangible assets of the firm, including within the latter its IP. In the third section we present estimates of the model for all firms and separate estimates for the two groups of service firms and manufacturing. Finally, we carry out further analysis of the financial services sector, exploring some different ways of estimating the model using alternative econometric approaches.

2 DATA OVERVIEW

The data used in the analysis below is drawn from the Oxford Intellectual Property Research Centre database of firm-level IP activity. The unique aspect of the database is that it contains data on the intellectual property activity of around 1300 large UK companies. More specifically, data on three forms of IP has been matched to firms, namely: patents published via the UK, patents published via the European Patent Office (EPO – which designated the UK *inter alia*), and trademark applications via the UK office.[2] The matching process is complex since it checks not only whether the parent company is IP active, but also whether any of its wholly owned subsidiaries are also active (further details are in Greenhalgh et al. 2003, appendix). Once the activity of all subsidiaries has been assessed these figures are then consolidated back to the parent firm. The database also contains firms' (consolidated) financial accounts obtained from Company Analysis (Extel Financial 1996; Thomson 2001) and, for some data in 2000, from 'FAME' (Bureau van Dijk 2004).

In this chapter, we focus attention on firms in the manufacturing, utilities and financial services sectors over the period 1996 to 2000. Manufacturing firms have been the source of considerable analysis of the value of IP and R&D (for a summary see Hall 2000), but there is less analysis of utilities and virtually none of financial services.[3] As discussed in Chapter 11 in this volume, patenting activity is minimal in the 'finance, insurance and real estate' (FIRE) sector and the 'transport, communications, electricity, gas and water' (TCEGW) sector.[4] In contrast, trademark activity is substantial across all sectors. The observed levels and trends in patents and trademarks for the sample firms reflect economy-wide trends – see Greenhalgh et al. (2003). The rate of application for trademarks rose rapidly from the mid-1990s in all sectors. The Trade Marks Act 1994 introduced new possibilities for trademarks attached to shapes, containers, three-dimensional marks, sounds and smells. As well as firms taking advantage of these new options, it seems likely that the importance of registered trademarks as a method of bolstering brand identity was enhanced by the increasing competition via external trade during this decade. Domestic changes also played a role, for example UK financial services have been subject to demutualization and high levels of merger/takeover, which has led to rebranding.

Figure 7.1 shows the percentage of firms that use one of the forms of IP at least once in the five-year period, which shows clearly that manufacturing firms are more active in patenting and trademarking, but also shows that trademarks represent the most common form of IP used by firms. What is not shown by the figure is the extent to which firms differ in their persistence of IP activity over the five-year period. For example, in the FIRE sector only around 7 per cent of firms took out a trademark in every year from 1996 to 2000, whereas in manufacturing and TCEGW the equivalent figure is around 17 per cent. A further issue revealed by preliminary analysis is the firm-specific volatility of IP activity over time. For example, Legal and General PLC – a large financial services firm – filed for 28 trademarks in 1998, but only two in 2000; Pilkington PLC – a glass-maker – had 14 UK patents publications in 1998 and only one in 2000. These large variations in IP activity through time are common in the data, although there are some firms that are much more persistent. Analysing whether such volatility is different for trademarking and patenting is beyond the scope of this chapter, but data inspection and basic statistics[5] suggest that trademark volatility is great, with many firms showing a single year of high activity. This would coincide with the view that firms abruptly decide to trademark a range of existing products.

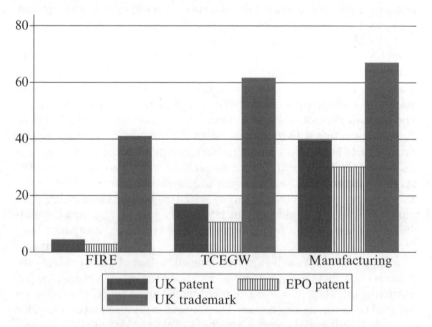

Figure 7.1   Extent of IP activity, by sector (1996–2000)

Table 7.1 Performance and trademark usage

	Finance, insurance and real estate (FIRE)			Transport, communications, electricity, gas and water (TCEGW)			Manufacturing		
	All	Active	Inactive	All	Active	Inactive	All	Active	Inactive
RoI %	9.1	17.1	6.0	17.3	19.8	12.8	15.9	17.3	13.2
RoA %	2.5	2.0	2.9	7.2	8.1	5.7	7.4	7.7	6.1
Tobin's q	0.61	0.43	0.66	1.1	1.2	1.0	0.77	0.84	0.65
Growth of employment (%)	25	41	20	28	36	7.8	9.6	14	-1.4

Note: 'RoI' is return on investment, defined as profit before tax divided by shareholders' funds. 'RoA' is defined as profit before tax divided by total assets. Tobin's q is the ratio of market value to total assets (market value is defined as shares outstanding (average in year) × price (end accounting period) plus creditors and debt less current assets, see Chung and Pruitt 1994). In each cell the figure is the median value using all data over the 1996 to 2000 period.

Do the large differences in prevalence of IP activity across firms and sectors affect firm performance? This is the focus of the analysis in the subsequent section but it is worthwhile first inspecting some basic measures of performance. Table 7.1 shows the median value of four different performance measures across sectors and, within each sector, between firms that have trademarked in the period 1996 to 2000 and those that have not. The former group of trademarking firms are entitled 'active' in the table, while those without any trademarks are 'inactive'. Table 7.1 shows the median value of four different performance measures: return on shareholders funds (RoI), return on assets (RoA), Tobin's q (which is the ratio of stock market value to book value) and growth in employment (1996 to 2000). In virtually all cases we see that trademark 'active' firms out perform 'inactive' firms – with the exception of RoA and Tobin's q for FIRE sector firms. These deviant results may arise because of the fact that accounting 'assets' for financial firms are not exclusively conventional capital but may include their financial assets.

Similar tables (not shown) for UK and EPO patent activity show a similar pattern of differential results between active and inactive firms. Although such statistics are only indicative, since there are no formal tests or allowance for other broad influences on performance, they do suggest that firms' use of the IP system is potentially important (as intuition would suggest).

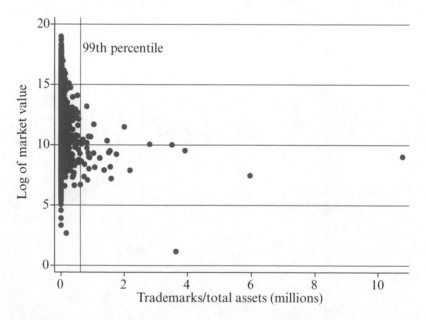

Figure 7.2   Market value versus trademarks to tangible assets ratio

Clearly, these statistics only indicate an association between IP activity and performance, rather than establishing any causation in such a relationship. In fact, it seems obvious that use of the IP system would have to be part of an integrated firm-level strategy to ensure high performance.

A final issue that needs to be addressed concerns the presence in the data of outlier observations. This can become a serious issue in regression analysis if a small number of influential observations dramatically affect the results. The regression analysis below uses the ratio of patents or trademarks to tangible assets as a proxy for the intensity of IP activity. As an example of this issue, Figure 7.2 shows a plot of the log of market value against the ratio of trademarks to tangible assets. One can see that there are a small number of data points that might affect the analysis of the relationship between market value and trademark activity. For this reason the regression analysis below often restricts the sample to IP intensity values below the 99th percentile of the distribution (this value is shown in Figure 7.2 by the vertical line).

3   A MODEL OF MARKET VALUE AND IP ACTIVITY

This section outlines a formal model that links the market value of a firm to its IP activity. It is based on Griliches (1981) who assumes that the market value (V) of the firms is given by

$$V = q(A + \gamma K)^\sigma \qquad (7.1)$$

where A is the book value of total assets and K is the stock of intangible assets not included in the balance sheet. The parameter q is the 'current market valuation coefficient' of the firm's assets, σ allows for the possibility of non-constant returns to scale, and γ is the ratio of shadow values of intangible assets and tangible assets (that is, $\dfrac{\partial V}{\partial K} \Big/ \dfrac{\partial V}{\partial A}$).[6] To estimate equation (7.1) many authors take natural logarithms and use the approximation $\ln(1+\varepsilon) \approx \varepsilon$ to yield

$$\ln V = \ln q + \sigma \ln A + \sigma\gamma\, \frac{K}{A} \qquad (7.2)$$

Researchers then use various proxies for K in empirical estimation, such as IP or R&D data but also including any data available on advertising, cash flows or other firm-level characteristics. Since market valuations can vary across industries, it is also standard to control for industry effects by including dummy variables. In this chapter we focus attention on using data on UK patent publications (*UKP*), EPO patent publications (*EPOP*), trademark applications (*TM*) and R&D as proxies for K in (7.2). Thus, with i indicating a firm and t a time period, the basic regression equation is

$$\ln V_{it} = \alpha_j + \alpha_t + \sigma \ln A + \beta_1 \frac{UKP_{it}}{A_{it}} + \beta_2 \frac{EPOP_{it}}{A_{it}} + \beta_3 \frac{TM_{it}}{A_{it}} + \beta_4 \frac{R\&D_{it}}{A_{it}} + \eta X + u_{it}$$

$$(7.3)$$

where q has been replaced by industry (α_j) and time dummies (α_t), X represents any further control variables and u_{it} is an error term. At the outset it is important to understand what information the coefficient estimates (the βs) from (7.3) convey. Since the IP measures are in units (that is, number of trademarks), rather than monetary terms, it is not possible to relate the coefficients directly to the γ coefficient in (7.1) (the shadow value of investment in intangibles). Instead, the coefficients indicate the proportional increase in average market value as IP intensity increases.

The availability of panel data means that it is possible to estimate (7.3) in a number of different ways. Assuming that the coefficients are constant across time, a standard choice is often that of using a fixed effects estimator. This estimator controls for a time invariant, firm-level effect and hence estimates coefficients based on changes within a firm's data through time. For those not familiar with such econometric models, the intuition is to test whether a change in a firm's IP activity is associated with a change in market value. However, especially in the case of IP, it may be that the market's reaction to such a change may differ from its valuation of a firm's average level of IP activity. Furthermore, in practice, inter-temporal volatility of the explanatory variables may also cloud the results.[7]

A final problematic issue concerns the possible lag structure in terms of the impact of IP activity on market valuations. Clearly, one might expect the stock market to react immediately as, in theory, the share price reflects the expected future performance of the firm. However, given that IP activity may well interact with other firm-specific investments and decisions, there may be a lag in impact between obtaining the IP asset and the reflection of its value in the share price. For all these reasons we choose initially to use the 'between' estimator, which uses the average values of variables over the five-year period for each firm to create what is essentially a cross-section estimator of (7.3).

Table 7.2   Between estimator regression results for market value

	All	All	FIRE	TCEGW	Manu.	Manu.
Log of total assets (mill)	1.010 [66.31]***	1.011 [65.43]***	0.990 [38.35]***	1.024 [25.40]***	1.012 [45.05]***	1.01 [44.18]***
UK patent/total assets (mill)	-5.370 [1.28]	-5.540 [1.35]		332.465 [0.73]	3.092 [0.96]	3.278 [1.04]
EPO patent/total assets (mill)	16.086 [4.90]***	11.039 [3.27]***		60.493 [0.19]	9.972 [3.81]***	3.887 [1.38]
Trademark/total assets (mill)	1.267 [1.80]*	0.839 [1.20]	29.122 [2.75]***	1.338 [0.93]	0.931 [1.36]	0.513 [0.77]
Debt/shareholders' equity	0.000 [0.74]	0.000 [0.78]	0.027 [1.18]	0.001 [0.08]	0.000 [0.67]	0.000 [0.74]
Intangible assets/total assets	1.852 [5.88]***	1.822 [5.86]***	2.062 [2.47]**	0.746 [0.69]	1.934 [5.09]***	1.911 [5.17]***
R&D expenditure/total assets		4.562 [4.86]***				4.525 [4.68]***
R&D dummy (some R&D 1996–2000)		0.023 [0.26]				0.07 [0.70]
Constant	-1.224 [2.26]**	-1.236 [2.31]**	-1.955 [4.22]***	-0.519 [0.82]	-1.248 [2.09]**	-1.227 [2.11]**
Observations	3030	3030	880	353	1819	1819
Number of firms	673	673	193	77	405	405
R-squared	0.91	0.91	0.92	0.93	0.89	0.89
F test: industry dummies	6.56	6.24	13.83	1.26	3.33	2.57

Note: The dependent variable is the natural log of market value (mv), where 'mv' is defined as shares outstanding (average in year) × price (end accounting period) plus creditors and debt less current assets (see Chung and Pruitt 1994). The sample contains only those firms which have three or more years of data during the five year period (1996 to 2000). The between estimator, weighted according to how many years firm has been in sample, is used with t-statistics in parentheses (* significant at 10 per cent; ** significant at 5 per cent; *** significant at 1 per cent). The industry F-test row shows the F value from a test of the null that all industry dummies are equal.

MARKET VALUE REGRESSION ANALYSIS

Table 7.2 above contains the regression analysis of the determinants of the market value of the firm. The need for a stock market valuation excludes 31 per cent of the sample firms, since these do not have their shares listed on a stock market. As indicated in the data overview section, the presence of outlier observations might influence results. This does, in fact, turn out to be the case and the sample used in Table 7.2 excludes those firms above the 99th percentile for any IP intensity measure.[8] All regressions contain industry dummies at the two-digit level. In addition, two control variables are added, namely, the debt to shareholders' equity (which models the debt burden of the firm) and the ratio of intangible assets in the balance sheet to total tangible assets (this accounting measure of intangible assets relates to items such as goodwill purchased in takeover deals and bears little relationship to current IP activity).

The first column of regression results pools firms from all sectors and enters the IP variables as a ratio to tangible assets (as per equation (7.3)). The results indicate that the EPO patent ratio has a statistically significant positive association with market value. The coefficient magnitude indicates that a 0.01 rise in this ratio is associated with a 16 per cent increase in market value (the standard deviation for this sample is 0.011). The coefficient on the UK trademark variable is also significant at the 10 per cent level, with the magnitude indicating a 0.01 rise in the ratio would increase market value by only 1 per cent, but as the standard deviation is 0.07 for the trademark variable, then comparing firms which are one standard deviation apart gives a difference of 7 per cent in market value. The UK patent to assets ratio has an insignificant coefficient, but this could be due to multicollinearity, as the correlation coefficient for UK and EPO patents is 0.28. The second column adds an R&D intensity variable and an R&D dummy variable. The former is significant and also reduces the significance and magnitude of the coefficient on the EPO patents and trademark variables, indicating correlation between these regressors.

The next three columns of Table 7.2 show the results for specific sectors. For the FIRE sector the patent-based variables are excluded, since these are positive for such a small number of firms. The coefficient on the trademark ratio is statistically significant; its magnitude indicates that a one standard deviation increase (0.008) in the trademark to assets ratio is associated with a 23 per cent increase in market value. For the transport, communications and utilities sector (TCEGW) there are no significant coefficients for the measures of intellectual property, nor for the accounting intangible assets, which are significantly positive for both the other sectors. Manufacturing firms show the expected positive effect of higher European patenting rates, but trademarks are not significant (Greenhalgh and Rogers 2006 analyse a longer panel of firms and also find no significant effects of trademarks on market value in manufacturing). These results suggest that stock market analysts are unimpressed with increasing product variety in the absence of patentable innovations in manufacturing, but view more positively such product novelty in financial services. The final column of Table 7.2 adds the R&D variables for manufacturing and, as in the full sample, shows that the R&D intensity variable reduces the significance of EPO patents and trademarks.

THE FINANCIAL SERVICES SECTOR: FURTHER ESTIMATES

Table 7.2 provided some initial evidence concerning the valuation of trademarks in the FIRE sector. The results suggest that a higher intensity of trademark usage is associated with a higher stock market valuation, based on the between estimator. An alternative method of using the data is the within, or fixed effects, estimator. This transforms the data to deviations from the within-firm means and then estimates coefficients on the basis of these deviations. Such estimates are presented in Table 7.3.

Using this estimator (Table 7.3, column 1) we find that the coefficient on the trademark to tangible assets ratio is positive, but with a coefficient of only 3.7 and not statistically significant. The interpretation of these conflicting estimates is difficult. Suppose that the stock market has all the necessary information about the individual firms in terms of their quality of management, and suppose also that well-managed firms are more active in their use of the trademark system. Then the inclusion of a firm fixed effect which is correlated with the trademark variable would render the trademark variable statistically insignificant. Whether this indicates that our previous result was erroneous depends on the view as to whether it is the quality of management that matters most, or the protection of product varieties from imitation that is significant for future profits. An alternative interpretation of the insignificant result in the within estimator is that the inter-temporal volatility in the trademark variable introduces substantial 'noise' in the variable and this biases the coefficient towards zero (owing to standard statistical properties of the estimation procedure).

An additional issue of interest is whether there is any evidence that the market valuation of trademarks has changed over the period 1996 to 2000. As discussed, there has been a rapid growth of trademark activity in the FIRE sector; hence a basic hypothesis might assert that the value of trademarking to firms has increased. To test this hypothesis the trademark

Table 7.3 FIRE sector: within and pooled OLS regression results for market value

	Within estimator – firm fixed effects	Within estimator – firm fixed effects	Pooled data estimated with OLS, robust standard errors
Log. total assets (mill)	0.824	0.812	0.980
	(16.66)***	(16.22)***	(55.05)***
UK trademarks/total assets (mill)	3.737	−22.842	−20.001
	(1.30)	(−2.81)**	(−1.24)
UK trademarks/total assets (mill) × trend in years		7.642	9.191
		(3.49)***	(2.07)**
Debt/shareholders' equity	0.008	0.009	0.012
	(1.70)*	(1.76)*	(2.33)**
Intangible assets/total assets (mill)	0.603	0.552	1.386
	(1.72)*	(1.58)	(3.34)***
Constant	1.470	1.620	−1.818
	(2.25)**	(2.66)***	(−5.43)***
Observations	880	880	880
No. of firms	193	193	193
R-squared	0.84	0.84	0.88
F test: firm fixed effects	8.94	9.03	NA
F test: industry dummies	NA	NA	28.16

Notes: *   Significant at 10 per cent
        **   Significant at 5 per cent
        ***   Significant at 1 per cent

ratio is interacted with a trend term and this is entered in both the fixed effect and a pooled OLS estimation (Table 7.3, columns 2 and 3). In both cases the interaction term is positive and significant. The magnitude of the coefficients suggests that the share market's positive valuation of trademarking only occurred in 1998 and after; this result is also confirmed by repeated single-year, cross-section regression estimates (results not shown), in which the coefficient of trademarks is not significant for 1996 or 1997, but is strongly significant for each of the years 1998, 1999 and 2000.

Finally, we have conducted similar additional analysis for the TCEGW and manufacturing sectors. For the TCEGW sector we find little evidence of any significant role for IP using alternative estimators, confirming the thrust of the results in Table 7.2. The only exception is, as with the FIRE sector, that there is some evidence that trademarking generates additional market value in the later years of the sample. For the manufacturing sector, one finding is that entering the IP variables separately in between estimations results in significant coefficients on each of the IP variables. This indicates that, on average, R&D and IP activity are complementary and generate value accordingly. However, our analysis of manufacturing firms using within estimators and trend analysis did not reveal any significance for IP activity.

CONCLUSIONS

We have explored the use of the intellectual property system by two services sectors in comparison with manufacturing. We find that the growing financial services sector has made increasing use of trademarks and this has recently begun to be reflected in increased share prices for these users of trademarks. In contrast, despite their widespread use in the transport, communications and utilities sector and in manufacturing, trademarks are not significant determinants of the stock market value of firms in these sectors. For manufacturing, it is patenting via the European Patent Office which is reflected in a higher share price, whereas none of the IP variables showed returns for the transport, communications and utilities firms.

NOTES

1. The database developed for analysis in this chapter was derived by Mark Longland at the Oxford Intellectual Property Research Centre (OIPRC), St Peter's College, working with the authors and with an earlier collaborator, Professor Derek Bosworth. Funding was received at various times from the ESRC, the Leverhulme Trust and the UK Patent Office. The current development of the database, to include more service sector firms, is with the

144 *IP and company performance*

support of ESRC award RES-334-25-0002 under The Evolution of Business Knowledge Programme. We are grateful to St Peter's College for accommodation and administrative support for this research.

2. Note that UK and EPO patents can, at first approximation, be considered substitutes: both offer protection in the UK market. Furthermore, it is possible to extend the coverage of a UK patent publication to other countries by using the Patent Cooperation Treaty.
3. The creation of data for the financial services sector is made possible as part of a ESRC grant (RES-334-25-0002) under the Evolution of Business Knowledge research project.
4. The fact that there is any patenting activity in the FIRE sector may be surprising. However, two firms – BTG Plc and Scipher Plc – account for the bulk of these applications. Both of these firms are in the 'holding and other investment offices' industry and are, essentially, firms that develop and commercialize intellectual property.
5. The mean of the intra-firm standard deviation of trademarks is 8, whereas for patenting activity it is less than 2. Generally, it is better to use the coefficient of variation in such cases, but the extreme skewness of the underlying data implies the need for a much more rigorous analysis.
6. The partial derivative of K with respect to V ($\partial V/\partial K$) indicates the impact of a change in intangible assets on market value. By partially differentiating equation (7.1) with respect to K and A, one can show that the ratio of the two partial derivatives equals γ. For example, if $\gamma > 1$ this indicates that intangible assets (K) have a greater impact – or shadow value – than tangible assets.
7. This happens either because the volatility creates influential observations or because the measurement error in the underlying variable attenuates the coefficient estimates; see, for example, Johnston and DiNardo (1997).
8. For the full sample, this restriction excludes 97 observations. The full sample results show a similar pattern of significance to those in Table 7.2. However, the coefficient on EPO patents is lower (it is never above 5), while the coefficient on trademarks is lower (at 4.8) in the FIRE regression. Note that the 99th percentile is calculated for each regression (for example, the FIRE sector regression excludes firms with a trademark to asset ratio above the 99th percentile for firms in this sector).

REFERENCES

Bureau van Dijk (2004), 'Fame: UK and Irish company information', DVD ROM Update 182 August.
Chung, K. and S. Pruitt (1994), 'A simple approximation of Tobin's q', *Financial Management*, **23** (3), 70–74.
Department of Trade and Industry (2003), *Innovation Report – Competing in the Global Economy: The Innovation Challenge*, and the accompanying DTI Economics Paper No. 7 of the same title, both December.
Extel Financial (1996), Company Analysis, online database (now discontinued).
Greenhalgh, C.A. and M. Rogers (2006) 'Intellectual property, competition and thge value of UK firms', in C. Peeters and B. van Pottelsberghe de la Poterie (eds), *Economic and Management Perspectives on Intellectual Property Rights*, Basingstoke: Palgrave Macmillan.
Greenhalgh, C.A., M. Longland and D. Bosworth (2003), 'Trends and distribution of intellectual property: UK and European patents and UK trade and service marks 1986–2000', Section B of a report to the Patent Office on a project titled *The Extent and Value of Intellectual Property in United Kingdom Firms*.
Griliches, Z. (1981) 'Market value, R&D, and patents', *Economic Letters*, **7**, 183–7.

Hall, B. (2000), 'Innovation and market value', in R. Barrell, G. Mason and M. O' Mahoney (eds), *Productivity, Innovation and Economic Performance*, Cambridge: NIESR/Cambridge University Press.

HM Treasury and Inland Revenue (2001), *Increasing Innovation, A Consultation Paper*, Budget 2001.

Johnston, J. and J. DiNardo (1997), *Econometric Methods*, 4th edition, New York: McGraw-Hill.

Thomson (2001), Company Analysis, online database (now discontinued).

8. Market valuation of Australian intellectual property

William Griffiths and Elizabeth Webster

1 INTRODUCTION

Company-level 'market value' studies seek to estimate the returns to investment using stock market, book value and intellectual property (IP) data. These studies, which were initiated by Griliches (1981), aim to establish whether intangible assets, especially those arising from innovation, contribute to future company profits. In some ways this issue is trivial, since we would not expect companies to repeatedly invest in intangible capital unless they previously had positive returns. Predictably therefore, we find that significant and positive relationships between patents and the value of the company have become a 'stylized fact' around the world. Instead of seeking to reconfirm this 'fact', applied economists are now using this model to test whether the value of innovative activities varies with characteristics such as company size, industry and competition, among other things.

This chapter uses annual data from over 300 Australian companies from 1989 to 2002 to examine the relationship between the effort companies make creating intangible assets activity and future anticipated profits. Although there have been other company level estimations of this model (that is, Bosworth and Rogers 2001), there have been no previous Australian company studies which span a long time period before. This type of data set, which is called 'panel data', is a combined cross-sectional time-series data. Panel estimation techniques use the information embodied in this data to control for unmeasured-company characteristics that do not vary over time. Examples of these characteristics include the expertise of a specific manager or a particular customer market advantage which are constant over the data period. Our study is used not so much to derive estimates of the value of innovative activities, but to identify whether the value of Australian IP to companies has been rising or falling over time.

We begin with an introduction about what market value studies are and then present results from a fixed-effects panel estimation of company value to determine whether there have been trends in the value of different forms of company IP over time.[1] Our evidence suggests that the average present value of patents in Australia has been falling over the last 14 years, but the value of trademarks has been rising. The trend for designs is less clear. We conclude with a discussion of the limitations of these studies and some common misconceptions about what they tell us.

2 WHAT ARE MARKET VALUE EQUATIONS?

Market value equations begin with the identity:

$$V \equiv q(A + K) \tag{8.1}$$

where V is the current economic value of the firm (total value of equity plus total liabilities), K is the historic (that is, accumulated) cost of intangible assets, A is the historic value of tangible assets and q reflects the current market valuation of these assets (such that qA and qK are the market values of tangible and intangible assets respectively).[2] Historically, most investment activity by firms was embodied in tangible forms such as land, plant and equipment.[3] The formal accounting system, which defined explicit journals for these items, then produced balance sheets such that across firms as a whole, V equalled qA.[4]

However, a growing divergence between the 'book value', A, and the economic value of companies, V, has become apparent over time (see Webster 2000). This value gap has been attributed to the growth of assets typically not recognized by the generally-agreed-accounting principles, such as investments into R&D, workforce skills, marketing and the organizational architecture of the firm. Expenditures on most of these items are classified in accounts as 'variable expenditures' and do not enter the assets ledger even though they make long-term contributions to revenues and profits. Accordingly, there are no data for intangible assets, which is comparable to data produced for tangibles.[5]

In order to show that innovation activities create some of these 'missing' assets, economists use indices such as patent and trademark application counts in lieu of K in equation (8.1). In some cases, advertising expenditure as a proxy for marketing and brand-name capital has also been used (Chauvin and Hirschey 1997; Hall 1993) but estimates involving measures of investment in the skills of the workforce and the organizational architecture are largely, if not wholly, absent from the economic literature.

Data on tangible capital, A, is derived from company accounts and K is represented, but not measured, by variables which mimic the stocks of intangible assets, that is, the accumulation of past investments into intangible capital. In practice, it is common to either artificially constructing stocks of IP assets from investment flows – such as R&D expenditure, new patent applications and/or new trademark applications – or simply use flow data in lieu of K. One advantage of the estimations used in this chapter is that we are able to replace K with an auxiliary relationship involving actual stocks of patents, trademarks and designs in-force from grant and renewal data derived using data from the central registrar (IP Australia).

While the original intention of Griliches' (1981) first market value equation was to establish the place of innovation activities in the missing accounting data, the basic format of these equations has subsequently been used to establish whether secondary interactive characteristics make patents or R&D activity[6] more or less valuable, *ceteris paribus*. In terms of equations (8.2) and (8.4), these characteristics constitute part of r, which in our fixed-effects estimation are called the fixed effects. Tested characteristics have included market power (Bosworth and Rogers 2001; Blundell et al. 1999; Connolly 1986; Toivanen et al. 2002), a measure of the effectiveness of patents for preventing imitation (Cockburn 1988), the debt ratio (Toivanen et al. 2002), sales revenue (Hall 1993, 2003; Bosworth and Rogers 2001; Toivanen et al. 2002), union power (Connolly 1986), and profits or cash-flows (Bosworth et al. 2000). Industry dummy variables are often included to capture more ill-defined factors such as union power and import penetration which are believed to vary by industry but difficult to collect on a firm-by-firm basis.

Overall, these studies find that patents are more valuable – as judged by the stock market – in firms where patents are regarded by managers as being more effective, in firms with lower debt ratios, and when the growth in a firm's sales revenue is strong (although this result is not consistently found). There was no clear evidence that market power affected the market valuations. Many studies, including this one, also find that either new patent applications,[7] or R&D expenditure, have a positive and significant effect on the firm's market value, but not both together (see Toivanen et al. 2002, for example).

3   THE EFFECTS OF IP STOCKS ON THE MARKET VALUE OF AUSTRALIAN COMPANIES

The effects of patents, trademarks and designs on company value may be used to first, approximate the present value of the registered IP, together with other correlated intangible assets, and second, to detect whether there has been a change in this value over time. Unlike most studies in this genre, we use data on IP stocks or IP 'in-force'. Data on patents, trademarks and designs 'in-force' is not usually available to researchers who have to rely upon patent application (flow) data. Since, we are modelling assets vis-à-vis values, the correct left-hand side variable in the estimating equation is IP stocks, not applications.[8] Data on stocks of patents pending has also been used alongside stocks of patents in-force since there are often long time delays between an application and a patent examination decision.

We assume that a reasonable measure of intangible assets, $\frac{K}{A}$, is a weighted index of patents, trademarks and designs such that

$$K = aP + bPP + cT + dD$$

where P, PP, T and D represent the number of registered stocks of patents, patents pending, trademarks and designs respectively, and a, b, c and d are coefficients to be estimated.

Accordingly, we use a mathematical transformation to get the equation:[9]

$$\ln\left(\frac{V}{A}\right) \approx r + a\left(\frac{P}{A}\right) + b\left(\frac{PP}{A}\right) + c\left(\frac{T}{A}\right) + d\left(\frac{D}{A}\right) + \varepsilon \qquad (8.2)$$

where 'ln' means a natural logarithm. To estimate (8.2), accounting and share market data[10] for all Australian-owned parent companies and the highest accounting unit of local foreign companies with an annual turnover over $50 million were matched to patent, trademark and design titles from the IP Australia data base.[11] Linking was made if the applicant name matched either the name of the parent or one of its subsidiaries.[12] Our final sample consisted of 308 publicly-listed companies from 1989 to 2002.

The average value of companies in our sample over the whole period was A$6628 million (1989–90 prices). The average stocks per company of patents and patents pending were 4.6 and 0.4 and the average number of granted trademark and design stocks was 60.4 and 8.0.

Four versions of equation (8.2) were estimated. In all cases the parameter r, measuring the market valuation of assets, was assumed to vary across firms, but not over time for a given firm.[13] Estimates of r (which is called 'the fixed effect') can be derived from the statistical programme and separately analysed, however we have not done this for the present chapter.[14]

The first column of Table 8.1 contains estimates of the first version of equation (8.2). As described above, the variables representing intangible assets are patents, patents pending, trademarks and designs, each expressed as a ratio relative to tangible assets. We found that all granted patent stock variables were significant and positive but the patents pending variable

Table 8.1 Effects of IP variables on company value, fixed effects estimation

Ln(Company value/tangible assets)	Coef. Unweighted	t	Coef. Weighted by days	t	Coef. Unweighted	t	Coef. Weighted by days	t
	1		2		3		4	
Patents/tangible assets	607.69**	3.2	0.2088**	5.13	2582.2**	5.83	1.177**	6.17
Pending patents/tangible assets	911.17	0.77	0.0095**	2.93	9812.2*	2.52	−0.005	−1.34
Trademarks/tangible assets	91.58**	4.61	0.1913**	6.34	−17.43	−0.71	0.124*	2.72
Designs/tangible assets	523.35**	7.04			101.61	0.85	−0.085**	−5.18
Patents*time/tangible assets					−177.90	−3.83		
Pending patents*time/tangible assets					−873.91*	−2.06		
Trademarks*time/tangible assets					20.17**	6.44	0.006**	8.22
Designs*time/tangible assets					19.68	1.43	−0.004	−0.76
Constant (the average r across all firms)	0.37	39.37	0.3856	42.05	0.35	37.29	0.353	36.07
R²– within	0.096		0.053		0.129		0.094	
Number of observations	2446		2446		2446		2446	
Number of companies	308		308		308		308	

Note: **, * Significant at the 1 and 5 per cent levels respectively.

was not significant, suggesting that stock market investors do not value applications prior to grant. This may arise because investors expect heavy costs associated with product commercialization in the early stage of the product life cycle.

To translate these estimates into financial terms, we derived and evaluated the partial derivatives which gave us the increase in company value for an additional patent, trademark or design, while holding everything else constant. Evaluating these derivatives, we find that the value of an additional patent (with other unmeasured and correlated investments) adds, on average, A\$933000 to the value of the company, all other things held constant. The additional values for trademarks and designs were A\$141000 and A\$803000 respectively.[15]

The second estimation weights the IP stock by the age (in days) of the average granted title and reveals a similar pattern to the unweighted equation. This suggests that the additional information embodied in the renewal data adds little to the total explanatory power of the equation.

To assess whether these values are rising or falling over time we make the coefficients a, b, c and d linear functions of time. For example, we write

$$a_t = \alpha_0 + \alpha_1 t$$

where α_0 and α_1 are unknown coefficients and t is a time index. Making this and similar substitutions for b, c and d into equation (8.2) leads to a model with time interacting with the IP variables. The results for this model appear in columns 3 and 4 of Table 8.1. The first unweighted estimates indicate that patents have been falling in value but trademarks and designs have been rising in value. However, these trends are at the expense of the significance of the trademark and design stock variables. The decline in patent value is unlikely to be due to poor general macroeconomic conditions, for over the same time, the economic value of companies (deflated to 1989–90 dollars) exhibited a strong positive trend. However, macroeconomic conditions may explain some of the rise in value of trademarks and designs.

The main difference found in the final estimation, which considered weighted IP stocks with time trends, was the significant and positive effect of the value for designs. This, however, was achieved at the expense of its time trend.

Both the time trend equations implied that the average present value of a patent fell from 1989 to 2002 possibly reflecting a lower intrinsic value of the invention over time or more competitive markets resulting in lower profit margins for new products. However, we have no direct evidence for either of these hypotheses. Over the same time horizon, the average present value of a registered trademark rose and this may be due to the rising importance of branded goods and services in the economy, or the anti-competitive benefits to firms of using brands as barriers between themselves and rival companies.

4   WHAT DO MARKET VALUE STUDIES NOT TELL US?

While market value studies seemingly imply that intangible assets are 'significant', it is also important not to overstate what they can do. Specifically, they do not tell us whether investing in inventive activity is profitable. They do not indicate what the value of invention is, as distinct from correlated investments such as training, marketing and reorganization. They do not show whether the legal registration of IP adds (company) value above and beyond the inventive process. And they cannot prove that the stock market correctly values inventions and IP. The following sections discuss each of these issues in turn.

4.1   Whether Investing in Inventive Activity is Profitable

The attribution of a change in company value to a change in a particular asset is driven by the correlation between value and ownership of the asset over time and across firms. We reason that a change to the ownership of company assets causes company values to change because the latter reflects prospective returns based on current knowledge. The stock market's expectations of future profits should only change after pertinent information about the firm becomes 'known'. Since most of our IP variables are 'announced' for the purposes of our statistical estimation after significant costs have already been incurred, the recorded change to company value will only quantify the prospective returns from that time forward. Past expenditures are sunk costs and would have been factored into the share price at the time they were known. A rise therefore in the economic value of a company as a result, for example, of a new patent being applied for, will indicate that the stock market expects the future revenues less prospective costs to be positive, regardless of how much it cost the company to date to create the invention. However, this does not signal profitability. Unless we know the overall costs of inventing the idea or device, we cannot know whether the whole inventive activity was profitable or not.

To illustrate this point, consider a simple example where there are two time periods; in time period 0, the company invests an additional $1000 into an innovation project, and in time period 1, the company reaps all its additional profits from this innovation.[16] All innovation is financed through borrowings at the annual rate of 10 per cent. Further, assume stock markets predict profits correctly and therefore there is no risk.

The change to company value at time 0 is:

$$\Delta \text{Equities} + \Delta \text{Liabilities} \equiv \Delta \text{ present value of expected profits} = \frac{\Delta \text{ profits}}{(1 + 0.1)}$$

In case 1 (shown in Table 8.2), the original investment of $1000 yields profits of $1100, which is just enough to repay the loan and interest. Consequently, shareholders do not receive additional dividends and the share price, at time 0, does not rise in anticipation. The value of the company will rise by $1000 (wholly due to the change in liabilities) even though the whole innovative activity is only just profitable. In case 2, we have the same $1000 investment into innovation, but expected profits are only $1050. The cost of the loan is accordingly partly financed through lower than normal dividends which causes the share price to fall at time 0. Even though this is clearly an unprofitable investment, the value of the company still rises at time 0 by $955. In case 3, we have the converse situation whereby profits of $1200 are expected. In this example, the value of the company increases by $1091. A parallel situation exists if the innovation was financed through new share issues. The value of the company will still rise even if the true profitability of the investment is negative. While it is true that in case 2, the value of the company would decline prior to time 0 as investors perceive a poor investment being undertaken, our market value studies only record the change in company value at or subsequent to time 0.

Table 8.2 Effects on company value of good and bad investments

Time 0 Cost of investment	Time 1 Δ Profits	Change to firm value in time 0 Δ Equities	Δ Liabilities	Δ (Equities + Liabilities)	
1 $1000	$1100	0	$1000	$1000	Average investment
2 $1000	$1050	−$45	$1000	$955	Bad investment
3 $1000	$1200	+$91	$1000	$1091	Good investment

This example illustrates how, unless we know all the costs of investments into the intangible activities, we cannot tell from examining only changes to the value of companies whether the activity has been profitable or not. In each case the value of the company at time 0 will rise so long as profits, from that point in time forward, are positive. Unless we know the relative costs of different projects, we cannot even rank the profitability of the various investment activities using market valuation models.

When patent, trademark or design data are used in the regression analysis as proxies for intangible investment, we have no measure of the costs of acquiring these assets and no way of deriving profitability conclusions from a market value equation. In estimations where R&D expenditure data are available, it is possible to deduce the rate of profitability so long as the R&D figures capture the full cost of the activity. However, as discussed in the next section, this latter qualification also causes us difficulties.

4.2   What the Value of Invention is, as Distinct from Correlated Investments

Econometric models essentially calculate effects of one variable on another, separate from all other causes, through disaggregating statistical correlations. However, if two causal factors are closely correlated and one is not measured, then statistically we will be ascribing the effects of both factors to the measured factor. There is a view from the theoretical literature that many intangible activities are correlated in this way, although the evidence for this is scant. If, for example, R&D activity is correlated with expenditures on workforce training, then measures of the effects of changes to R&D on company value will inadvertently include the effects of training. The point is that if we do not have measures of the non-invention intangible investment activities, then we may be overstating the effects of inventive activity on market value in our econometric estimations.

4.3   Whether Higher Company Value is Due to the Invention or the IP Title

Studies that use registered IP as proxy variables for the extent of the inventive process will, for the same reasons discussed above, conflate the value of the invention with the value of the IP title. It is possible that the invention has no value to consumers and is unlikely to be commercialized, but the IP title adds considerably to company profits because it is being used anti-competitively to block and intimidate would-be rivals. The latter, which occurs when firms take out the maximum number of patents they can for any given invention in a bid to confuse and overwhelm competitors, is referred to in the literature as 'patent bombing'. Alternatively, legal protection may add very little to the commercial value of a given invention.

Market value studies are simply not able to distinguish the separate contribution of the invention and the IP title to company value. This difference matters from the manager's perspective since committing to an invention and paying for the cost of a patent, trademark or design title are separate decisions for the firm. Good returns from an innovation may be forthcoming if the firm seeks to protect itself from copying through use of secrecy or lead-time advantage rather than a patent.

4.4   Whether the Stock Market Correctly Values Inventions and IP

Market value studies rely on the economic 'law' of competition, which compels stock markets investors to make unbiased predictions of future profits. However, we know that stock markets regularly make systematic errors, most recently the NASDAQ crash of 2000 and the general stock market slump of 1987. This occurs because good investments on the stock market include a substantial amount of capital gain. To make a capital gain, you have to predict what shares other investors will buy and similarly they need to predict what you will buy. This can lead to a circular or infinite regress situation whereby investors may value certain shares, or forms of IP, simply because they believe other investors will.

Perhaps over the long run, objective factors (whether inventions are on average a profitable activity) may dominate subjective factors (what other share market investors will buy) but the former may take many years, even decades, to prevail. In the mean time, for shorter time horizons, such as those typically used for market value studies, we do not know whether there is a systematic under or over market valuation of IP.

5   CONCLUSION

Market value equations cannot tell us whether the innovation process has been profitable, nor whether any prospective profits are attributable to the innovative activities or other associated activities. They can however indicate the direction of trends in the value of the different IP components. If we accept that on average, over the period 1989–2002, stock market investors made reasonable predictions of future company profitability, our results show that the average value of patents has been falling over time, while the average value of trademarks has been rising. The trend for design values is less clear.

There are several possible reasons for these developments. The value of patents may be falling because either examiners are increasingly prepared to pass applications with lower levels of inventive step, the mix of applications by technology is changing in favour of less valuable inventions, or because the market for products, which embody patented material is becoming more competitive thereby yielding lower profit margins. There may be a hidden selection process going on whereby, over time, owners of the more valuable inventions are deciding not to use patents to prevent imitation, but other non-patent forms of appropriability.

The value of trademarks, on the other hand, may be growing because increasingly new brands, especially formally-registered brands, are seen as critical to the marketing and commercialization of product lines. This may reflect a deeper change in the way goods and services are standardized and packaged. Alternatively, rising trademark values may reflect a rise in the examination threshold. Although given the strong growth in the absolute number of trademarks per unit of GDP in recent years, this is unlikely.[17]

ACKNOWLEDGEMENT

We would like to thank Mitch Cassellman, Paul Jensen and Derek Bosworth for their generous time reading this chapter.

NOTES

1. For further details on the fixed-effects estimation method see Carter Hill et al. (2000).
2. Characteristically, equation (8.1) is transformed to make it more convenient for estimation after inclusion of an auxiliary relationship to explain the unmeasurable K, and to accommodate a more general formulation than (8.1). The transformation makes both formulations suitable for ordinary least squares estimation, although it is not strictly necessary; non-linear least squares can be used as an alternative. If we pursue the linear route, we first divide by A and take natural logs to get: $\ln(V/A) \equiv \ln q + \ln(K/A + 1)$ Recognizing that intangible assets K are small relative to tangible assets A, this expression can be simplified using the result that $\ln(1 + x) \approx x$ when x is small (the tolerance limit for x is 0.045): $\ln(V/A) \approx \ln q + (K/A)$ If we set $q = \exp(r)$, where r represents the various market valuation factors and include a random error term ε, then the equation becomes: $\ln(V/A) \approx r + (K/A) + \varepsilon$. A more general variant of (8.1) is to allow for economies of scale, such that: $V \equiv q(A + K)^{\sigma}$ where $\sigma > 1$ when economies of scale exist. In this case, following transformations similar to those used to derive equation (8.2) yields: $\ln V \equiv r + \sigma \ln A + \sigma K/A + \varepsilon$. One advantage of this formulation is that when $\sigma > 1$ the tolerance limit for the approximation to $\ln(1 + K/A)$ rises above 0.045 so this model is more flexible than (8.2). However, we found that when the model in equation (8.4) was estimated, we found an estimate for σ of about 0.6, which implies an implausible level of diseconomies of scale. Consequently, the results that we present below in Table 8.2 are extensions of the functional form in equation (8.2).
3. Tangibles also includes liquid items such as cash.
4. Since V is a value and A and K are accounting costs which include economists, profit and loss (normal or otherwise), then q will not necessarily equal one.
5. Formal accounting data on intangible assets only includes expenditures on some externally procured items such as patent attorneys' fees and licences. Since most intangibles are produced in-house as intermediate capital items, these estimates are a sub-set of the true level of intangible assets. Webster (1999, p. 56) estimates that, on average, measured intangibles are less than a quarter of the true level of intangible assets.
6. A limited number of studies have also used other innovation measures such as 'innovation counts' which are derived from mentions of innovations in trade journals or external expert assessments of companies' innovations. These measures are not widely available and usually only exist for limited time periods.
7. See the summary in Bosworth and Rogers (2001), table A1 and Hall (2000), table 1.
8. Application data, however, can be used to capture the new news effects.
9. If we assume there is a non-IP related level of intangible capital proportional to the level of tangible assets, then this effect becomes included in the parameter r.
10. These data were sourced from the IBISWorld and the AGSM databases.

11. Only applications from Australian resident entities were matched.
12. A company is defined as a subsidiary of a parent if the latter owns at least 50 per cent of the former.
13. Within the context of our panel data, this assumption can be accommodated by estimating either a fixed effects or a random effects model. Given the possibility of possible correlation between a firm's *r* and values of it's right-hand-side variables *A*, *P*, *T* and *D*, we opted for fixed effects estimation (Judge et al. 1985).
14. We do this in a related piece of research (Griffiths and Webster 2004).
15. Derivatives has been evaluated at the mean levels of all variables.
16. The same logic holds if the innovative activity were wholly financed through retained earnings.
17. See Jensen and Webster (2004).

REFERENCES

Blundell, R., R. Griffith and J. Van Reenen (1999) 'Market share, market value and innovation in a panel of British manufacturing firms', *Review of Economic Studies*, **66**, 529–54.

Bosworth, D. and M. Rogers (2001), 'Market value, R&D and intellectual property: an empirical analysis of large Australian firms', *Economic Record*, **77**, 323–37.

Bosworth, D., A. Wharton and C. Greenhalgh (2000), 'Intangible assets and the market valuation of UK companies: evidence from fixed effects models', in *Oxford Intellectual Property Research Centre*, vol. 2, April, St Peter's College, Oxford.

Carter Hill, R., W. Griffifths and C. Judge (2000), *Undergraduate Econometrics*, Chichester: Wiley.

Chauvin, K.W. and M. Hirschey (1997), 'Market structure and the value of growth', *Managerial and Decision Economics*, **18**, 247–54.

Cockburn, I. and Z. Griliches (1988), 'Industry effects and appropriability measures in the stock market's valuation of R&D patents', *American Economic Review*, **78**, 419–23.

Connolly, R.A., B.T. Hirsch and M. Hirschey (1986), 'Union rent-seeking, intangible capital and market value of the firm', *Review of Economics and Statistics*, **68**, 567–77.

Griffiths, W. and E. Webster (2004), *Trends in the Value of Intellectual Property in Australia*, Vol. 18/04, working paper, Intellectual Property Research Institute of Australia Centre for Microeconomics, Department of Economics and Melbourne Institute of Applied Economics and Social Research, Intellectual Property Research Institute of Australia, University of Melbourne: Melbourne.

Griliches, Z. (1981), 'Market value, R&D and patents', *Economics Letters*, **7**, 183–7.

Hall, B. (1993), 'The stock market's valuation of R&D investment during the 1980s', *American Economic Review*, **83**, 259–64.

Hall, B.H. (2000), 'Innovation and market value', in R. Barrell, G. Mason and M. O'Mahony (eds), *Productivity, Innovation and Economic Performance*, London and Cambridge: National Insititute of Economic and Social Research and Cambridge University Press.

Hall, B. and R. Oriani (2003), 'Does the market value R&D investment by European firms? Evidence from a panel of manufacturing firms in France, Germany and Italy', in DRUID conference and EEA-ESAM Elsinore and Stockholm.

Jensen, P. and E. Webster (2004), 'Recent patterns of trade marking activity in Australia', *Australian Intellectual Property Journal*, **15** (2), 112–26.

Judge, G.G., R. Hill, W. Griffifths and T. Lee (1985), *The theory and practice of econometrics*, New York: Wiley.

Toivanen, O., P. Stoneman and D. Bosworth (2002), 'Innovation and the market value of UK firms, 1989–1995', *Oxford Bulletin of Economics and Statistics*, **64**, 39–61.

Webster, E.M. (1999), *The economics of intangible investment*, Cheltenham, UK and Northampton, MA, USA: Edward Elgar.

Webster, E.M. (2000), 'The growth of intangible enterprise investment in Australia', *Information Economics and Policy*, **12**, 1–25.

9. Innovation scoreboards: an Australian perspective

Paul H. Jensen and Alfons Palangkaraya

1 INTRODUCTION

Innovation is generally recognized by economists as the ultimate engine of growth and prosperity. As Gans and Stern (2003, p. 7) state: 'World class competitiveness and prosperity depends on ... the ability to develop and commercialise "new-to-the-world" technologies, products and business organizations.' This insight has spawned burgeoning interest in the analysis of innovation and its determinants at both the national level and the company level. While governments are typically interested in aggregate measures of innovation so that a nation's performance can be benchmarked against others, it is at the firm level where most of the innovative activity actually occurs: firms take the risks involved in commercializing the inventions which ultimately drive the growth of the domestic economy. As a consequence, measurement of companies' innovative performance has also received a lot of attention from academics, policy-makers and business analysts.

However, measurement of innovation at either the national or company level is difficult for a number of reasons. First, an innovation (by its very definition) is something that is 'new', which makes it difficult to construct a measure of innovation which is general enough to be used to compare to other innovative outputs. Second, the innovation process typically takes many years and involves managing numerous risks. As a result, the relationship between inputs (such as R&D expenditure) and outputs (such as patents) is potentially non-linear and it is unclear how these factors can be accounted for in a single measure of innovation. Finally, much of what is innovative within a firm – particularly, process innovations and development of intermediate goods – is invisible to the outsider. Thus, commonly used measures of innovative performance such as R&D expenditure or the number of patents may be imperfect proxies of innovative activity. However, much progress has been made on the empirical measurement of innovation, including the use of multiple indicators measures of innovation which capture more than just that which is easily observable (such as patent activity).

Bearing these issues in mind, the aim of this chapter is to construct an index which enables us to measure innovative activity at the company level. This innovation index reflects many of the recent developments in the academic literature aimed at deepening our understanding of what constitutes innovative activity within the firm and therefore provides an accurate picture of the current state of innovative activity. The index is then used to compile an 'innovation scoreboard', which is simply each firm's indexed 'score' in a given year, which forms the basis of our comparison of the innovative performance of Australian companies over the period 1998–2003.[1] Using the results of the innovation scoreboard enables the following questions to be addressed: which Australian companies are the most innovative? In what sectors do they operate? How does their innovative performance change over time?

2   DEFINING INNOVATION

Economists often argue that the search for new and improved goods and services – which is often referred to as 'innovation' – is one of the primary drivers of economic development in capitalist nations. But the term 'innovation' is often used in a very ambiguous and imprecise fashion, which causes much confusion. In particular, does innovation include only final goods and services or are improvements in production processes also important? Furthermore, should changes in work culture or management practice also be included in the definition? Are invention and innovation synonymous? For the purpose of this chapter, it is worth reflecting on issues relating to the definitions of innovation and invention.

The classic economic representation of innovation is contained in Schumpeter (1934), who articulated five aspects of innovation: product innovation, process innovation, organizational innovation, input innovation and market innovation. Although these aspects are not mutually exclusive, using this taxonomy enables us to get a clearer picture of what we are referring to when we talk of 'innovation'. Product innovation refers to the creation of new (or improved) goods or services that are launched on to the market. Process innovations, on the other hand, refer to changes in the way in which goods and services are produced. Organizational innovation refers to changes in the architecture of production and accounts for innovations in management structure, corporate governance, financial systems or changes in the way workers are paid. Market and input innovations refer to improved ways of sourcing supplies of raw inputs or intermediate goods and services as well as opening up new market opportunities (which could relate to either creating new domestic or export markets).

While this framework provides a means of categorizing the different kinds of innovation, it also implicitly outlines another important dimension of innovation: whether it constitutes something that is new to the world or something that is new to the firm. The former is a narrow definition of innovation that only includes inventions,[2] while the latter is a much broader definition that includes imitation and adaptation of existing products as well as invention. It is the second definition of innovation (that is new to the firm) that we use here. The extent of novelty included in the definition of innovation is a critical factor in understanding the effects of innovation since the risks and returns of the two definitions are fundamentally different.[3] Moreover, it is important to understand the distinction between invention and innovation when deciding how to measure the relevant phenomenon: using patents, for example, may be a good measure of invention but not innovation.

3 MEASURING INNOVATION

One of the difficulties with measuring innovation is that it is a dynamic process which has no beginning and no end: it is a process in which products and processes are in a constant state of flux. The innovation process follows a complex pathway which involves feedback loops generated by on-the-job learning, trial-and-error and other discontinuities in production. Capturing the complexity of this process with a simple, static indicator is difficult since much of the innovative activity that occurs within a firm may not be easily observed. In attempting to make innovation measurement tractable, some assumptions about the beginning and end of the innovation pathway have to be made. The standard convention is that innovation begins with R&D. Following this, some outputs may become encoded into patents and/or trademarks, integrated into business secrets or embodied in tacit organizational knowledge. With good management and fortune, this may evolve into new products or production technologies.

Given this innovation pathway, there are a number of single indicator proxies for innovation that could be used. For example, company R&D expenditure data could be (and often are) used as a proxy for innovation. However, not all firms that collect R&D data report it in their annual reports even though this is required by many national accounting standards. Thus, there may be substantial holes in our understanding of innovation if we simply rely on R&D data. Furthermore, it is not clear whether we should be using what is essentially an input into the innovation process (R&D expenditure) or outputs of the process (such as patents or trademarks).

In this section, we consider issues related to the use of single indicator innovation proxies and then consider some of the benefits of adopting a multi-indicator approach to develop a composite measure of innovation.

3.1   Single Indicator Approach

As already mentioned, innovative activity could be measured using a number of single indicators such as R&D expenditure, patent counts or the number of new products introduced over any given period of time. However, each of these proxies suffers from a common problem: the units of measurement are heterogeneous. Since the act of measuring is concerned with quantifying commensurate elements of an activity, measurement can only be achieved if the units of input/output are homogeneous. What does it mean to say that a company has 100 patents if the effort that went into creating each patent is substantially different? Is a dollar spent in one company on R&D equivalent to that spent in another company and, if not, does comparing R&D expenditure tell us anything about either company's innovative activity?

Each of the single indicator innovation proxies also suffer from some specific problems. Patents, for example, are known to have considerable biases in terms of their ability to measure innovation since many innovations are not patentable (because they do not fulfil the patenting requirements of novelty and inventiveness). In addition, only firms who believe that the legal protection offered by patents is more valuable than it costs will attempt to apply for it. Accordingly, inventions in technical fields not well covered by patent laws (for example, software programs) and inventions that can be protected by other methods (for example, secrecy, copyright or keeping ahead) are less likely to be captured using a simple single indicator of innovation. Similarly, inventions that are otherwise hard to imitate – usually because they are embedded in complex production systems – are expected, a priori, to have a lower correlation between patent rights and innovation (see Arundel and Kabla 1998). There is also some other empirical evidence to suggest that patents are biased towards firms in manufacturing industries (see Jensen and Webster 2004).

Another problem with single indicators of innovation is that it forces a decision to be made with regard to which end of the innovation pathway provides more valuable information regarding innovative activity. For example, a choice must be made as to whether to use R&D expenditure or new products (which lie at opposing ends of the innovation pathway). While there may be some persuasive reasons for using new products as a measure of innovation, the further we progress down the innovation pathway, the more we are using a measure of innovation based on the successful launch of a product, rather than innovation per se. Since innovation is a risky activity, many investments in research (and development) may not actually result in any new product being launched on the market. However, these problems are not insurmountable. They simply reflect the fact that innovation is an easy concept to understand but a difficult one to measure. One way in which we can overcome some of the shortcomings of single indicators is the use of multi-indicator measures of innovation.

3.2 Multi-indicator Approach

In order to illustrate the potential weakness of a single indicator approach for measuring innovation, consider the following example from Feeny and Rogers (2003). Let us say there are two firms of the same size and other characteristics which spend $1 million and $5 million on R&D, respectively. In addition, assume that the first firm produces two patents, whereas the second firm produces only one patent. If we measure innovative activity based on a single indicator such as R&D expenditure, then the first firm is least innovative. However, if we use the number of patents produced, the same firm becomes the most innovative.

The potential problem with the single-indicator approach can be illustrated using a Venn diagram as in Figure 9.1 (Hagedoorn and Cloodt 2003). In the diagram, the space defined by the square box represents the true innovative performance and the space defined by each overlapping circle as the part of innovative performance measured by any single indicator. Notice that the circles may overlap with each other, indicating that two or more indicators may provide the same information regarding innovative performance. The greater the overlap between the circles, the more likely it is that one single indicator will be an adequate proxy for innovative activity. However, a complete overlap is highly unlikely since not all inventions that

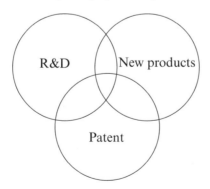

Figure 9.1   The relationship between innovation proxies

resulted from R&D investment can or will be patented, for various reasons explained before. In addition, not all patents will be incorporated into new products and not all new products result from R&D investment.

4   THE INNOVATION SCOREBOARD[4]

The aim of the construction of the Australian innovation scoreboard is to measure the innovativeness of Australian companies. As such, the scoreboard serves as a benchmarking and competitor analysis tool for Australian companies in terms of innovative performance. Investors and policy-makers, for example, can use the scoreboard to compare the extent and outcomes of innovative activities across companies and industries. Thus, the scoreboard is a particularly useful tool when the number of companies to be compared is large enough to render a thorough and in-depth comparison among them impractical. In this section, we discuss the construction of the index which is used to build the innovation scoreboard and demonstrate some useful ways in which the index can be used.

4.1   Construction of the Innovation Index

Given the problems with the single indicator approach, we use a multi-indicator innovation index which combines measures of innovative activities. The innovation index is based on the following formula:

$$I = \lambda_1 \left(\frac{R}{A} \right) + \lambda_2 \left(\frac{P}{A} \right) + \lambda_3 \left(\frac{T}{A} \right) + \lambda_4 \left(\frac{D}{A} \right) \qquad (9.1)$$

where λ_j denotes the intensity of the j-th measure of innovative activities – R&D expenditure (R), patent applications (P), trademark applications (T) and design applications (D) – with respect to A, which is the replacement value of tangible assets. Each of these single indicators provides us with information about the extent of innovative activity within a firm at different stages of the innovation pathway. R&D expenditure, for example, captures both the initial investment made in conducting research about a potential innovation and the subsequent expenditure made in conducting the trials necessary to ensure that the innovation actually works. Trademarks, on the other hand, reflect the outputs of innovative activity: they are typically observed after the R&D process has been completed and new products (or modifications of existing products) are launched on the market. The effect of combining these single indicators into an innovation index is to provide us with a much more comprehensive picture of the breadth and depth of innovative activity across all stages of the innovation pathway.

To compute the innovation index, we need to know the importance of each individual component. That is, we need to know the values of the weighting factors (the λ_js). In order to estimate these values, we analyse the relationship between innovative activities and the market value of the company.

Following Griliches[5] (1981), we express the market value (V_{it}) of company i at period t as:

$$V_{it} = V(A_{it}, K_{it}) \qquad (9.2)$$

where A_{it} is the replacement value of tangible assets and K_{it} is the replacement value of intangible assets. The regression function to obtain estimates of λ_j is then derived by assuming a specific functional form for equation (9.2) as shown below:

$$V_{it} = b(A_{it} + \lambda K_{it})^\sigma \qquad (9.3)$$

where b denotes the 'current market valuation coefficient' of the company assets, σ is the degree of returns-to-scale, and λ expresses the relative shadow value of intangible assets to tangible assets. Taking the logarithmic values of both sides of equation (9.3), subtracting $\log A_{it}$ from each side, utilizing the approximation $\log(1 + c) \approx c$, using the book value of intangible assets (B_{it}), R&D expenditure, patent, trademark and design applications as proxies for K_{it}, and assuming $\sigma = 1$, we get:

$$\log\left(\frac{V_{it}}{A_{it}}\right) = \log b + \hat{\lambda}_1\left(\frac{R_{it}}{A_{it}}\right) + \hat{\lambda}_2\left(\frac{P_{it}}{A_{it}}\right) + \hat{\lambda}_3\left(\frac{T_{it}}{A_{it}}\right) + \hat{\lambda}_4\left(\frac{D_{it}}{A_{it}}\right) + \gamma\left(\frac{B_{it}}{A_{it}}\right) + \beta X_{it} + u_{it}$$

$$(9.4)$$

In order to capture variation in market valuation of companies across industries and aggregate movement across time, the regressions also include year and two-digit industry dummy variables as part of X_{it}. Equation (9.4) is then estimated with ordinary least squares using firm level data on patent, trademark and design applications (from IP Australia), market value data (from SIRCA) and accounting data (from IBISWorld). Since not all companies are listed in the Australian Stock Exchange or appear in the SIRCA database and not all companies report any R&D expenditure,[6] we only include those with observed market values and/or R&D expenditures in the relevant analyses.

To assess the importance of non-R&D reporting companies, we compared the relative distribution of those companies with and without R&D expenditure across sectors in our sample data in 2003 with the relative distribution of sectoral R&D expenditures in the 2002/03 Business Expenditures on Research and Development (BERD) (ABS 2004). Overall, even though there are less than one third of 875 companies included in the 2003 sample with reported R&D expenditures, those companies account for more than 60 per cent of the total BERD in the same period.

The coefficient estimates $(\hat{\lambda}_1 \ldots \hat{\lambda}_4)$ are substituted for $(\lambda_1 \ldots \lambda_4)$ in equation (9.1), respectively, to compute the innovation index. Feeny and Rogers (2003) estimated equation (9.4) using the 1996–98 data for 300 companies.[7] Using their estimation results, we compute innovation scores for each company in each year using the following:

$$I_{it} = 2.409\left(\frac{R_{it}}{A_{it}}\right) + 6.822\left(\frac{P_{it}}{A_{it}}\right) + 1.132\left(\frac{T_{it}}{A_{it}}\right) + 0.385\left(\frac{D_{it}}{A_{it}}\right) \qquad (9.5)$$

4.2   Innovative Performance in 2003

Using this approach, we can construct the innovation index for 2003. In this section, we report results from the innovation scoreboard in order to analyse which industry sectors are the most innovative and which companies are the most innovative.[8] Table 9.1 shows the average innovation scores of companies in the top six industry sectors along with the corresponding intensity levels of innovative activities in these sectors.[9] The most innovative sector in the sample, photographic and scientific equipment, consists of four companies. Altogether, these four companies had an average score on the innovation index of 46.5, spent approximately 9.3 per cent of their total revenues on R&D and filed an average of six patent and three trademark applications. In contrast, companies in the property and business services industry sector had an average score on the innovation index of 11, spent 3.8 per cent of revenues on R&D and applied for three trademarks.

In addition to analysing inter-industry variation in innovative activity, the innovation scoreboard can also be used for company benchmarking and/or competitor analysis purposes. Table 9.2 lists the ten most innovative Australian companies in 2003.[10] Note that the innovation scores shown in the second column of Table 9.2 are normalized values with respect to the highest score in that period. Thus, the most innovative company – Cochlear – received a score of 100 while the second company on the list – Varian Holdings – scored 77. Given the construction of the index, this can be

Table 9.1 *Top six innovative industry sectors in 2003*

Industry sector	No. of companies	Innovation score[a]	R&D/revenue[a]	Patent applications[a]	Trademark applications[a]	Design applications[a]
Photographic and scientific equipment manufacturing	4	46.5	9.3%	6	3	0
Scientific research	1	29.0	9.1%	15	6	0
Electronics and electrical equipment and appliance manufacturing	13	14.6	4.9%	2	5	1
Printing, publishing and recorded media manufacturing	1	14.0				
Industrial machinery and equipment manufacturing	15	11.4				
Property and business services	17	11.0	3.8%	0	3	0
All	51		2.6%	2	4	1

Note: [a] Average per company.

167

interpreted as meaning that the innovative performance of the second-ranked company is 23 per cent lower *relative* to Cochlear.

If we compare the ten most innovative firms listed in Table 9.2 with the rest of the firms in the industry, we can see that they spend a lot more on R&D expenditure, both in absolute and relative terms, than the average firm in the industry. In fact, the ten most innovative firms spend an average of 11.2 per cent of their revenue on R&D, while the average firm in the industry only spend an average of 1.6 per cent of their revenue on R&D. Similarly, there is a significant difference between the top ten most innovative firms and the average firm with regard to patenting activity. The most highly innovative firms in 2003 had an average of 7.7 patent applications, whereas the average firm had only 1.1 patent applications. Thus, patenting and R&D appear to be important determinants of scoring highly on the innovation index.

Similar conclusions can be drawn when we compare the average innovation score of the ten most innovative companies with the average score of the top 50 companies. Specifically, the top ten companies score more highly on both R&D and patenting activity. The average firm in the top 50 most innovative firms, however, receives higher scores in both trademarks (4.2 applications) and designs (2.4 applications) than the average firm in the top ten (with 2.6 and 0.1 trademark and design applications, respectively).

To better understand what possibly differentiates the most innovative firms from the rest of the industry, we match our sample with the results of a recent series of business surveys conducted by the Melbourne Institute in collaboration with the Business Council of Australia and the Committee for Economic Development of Australia. This survey has been conducted annually from 2001 and, for our purposes, contains three groups of relevant questions.[11] The first one asks a senior manager from each company how he/she rates the extent to which various methods of information gathering are used by the company in order to assess its business environment. The second group asks about the flexibility of the company in changing its strategic plan whenever faced with various contingencies. Finally, the managers are asked to what extent their competitive strategy focuses on a given list of potential competitive strategies.

Figure 9.2 compares the average score of some of the principal factors identified using factor analysis based on these three groups of questions for the top ten, top 50 (excluding those in the top ten) and the rest of the companies. In one of his widely read business/management books, Drucker (1986) lists various sources of innovative opportunities such as the development of new knowledge, the emergence of unexpected outcomes, or demographic shifts, and points out that only those entrepreneurs who can systematically identify and adapt to these changes are the ones who become successful innovators.

Table 9.2 Top ten innovative companies in 2003

Company name	Innovation score	2002–03 R&D expenditure ($000); % revenue; % assets			IP applications in 2003 Patents; trademarks; designs			Sector
Cochlear	100	37030	12.8	16.1	30	0	1	Electronics
Varian Holdings (Australia)	77	12192	9.5	19.1	5	0	0	Photographic and scientific equipment
ResMed Holdings	63	24593	8.7	9.4	21	9	0	Photographic and scientific equipment
Stargames	58	5127	8.3	11.3	2	7	0	Machinery and equipment wholesaling
Alcatel Australia	58	66119	17.4	30.4	0	2	0	Electrical and electronics equipment wholesaling
Schefenacker Vision Systems	40	9652	6.4	9.9	4	0	0	Glass manufacturing
Robert Bosch (Australia)	39	42528	4.9	11.2	13	2	0	Motor vehicle and parts manufacturing
Mincom	39	12632	7.5	17.2	1	0	0	Computer services
MYOB	38	14264	18.6	14.4	1	6	0	Computer services
Solution 6 Holdings	33	43160	17.9	16.1	0	0	0	Computer services
Top 10 average	55	26729	11.2	15.7	7.7	2.6	0.1	
Top 50 average	23	16908	5.2	6.5	3.2	4.2	2.4	
Industry average	6.1	6997	1.6	2.0	1.1	3.5	0.7	

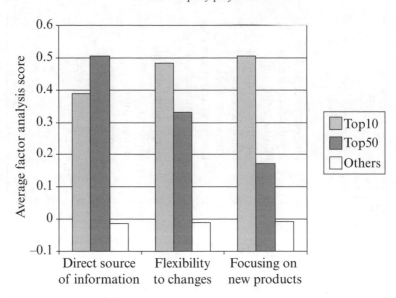

Figure 9.2   Sources of innovative opportunity

Indeed, from Figure 9.2, these are more or less how the most innovative companies seem to differ from the rest. For example, we can see that the most innovative companies are more likely to pursue information from primary sources such as their clients and conduct their information gathering more systematically. In addition, they are more ready to adapt their strategic plan in the face of external changes. Finally, they are more inclined to focus on developing new products or exploiting early signs of opportunity provided by the market.

4.3   Trends in Innovative Performance, 1998–2003

Over time, a company's innovative performance will probably change: some companies may gain in terms of their innovativeness, while others may be unable to sustain their past performance. By computing the innovation scores for each company using annual data from 1998 to 2003, we can track how the innovative performance of the companies has changed.[12] At the company level, the changes in innovative performance have been quite dramatic. For example, as shown in Figure 9.3, the innovative performance[13] of Cochlear resembles an inverted-U pattern, whereas Varian's pattern of performance looks like a regular U-shape. Much of the U-shaped pattern of Varian's innovative performance is due to the reduction of R&D expenditures in the first half of the period and their revival at the later

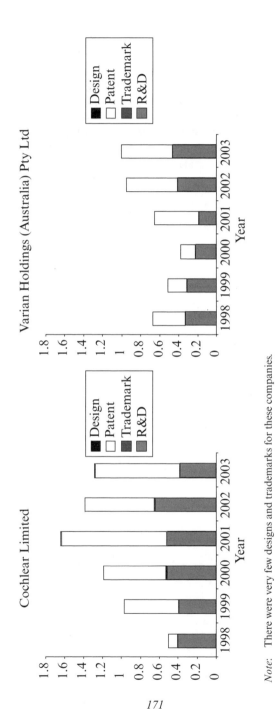

Note: There were very few designs and trademarks for these companies.

Figure 9.3 Patterns of innovative performance for two Australian companies, 1998–2003

half. A carefully designed and executed case study would help us uncover the underlying reasons for the fluctuation of R&D expenditures or other components of the innovation index. However, this is outside the scope of the present chapter.

Another way to assess the importance of variations in innovative performance across companies and over time is to look at changes in the distribution of the top performing companies. The more important within and between company heterogeneity is, the more significant the change in ranking of companies over time. Knowing the degree of such heterogeneity is an important step in understanding the underlying drivers of company innovative performance or to design any industrial policy to stimulate innovation.

Table 9.3   Top 20 innovative companies, 1998–2003

Company	Rank					
	2003	2002	2001	2000	1999	1998
Cochlear Ltd	1	1	1	2	2	10
Varian Holdings (Australia) Pty Ltd	2	7	5	11	5	8
ResMed Holdings Ltd	3	3	7	1	1	1
Stargames Ltd	4					
Alcatel Australia Ltd	5	20	17	16	14	7
Schefenacker Vision Systems Australia Pty Ltd	6	2	10	3	11	
Robert Bosch (Australia) Pty Ltd	7					
Mincom Ltd	8	14	12	8		5
MYOB Ltd	9					
Solution 6 Holdings Ltd	10	19			10	
Amrad Corporation Ltd	11	5	6	6	7	4
Marley Plastics Australia Holdings Ltd	12	48				
Thales Underwater Systems Pty Ltd	13					
NEC Business Solutions Ltd	14	15	3	7		
Ludowici Ltd	15		11	21		15
Aristocrat Leisure Ltd	16	17	2	4	16	3
MaxiTrans Industries Ltd	17					
Foxboro Australia Pty Ltd	18					
GUD Holdings Ltd	19	18	24	27	20	13
ANCA Pty Ltd	20					

Table 9.3 shows the ranking of the top 20 companies in 2003 over the period 1998–2003. From Table 9.3 we can see that approximately half of the companies have been among the top 20 throughout the period. This suggests that there has been some persistence in innovative performance over the years. Cochlear, for example, has been the top-ranked company since 2001, and was ranked second for two consecutive years before that. However, there has also been some considerable entry and exit in the list of top 20 innovative companies. For example, there are a number of companies – such as Stargames, Robert Bosch (Australia), and MYOB – which appeared in the top 20 for the first time in 2003. At the other extreme, there were companies ranked as high as second, sixth and eighth in 1998 that were no longer among the top 20 in 2003. Further analysis would allow us to analyse why certain companies seem to be able improved their relative performance while others were unable even to maintain their position.

5   LIMITATIONS OF THE INNOVATION SCOREBOARD

Earlier in this chapter we argued that there are potential difficulties surrounding the use of single indicator measures of the innovative performance at either the company or national level. To address these issues, we constructed a multi-indicator measure of innovation, which takes into account both efforts and outcomes related to innovative activities within a company. While this index approach is better than a single indicator approach, there are still a number of problems with the innovation scoreboard which should be noted when using it for benchmarking or competitor analysis.

In this section, we discuss two potential biases in our measurement and analysis of Australian company innovation. The first is that the index does not address the possibility of heterogeneity in defining innovation and valuing innovative investment both across companies and across sectors. Instead, we assume that a dollar spent on R&D in biotechnology has the same value (in terms of its effect on a company's measured innovative activity) as a dollar spent on R&D in the motor vehicle industry. Moreover, we assume that the value of a patent granted to one firm has the same value as that granted to another firm. This assumption of homogeneity in both the inputs and outputs of the innovation process is clearly unrealistic, especially in light of emerging evidence that the distribution of patent value is highly skewed: that is, only a very small proportion of patents generate substantial economic rents (see Allison et al. 2004). Including patents which have little economic value in our measure of innovation seems to be counter-intuitive but it is very difficult to differentiate valuable patents from the rest: some have tried to use patent citations as a proxy for value but even this has its limitations (see Narin 1999).

It is also apparent that patents (and trademarks) might not be the only way companies protect their inventions. In fact, companies such as Coca-Cola often rely on trade secrecy to protect inventions and there is evidence suggesting that trade secrecy is a more important source of protection than patents (see Cohen et al. 2000). Unfortunately, data on the use of trade secrecy is not readily available. As a result, we are not able to include such measures in the specification of the company market value function which may result in a classic 'omitted variable bias' in the estimation of the regression coefficients ($\hat{\lambda}_1 \ldots \hat{\lambda}_4$) on which the innovation index is based.[14] One common solution to this problem is to include a fixed-effect term in equation (9.4) and estimate it in a panel data analysis framework. The idea is that the fixed-effect term would capture any unobserved company heterogeneity that affects the company's market value and is not yet accounted for by other observed characteristics.[15]

The second problem with the innovation scoreboard is that it does not include any data on small and medium enterprises (SMEs) since accounting data on these firms are difficult to obtain. Data on the patent, trademark and design activity by SMEs is available but, without data on R&D expenditure, it is not possible to construct the innovation index for these firms. Unfortunately, the accounting data set used to construct the innovation scoreboard – IBISWorld – does not include data on SMEs. This may constitute a major problem since it is possible that there are SMEs that are highly innovative but will not be reported as so.

However, the extent of this problem is unclear since there is no conclusive empirical evidence supporting the notion that firm size is related in any systematic way to innovativeness. Schumpeter (1934) argued that large firms are more innovative since they have the retained earnings with which to reinvest in risky innovative activities. However, it has also been argued that SMEs may have some distinct advantages in innovation since they may have better information about the function that relates expected profitability of an innovation to development expenditure (see Arrow 1983) and that they may have less inertia than large firms and are therefore able to recognize (and take advantage of) market niches (see Rogers 2004).

6 CONCLUSION

This chapter has examined two interrelated issues in the study of the innovativeness of Australian enterprises: first, how to construct a multi-indicator innovation index and, second, how to interpret and analyse the index. Overall, in illustrating various ways to interpret the computed index, we found that a multiple indicator that takes into account both innovative inputs and inputs can be quite illuminating. For example, in a cross-section analysis, by combining with an enterprise survey data, we learned that our innovation index confirmed the popular notion that top innovators were those which were more active in pursuing direct information about their business environment and more willing to change whenever presented with opportunities. Adding the time-series dimension, interestingly, we also found the indicator's ability to capture the degree of persistence in innovative performance of top-ranked enterprises, as well as the wide variations of performance across companies, sectors and over time. For the future, a more detailed study of the underlying factors of these findings would help explain some of the determinants of innovative activity at the company level.

NOTES

1. The analysis draws on the innovation index reported in the annual series 'Research and Development and Intellectual Property (IP) Scoreboard' published jointly by the Intellectual Property Research Institute of Australia (IPRIA) and the Melbourne Institute of Applied Economic and Social Research in collaboration with IP Australia and IBISWorld.
2. Note that only inventions that are eligible for patenting since a requirement of patents is that they are novel (that is, new to the world).
3. Innovation that is new to the world is a much riskier prospect than innovation that is new to the firm and therefore involves higher expected returns since a risk-averse inventor will charge a premium for bearing risk.
4. The discussion in this section draws on Feeny and Rogers (2003).
5. See also Hall (2000) and Hall and Oriani (2004).
6. It is not clear whether or not those companies which do not report any R&D expenditure are actually zero spenders in terms of R&D or whether this observation is just missing.
7. The sample period is chosen simply based on the availability of market value data at the time the analysis was conducted.
8. See IPRIA (2004) for a more detailed presentation of the results.
9. Due to the limited size of the sample within each sector, in particular scientific research and printing, publishing and recorded media, the ranking of the sectors should be taken as indicative only.
10. Note that there is an important caveat to this statement: because of data constraints, only medium and large companies are included in the innovation scoreboard. The implications of this are discussed in section 5 of this chapter.
11. See the second appendix of Griffiths and Webster (2004) for a more detailed description of this survey.
12. See IPRIA (2000), (2001), (2003) and (2004) for more detailed results.
13. The innovative performance score is the actual value of I_{it} for each company in each year rather than the normalized score described earlier.
14. Griffiths and Webster (2004) found strong evidence that unobservable characteristics that are correlated with variables such as work culture and managerial style influence the company's decision regarding which appropriability methods to use to protect their invention.
15. Note that this solution only fixes the estimates of the weights of the innovation index. It still has not fixed the bias against companies which rely more on trade secrecy rather than patents.

176   *IP and company performance*

REFERENCES

Allison, J.R., M.A. Lemley, K.A. Moore and R.D. Trunkey (2004), 'Valuable patents' *Georgetown Law Journal*, **92** (3), pp. 435–80.

Arrow, K.J. (1983), 'Innovation in large and small firms', in J. Ronen (ed.), *Entrepreneurship*, Lexington, MA: Lexington Books.

Arundel, A. and I. Kabla (1998), 'What percentage of innovations are patented? Empirical estimates for European firms', *Research Policy*, **27**, 127–41.

Australian Bureau of Statistics (ABS) (2004), *Research and Experimental Development, Businesses Australia*, cat. no. 8104.0, September.

Cohen, W.M., R.R. Nelson and J.P. Walsh (2000), 'Protection their intellectual assets: appropriability conditions and why US manufacturing firms patent (or not)', NBER working paper series 7552, Washington, DC: National Bureau of Economic Research.

Drucker, P.F. (1986), *Innovation and Entrepreneurship: Practices and Principles*, New York: Harper and Row.

Feeny, S. and M. Rogers (2003), 'Innovation and performance: benchmarking Australian firms', *Australian Economic Review*, **36** (3), 253–64.

Gans, J. and S. Stern (2003), 'Assessing Australia's innovative capacity in the 21st century', Melbourne Business School working paper 2003–16.

Griffiths, W. and E. Webster (2004), 'The determinants of research and development and intellectual property usage among Australian companies, 1989 to 2002', Melbourne Institute working paper no. 27/04.

Griliches, Z. (1981), 'Market value, R&D, and patents', *Economic Letters*, **7**, 183–7.

Hagedoorn, J. and M. Cloodt (2003), 'Measuring innovative performance: is there an advantage in using multiple indicators?', *Research Policy*, **32**, 1365–79.

Hall, B.H. (2000), 'Innovation and market value', in R. Barrel, G. Mason and M. O'Mahoney (eds), *Productivity, Innovation and Economic Performance*, Cambridge: Cambridge University Press.

Hall, B.H. and R. Oriani (2004), 'Does the market value R&D investment by European firms? Evidence from a panel of manufacturing firms in France, Germany, and Italy', National Bureau of Economic Research working paper 10408.

International Property Research Institute of Australia (IPRIA) (2004), *R&D and Intellectual Property Scoreboard 2004: Benchmarking Innovation in Australian Enterprises*, Intellectual Property Research Institute of Australia, University of Melbourne.

Jensen, P.H. and E. Webster (2004), 'Examining biases in measures of firm innovation', IPRIA working paper 05/04, Melbourne: University of Melbourne.

Narin, F. (1999), 'Tech-line background paper', vol. mimeo CHI Research, Haddon Heights, NJ.

Rogers, M. (2004), 'Networks, firm size and innovation', *Small Business Economics*, **22**, 141–53.

Schumpeter, J.A. (1934), *The Theory of Economic Development: An Inquiry into Profits, Capital, Credit, Interest and the Business Cycle*, Cambridge, MA: Harvard University Press.

PART IV

Understanding the use of intellectual property by firms

10. Intellectual property and company performance: company case study evidence

Derek Bosworth

1 INTRODUCTION

It is generally recognized that IP only gives competitive advantage if it is not also used by rivals. This can be achieved in a variety of ways, most of which, perhaps with the exception of speed to market, involve IPRs.[1] These IPRs take many forms: patent protection for inventions, trademark (TM) protection for brands, trade secrets for in-house knowledge enabling faster speed to market, and so on. Essentially, their aim is to protect the discretionary investments of individuals and companies in various creative activities (that is, R&D, marketing, design, composition, and so on), enabling them to recoup their investment expenditures. It is argued that the absence of IPRs would reduce if not eliminate the incentives for creative activity, for example, reducing the flow of inventions, and thereby adversely affecting the dynamic performance of companies.

This chapter takes the IPR system as it currently stands and explores how IPRs can be used by companies to improve their dynamic performance. It illustrates the main points using examples taken from a large number of individual case studies. The case study literature is quite distinct from the econometric estimates. Not only do the two approaches use different methods and data (for example, individual, often in-depth interviews versus large-scale data interrogated using econometric methods), they also have very different foci. The case study evidence, taken in the round, is able to offer a much broader perspective, and can be used to add some flesh to the bones provided by the econometric estimates.

One stream of the literature portrays IP as a particular category of intellectual capital (IC), which is argued to comprise human capital, relational capital and organizational capital, where the last of these can be subdivided into IP and infrastructure capital (Brooking 1998, p. 13; Lynn

179

1998, p. 14). While it is useful to categorize the assets in this way, doing so tends to underplay the dynamic interaction between assets, the major differences in the mix of such assets across organizations and the manner in which assets such as IP play a core role in business strategy. Given the diverse range of assets that the literature on IC covers, it adds little to our understanding of the management and value of IP; the case studies reported by Lynn (1998, pp. 22–37) say nothing about IP per se.

This chapter draws upon information built up during case studies of IP and IPRs by the author and illustrates them with examples drawn from other sources, such as the WIPO SME case study website.[2] Section 2 considers the value of patent disclosure to performance as a source of technical information that firms can use in their creative activities, as a strategic device to hinder other companies inventive activities and as a 'shop window' to potential clients. Section 3 examines patent (and other IPR) watching and search mechanisms for discovering what rivals and potential takeover targets and collaborators are doing. Section 4 looks at the use of patenting as a mechanism for triggering rewards that incentivize employees. Section 5 considers the role that IPRs play not only in attracting investors, but also as collateral for raising funding. Section 6 turns to the role of IPRs in allowing the licensing of the firm's technology. Section 7 considers the use of cross-licensing and patent pooling to improve the freedom to operate and increase access to technologies owned by other companies. Section 8 looks at IP and IPRs as a key strategic focus of the enterprise. It attempts to show how different IP and IPR strategies are woven into the business strategy of the firm. Section 9 examines the role of IPRs in protecting the firm against infringement, thereby enabling it to recoup its R&D and marketing outlays and improve its dynamic performance. Finally, Section 10 outlines the main conclusions from this chapter.

2 THE VALUE OF DISCLOSURE

2.1 As a Source of Technical Information

Patents are used by some companies as a source of technical information. The technical information disclosed in the patent should describe the invention sufficiently well to enable any person 'skilled in the art' (at the time of the invention) to reproduce the invention without undue experimentation. In the surveys that take place on sources of information, patent disclosure normally comes towards the bottom of the ranking, although such surveys generally show it to be much more important for larger companies, particularly in sectors such as chemicals, electronics and engineering. However, examples can also be found on the WIPO database about individual inventors and

SMEs.[3] One describes how Takashi Ishikawa gave up working as a carpenter to launch a new business. He wanted to invent a method of reducing the high death rate from cerebral apoplexy caused by low winter temperatures in Japan. The solution used strong iron plates with added heat insulation on one side for the exterior walls. Given the urethane filling in the mattress of his futon kept him warm, he decided to investigate whether it could act as the insulating material. Ishikawa consulted patent disclosures, to obtain a wide range of useful technical information on urethane, but also discovered that the basic patent was due to expire in 1971 and related patents in 1973, allowing him to use the prior art without paying a licence fee. Takashi Ishikawa is now President of IG Kogyo, which has the highest domestic share in the market for heat-insulated metal sidings for exterior walls, and exports the product overseas. Today IG Kogyo owns more that 10 000 individual IPRs, which is exceptional for a relatively small company.

2.2 As a Strategic Device

Baker and Mezzetti (2001) argue that firms disclose a surprisingly large amount of information in their patents. Conventional wisdom suggests that such disclosures are made for defensive purposes; as the firm does not plan to pursue the technology, the information is disclosed to prevent rival companies from patenting. The authors, however, argue that there is another reason – if an invention of a given quality would have been granted patent protection prior to the disclosure, the disclosure raises the height of the hurdle to be jumped, extending the patent race. They study 13 854 utility patents issued by the United States Patent and Trademark Office (USPTO) from 1996 to 2001, for which IBM was the assignee. They found that 2310 of them cite at least one article from the *IBM Technical Disclosure Bulletin* as 'prior art'. The prior art consists of all earlier received knowledge, patents or published papers which a searcher in the patents office thinks are close to the invention (Irish 2000, p. 72). Thus, approximately one in six IBM patents cite IBM's own disclosures, suggesting the disclosures could not have been defensive. They check if IBM changed their policy, and returned to areas where they had originally made a decision not to work. In practice a sufficiently high proportion of the citation lags are so short to suggest that this is not the case. They conclude that IBM is often disclosing information about technologies it is actively pursuing.

2.3 As a Shop Window

In a case study of Lotus Cars, it became clear that various forms of IP and IPRs are used an important 'shop window' (Bosworth and Pitkethly

2004). Lotus is a medium sized UK-based company.[4] Lotus Cars has two main divisions: (1) sports car production; (2) engineering consultancy, which provides engineering solutions, primarily for original equipment manufacturers in the automobile sector. This takes place in several ways. First, the company partially discloses ideas and concepts at technical conferences and fairs. The engineering consultancy division relies heavily on learning from other players in the sector, including competitors and clients. Presenting state-of-the-art ideas helps to raise Lotus's profile with potential clients and is part of the sharing of knowledge that helps Lotus make new technological advances. Second, the company constructs demonstration vehicles embodying its technologies to demonstrate to potential clients that it could be engineered into their vehicles. Finally, Lotus use patents as a form of accreditation of their technological prowess. This is particularly important in the Asia Pacific, as the patents in these markets form 'shop windows' that promote and enable the selling of services or licences into those territories.

Copyright collectives also form a shop window in which composers, musicians and the like can display their music. Examples include the American Society of Composers, Authors, and Publishers (ASCAP) and Broadcast Music Incorporated. These organizations act as non-exclusive licensing agencies for composers, issuing most of the US public performance licences permitting copyrighted songs to be played for public consumption. These organizations gather together large numbers of compositions, which allow them to issue 'blanket licences' for all the music in their catalogues. This reduces transaction costs for radio and television stations using large volumes of music. The ASCAP distributes a proportion of the blanket licensing revenues to the individual copyright holders, based on the estimated number of uses of each composition.

3   TO MONITOR WHAT COMPETITORS AND POTENTIAL COLLABORATORS ARE DOING

One reason to monitor the patenting, TM and other IPR activities of companies is to ensure other firms do not infringe the company's IPRs and, likewise, that the company does not infringe other firms' IPRs. This can also save costly R&D effort in areas where patented inventions already exist. IP Australia report the case of L&R Ashbolt, a specialized surface engineering company,[5] which use IP Australia to carry out extensive patent searches in Japan, the UK, the USA and elsewhere. The company argues that,

IP Australia's patent search facility ensures we won't waste valuable time and dollars developing something on which someone else has spent $100,000 and two years. We don't copy patents that already exist – they just give us an idea of a direction we could follow and improve on. Examining competitors' patents also provides us with invaluable marketing knowledge.

A good patent or TM search provides an indication about likely infringement, but no patent search is foolproof. In a similar way, TMG, a small Spanish firm producing metal fixing elements for the illumination sector, makes extensive use of technological watching services of the Spanish patent office to monitor competitors' products and the market. In addition, TMG's personnel undertake regular field surveillance of technological developments by attending professional meetings and industrial fairs.

Burrone outlines the concept of 'freedom to operate' (FTO), which relates to the likelihood that an inventing company will infringe other firm's patents in areas of technology they want to develop and allow access to technology that will be useful in their inventive efforts. For example, Cambridge Antibody Technology, Micromet AG and Enzon Pharmaceuticals signed a non-exclusive cross-licence agreement in September 2003.[6] This gave all the parties substantial FTO by allowing access to each other's IP, with a view to developing new therapeutic and diagnostic antibody products. Such agreements have become common in certain sectors, reducing the likelihood of infringement and litigation. In the extreme, invention may be blocked for one company by the patents of another, and vice versa. Hence, some agreement between the companies to allow access to each other's technology makes sense. Note that the issue is not always to do with competitors, it relates to any area of technology that would be useful in the invention process. There are many ways of overcoming a lack of FOT, including not inventing, inventing around the patent, operating in markets where patents have not been taken out, purchasing the blocking patent, licensing, cross-licensing and patent pooling. A number of these are discussed below.

4 TO INCENTIVIZE RESEARCHERS

The award of patent rights to an organization can be used to incentivize employees. There is a long history of debate in the USA over the protection of IP, in particular patenting, by the universities (Mowery and Sampat 2000). Perhaps the most significant move was the introduction of the Bayh–Dole Act, 1980, which permits universities and other non-profit institutions to obtain patent rights over the outputs of federally sponsored research (Cohen and Walsh 2000). The rationale for Bayh–Dole lay in the belief that there was an under-exploitation of commercially valuable knowledge within the universities and other research institutions that received federal funding. The argument was that the award of patents to universities would 'incentivize' downstream research and commercialization by private sector companies, as well as encouraging technology transfer by universities (Mazzoleni and Nelson 1998). This has led to universities using patenting activity as a basis for rewarding staff who invent, through salaries and/or promotion.

The US Stevenson–Wydler Act, enacted in 1986 (and amended by the National Technology Transfer and Advancement Act, 1995), mandated the sharing of not less than 15 per cent of the royalties and other payments received by the employer with the employee-inventors if the rights are assigned to a US government agency or a prime contractor. The logic is that employees would file the appropriate paperwork if there were stronger incentives. In the case of the University of Kentucky, for example, the university reports that it usually takes one of the following approaches to structuring an IP licence agreement: royalties, licence initiation fee, milestone payments or equity in the company.[7] After the recovery of patent costs, the UK returns 40 per cent of all royalties to the inventor(s), 20 per cent to the inventor's department, 20 per cent to the inventor's college and the remaining 20 per cent is reinvested in research programmes and activities within the university.

Private sector employers are less likely to share royalties with employee-inventors, nevertheless, they are likely to result in cash awards, salary increases, promotions, public praise and prestige for employee-inventors. There appear to be few case studies of this topic, however, Sosnin (2000) reports that, when an invention leads to a patent, Motorola pays a bonus to the employee or employees. This mechanism encourages employees to share their expertise and endure the lengthy and resource intensive patenting process. The author reports that both Motorola and IBM see patent incentive programmes as being useful in raising the awareness of staff about the importance of IP. Motorola's programme gives a cash bonus to inventors when the application for a patent is filed and another bonus when granted. The company also gives a further reward when an employee achieves their tenth patent. If a patent generates revenues for the company, Motorola generally gives the inventor between $10 000 and $40 000, depending on the estimated commercial value of the patent. Sosnin (2000) also reports on a similar system operating at HNC Software, a much smaller San Diego based company.

It is important in such incentive programmes that the employee's contract makes it clear that the company owns the patent. In some contracts, employees assign all rights to the company, while others cover all inventions related to the company's business. Such contracts invariably include a confidentiality clause requiring employees to keep the invention secret. The absence of such agreements can result in litigation between the employee and the employer. Other messages from companies using such schemes were to consult employees early in the process to find out what motivates them, to make procedures standard, as with Motorola and HNC, with in-house forms that allow employees to alert the company to potential patentable inventions and to designate an administrator for patent applications so all parties have a single point of contact.

5   AS A SOURCE OF FUNDING

5.1   Using IP to Attract Investors

As patents give the owner a monopoly to exploit the technology for up to 20 years, this provides a major incentive for investors to commercialize and exploit the invention, in their search for abnormal profits. Further incentive is given by the presence of strong TMs that clearly identify and distinguish the associated product and company from others operating in the same area. Burrone (WIPO SME website) argues that systematically evaluating the company's FTO prior to launching a new product is not only a way of minimizing the risk of infringing, but also a way of improving the chances of finding business partners and attracting investors to support the company's business plans.

Strong IP protection provided an incentive to investors in the development and commercialization of Emergency Autotransfusion Set (EAT-SET). The EAT-SET, invented by Dr Ovadje in Lagos, is a technique for recovering blood out of the body during operations, filtering it and then re-infusing it into the patient. It prevents the transmission of diseases, avoids immunological complications of standard transfusion procedures and permits more flexible use of blood bank supply.[8] The project started in 1989, financed by the Nigerian government with just US$120, before attracting further funding from the United Nations Development Programme. With UNDP's help Dr Ovadje acquired patent and TM protection for EAT-SET in nine foreign countries. In 2001, EAT-SET Industries was established to commercialize the invention and to design new medical tools appropriate to developing countries, which cannot afford more sophisticated technologies. Intellectual property rights stimulated investment in the company, which has grown from US$120 in 1989 to nearly US$100000 and, it is now reported that investors are willing to put in US$1 million.

5.2   As Collateral for Borrowing

Access to funding is essential for funding strategic investments. Historically, funding has been raised against tangible assets, but this is increasingly difficult in a more knowledge-based economy. This implies at least two things. First, that companies account for their intangible assets, particularly IP protected by IPRs (as this is the more easily quantified form of intangible). Second, that banks and other funding institutions have the capacity to measure the value of such intangibles and are willing to loan money using them as collateral. In the absence of these two factors, technological change and growth in the knowledge-based economy will be restricted. Table 10.1 provides evidence of the use of IP, protected by IPRs, as collateral for borrowing.

Table 10.1   Use of IP/IPRs as surety

Borrower	Type of IPR	Transaction Value	Year
Borden	Trademarks	$480 m	1991
Disney	Copyright portfolio	$400 m	1992
Liggett	Trademarks	$150 m	1992
Chemical Company	Patent portfolio	$100 m	1994
Calvin Klein	Trademarks	$58 m	1993
GE Capital	Trademarks	NA	1995
Fashion Company	Trademarks	$100 m	1996
News Corporation	Copyright	$260 m	1996
Nestlé	Trademarks	NA	1996
David Bowie	Copyright portfolio	$55 m	1997

Source: Bezant and Punt (1997, p. 46).

The Australian Broadcasting Authority provides a practical example in its accounts for 1997–98 (see Figure 10.1).[9] Even though real liabilities have always been less than total real assets, they have always exceeded the real value of tangible assets. Thus, overall, ABA has borrowed against the value of its radio licences, which, in many cases, were obtained for negligible amounts. However, borrowing against intangible assets was much less in 1997–98 (A$175 m) than in 1987–88 (A$797).

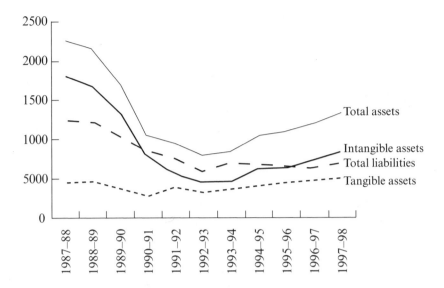

Figure 10.1   Australian Broadcasting Authority: real tangible, intangible and total assets, and real total liabilities, 1987–88 to 1997–98 [$m, 1997–98 prices]

6   TO ENABLE LICENSING OF OWN-TECHNOLOGY, TRADEMARKS, AND SO ON

Licensing implies that the IPR holder gives written authorization for another firm to use the patented technology for 'specified activities', in 'delimited markets', for a given period of time and defines what constitutes misuse (Chen 1996, p. 165). This applies to patents, TMs, copyright, and so on, as well as to franchising, which may involve no transfer of technology per se. In so far as trade secrets are also transferred, the agreement will also contain a confidentiality clause, restricting the information the licensee can disclose to third parties. Note that, while patent disclosure should enable someone 'skilled in the art' to repeat the invention, this will not be enough if the licensee is not sufficiently 'skilled in the art' (WIPO 1998, pp. 1 and 63–6). In addition, the patent says nothing about how best to commercially exploit the invention. The benefits of such an agreement to each party depends crucially on the transfer of know-how and technology, the terms and conditions of the licence, including the size and periodicity of royalty payments, and whether the agreement is exclusive or non-exclusive (see WIPO 1998, pp. 71–85).

The example of licensing given in many textbooks is the float glass process invented by Pilkington in 1959. The invention was protected by patents, which expired in the mid-1970s, and know-how protected by trade secrets. The invention radically improved the quality and reduced the price of glass. As Teece (2000, p. 225) points out: 'The consumer benefits flowing from lower prices, high quality and increased output, and the private benefits to licensees, dwarfed the returns to Pilkington itself.'[10] So why did Pilkington license the technology? Teece (2000, pp. 225–76) provides an excellent review of this case, along with estimates of the private and social returns from licensing. The present discussion is limited to the motivation for Pilkington undertaking licensing, rather than sole exploitation.

The answer to 'why licence?' can be traced to the characteristics of the company at the time of the invention. At that stage, Pilkington was a medium-sized, privately owned company, without access to major financial or managerial resources. Its resources had been depleted by the expensive R&D process that led to the invention. To fully exploit the invention itself, the company would have needed to be a large, global player, with the corresponding management skills and access to major funding. As a consequence, to commercialize the invention broadly and quickly, Pilkington licensed the technology to existing plate glass producers, which had the necessary industry knowledge and experience to successfully introduce it. The first non-exclusive licence was granted to PPG, a US plate glass manufacturer in 1962 and, by 1970, every remaining plate glass manufacturer in the world had licensed the technology. As the costs of production continued to fall, the process then replaced the previously cheaper, but lower quality, sheet glass. The licences were restricted to each producer's domestic market. Thus, competition was maintained in each market, and the price of glass was significantly lower than if Pilkington had been able to individually exploit it's monopoly worldwide. Over time, Pilkington's financial position improved with the flow of royalties and sales, and it became an international player, hence its strategy for exploiting the invention also changed (see Teece, 2000).

In a case study of Bishop Steering, IP Australia report that this Sydney-based firm profits from licensing its IP without losing ownership of the technology. Bishop, amongst the world leaders in power steering technology, has more than 500 patents and patent applications, earning more than A$7 million each year in royalties, mainly from overseas licensees. Bishop licenses some of the largest automotive and component manufacturers in the world and 25 per cent of all motor vehicles produced each year incorporate their technology. As in the case of Lotus, the royalties are largely reinvested in R&D. They adopted a licensing, rather than production strategy, which avoided the need to establish major manufacturing facilities and allowed entry into overseas markets without establishing overseas facilities. Bishop initially exclusively licensed its technologies; however, as its products became more accepted, in the early 1980s these licences were renegotiated, making them non-exclusive. This allowed Bishop to substantially broaden the user base of its technologies. As in the case of Lotus, working in broadly the same sector, it is difficult to build upon existing technologies if the company loses ownership of key patents in that area.

Teece (2000, pp. 209–11) provides an empirical exploration of the effects of Texas Instruments' (TI) change in licensing strategy since 1985 on its competitive and innovative position. The more aggressive licensing stance was a considerable risk, given it might have prompted other firms to challenge TIs' patents. In addition, Teece (ibid.) notes that, 'patent assertion against customers and partners is an especially sensitive area'. In practice, the benefits of the policy were enhanced by the stronger US treatment of IPRs after 1982. The result was cumulative royalty earnings of $1.8 billion from 1986 to 1993. As well as improving the company's bottom line, Figure 10.2 demonstrates that it enabled TI to maintain its R&D spend at a time of sector downturn. Teece (2000, p. 210) argues that TIs' IP portfolio also enabled the company to negotiate co-operative R&D agreements, including those with Hitachi, involving a series of projects relating to DRAM memory chips. The author argues that, 'TIs' ability to supply technology, supported by it's IP rights, was crucial to these agreements'.

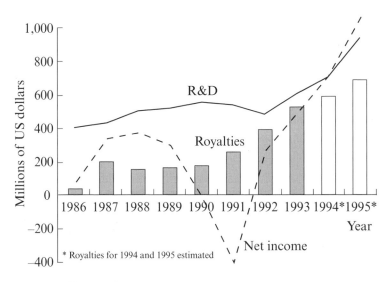

Source: Teece (2000, p. 210).

Figure 10.2   Texas Instruments: royalty earnings, net income and R&D

7   TO INCREASE FREEDOM TO OPERATE AND SECURE TECHNOLOGY FROM OTHERS

Patents can be viewed in two ways. They are: (a) a barrier to others using an inventive idea; (b) a lever to enable access to others' inventive ideas. Where a new field requires the use of disparate inventions (as was the case of radio), individual patents block the development of the technology. Only where these patents are in some sense shared or pooled, can the technology emerge. This can be done in a variety of ways (see also the discussion of FTO above).

7.1   Patent Pools

Patent pooling often occurs where overlapping or complementary patents owned by different parties are mutually blocking inventions. A patent pool involves two or more companies in a particular area of technology pooling their patents and establishing a clearing house for patent rights. Teece (2000, p. 194) argues that pooling is different from cross-licensing, as each member accesses the pool on the same terms and conditions. Merges (1998) adds that, such pools also generally offer standard licensing terms to potential licensees who are not pool members. He notes (p. 10) that,

> The most well-documented industry-wide pools arose in the automobile and aircraft industries around the turn of the twentieth century. In these cases representatives of the various members participate in the valuation of the patented technology. Each licensee of pooled technology is charged a royalty that is agreed upon by the pool committee. This basic structure appears in pools covering not only autos and aircraft, but also sewing machines, bathtubs, door parts, seeded raisins, coaster brakes, and a variety of other technologies.

He terms these 'mega-pools'. As an example of small pools, Merges (1998, pp. 24–5) reports on a 'simple contract' pooling agreement in the davenport bed industry in the 1930s,

> On November 3, 1916, a written agreement was entered into between the owners of … various patents [pertaining to folding davenport beds and similar devices], which provided for the granting of an exclusive license to the Seng Company … to manufacture and sell under all of said pooled patents, the specified royalties to be divided in stated proportions among the parties to said agreement. Of the total amount of said royalties, 33 per cent was allotted to the Pullman Couch Company. … The license contract of November 3, 1916, was signed by the Davoplane Bed Company and also by the Pullman Couch Company, as well as by [two inventors], individually. The Pullman Couch Company 'submitted' 13 patents to be controlled by the pool agreement, including two of the Bostrom patents, and the Davoplane Bed Company 'submitted' 7 patents, including one of the Bostrom patents. [An individual inventor] likewise 'submitted' one patent.

More recently, patent pools have been formed in the digital media area, used in consumer electronics products. Burrone (WIPO SME website) notes the patent pool formed by Sony, Philips and Pioneer for inventions that are essential to comply with certain DVD-Video and DVD-ROM standard specifications. Merges (1998, p. 28) notes that the MPEG2 pool and the DVD pools form an interesting new breed of patent pool, narrower than the mega-pools, as they only involve a single technology (rather than all patents in the sector), but broader than the simple contract pools, as they include various adjustment mechanisms (that is, for adding new patents and adjusting royalty shares).

7.2   Cross-licensing

Cross-licensing occurs when two (or more) companies exchange licences in order to be able to use the patented inventions of the other párty (or parties); see the case of the three pharmaceutical companies outlined above. Cross-licensing requires that the companies have well-protected patent portfolios of value to the other partners. Teece (2000, p. 206) reports on two types of cross-licences found in the semiconductor sector. First, 'capture agreements' enable the parties to use all the patents in the defined area of technology for a fixed period (often five years), including any patents taken out during that period.[11] Under this type of agreement, the parties have a right to use this cohort of patents until they expire. Second, in 'fixed period agreements' the right to use the patents terminates at the end of the agreed fixed period, and further use requires a new agreement. Teece notes that the use of 'capture agreements' became widespread in the sector because of their adoption by AT&T and IBM, but TI became the leader in the use of 'fixed period agreements', which are now increasing in popularity because of their flexibility, allowing adjustment in terms and conditions after the fixed period.

7.3   Access to Know-how and Technology

The rationale for undertaking cross-licensing can be illustrated using the press release[12] relating to the Cambridge Antibody Technology (CAT), Micromet AG and Enzon Pharmaceuticals agreement of 2003 (discussed above). Christian Itin, Micromet's Chief Business Officer commented: 'The SCA IP estate consolidated between Enzon and Micromet in 2002 and the CAT–MRC IP estate to antibody phage display are robust in their respective spaces. The present transaction provides each of the companies access to relevant complementary IP, supporting each company's business case on attractive commercial terms.'

Peter Chambré, CAT's Chief Executive Officer, commented,

We view this cross-license agreement with Micromet and Enzon as important to our commitment to the development and commercialisation of therapeutic antibodies. Not only does CAT obtain access to a broad commercial opportunity in SCA, but through this agreement CAT enjoys greater flexibility in respect of its collaboration partners. All three companies stand to benefit from this consolidation of intellectual property which underpins the exploitation of antibody-based drugs.

Uli Grau, Enzon's Chief Scientific Officer, commented: 'With this cross-licence Enzon is able to strengthen our leading position in the growing field of antibody therapies, which we intend to leverage to expand our product portfolio.'

7.4   Freedom to Operate

Teece (2000, p. 211) also refers to this as 'freedom to design'. The cases of RCA, IBM and TI all had elements of the need for FTO (ibid. pp. 215–16). RCA was faced by the need to access a wide range of patented technologies in order to manufacture radios. It did this by acquiring exclusive cross-licensed rights to the necessary technologies, and then licensed them out to other manufacturers, leading to its long-term dominant position in the market. Teece (2000, p. 215) argues that IBM's main concern was design freedom and access to the widest range of technologies, hence, the central role played by cross-licensing in its IP strategy. TIs' concern was FTO in semiconductors, characterized by high levels of patent concentration. Given the rather dominant nature of these large and powerful companies, they also earn considerable royalties from these cross-licences. In addition, Teece (2000) explains how these companies set about the licensing process, which can differ between licences and between companies.

8   AS A FOCUS FOR MANAGEMENT BEST PRACTICE

The introduction indicated that IP was only a part, although an integral part, of the IC of the enterprise, which accountants value as 'intangible assets'. Figure 10.3 shows the breakdown between the value the market placed on a number of companies and their balance sheet net assets (Buchan and Davies 1997). Today, for many companies, managing tangible assets focuses on the tip of the iceberg. The value of the tangibles reflects little more than the value an accountant thinks they might be sold for, independent of the core business. Thus, the intangibles are the core of the business and need to be integrated within the business strategy of the company. The remainder of this section demonstrates the need for a holistic approach to company decision-making, which integrates IP and IPRs.

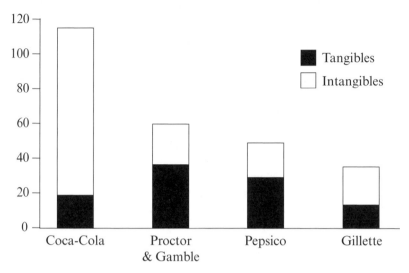

Source: Buchan and Davies (1997).

Figure 10.3   Sources of value: tangibles and intangibles

A case compiled by IP Australia discusses the IP strategy of the Dome Group of companies, producing ground coffee, which demonstrates the need for a holistic approach. The more extensive and aggressive IP strategy followed the appointment of John Groppoli as a director. Dome's strategy therefore is to protect and manage their IP assets. From a practical perspective this involves registering TMs with IP Australia and abroad, giving protection in the specified classes of the register. They also register their business name in each Australian state, to avoid inadvertent infringement. The company searches for any infringement using IP Australia's registered TM database, company names registers, telephone listings and the internet. Infringement is dealt with by letter in the first instance. Dome actively manage their trade secrets via confidentiality agreements with franchisees and through outlining the consequences of abuse in employee contracts. They strictly manage their franchise image, providing a guide on how franchisees can use their registered TMs, which precludes the use of the Dome name in franchisee company names. Finally, they place copyright notices on all press releases, marketing materials, training manuals, and so on, and ensure that all their externally produced materials are Dome copyright.

The case study of Lotus Cars provided an example where IP and the associated IPRs were fundamental to the business, and IP/IPR strategies were inextricably interwoven with the overall business strategy (Bosworth and Pitkethly 2004). Management of IP/IPRs was detailed and rigorous, with management processes to handle the risks and uncertainties (that is, whether to renew a patent or not) not only in place, but under review to see if better systems could be devised. Technological change and marketing were twin blades of the scissors that were brought together to obtain new business and increase the value of the Lotus brand. In addition, IPRs were used in a wide range of ways to benefit the company. Patents were used as a 'shop window' to attract clients as well as to protect core knowledge that underpins current projects and future areas of research. Trademarks were used to protect not only the company logo, but three-dimensional marks were used to protect the 'shape' of cars the company had produced. Patents and TMs were used in licensing activity, for example, in badging cars which Lotus had worked on for other companies.

Bishop Steering (IP Australia website) also take a holistic approach to their IP. In particular, they adopt what they call a 'layered IP structure' which protects not just the product, but also the process. Sharyn Ch'ang, from the Sydney law firm Gilbert & Tobin, who handle Bishop's account, argues that

> The time and dollars spent on adequately protecting IP is the best business insurance you can have. However, protecting the assets is not an end in itself. One's real commercial objective is to exploit the assets to generate revenue and to maximise profit and success, a strategic approach, encompassing all the elements above, is needed.

Her philosophy is that the company must: (1) identify all the IP they own; (2) record appropriate details about those assets in an IP asset register; (3) audit it periodically; (4) protect it wisely, using the most appropriate legal mechanisms; (5) value each IP asset and reflect this in the balance sheet; (6) ensure commercialization of new IP does not expose the company to risk – clear any new products and processes before marketing; (7) commercialize the property; (8) attribute ownership of IP so that others know who owns it; (9) enforce their rights when they are infringed or threatened; (10) develop and adhere to corporate policies and practices about handling and managing IP.

9   AS PROTECTION AGAINST INFRINGEMENT

Imitation of one company's new products or processes by another can have a devastating effect on sales, profits and brand value.

9.1 Protecting an Invention

Earlier, the discussion noted TIs' more aggressive stance to licensing fees in the 1980s. Here the discussion demonstrates that this was paralleled by increased litigation over patent rights, where it considered infringement to have taken place. In January 1986, TI filed suits against a number of Asia Pacific semiconductor manufacturers – Fujitsu, Hitachi, NEC, Oki Electric, Toshiba and Samsung – on the grounds that these firms were infringing its patents. A lengthy battle ensued, resulting in companies paying royalties of around $191 million in 1987, about the same as the companies made in profit from their operations (Pollack 1988). Granstrand (1999, p. 6) outlines a number of cases of damages awarded by the courts, the largest of which was US$1200 million, paid by Honeywell to Litton (overturned on appeal). The first half of 2002 saw a number of major patent damage awards and settlements, as shown in Table 10.2.

Table 10.2   Patent damages and settlements, USA, first half 2002

Patent damage award amount	
IGEN International Inc. v. Roche Diagnostics GmbH	$505 million
City of Hope National Medical Center, Arthur Riggs and Keiichi Itakura v. Genentech Inc.	$500 million
Internet Magic Inc. v. Netfax Inc	$114 million
BJ Services Co. v. Halliburton Energy Services Co	$98 million
Applied Biosystems/MDS Sciex v. Micromass Inc	$47 million
Patent damage settlement amount	
Intergraph Corp. v. Intel Corp	$300 million
ADC Telecommunications Inc. v. Thomas & Betts Corp. and Augat Communications Products Inc.	$30 million
Business Objects v. Cognos Inc.	$24 million
Berlex Laboratories Inc. v. Biogen Inc.	$20 million
Jupiter Media Metrix Inc. v. NetRatings Inc.	$15 million

Source: *The Recorder* 15 August 2002.

However, there is always a danger to the litigant; litigation by patent-holders often results in the alleged infringers making a counterclaim, challenging the validity of the litigant's patents. Choi (2003, p. 1) discusses the US case of Gemstar-TV Guide International Inc., which at the time held more than 190 patents relating to interactive television programming, and whose value was heavily dependent on its patent protection. This litigious company was established as the result of patent litigation between Gemstar and TV Guide. The Department of Justice approved the merger in 2000 as a settlement of disputes in which Gemstar sued TV Guide for the infringement its patents for on-screen interactive information about television programme listings. However, the merged company's IPR litigation against EchoStar, Scientific-Atlanta, Pioneer and SCI Systems failed in a key judgment by the International Trade Commission, and Gemstar's shares fell to a quarter of their earlier value.

Such cases are more generally settled out of court, often resulting in patent pooling or cross-licensing arrangements. Choi (2003, p. 2) gives the example of the litigation between Owens and Hartford between 1916 and 1924. The two companies held competing patents on processes for making glass containers. Owens held a patent on the 'suction-feeding' device and Hartford the 'gob-feeding' device. The companies settled their differences by cross-licensing. This was followed, in 1932, by an infringement claim by Hazel relating to the gob-feeding process. Although this claim was rejected by the courts, Hazel threatened to appeal and the two companies then agreed to cross-license. Choi reports that this also led to licence agreements between Hartford and other claimants.

9.2   Protecting a Design

Jain (WIPO SME website) reports on a small goldsmiths firm in Southern India. The firm designed and made ornaments sold directly to customers. They discovered that a large Indian conglomerate jewellery retail outlet was selling items based on their designs. They approached an IP attorney. Although they had not registered their designs under Indian design law, they were able to produce paper-based sketches and drawings of the items (protected automatically by copyright), which indicated the evolution of the designs. When legal notice was served, the conglomerate claimed to have developed the designs independently, and it was just chance that they looked alike. However, the goldsmiths were able to show that the conglomerate had purchased a few pieces of these items from them as New Year gifts. The absence of registered design protection threatened to make it very difficult to prove infringement. In this case, however, the meticulous record-keeping, not only of drawings and designs (dated, numbered, signed and properly filed), but also business transactions, allowed the goldsmiths to build a case under copyright law. The conglomerate agreed to settle out of court, paying a lump sum, agreeing to stop manufacturing the items and outsourcing their requirements over the next five years to the small firm – what started as an IP dispute turned into a business opportunity.

9.3　Protecting a Brand

Yang and Bosworth (2002) report on a case study of Manchester United's (MU) experience in China. This case indicated two main problems with MU's TM activity in China: (1) inconsistencies in the registration and administrative procedures; (2) counterfeiting of MU products. The present discussion concentrates on the second issue. Manchester United has found itself the subject of extensive counterfeiting, particularly in the Asia Pacific, of its kit, sports items and 'fanzine'. The cause of counterfeiting could be traced to the popularity of the brand in the face of inadequate purchasing power.

In addition to independent counterfeiters, MU faced problems with production overruns from companies that it licensed to produce international markets. Maintaining management control proved difficult owing to the distance and policing costs between the UK and China. Manchester United's only representative in the Asia Pacific in this regard was a TM agent in Hong Kong. The failure to discourage or prevent this form of counterfeiting was not helped by the rather loose wording of the contracts with the manufacturing companies. Other factors included the rather arm's length approach of the Chinese authorities and the inadequate penalties that were in place for infringement.

10　CONCLUSIONS

While econometric methods are able to provide important insights about the value of intangibles, to date they have thrown little light on the ways in which such assets are built or exploited. What becomes clear from the case study literature is that the way in which IPRs are used by companies is more complex than standard economic models suggest. The discussion has illustrated that there many different ways in which IPRs impact on performance, for example, as a shop window to attract new clients or as a strategic mechanism for making it harder for competitors to jump the novelty hurdle. It has also demonstrated the more holistic way in which companies protect their IP, with combinations of patents, TMs, trade secrets, and so on. This suggests that there are important synergies between the different IPRs, which could be explored in future case study and econometric work.

NOTES

1. The authors treat trade secrets as a form of IPR.
2. www.wipo.int/sme/en/.
3. Taken from *Experience of Japan* published by the Institute of Intellectual Property, Tokyo.

4. Although a wholly owned subsidiary of Proton, it operates entirely independently of its parent (Bosworth and Pitkethly 2004).
5. www.innovated.gov.au/Innovated%5Ccase_studies%5CAshbolt.pdf.
6. www.cambridgeantibody.com/html/news/press_releases/2003/2003_09_03_micromet_enzon.htm.
7. www.rgs.uky.edu/ip/licensing.html.
8. www.eatset.com.
9. www.aba.gov.au/radio/research/projects/commerc79_98/profit.htm.
10. Teece (2000, p. 225) estimates that Pilkington realized US$5.3 billion from the process, compared with a social benefit of around US$110 billion (both figures in constant, 1992 prices) – a smaller fraction than is normally the case.
11. The agreement may exclude certain key patents.
12. www.cambridgeantibody.com/html/news/press_releases/2003/2003_09_03_micromet_enzon.htm.

REFERENCES

Baker, S. and L. Mezzetti (2001), 'Disclosure and investment as strategies in the patent race', working paper, School of Law, University of North Carolina.

Bezant, M. and R. Punt (1997), *The Use of Intellectual Property as Security for Debt Finance*, London: Arthur Anderson and the Intellectual Property Institute.

Bosworth, D.L. and R. Pitkethly (2004), '*Group Lotus PLC: IP management and business strategy at Group Lotus PLC*', research report to the UKPO and the EPO, Oxford Intellectual Property Research Centre, St Peter's College, Oxford.

Brooking, A. (1998), *Intellectual Capital: a Core Asset for the Third Millennium Enterprise*, London: Thompson Press.

Buchan, E. and N. Davies (1997), 'Mergers and acquisitions', in R. Perrier (ed.), *Brand Valuation*, London: Premier Books.

Chen, M. (1996), *Managing International Technology Transfer*, London: International Thomson Business Press.

Choi, J.P. (2003), 'Patent pools and cross-licensing in the shadow of patent litigation', CESIFO working paper no. 1070, category 9: industrial organization, November.

Cohen, W.M. and J. Walsh (2000), 'Public research, patents and implications for industrial R&D in the drug, biotechnology, semi-conductor and computer industries', working paper, Carnegie Mellon University.

Granstrand, O. (1999), *The Economics and Management of Intellectual Property*, Cheltenam, UK and Northampton, MA, USA: Edward Elgar.

Irish, V. (2000), 'How to read a patent specification', *Engineering Management Journal*, April, 71–3.

Lynn, B.E. (1998), *The Management of Intellectual Capital: The Issues and the Practice*, Hamilton: Society of Management Accountants of Canada.

Mazzoleni, R. and R.R. Nelson (1998), 'Economic theories about the benefits and costs of patents', *Journal of Economic Issues*, **32** (4), 1031–52.

Merges, R. (1998), 'Institutions for intellectual property transactions: the case of patent pools', working paper, School of Law, University of California at Berkeley, (revised 1999).

Mowery, D.C. and B. Sampat (2000), 'University patents and patent policy debates: 1925–1980', presented at the Conference in Honour of Richard Nelson, Columbia University, 13–15 October.

Pollack, A. (1988), 'The new high-tech battleground', *New York Times*, section 3, 3 July.

Recorder, The (2002), *Patent Damages*, Thursday 15th August, p. 1, available at www. therecorder.com; reprinted at www.townsend.com/files/patentdamages.pdf.

Sosnin, B. (2000), 'A pat on the back', *HR Magazine*, March, pp. 1–2, available at http://www.findarticles.com/p/articles/mi m3495/is_3_45/ai 60904386.

Teece, D.J. (2000), *Managing Intellectual Capital*, Oxford: Oxford University Press.

World Intellectual Property Organization (WIPO) (1998), *Introduction to Intellectual Property: Theory and Practice*, London: Kluwer.

Yang, D. and D. Bosworth (2002), 'Manchester United versus China: the "Red Devils" trademark problems in China', working paper, www.derekbosworth. com.

11. Use of intellectual property by the UK financial services sector[1]

Mark Rogers and Christine Greenhalgh

1 INTRODUCTION

The purpose of this chapter is to provide new information on the intellectual property activity of UK financial sector firms. The database we have constructed allows us to document trademark applications, and UK and European Patent Office (EPO) patent publications for a sample of large UK companies over the period 1996–2000. Why should we be interested in this sector's intellectual property activity when most economic studies of R&D and IP confine themselves to an examination of firms in manufacturing industries?

Data from the Office of National Statistics (2004) shows that the 'financial services' sector accounted for 8.9 per cent of total gross value added in 2002, up from 8.2 per cent in 1992.[2] In comparison manufacturing accounts for around 19 per cent of gross value added. In terms of employment, the financial services sector accounts for around 16 per cent of total employment, with manufacturing having around 14 per cent of the total (Begum 2004, Labour Force Survey data). While the changing structure of the UK economy and the growing contribution of service sector firms has been well documented via such aggregate statistics, Greenhalgh and Gregory (2001) also stress the expanding role of financial and professional services as suppliers of intermediate inputs, reflecting increased inter-industry specialization. These authors have demonstrated that this rise in intermediate demand dwarfs even the large rise in direct final demand for services output. The same authors also calculated the extent to which services (especially financial services) acted both as suppliers of productivity growth via labour-saving production and as transmitters of R&D investments by manufacturing, through service sector use of hardware products developed in sectors such as electronics. Thus the financial services sector has come to play a role traditionally occupied solely by manufacturing, as an engine of productivity growth and as a key sector in the transmission of innovation, with consequent beneficial externalities yielding social returns within the economy.

A key feature of this growth through innovation was the rise of service product differentiation, within a financial sector that was able to increase rapidly its product range, using tools bought in from both manufacturing (for example, electronics and communications hardware) and other new services (such as computer software). Thus, although manufacturing has traditionally been seen as the sector most naturally associated with R&D and the patenting of tangible innovations, we expect to find evidence of innovation in services being reflected in a rise in registered trademark applications for the protection of new services. Despite widespread use of the trademark system, the literature on the value of trademarks in manufacturing is rather limited by comparison with that evaluating the returns to R&D and patents. However, the acquisition of a new trademark has been shown in an earlier study (Greenhalgh and Longland 2005) to have considerable value for manufacturing firms (increasing the firm's value added). We are interested to document the level and growth of acquisition of these IP assets for financial services, as a complement to our examination of whether they have similar economic value to these firms as to those in manufacturing, a topic we addressed in our analysis of the market value of IP in Chapter 7 (Greenhalgh and Rogers 2006).

2 THE OIPRC DATABASE

The foundation for the database used in our analysis is firm-level financial information obtained from 'Company Analysis' (Extel Financial 1996; Thomson 2001).[3] Specifically, we use balance sheet, profit and loss and associated accounting data from the published consolidated accounts of UK firms. The financial data included the usual items, such as sales, profits and R&D expenditure, where separately reported, and the end of accounting period share price if the company was publicly quoted, together with information on the industrial classification (SIC) for the principal product. The unique aspect of the database is that data on three forms of IP have been matched to the firm-level financial data: patents published via the UK, patents published via the European Patent Office (which designated the UK *inter alia*) and trademark applications via the UK office. These IP data were obtained from a range of sources (a list of data sources is given after the References). This chapter reports on the IP activity of firms in the finance, insurance and real estate sector and, in particular, how the activities of these firms compare with those in a wide range of manufacturing industries, and with transport, communications and utility firms.

In order to assess accurately the IP assets acquired by these companies, we needed to know which firm names formed part of the group reporting the (consolidated) accounts, in order to include all the IP that might have contributed to the overall performance of the financial group. We obtained 'Who Owns Whom' information as of December 2001 (Dun and Bradstreet International 2001) to determine the family trees of the (mainly UK-based) parent firms. (Difficult cases were resolved with the help of the Fame database – Bureau van Dijk 2003.) Searches for patent and trademark records were then conducted for the names of each parent and all of its subsidiary companies.

3   THE EXTENT OF IP ACTIVITY

Table 11.1 shows some summary statistics of the activity within each of the three broad sectors, namely, finance, insurance and real estate (FIRE), transport, communications, electricity, gas and water (TCEGW) and manufacturing. The top row of the table shows that the database has more firms in manufacturing than in either of the other sectors and, in terms of value added or employment, this sector is also larger.[4] However, the growth of value added and employment has been much higher in FIRE than in other sectors; in fact, firms in the other two sectors reduced their total employment over the sample period.

The central panel of Table 11.1 summarizes information on the IP and R&D activities for the sectors. Over the five years of available data the 317 firms in the FIRE sector made 4828 trademark applications, that is, around 15 per firm or five per thousand employees. While this is a substantial indication of new service products being offered, it is still a significantly lower rate of acquisition of these intangible assets than in TCEGW and manufacturing, where the typical firms registered 47 and 30 trademarks respectively, or at least seven per thousand employees.

Table 11.1 also shows that firms in the FIRE sector did obtain some patent publications. However, for EPO patents, two firms – BTG Plc and Scipher Plc – account for 218 of these applications, the vast majority of those recorded. Both of these firms are in the 'holding and other investment offices' industry and are, essentially, firms that develop and commercialise intellectual property. For UK patents, these two firms account for 44 of the 107 patents, with a range of other firms, especially banks, accounting for the others. We should also note at this stage that UK and EPO patents are substitutes to a large extent: both offer protection in the UK market and it is possible to extend the coverage of a UK patent publication to other countries.

Table 11.1 Activity by sector

	Finance, insurance and real estate (FIRE)	Transport, communications, electricity, gas and water (TCEGW)	Manufacturing
Number of firms	317	145	665
Value added (£bn, 2000)	59	34	146
% increase in value added (1996–2000)	36.0%	–15.4%	18.8%
Employment (000s, 2000)	947	894	2,851
% increase in employment (1996–2000)	28.9%	–11.6%	–1.3%
Total trademarks (1996–2000)	4828	6889	20074
Total UK patents (1996–2000)	107	141	2700
Total EPO patents (1996–2000)	226	535	4078
Total R&D (£m, 2000)	8	530	10857
Growth in trademarks (2000 vs 1996)	194%	59%	62%
Growth in UK patents (2000 vs 1996)	57%	65%	17%
Growth in EPO patents (2000 vs 1996)	43%	70%	26%

A further issue that stands out in Table 11.1 is that, as anticipated in the introduction, the FIRE sector has a negligible amount of reported R&D compared with the other sectors. Again, the bulk of the £8 million is carried out by BTG Plc and Scipher Plc (around 95 per cent) with only two other firms reporting small amounts. Over the entire 1996–2000 period there are only three other FIRE firms (apart from BTG and Scipher) that report any R&D in their accounts. This means that most firms in this sector are not likely to have benefited from the recent introduction of the R&D tax credit in the UK.

The last three rows of Table 11.1 show the growth in total numbers of trademarks and patent publications between the years 1996 and 2000. The relatively high rate of growth of trademarking for the FIRE sector stands out, although trademark growth is also considerably higher than patenting growth in manufacturing. Was this growth concentrated or dispersed over the firms in the sample?

Table 11.2 shows the percentages of firms that have used the three different forms of IP over the entire five-year period. Clearly, for firms in the FIRE sector, it is trademarking that dominates their interaction with IP, with 41 per cent of firms taking out one or more trademarks. Even so, this is a lower percentage than in either of the other two sectors. At this point it may be worth clarifying that 'trademark' can relate to a good or service (at least since 1984 when registration of 'service marks' were formally allowed), so there is no legal reason why differences should exist.

Table 11.2   Percentage of firms undertaking IP activity, by sector

	Finance, insurance and real estate (FIRE)	Transport, communications, electricity, gas and water (TCEGW)	Manufacturing
Firms that trademark in one or more years (1996–2000)	41.0	60.0	64.8
Firms that (UK) patent in one or more years (1996–2000)	4.4	16.6	38.2
Firms that (EPO) patent in one or more years (1996–2000)	2.8	10.3	29.0

A further issue to explore is whether the proportion of firms undertaking IP activity has changed through time. Figure 11.1 shows these statistics for trademark activity. It is clear that while firms in both the FIRE and TCEGW sectors have been increasingly using trademarks, the opposite has happened in manufacturing. Even so, by 2000 the annual trademarking propensities

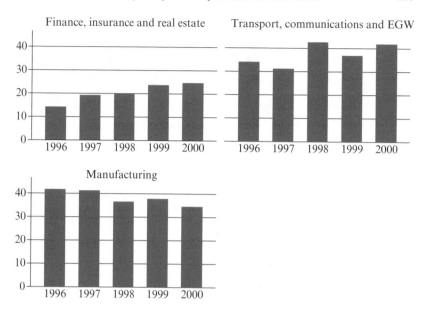

Figure 11.1   Percentage of firms trademarking, by sector and year

are still higher in manufacturing (and in utilities) than in FIRE. (Although not shown here, the equivalent bar charts for UK and EPO patenting show no trend for the FIRE sector.)

Table 11.3 breaks down the FIRE sector into its component two-digit industries. This table reveals the large differences in structure within the FIRE sector. The 'depository institutions' industry contains the major banks present in the UK, such as RBS, Barclays, HSBC and the like. Table 11.3 shows how this industry accounts for a huge slice of the value added in the FIRE sector. In terms of absolute numbers of trademarks banking also dominates, with almost 49 per cent of the sector total, followed by insurance carriers (such as CGNU, Friends Provident, Royal and Sun Alliance) with 18 per cent. However, in terms of trademarks per employee, which is a measure of the intensity of trademark activity, banking and insurance are respectively second to last and last. In contrast, the 'security and commodity brokers' industry, which comprises 33 very small firms, has 28.8 trademarks per thousand employees over the 1996–2000 period.

The Appendix contains trademark 'scoreboards' for each of the seven sub-sectors itemized in Table 11.3. These list all FIRE firms in the database that have some IP activity, along with their average number of trademarks per year. These scoreboards demonstrate that, even within the most active sectors of banking and insurance, there is extreme skewness in the

Table 11.3 Trademark activity by FIRE industry

Industry (two-digit US SIC)	Number of firms	Total trademarks (1996–2000)	Value added (£bn, 2000)	Employment (000s, 2000)	Trademarks per 1000 employees
Depository institutions (60)	24	2364	42.8	564	4.2
Non-depository institutions (61)	33	514	6.0	75	6.8
Security and commodity brokers (62)	33	141	0.6	5	28.8
Insurance carriers (63)	32	889	4.3	235	3.8
Insurance agents brokers and service (64)	8	45	0.3	6	7.6
Real estate (65)	117	530	3.2	44	12.2
Holding and other investment offices (67)	70	345	2.0	19	18.4
Total	317	4828	59.3	947	5.1

distribution of trademark applications. The typical pattern in all the sub-sectors is that just a few firms have very high rates per firm, a few more have low rates, but the majority have acquired no new trademarks in the period. This underlines our assessment that, as yet, the acquisition of IP assets is not a typical activity for firms in the financial services sector.

Even so, a few of our financial firms are matching the performance of firms in any sector, as shown by those reaching the top ten of the most recent statistics (Patent Office 2004). Our figures are not commensurate with these for a number of reasons: first, our figures for a given firm name relate to the group of firms (subsidiaries and associates) operating under the control of this parent firm; second, we are only able to record trademark applications, not successful registrations; and finally, these official statistics relate to a later year. Taking three examples from manufacturing: Glaxo Group Ltd, Unilever plc and Imperial Chemical Industries plc, firms which between them held the top two positions in 2002 and 2003 with rates ranging from 78 to 118 trademarks per year, we see that the trademark activities of Royal Bank of Scotland (including NatWest)[5] and Barclays have been sustained over 1996 to 2000 at comparable rates to these major chemical and consumer product companies.

4   THE DETERMINANTS OF TRADEMARK ACTIVITY FOR FINANCE SECTOR FIRMS

As shown in Table 11.2, around 41 per cent of finance sector firms applied for at least one trademark over the 1996 to 2000 period. In contrast, there were very few finance sector firms that applied for patents. In this section we investigate the characteristics of firms that applied for trademarks. We have already seen that the bulk of trademarking is from depository institutions – essentially the large banks that are familiar names on the high street. However, Table 11.3 also indicates that this industry has one of the lowest trademark rates per employee. This section analyses in more detail the relationships between trademarking, firm size and other firm-level characteristics.

One factor that may determine trademarking is the size of the firm with, perhaps, larger firms having more resources and management expertise to capitalize on IP. Figure 11.2 shows a plot of total trademarks against average employment (both taken for the period 1996–2000). It is clear that while there is evidence of a positive relationship, the plot shows the wide dispersion in trademarking. The Royal Bank of Scotland (RBS) and Barclays dominate the graph, both averaging over 100 trademarks per year. Over the period 1996–2000, the RBS registered a total of 861 trademarks and Barclays 559. In contrast, HSBC Holdings PLC which is a larger bank than either RBS or Barclays – applied for 108 trademarks. The plot therefore shows that there are substantial differences across firms in their strategy towards trademarking. Using employment as a measure of firm size has its drawbacks, since firms vary in income or assets per employee. However, the graph of trademarks versus total assets shows a similar pattern to Figure 11.2.

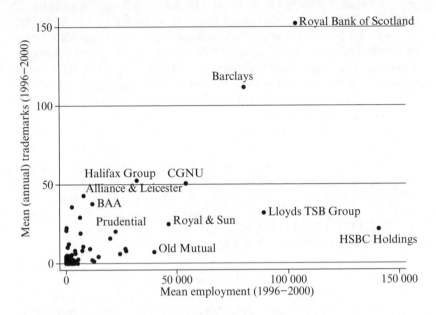

Figure 11.2   Trademarks and employment

Although there is clearly considerable heterogeneity in firms' trademarking activity, it is worthwhile analysing the average relationship between firm size and trademarking. Given the skewed nature of the distribution of both trademarks and firm size, it is normal to analyse this using a double log functional form. Figure 11.3 plots the relationship between the log of total trademarks (1996–2000) and log of average employment. The figure also shows the regression line that can be fitted through the data points. The specific equation for the regression is

$$\log TM = -1.94 + 0.39\log(employment) \qquad (11.1)$$

with both intercept and coefficient significant at the 1 per cent level. This indicates that a 1 per cent increase in employment yields, on average, only a 0.39 per cent increase in trademarks, so as firm size increases, the average number of trademarks per employee falls. This feature of the financial services sector mirrors findings for manufacturing and utilities, for which smaller firms showed greater intensity of both UK patent and UK trademark activity per employee (Greenhalgh and Longland 2001). The significance and magnitude of this regression relationship is robust to controlling for industry differences at the two-digit SIC level (that is, those shown in Table 11.3). Later in this section we develop this type of regression analysis; however, prior to this we consider two additional firm characteristics: whether the firm is listed on the stock market and the extent of diversification.

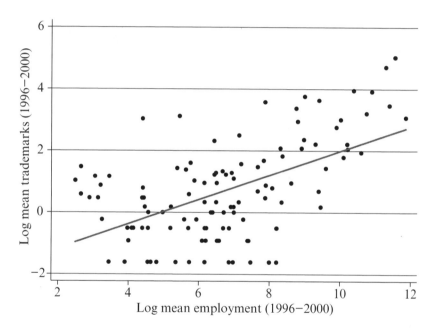

Figure 11.3   Log of total trademarks versus log of employment

Around 65 per cent of firms in the sample are listed on the stock market (the percentage varies slightly year-on-year). Table 11.4 below shows a cross-tabulation of listed status against whether the firm trademarked in a year (that is, there are 1585 observations (=317 firms × 5 years) in the table). As can be seen from the table, there is little difference in the propensity to trademark for listed and non-listed firms. This suggests that the greater media and investor exposure associated with listed status does not influence the decision to trademark.

Table 11.4   Trademarking and stock market listing (1996–2000)

	No trademark	Trademark(s)	Total
Unlisted	438	118	556
%	34.7	36.7	35.1
Listed	825	204	1029
%	65.3	63.4	64.9
Total	1263	322	1585
%	100	100	100

Note: A chi^2 test (0.43) rejects the null hypothesis of a significant association.

A second characteristic of interest is the extent of firm diversification. There is an extensive debate concerning whether focused firms have greater performance or whether diversification does, on average, yield economies of scope (see Rogers 2001). The available data only allow a crude measure of diversification: the number of four-digit US SIC codes that the firm reports to be active in. Using these data, a dummy variable called 'high' diversification is created if the firm has activities in four or more four-digit SICs and this is tabulated against trademarking in Table 11.5. This table shows that while the aggregate propensity to trademark in a given year is 20.3 per cent, for firms with 'high' diversification the figure is 27.9 per cent. It is likely that 'high diversification' is closely linked to firm size; hence there is the possibility that firm size is driving the relationship seen in Table 11.5, something we analyse below using multivariate regression analysis.

Table 11.5   Trademarking and diversification (1996–2000)

	No trademark	Trademark(s)	Total
Low diversification	827	153	980
%	84.3	15.6	
High diversification	436	169	605
%	72.1	27.9	
Total	1263	322	1585
%	79.7	20.3	

Note: A chi^2 test (53.1) supports the null hypothesis of a significant association.

Table 11.6 shows a series of regressions on all available firm-year observations in the data. The first column shows the results from a probit model, where the dependent variable is a dummy for whether a firm trademarks in a given year. As can be seen, it is firm size that dominates the regression, showing a positive and highly significant coefficient. The regression also controls for listed status, diversification, industry dummies (at two-digit level) and a time trend. Note also that the time trend is positive and significant, suggesting that the proportion of firms trademarking is increasing through time, confirming the indication from Figure 11.1. The second column of results uses the log of trademarks as the dependent variable. This effectively removes firms with zero trademarks in a given year, hence substantially reducing the sample size. The results confirm the relationship between firm size and number of trademarks, although the coefficient is lower that in the simple regression shown in (11.1). As with the probit regression, the results also show no role for listed status or the extent of diversification. Furthermore, in this regression the time trend is positive, although not significant, suggesting that the average number of trademarks per firm has not been rising (significantly) over the period. The final column of the table considers the determinants of the *intensity* of trademarking, where this is measured by trademarks per employee. This is, in effect, a method of controlling for the impact of firm size. The results from this regression indicate trademark intensity has a *negative* relationship with firm size: larger firms make less trademark applications per employee. In

Table 11.6   Multivariate regression analysis

Estimator Dependent variable	Probit Trademark dummy	OLS Log(trademarks)	OLS Trademark per employee
Log of employment	0.383	0.326	–0.067
	[12.68]***	[6.38]***	[1.79]*
Listed (=1)	–0.188	0.015	–0.093
	[1.44]	[0.08]	[0.93]
High diversification (=1)	0.028	–0.05	0.084
	[0.26]	[0.28]	[0.99]
Time trend	0.179	0.066	0.003
	[4.72]***	[1.25]	[0.38]
Constant	–3.083	–0.613	0.484
	[8.49]***	[1.59]	[1.88]*
Observations	1101	266	266
R-squared	0.35	0.27	0.2
F test: Joint sig. of ind. dummies	22.1	2.67	0.63
Prob>F	0.00	0.02	0.70

Note: t-statistics are shown under each coefficient; * means the coefficient is significantly different from zero at the 10 per cent level; ** significant at 5 per cent; *** significant at 1 per cent. These OLS estimates have White's robust standard errors.

the trademark intensity regression, the other coefficients on the explanatory variables are not significantly different from zero indicating, for example, that there has been no upward trend in trademarking per employee over the sample period.

5 CONCLUSIONS

The strong growth and development of the financial services sector in the UK has been accompanied by a rise in the acquisition of intangible assets in the form of intellectual property rights held by firms in this sector. The main type of IP asset acquired was trademarks, with only a few venture capital companies reporting R&D expenditure or acquiring patents. This pattern is consistent with the development of new varieties of financial services products, using new process technology bought-in from the manufacturing sector. Over the 1996–2000 period 41 per cent of finance sector firms took out one or more trademarks. The number of trademark-active firms in each year is lower than this, but did increase over time (from 14.2 per cent in 1996 to 24.6 per cent in 2000). Despite this growth, the incidence of new trademarks during 1996–2000 for financial service firms was still zero in over three-quarters of finance sector firms in any given year; this is below the rates in the manufacturing and utilities sectors.

Although large firms account for much of the observed trademark activity, smaller firms make more trademark applications per employee. These patterns can also be seen by looking at separate industries within the finance sector. The 'depository institutions' industry, which contains the large banks, accounts for almost half of all trademarks in the finance sector database; in contrast, the smaller firms in the 'security and commodity brokers' industry together account for only around 3 per cent of finance sector trademarks, but have the highest number of trademarks per employee. We find no significant association between whether a firm is stock market listed and its propensity to acquire trademarks. There does appear to be a bivariate association between a measure of firm diversification and trademarking (firms that are active in four or more four-digit SICs are more likely to trademark), but we cannot rule out that this association is due to a firm size effect.

NOTES

1. The financial services database developed for analysis in this chapter was derived by Mark Longland at the Oxford Intellectual Property Research Centre (OIPRC), St Peter's College,

working with the authors and with the financial support of ESRC award RES-334-25-0002 under The Evolution of Business Knowledge Programme. Funding was received at various times from the ESRC, the Leverhulme Trust and the UK Patent Office for the development of the comparison database on manufacturing and utilities firms. We are grateful to St Peter's College for accommodation and administrative support for this research.
2. 'Financial services' contains banking, insurance, pensions, auxiliary financial services and real estate (dealing and estate agents). It excludes 'letting of dwellings', which accounts for around 7 per cent of gross value added.
3. The firms are primarily UK firms, but a few Irish firms were also included, amounting to less than 4 per cent of the sample in each of the three sectors analysed here.
4. These data are based on firms in the database, which is dominated by large firms that have publicly available accounts. Office of National Statistics data report that the gross value added (GVA) for the manufacturing accounting is £154 billion in 2000, with 'transport, communications and EGW' having a GVA of £84.5 billion. In contrast, the FIRE sector in the national accounts has a GVA of £240 billion and within this 'real estate, renting and business activities' having a GVA of £194 billion. Our interpretation is that this sector has a large number of small firms that are not covered by our database.
5. The RBS took over NatWest Bank in February 2000, hence our ownership data from December 2001 includes NatWest (and all of its 375 subsidiaries) as a subsidiary of RBS. Thus, in terms of the IP data, 'RBS' is RBS–NatWest for the entire period under analysis. In terms of financial data, only 2000 has consolidated data. To avoid dropping RBS from the sample, we adjust RBS employment and asset data to include those of NatWest in the years 1996–99.

REFERENCES

Begum, N. (2004), 'Employment by occupation and industry', National Statistics, www.statistics.gov.uk/downloads/theme_labour/emp_by_occ_ind.pdf.
Greenhalgh, C.A. and M.B. Gregory (2001), 'Structural change and the emergence of the new service economy', *Oxford Bulletin of Economics and Statistics*, **63**, special issue: The Labour Market Consequences of Technical and Structural Change.
Greenhalgh, C.A. and M. Longland (2001), 'Intellectual property in UK firms: creating intangible assets and distributing the benefits via wages and jobs', *Oxford Bulletin of Economics and Statistics*, **63**, special issue: The Labour Market Consequences of Technical and Structural Change.
Greenhalgh, C.A. and M. Longland (2005), 'Running to stand still? The value of R&D, patents and trademarks in innovating manufacturing firms', *International Journal of the Economics of Business*, November **12** (3).
Greenhalgh, C.A. and M. Rogers (2006), 'Market valuation of UK intellectual property: manufacturing, utility and financial services firms', chapter 7 of this volume: D. Bosworth and E. Webster (eds), *The Management of Intellectual Property*, Cheltenham, UK and Northampton, MA, USA: Edward Elgar.
Office of National Statistics (2004), 'Gross value added by industry groups, current prices', online data at www.statistics.gov.uk/.
Patent Office (2004), *The Patent Office Facts and Figures 2003*, Newport: Patent Office.
Rogers, M. (2001), 'The effect of diversification on firm performance', Melbourne Institute working paper 2/01.

DATA SOURCES

Bureau van Dijk (2003), 'Fame', online database.
Dun and Bradstreet International (2001), 'Who Owns Whom D&B Linkages', 2001/4 CD-ROM.
European Patent Office (2001), 'ESPACE Bulletin', vol. 2001/001, (August) December 1978–February 1996 CD-ROM.
European Patent Office (2002), 'ESPACE Bulletin', vol. 2002/002, (July) February 1978–July 2002 CD-ROM.
Extel Financial (1996), 'Company Analysis', online database (now discontinued).
Marquesa Search Systems Ltd (2002), 'Marquesa – UK Trade Marks (A)', CD-ROM March.
Patent Office (1997), 'ESPACE ACCESS-EUROPE', vol. 1997/001 (December).
Patent Office (2002), 'ESPACE ACCESS-EUROPE', vol. 2002 (September).
Thomson (2001), 'Company Analysis', online database (now discontinued).
WIPO (1997), 'Industrial Property Statistics', 1995 CD-ROM.
WIPO (2003), 'Industrial Property Statistics', 1996–2000, www.wipo.org.

APPENDIX: RANKINGS OF FINANCE SECTOR FIRMS WITH IPR ACTIVITY, BY INDUSTRY

Note: Companies shown are only those with some intellectual property during 1996–2000.

Depository institutions	Trademarks (average per year 1996–2000)	UK patents (average per year 1996–2000)	EPO patents (average per year 1996–2000)	Trademarks per 1000 employee (average)	Growth in total assets (1996–2000)	Growth in share price (1996–2000)
Royal Bank of Scotland Group PLC	152.2	4.4	0.2	1.47	28.9	NA
Barclays PLC	111.8	2.2	0.2	1.39	70.0	107.1
Alliance & Leicester PLC	43.0	0	0	5.37	44.2	
Household International, UK Ltd	35.8	0	0	13.72		
Lloyds TSB Group PLC	32.0	0.2	0	0.36	47.9	64.5
HSBC Holdings PLC	21.6	0.2	0	0.15	104.6	−16.9
Bradford & Bingley PLC	19.0	0	0	2.89		
Bank of Scotland Gov. & Co. of	15.8	0	0	0.80	82.2	121.4
Abbey National PLC	9.2	0.2	0	0.34	64.8	59.3
Standard Chartered PLC	7.8	0	0	0.29	62.8	34.1
AIB, Allied Irish Banks PLC	6.0	0	0	0.25	93.9	99.3
Bank of Ireland Gov. & Co. of	4.2	3.2	0	0.29	158.2	−3.8
Close Brothers Group PLC	3.4	0	0	3.94	146.6	216.7
Anglo Irish Bank Corporation PLC	1.4	0	0	2.94	168.6	119.4
London Scottish Bank PLC	1.2	0	0	1.11	60.1	23.9
Cheshire Building Society	0.4	0	0	0.82	58.7	
Secure Trust Banking Group PLC	0.4	0	0	0.90	52.7	−34.1
Northern Rock PLC	0.2	0	0	0.06	64.3	
Bank of England	0	0	0	0.00		
Leopold Joseph Holdings PLC	0	0	0	0.00	76.7	54.6
Principality Building Society	0	0	0	0.00		

Note: Royal Bank of Scotland Group PLC represents consolidated RBS and NatWest even though the takeover only occurred in 2000.

Non-depository institutions	Trademarks (average per year 1996–2000)	UK patents (average per year 1996–2000)	EPO patents (average per year 1996–2000)	Trademarks per 1000 employee (average)	Growth in total assets (1996–2000)	Growth in share price (1996–2000)
Halifax Group PLC	52.4	0	0	1.64	58.0	
Provident Financial PLC	6.2	0	0	1.46	44.7	96.8
Skipton Building Society	5.4	0	0	2.14	80.0	
Chelsea Building Society	3.4	0	0	5.43	75.9	
Derbyshire Building Society	2.6	0	0	3.90		
Schroders PLC	2.6	0	0	0.47		
Britannia Building Society	2.4	0	0	0.90	−5.9	
Nationwide Building Society	2.0	0	0	0.17	75.8	
Singer & Friedlander Group PLC	1.4	0.2	0.2	1.12	32.4	128.9
Intermediate Capital Group PLC	0.8	0	0	31.01	161.7	143.8
Coventry Building Society	0.6	0	0	0.75	72.0	
London Forfaiting Company PLC	0.6	0	0	3.30	−65.3	−88.1
Newcastle Building Society	0.6	0	0	1.26	54.7	
Paragon Group of Companies PLC	0.6	0	0	1.20	43.8	58.9
Park Group PLC	0.6	0	0	0.63	−44.1	−82.5
Kensington Group PLC	0.4	0	0	7.34		
Leeds & Holbeck Building Society	0.4	0	0	0.59	43.5	
Yorkshire Building Society	0.4	0	0	0.25	60.1	
Portman Building Society	0.2	0	0	0.19	70.9	

Security and commodity brokers	Trademarks (average per year 1996–2000)	UK patents (average per year 1996–2000)	EPO patents (average per year 1996–2000)	Trademarks per 1000 employee (average)	Growth in total assets (1996–2000)	Growth in share price (1996–2000)
London Stock Exchange PLC	10.2	0	0	16.44	-2.9	
DBS Management PLC	5.0	0	0	15.67		
Web Angel PLC	2.8	0	0	233.33	165.3	-73.0
Shore Capital Group PLC	2.4	0	0	96.97		
Charles Stanley Group PLC	1.8	0	0	5.89	161.3	120.0
ICAP PLC	1.6	0	0	0.61	374.6	
Walker, Crips, Weddle, Beck PLC	1.2	0	0	13.73	2.2	84.4
Towry Law PLC	0.8	0	0	2.12		
Kiln PLC	0.6	0	0	2.00		
Numis Corporation PLC	0.6	0	0	9.97	141.6	187.2
Savoy Asset Management PLC	0.4	0	0	0.00		
Berry Birch & Noble PLC	0.2	0	0	0.95	10.4	68.9
Durlacher Corporation PLC	0.2	0	0	4.07	1468.9	-71.2
Inter Alliance Group PLC	0.2	0	0	2.10		
Millfield Group PLC	0.2	0	0	6.38		

Insurance carriers	Trademarks (average per year 1996–2000)	UK patents (average per year 1996–2000)	EPO patents (average per year 1996–2000)	Trademarks per 1000 employee (average)	Growth in total assets (1996–2000)	Growth in share price (1996–2000)
CGNU PLC	50.6	0.2	0	0.94	255.5	58.3
Friends Provident PLC	29.2	0	0	4.64		
Royal & Sun Alliance Insurance Group PLC	24.8	0	0	0.54	29.3	28.9
Prudential PLC	20.2	0	0	0.91	97.5	119.1
Legal & General Group PLC	10.6	0	0	1.36	136.0	–50.4
Standard Life Assurance Co	9.2	0	0	0.85	68.9	
Britannic PLC	8.0	0	0	1.99	153.5	41.6
Old Mutual Plc	7.0	0	0	0.18	16.3	
National Farmers Union Mutual Insurance Society Ltd	4.4	0	0	2.06		
Liberty International Holdings PLC	3.6	0	0	3.53		
Scottish Provident Institution	2.0	0	0	0.94		
Amlin PLC	1.4	0	0	2.13	95.1	–6.8
Eagle Star Holdings PLC	1.2	0	0	0.09		
Domestic & General Group PLC	0.4	0	0	0.58	17.8	–70.9
Independent Insurance Group PLC	0.4	0	0	0.24	107.6	–32.9
Ockham Holdings PLC	0.4	0	0	0.56	680.0	2.7
Hiscox PLC	0.2	0	0	0.65	167.0	20.4
Irish Life & Permanent PLC	0.2	0	0	0.07	294.3	72.7
Insurance agents brokers and service						
Innovation Group PLC	4.4	0	0	314.29	349.2	24.7
Cox Insurance Holdings PLC	3.0	0	0	2.77	9.6	–83.5
Bradstock Group PLC	1.0	0	0	1.68	35.0	167.1
Jardine Lloyd Thompson Group PLC	0.6	0	0	0.17		

Real estate	Trademarks (average per year 1996–2000)	UK patents (average per year 1996–2000)	EPO patents (average per year 1996–2000)	Trademarks per 1000 employee (average)	Growth in total assets (1996–2000)	Growth in share price (1996–2000)
BAA PLC	37.8	0.2	0	3.15	37.5	21.1
Capital & Regional PLC	20.8	0	0	254.90	249.1	8.3
Countrywide Assured Group PLC	8.0	0	0	1.09	140.3	8.0
Marylebone Warwick Balfour Group PLC	4.2	0	0	19.23	425.6	101.3
Hammerson PLC	4.0	0	0	14.34	77.2	14.7
Land Securities PLC	3.6	0	0	5.54	34.3	13.8
Emerson Developments, Holdings Ltd	2.8	0	0	7.87		
Swan Hill Group PLC	2.6	0	0	5.50	20.4	−21.8
Saville Gordon Estates PLC	2.2	0	0	26.63	187.9	50.4
Savills PLC	2.2	0	0	0.69	375.8	76.9
Armstrong Brooks PLC	1.8	0	0	128.57		
Minerva PLC	1.6	0	0	69.57	208.2	
Northacre PLC	1.6	0	0	88.89		
Britannia Hotels Ltd	1.0	0	0	0.92		
Canary Wharf Group PLC	1.0	0	0	1.76	167.4	
Freeport PLC	1.0	0	0	6.87		
London Merchant Securities PLC	1.0	0	0	10.35	87.9	38.4
DTZ Holdings PLC	0.8	0	0	0.56	144.9	161.2
Bailey, NG Organisation Ltd	0.6	0.6	0	0.16		
Workspace Group PLC	0.6	0	0	6.24	191.5	249.3
Chesterton International PLC	0.2	0	0	0.11	−2.5	−52.2
Hercules Property Services PLC	0.2	0	0	1.63	2019.6	58.0
Liberty International PLC	0.2	0	0	0.21		
OEM PLC	0	0.4	0.2	0.00	65.9	−19.8

Holding and other investment offices	Trademarks (average per year 1996–2000)	UK patents (average per year 1996–2000)	EPO patents (average per year 1996–2000)	Trademarks per 1000 employee (average)	Growth in total assets (1996–2000)	Growth in share price (1996–2000)
Scipher PLC	22.6	8.4	14.4	96.58	640.7	
Caledonia Investments PLC	12.2	0	0	9.72	13.5	3.6
Guinness Peat Group PLC	4.8	0	0	3.60	3.0	33.3
3i Group PLC	3.8	0	0.2	4.82	69.2	119.4
Comprehensive Business Services PLC	3.2	0	0	101.59		
Liontrust Asset Management PLC	3.2	0	0	152.38	1208.9	
Henderson Smaller Companies Investment Trust PLC	2.4	0	0	0.00	13.3	24.7
Exeter Investment Group PLC	1.6	0	0	19.85	209.4	
IG Group PLC	1.6	0.6	0	18.88		
AMVESCAP PLC	1.4	0.4	0	0.34	949.1	429.5
BTG PLC	1.2	0	29.2	6.54	281.6	45.0
Colt Investments Ltd	1.2	0	0.4	1.20		
Brewin Dolphin Holdings PLC	1.0	0	0	1.22	319.0	26.8
Aberdeen Asset Management PLC	0.8	0	0	2.99	80.1	580.4
Beeson Gregory Group PLC	0.6	0	0	7.38		
Medi@Invest PLC	0.6	0	0	9.60		
Retail Decisions PLC	0.6	0	0	11.32	438.8	
Pantheon International Participations PLC	0.4	0	0	0.00	41.9	69.4
BRIT Insurance Holdings PLC	0.2	0	0	1.92	151.9	–29.4
Evolution Group PLC	0.2	0	0	0.00		
Rathbone Brothers PLC	0.2	0	0	0.42		
Gresham House PLC	0	0	0.2	0.00	231.9	1728.9

12. Understanding the patenting behaviour of firms

Carine Peeters and Bruno van Pottelsberghe de la Potterie

1 INTRODUCTION

The present book is about intellectual property (IP), 'once considered the most boring subject in the world' (Rivette and Kline 2000, p. 1). The authors of *Rembrandts in the Attic* demonstrate that the ownership of ideas is now becoming part of the day-to-day business life, policy debates and legal arguments. Publications on the strategic management of intellectual property (IP) have indeed recently flourished (for example, Glazier 2000; Parr and Sullivan 1996), together with a vast economic literature, with both theoretical and empirical contributions.

This chapter aims at contributing to the literature dedicated to the identification of the factors underlying the large variance observed across firms in terms of patenting behaviour. The theoretical framework suggests that a firm's patenting behaviour is determined by three types of factors. The first concerns the innovation strategy of a firm and its general attitude towards intellectual property. The second is related to the perceived barriers to innovation and to patenting. The third takes into account firm- and sector-specific characteristics, such as size, age and market structure. Several concepts and relations discussed in this chapter have already been highlighted by a number of authors. However, this chapter adds to the existing literature in the sense that it identifies new potential explanatory factors of a firm's patenting behaviour. It includes these determinants from an integrated perspective, putting together different concepts that are generally addressed in separate pieces of research.

An original survey database of 148 large firms based in Belgium in 2001 is used for the empirical analysis. Two econometric models are used in order to explain the probability for a firm to have a patent portfolio (that is, at least one patent) and the size of this portfolio. The results indicate that various dimensions of an innovation strategy do affect the patenting behaviour of firms. In particular, a focus on more basic and applied research, an innovation strategy that is product-orientated, and the propensity to enter into research and development (R&D) partnerships with knowledge-based institutions and with competitors appear to be key determinants. Some of the perceived barriers to innovation seem to correlate with the patenting behaviour of firms as well.

Section 2 sketches the theoretical framework and presents the survey data. Section 3 presents the measurement of the different dimensions of an innovation strategy. The measurement of the perceived barriers to innovation and to the use of the patent system is illustrated in section 4. The quantitative analysis is presented and interpreted in sections 5 and 6. Section 7 concludes.

2   THEORETICAL FRAMEWORK

Understanding the patenting behaviour of firms becomes an important concern. Indeed, innovation is an important driver of sustainable growth. As patents aim at protecting the intellectual capital embodied in inventions, policy-makers and company boards are increasingly scrutinizing the patenting performance of firms. Together with copyrights, trademarks and other legal mechanisms, patents are a central concern for any institution involved in the generation of knowledge.

Applying for a patent is a strategic decision that is not only driven by the desire to protect the innovation rents of firms (for example, Sherry and Teece 2004; Teece 1998). It is also a highly valuable tool for the following purposes:

- technological negotiations with competitors or with potential collaborators
- exclusion of rivals from a particular technological area
- licensing agreements and attraction of capital
- avoiding being blocked by competitors' patents

(see Chapter 10 of this book). These strategic considerations influence the propensity to patent of a firm.[1] Patents are therefore not only an indicator of innovation and technological success but also an indicator of strategic behaviour. In this respect the patenting behaviour might also be the result of an innovation strategy.

The theoretical framework underlying this chapter is provided in Figure 12.1. It is assumed that a firm's patenting behaviour is reflected in its patent portfolio and is influenced by three main categories of factors. The first relates to the innovation strategy of the firm and its general attitude towards IP. The second refers to the barriers a firm perceives as hindering its innovation activities or as preventing it from patenting its inventions. The last category includes the firm- and sector-specific variables, most of which are already largely discussed in the existing literature.

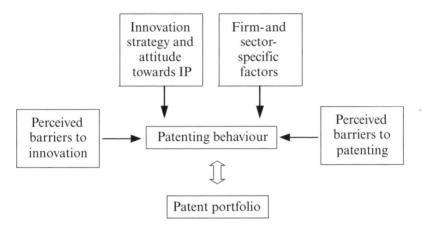

Figure 12.1   Theoretical framework

The various dimensions of an innovation strategy and the potential barriers to innovation and to the use of the patent system are explained and measured in the next two sections. In order to test and measure the relations depicted in the theoretical framework, data have been collected through a survey of 1301 large firms in Belgium. A total of 148 questionnaires were filled in and sent back, which represents a 11.4 per cent response rate. For statistical purposes the sample is stratified according to the firms' size and sector of activity. Small firms have between 50 and 199 employees, medium firms have between 200 and 499 employees, and large firms have 500 or more employees.[2] The sector classes are determined according to the OECD terminology:[3] high-tech (HT), medium high-tech (MH), medium low-tech (ML) and low-tech (LT) sectors. A category is added for all service firms: commerce, hotels and restaurants, transports, posts and telecommunications, insurances, financial services, real estate activities, and computer activities. Large firms account for 33 per cent of the sample, medium and small firms for 36 per cent and 31 per cent respectively. For simplicity of presentation, HT and MH firms are grouped into one category representing the firms in higher-technological opportunity sectors, and ML and LT firms are grouped into one category representing the firms in lower-technological opportunity sectors. The last category comprises all services companies. The sample is approximately equally distributed among these three categories. A complete description of the survey and an extensive statistical analysis of the results can be found in Peeters and van Pottelsberghe (2003a).

We assess a firm's patenting behaviour by looking at its portfolio of active patents. This departs from many existing studies that rely on patent applications data (for example, Brouwer and Kleinknecht 1999; Crépon et al. 1998; van Ophem et al. 2001). The patents in a firm's portfolio bear in themselves an element of 'quality' that is lacking in most existing studies. These patents have indeed been granted, which means that the inventive step of the underlying innovation has been recognized. Moreover these are 'active' patents in the sense that renewal fees have been paid. In the case of older patents this guarantees that the innovation profits they are supposed to protect are actually still protected, which is not the case with patent applications or even patent grant data.

3   MEASURING AN INNOVATION STRATEGY AND THE ATTITUDE TOWARDS IP

A first dimension of an innovation strategy is the extent to which a firm's innovative efforts rely on R&D. About 80 per cent of the firms included in the sample declare some kind of R&D activities. Besides knowing whether firms do R&D or not, the size of their R&D effort and orientation towards more basic and applied research or towards development work are also worthwhile investigating. If the positive relationship between the relative effort in R&D and patenting has been widely illustrated, there is little evidence so far about the content of R&D.[4] Since patents are by definition the codification of an invention, they might rather be the outcome of basic and applied research as opposed to development activities.

Figure 12.2 shows that surveyed firms claim to allocate on average 3.3 per cent of their sales to basic and applied research. The percentage is the highest for large and small firms, as opposed to medium-sized firms.[5] This U-shaped curve probably stands for the fact that firms, in order to grow from small to large scale, need resources that could otherwise be used for research. Medium firms would be in a kind of intermediate step where cost reductions, efficiency improvements and organizational adaptations are priorities to move towards large-scale production. Development activities account for an average of 4.3 per cent of sales of surveyed firms. The highest percentage is found among small firms (6.9 per cent). Research and development activities seem also more important to firms operating in high

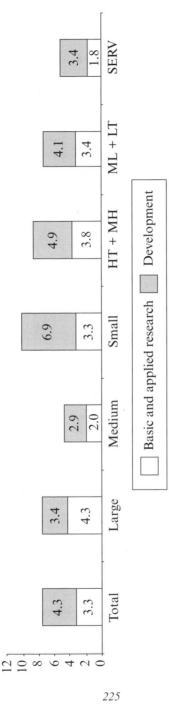

Source: Own survey, 148 responding firms, Belgium, 2001.

Figure 12.2   Average percentage of sales allocated to R&D in 2000

technological opportunity manufacturing sectors than in low technological
opportunity manufacturing sectors or in the services industry.

A firm's innovation strategy can also be characterized as more or less
outward-orientated reflected by its propensity to enter into research partnerships with other institutions. Potential collaborators include competitors,
vertical partners, universities, consultants, complementary firms and other
firms of the same group. These institutions form an external stock of
knowledge that might prove useful for the firms' own innovation activities,
as it might reduce their cost and their risk.[6] Firms were asked whether or
not they had launched a collaborative R&D agreement in the three years
preceding the survey. The question was asked for each of the potential
collaborators. Figure 12.3 shows that the average percentage of positive
answers is 46 per cent. It is the highest for large firms (62 per cent) and firms
operating in high-tech and medium high-tech sectors (57 per cent).

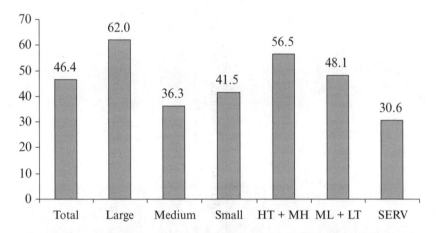

Source: Own survey, 148 responding firms, Belgium, 2001.

*Figure 12.3   Average percentage of positive answers to the seven R&D
collaboration questions*

Research and development collaborative agreements often imply a mutual
access to the partners' knowledge base. Therefore, partnering firms might
be more likely to seek patent protection for their inventions. In addition, a
firm's knowledge base becomes a tradable asset that can be very useful when
negotiating future collaborative agreements. Finally, knowledge developed
through collaborative R&D agreements may be more difficult to protect by
other means such as trade secrets, and partnering firms are likely to share the
cost of patent protection. Brouwer and Kleinknecht (1999) and van Ophem

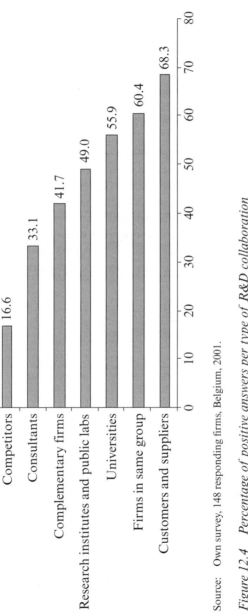

Source: Own survey, 148 responding firms, Belgium, 2001.

Figure 12.4   Percentage of positive answers per type of R&D collaboration

et al. (2001) show that the firms participating in research partnerships apply for more patents than the firms that focus more on internal research. As collaboration with a scientific institution like a public laboratory or a university is associated with a strong science base, it can induce a more active patenting behaviour than other kinds of partnerships.

Figure 12.4 shows that 68 per cent of surveyed firms participated in joint R&D projects with vertical partners (customers and suppliers). This is the most common type of R&D collaboration. At the opposite extreme, only 17 per cent of firms built R&D collaboration agreements with their competitors. Collaboration with sister companies of the same group is also quite common, whereas consultants are poorly rated. Approximately 56 per cent of firms collaborate with universities.

A third dimension of a firm's innovation strategy relates to the orientation of its creative activities. Two dichotomies are frequently investigated in this respect. The first is whether the innovation activities are aimed at developing new products or new processes. The second is whether the objective is to improve existing products and processes or to launch more radical innovations. Firms participating in the survey were asked to rate the strategic importance of these four types of innovation activities. Figure 12.5 shows the average percentage of firms that answered 4 or 5 on a 5-point Likert scale, indicating a high or very high strategic importance for each item.

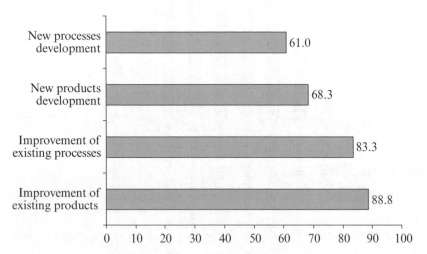

Source: Own survey, 148 responding firms, Belgium, 2001.

Figure 12.5   Percentage of 4 or 5 answers on 5-point Likert scale on the type of innovative efforts

Figure 12.5 suggests that firms tend to favour the improvement of existing products and processes to the launch of radical innovations. This behaviour seems to make sense given the importance of the required resources and inherent risks that make radical innovation much more difficult to implement than incremental innovation. In terms of the product versus process development dichotomy, Figure 12.5 tends to show a preference for product-orientatated innovation activities. No clear difference appears in firms' strategic orientations according to their size and sector of activity.

It is traditionally found that process innovations are less likely to be patented (Arundel and Kabla 1998; Brouwer and Kleinknecht 1999), as secrecy might offer a more appropriate protection mechanism for this type of innovation (Cohen et al. 2000). It is indeed more difficult to track down imitations of processes than imitations of products. Therefore, the publication of technical information that a patent requires might be more worthwhile in the case of a product innovation, for which infringement is easier to detect. In the case of process innovations firms might opt for a non-legal protection mechanism such as secrecy. Product innovations might be easier to imitate through reverse engineering and legally enforceable protection might prove to be more useful.

A firm's patenting behaviour might also be related to its general attitude towards intellectual property. This 'attitude' has been measured in the survey through six questions relating to:

- the existence of an active IPR strategy
- the discussion of IP issues at top management's meetings
- the existence of a centralized patent department
- the use of an evaluation process for the patenting of a firm's inventions
- the systematic assessment of the risk of imitation of inventions
- the regular scrutiny of competitors' patent applications to potentially fill patent litigation.

The results are presented in Figure 12.6. Less than 50 per cent of firms claim to have an active IPR strategy. This shows that more than half of the firms are either not interested in protecting their knowledge or favour other protection mechanisms, like secrecy or market lead. Approximately the same percentage of firms claims to have a centralized patent department that co-ordinates the IP strategy of the whole company. However, this percentage is higher for large firms that seem to stress the centralized management of their patent portfolio in almost three cases out of four.

Surprisingly, few firms take systematically into account the risk of imitation of their inventions. Most firms rather seem to consider imitation

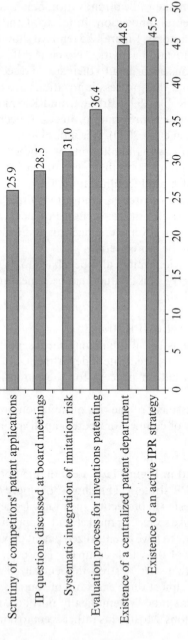

Source: Own survey, 148 responding firms, Belgium, 2001.

Figure 12.6 Percentage of 4 or 5 answers on 5-point Likert scale to six questions on the attitude towards IP

to be 'part of the game'. Furthermore, most firms do not feel the need to scrutinize the competitors' patent applications. Large and high-tech firms are, in fact, almost the only ones interested in technology-related business intelligence practices directed towards the protection of their knowledge base. More generally, there is an important difference between the highly positive attitude towards IP of large firms and firms active in high-tech and medium-high-tech sectors, and the relative indifference for the issue showed by other firms, as illustrated in Figure 12.7.

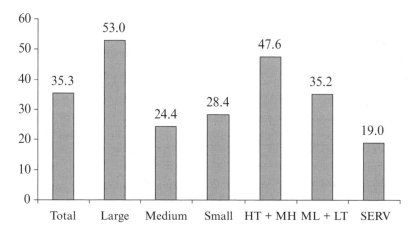

Source: Own survey, 148 responding firms, Belgium, 2001.

Figure 12.7   Average percentage of 4 or 5 answers on 5-point Likert scale to questions on attitude towards IP

While approximately 50 per cent of large firms operating in relatively high-tech sectors highly rate the different IP-related issues assessed in the survey, this percentage drops to about 25 per cent for firms with less than 500 employees operating in lower-technology fields or in the services industry. The difference observed between the various groups of firms remains valid when looking at the questions separately.

4   PERCEIVED BARRIERS TO INNOVATION AND PATENTING

Whatever the willingness of managers to build strong patent positions in certain technological areas, the development of a patenting portfolio makes sense only as far as there is some kind of innovative activity taking place in the firm. Therefore, the barriers firms perceive as hindering their innovative efforts are likely to influence their observed patenting behaviour. Survey results related to these perceived barriers are provided in Figure 12.8.

Cost- and risk-related issues are by far the most important barriers to innovation (about 60 per cent). The second type of obstacles comes from the resistance to change and the lack of qualified personnel (about 25 per cent of firms consider it as a major barrier). In third position come the external factors related to customers' rigidities and lack of reaction, and to regulations. Internal organizational issues come in the fourth position: poor communication, lack of leadership and internal rigidities. Finally other external factors like trade unions, lack of access to competent suppliers and an imperfect protection system are perceived as important barriers by less than 10 per cent of firms.

When the answers to all potential barriers are averaged, there are very few differences due to firms' size and sector of activity. Only small firms and firms in the services sector seem to perceive more barriers than the others. In order to deepen the analysis, the potential barriers can be grouped into four categories, as shown in Table 12.1.

Table 12.1   Average percentage of 4 or 5 answers on 5-point Likert scale, per category of potential barriers

	Total	Large	Medium	Small	HT + MH	ML + LT	SERV
Cost- and risk-related barriers	59.9	56.7	60.0	64.8	61.4	57.8	64.6
Internal lack of resources	24.7	26.2	20.6	29.6	27.1	21.6	27.7
Internal organizational barriers	15.2	18.6	14.4	13.6	15.1	17.2	14.2
External barriers: regulations and customers	10.9	9.7	17.2	7.8	7.2	12.3	17.1
Total	27.7	27.8	28.1	29.0	27.7	27.2	30.9

Source: Own survey, 148 responding firms, Belgium, 2001.

The higher importance of cost- and risk-related barriers with respect to other potential barriers holds, whatever the size and sector of activity of firms. This first group of barriers is, however, more highly rated by small and services firms than other firms. The second group is made of potential barriers arising from the lack of resources of firms: time, money, qualified personnel and leadership. These barriers hinder small firms the most, and firms operating in either high-tech sectors or in the services industry. The

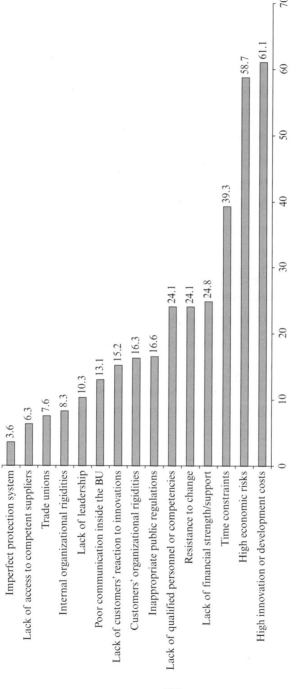

Source: Own survey, 148 responding firms, Belgium, 2001.

Figure 12.8   Percentage of 4 or 5 answers on 5-point Likert scale to 15 potential barriers to innovation

third group comprises mainly internal organizational barriers: resistance to change, lack of communication and internal rigidities. These elements are more important for large firms and for low-tech firms. The external barriers resulting from regulatory factors and customer-related issues hinder more the innovativeness of medium-sized firms and services firms.

The perception firms have of the effectiveness and cost of the patent system might influence their patenting behaviour as well. Actually, the advantage for a firm to patent an invention is not always clear since a patent offers protection to its holder at the high indirect cost of revealing important technical information. Applying for a patent does not seem to be the most popular protection mechanism for manufacturing firms, which often favour secrecy and lead time over competition.[7] The risk to have competitors 'inventing around' and the disclosure of critical information are the most important reasons why patents are not always considered as an efficient protection mechanism of innovation rents (Cohen et al. 2000; Levin et al. 1987; Scotchmer and Green 1990). The perceived barriers to using the patent system have been measured by asking firms to rate on a 5-point Likert scale the factors that reduce their propensity to rely on the patent protection mechanism. The results are reported in Figure 12.9.

The highest rated barriers relate to the lack of efficiency of the patent system. Many firms consider that the lead time on the market is more efficient than relying on the protection of a patent. More than half of the firms feel unable to prevent competitors from copying their technology, even if a patent protects it. Indeed, many firms (44 per cent) consider secrecy as more efficient. Another category of barriers relates to the cost of patents: the cost of protection in case of litigation and the cost of fees. Finally, only one out of five firms do not patent because they lack information about the IP system. It appears from Figure 12.10 that medium-sized firms and firms operating in relatively low-tech fields tend to perceive more limitations to the patent system than other firms.

5   EMPIRICAL IMPLEMENTATION

The patenting behaviour of a firm is measured through its patent portfolio. Two main models are used in order to identify the determinants of a firm's patenting behaviour. The first focuses on whether the firm has a patent portfolio or not, that is, the probability of the firm having at least one patent. The second intends to explain the size of this portfolio, that is, the number of patents the firm has in its patent portfolio.[8]

The empirical methodology is illustrated in Figure 12.11. The exogenous (explanatory) variables are listed in the left-hand-side box. They are grouped

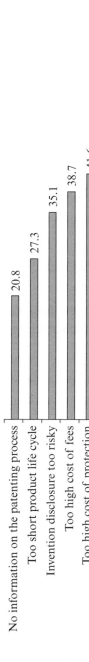

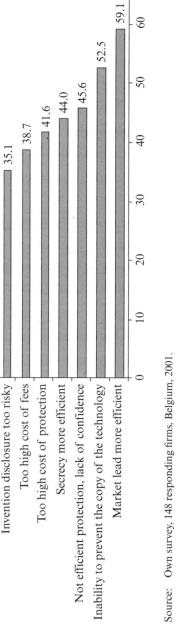

Source: Own survey, 148 responding firms, Belgium, 2001.

Figure 12.9 Percentage of 4 or 5 answers on 5-point Likert scale to nine potential barriers to patenting

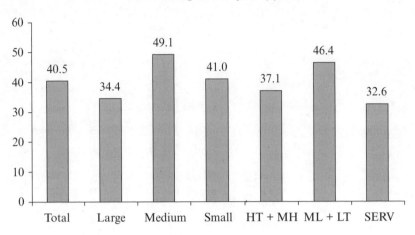

Source: Own survey, 148 responding firms, Belgium, 2001.

*Figure 12.10   Average percentage of 4 or 5 answers on 5-point Likert scale
to nine potential barriers to patenting*

into three categories: innovation strategy variables, indicators of perceived
barriers, and firm- and sector-specific factors. The econometric models that
are used and the corresponding dependent variables are listed in the middle
and right-hand-side boxes, respectively. A binary logit model is used to
estimate the probability that a firm will have at least one patent. A count
model with a negative binomial specification is used to estimate the size of
the patent portfolio.

Two types of explanatory variables are used for the empirical analysis:
binary and numerical variables. Some numerical variables consist of the
firms' coordinates on various factorial axes coming from factorial analyses
on several questions from the survey. They represent the type of institutions
with which firms enter into R&D partnerships, their general attitude
towards IP and their perceived barriers to innovation and to patenting.
A detailed description of the factorial axes is provided in Peeters and van
Pottelsberghe (2003b).

5.1   Innovation Strategy Variables

The innovation strategy variables include the share of basic and applied
research in the total R&D budget, the type of institutions chosen for R&D
partnerships, the relative importance of the development of new products
and of new processes in the firm's innovation strategy, and the importance
given to IP issues.

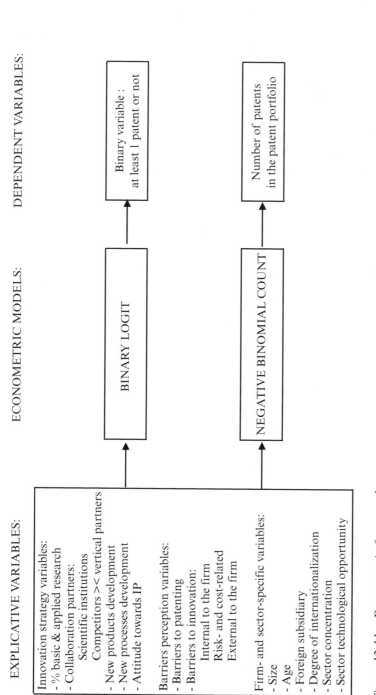

EXPLICATIVE VARIABLES:

Innovation strategy variables:
- % basic & applied research
- Collaboration partners:
    Scientific institutions
    Competitors >< vertical partners
- New products development
- New processes development
- Attitude towards IP

Barriers perception variables:
- Barriers to patenting
- Barriers to innovation:
    Internal to the firm
    Risk- and cost-related
    External to the firm

Firm- and sector-specific variables:
- Size
- Age
- Foreign subsidiary
- Degree of internationalization
- Sector concentration
- Sector technological opportunity

ECONOMETRIC MODELS:

BINARY LOGIT

NEGATIVE BINOMIAL COUNT

DEPENDENT VARIABLES:

Binary variable :
at least 1 patent or not

Number of patents
in the patent portfolio

Figure 12.11 Econometric framework

237

The share of the total R&D budget accounted for by basic and applied research activities measures the relative importance of research activities as opposed to development activities. The involvement in research partnerships is accounted for by two variables. They are based on a factorial analysis of the questions relating to the existence of collaboration agreements with different types of partners.[9] The first latent variable (obtained through the coordinates of each company on a factorial axis) reflects the extent of collaborations with universities and research institutes. The second reflects the collaborations with competitors and negatively relates to the use of consultants and vertical partners as innovation partners. Both variables are expected to have a positive impact on the firms' patent portfolio.

The main reason for a positive impact of partnerships with universities and research institutes would come from the basic nature of academic research. Collaborating with competitors implies reciprocal openness and access to the firms' knowledge base. There would therefore be a greater need for patent protection. The product-orientated or process-orientated strategy of the firm is measured with two dummy variables. They take the value of 1 if the firm answered 4 or 5 (on a Likert scale ranging from 0 to 5) to the question of the importance of product innovation and to the question of the importance of process innovation. A firm can therefore be orientated towards both types of innovations as well as neither of them. These two dummy variables are not mutually exclusive. The attitude of the firm with respect to IP is approximated by a latent variable (coordinates on a factorial axis) obtained through the factorial analysis of the six questions presented in Figure 12.6.

5.2   Barriers Perception Variables

Several potential barriers were listed in the questionnaire and had to be scored on a Likert scale (from 0 to 5). For each type of barrier (to innovation and to patenting) we performed a factor analysis with the scores of all potential barriers. The resulting latent variables (composed of the coordinates of the firms on the factorial axes) are used as explanatory variables. The first factor analysis reflects the perceived limitations of the patent system. A single latent variable seems to effectively summarize all the barriers to the use of the patent system assessed in the survey. This latent variable accounts for the perceptions of cost of fees and protection, the lack of effectiveness of the patent protection, the disclosure of important information and the lack of information on the patent system.

The second factor analysis concerns the perceived barriers to innovation. Three latent variables are built (using the firms' coordinates on three factorial axes) representing three categories of potential barriers to innovation. These variables are barriers due to internal organization, risk and cost factors, and external barriers. The internal barriers variable represents the firms' internal rigidities, employees' resistance to change, lack of relevant competencies, time constraints, lack of communication and lack of leadership. The risk- and cost-related barriers variable stands for the high costs and high economic risks associated with innovation and the lack of financial resources. The external barriers variable comes from the customers' rigidities and lack of reaction to new products, and from inappropriate public regulations.

5.3 Firm- and Sector-specific Variables

The last category of variables includes the firm's size, its age, the domestic or foreign nature of its ownership, its degree of internationalization, the sector concentration and technological opportunity indicators. Firm size is measured by the total number of employees in the firm or branch, and a positive relationship is expected with the patent portfolio. Firm age is the number of years, at the time of the survey, since the creation of the company. The square of the firm age is also introduced to check for a potential non-linear relationship with the firms' patenting behaviour. The firm's age could indeed influence its patent portfolio in two opposite directions. On the one hand, young firms may be more dynamic and have a less rigid structure favourable to innovation, but they probably would not have developed sufficient market power yet to partially protect their innovation rents. This may induce them to look for patent protection. On the other hand, older firms may have built over time a larger technological expertise protected by a larger number of patents. They also probably have more resources to sustain strong patenting strategies.

The domestic or foreign nature of a firm's ownership is proxied by a binary variable taking the value of 1 if the firm belongs to a foreign group and 0 otherwise. A common thought is that foreign firms are more innovative than local ones. As a consequence they might patent more (Baldwin et al. 2002). However, it could be argued that Belgian subsidiaries of foreign companies are less involved in patenting. Patents could indeed be managed at the group level, in the country of origin. The degree of internationalization is measured by the number of countries a firm is operating in. A firm is considered to operate in a country if it has customer contacts in this country. Firms operating in a large number of countries can be expected to develop strong patent portfolios because they face more international competition, which increases the need for protection because the number of potential imitators increases. This may translate into a more active patenting behaviour.

The sector concentration is proxied by the four-firm concentration ratio – that is, the total sales of the four largest firms in the firm's main sector of operation (in terms of sales) divided by the total sales of the sector of activity. The sector of activity is determined using the four-digit Nace code used in Belgium. This is an imperfect variable since it is measured at the Belgian level while a lot of firms face international competitors. Moreover, it is based on firms operating in the same kind of activity and does not necessarily reflect the firms' direct competitors. Finally, multi-product firms are attributed the sector code related to their most important product or service without taking into account their other activities. The technological opportunity variable is proxied by three dummy variables. The first takes the value of 1 if the firm belongs to a high-tech or medium high-tech sector and 0 otherwise. The second takes the value of 1 if the firm belongs to a medium low-tech or low-tech sector and 0 otherwise. The third takes the value of 1 if the firm belongs to the services industry and 0 otherwise.

6   EMPIRICAL RESULTS

Estimated results are presented in Table 12.2. The first column relates to the probability of having a patent portfolio (binary logit model) and the second column relates to the size of the patent portfolio (negative binomial model). The first strategic variable concerns the relative involvement in basic and applied research (as opposed to development activities). The parameters clearly indicate that the larger the portion of a firm's total R&D budget allocated to basic and applied research, the higher the probability it will have a patent portfolio and the larger the size of this portfolio. Basic and applied research projects are indeed more likely to lead to scientific breakthrough inventions, which are in turn more likely to be patented.

A second strategic variable relates to the extent to which firms enter into collaborative R&D and the type of partners they choose. Collaborating with scientific institutions has a highly significant and positive impact on the patenting behaviour of firms, both in terms of the probability of having a patent portfolio and in terms of the size of this portfolio. Most of these partnerships concern science-related innovation projects and require an open attitude towards bilateral access to knowledge bases. This level of openness and strong scientific content induce a higher propensity to patent the outcome of such collaborative research projects. Firms that build research partnerships with their competitors (as opposed to research partnerships with consultants and vertical partners) are also more likely to build larger patent portfolios. The parameters associated with this latent variable are positive and significant within the two models. The need for patent protection is higher for the firms that collaborate with competitors than for the firms that collaborate more with consultants or vertical partners.

Table 12.2   Econometric results: probability and size of the patent portfolio of a firm

	Binary logit	Negative binomial
Innovation strategy variables:		
% basic & applied research	0.0362**	0.0186*
	(0.0142)	(0.0096)
Collaboration partners:		
– *Scientific institutions*	3.8972***	2.7775***
	(1.1049)	(0.4954)
– *Competitors >< vertical*	4.8112**	1.3686**
partners & consultants	(2.0465)	(0.6979)
New products development	1.3439	2.6962***
	(1.4050)	(0.7583)
New processes development	−2.9630***	−1.2700***
	(1.0859)	(0.4134)
Attitude towards IP	0.5563*	0.3639**
	(0.3322)	(0.1686)
Barriers perception variables:		
Barriers to patenting	0.4577	0.1489
	(0.2862)	(0.1222)
Barriers to innovation:		
–*Internal*	0.0354	−0.2951**
	(0.3367)	(0.1461)
– *Risks and costs*	−1.1515**	−0.5669***
	(0.4953)	(0.1985)
– *External*	−1.2036***	−0.2428
	(0.3160)	(0.1757)
Firm- and sector-specific variables:		
– *Size*	0.0002	0.0005***
	(0.0004)	(0.0002)
– *Age*	−0.0798**	−0.0483**
	(0.0369)	(0.0220)
– *Age square*	0.0008***	0.0005***
	(0.0003)	(0.0002)
– *Foreign subsidiary*	0.4073	0.4696
	(1.0339)	(0.4572)
– *Degree of internationalization*	0.0185	0.0018
	(0.0259)	(0.0063)
– *Sector concentration*	0.0259	0.0228*
	(0.0223)	(0.0130)
– *High-tech*	0.2411	1.0186
	(1.1832)	(0.7897)
– *Service*	−1.1964	−1.1574
	(1.5977)	(0.9101)
Constant	−2.4079	−3.6194***
	(1.9075)	(1.2729)
McFadden R-squared	0.7118	
Pseudo R-squared		0.5669

Notes: S-E into parentheses. Significativity levels: * 10 per cent, ** 5 per cent, *** 1 per cent.
Source: Own survey, Belgium, 2001, 97 firms.

This patenting behaviour is probably due to the reciprocal openness to the knowledge base of the partners, and to their contractual relationship.

The third type of innovation strategy variables are a measure of the focus towards product innovations (new growth potential) and process innovations (cost reducing). The importance firms give to the development of new products has a positive and significant impact on the size of their patent portfolios, but not on the probability to have a patent portfolio. Conversely, a strong focus towards process innovation is associated with both a lower probability of patenting and with smaller patent portfolios. These results corroborate Arundel (2001)'s finding that process-orientated R&D is associated with a higher importance of secrecy as protection means. The disclosure of a process innovation might indeed lead other firms to use the technology, as infringements are difficult to track down and proving the paternity of a new process is not easy.

The general attitude towards IP also influences a firm's patenting behaviour in terms of the probability of having a patent portfolio and in terms of the size of this portfolio. A firm with a more active IPR strategy, where IP issues are tackled at board meetings, that assesses the risk of imitation of its inventions, that scrutinizes patent applications by competitors, and that has a centralized patent department will indeed have a more active patent behaviour than other firms.

The second type of factors that might affect the patenting behaviour of firms is related to their perception of the barriers to patenting and to innovation. In the theoretical part of this chapter we suggested that the firms that perceive high barriers to patenting would have a lower propensity to patent their inventions. The empirical results do not validate this assumption, as the estimated parameters associated with the perceived barriers to patenting are not significantly different from zero. This result is probably due to the fact that firms that have a substantial experience in patenting understand the potential shortcomings (in terms of effectiveness and cost) of the patent system and are as critical as the firms that do not patent.

The opposite is observed for the barriers to innovation, which matches our expectations: the higher the perceived barriers to innovation, the weaker is the probability for a firm to have at least one patent, and the smaller is its patent portfolio. The perceived barriers to innovation that are associated with risk and cost issues negatively affect the patenting behaviour of firms in the two models. The probability to have a patent portfolio is also negatively influenced by external barriers. The perceived internal barriers such as the employees' resistance to change, the organizational rigidities and the lack of relevant competencies affect mainly the size of the patent portfolio.

Some firm- and sector-specific variables also play an important role in explaining the patenting behaviour of firms. The parameter associated with the size of the firm is not significantly different from 0 in the first column (probit model) and is positive and significant in the second column (negative binomial model). These results suggest that large firms are not more likely to have a patent portfolio than smaller ones, but if they have one it is more likely to be larger. In terms of the age of the firm a U-shaped relationship is found with both the probability of having a patent portfolio and the size of this portfolio. Two effects might work in opposite directions. On the one hand, the need to protect the inventions might be more important for younger firms because they have no market power. On the other hand, older firms might have a large technological background covering more areas of technology over a longer period, and hence, have more patents.

The foreign nature of the firm and its degree of internationalization do not influence its patenting behaviour (the parameters are not significantly different from zero in both models). These results might be particular to small open economies. Operating in a concentrated market does not seem to play any role, except for the size of the patent portfolio.

7   CONCLUDING REMARKS

The objective of this chapter was to better understand the factors that influence firms' patenting behaviour, both in terms of the probability to have a patent portfolio and in terms of the size of this patent portfolio. The theoretical framework suggests that the patenting behaviour of firms can be influenced by three kinds of factors: the innovation strategy of firms and their general attitude towards IP; the barriers firms perceive to their innovation process and to the use of the patent system; and firm- or sector-specific factors like the age, the size or the market structure. An original survey of large firms has been used for the empirical implementation.

The four components of an innovation strategy that have been taken into account are the extent to which a firm is involved in basic or applied research (as opposed to development), the extent to which a firm enters into collaborative research with other institutions, the focus on new product or new process development, and the importance given to IP. All four components affect both the probability of a firm to have a patent portfolio and the size of this portfolio. Firms that (1) allocate a higher share of their R&D activities to basic and applied research; (2) enter into collaborative agreements with scientific institutions and with competitors; (3) are more focused on product innovation; and (4) give a higher importance to IP management have both a higher probability to have a patent portfolio and a larger patent portfolio. However, an innovation strategy that is more focused on process innovation and a higher propensity to enter into R&D

partnership with vertical partners and consultants translates into a lower probability to have a patent portfolio and a smaller patent portfolio.

The perceived barriers to innovation also correlate with the patenting behaviour. Our results suggest that firms that are better able to overcome internal organizational barriers (for example, internal rigidities, resistance to change) and to face risk-and cost-related barriers do have larger patent portfolios. At the opposite, the shortcomings of the patent system perceived by firms do not seem to influence their actual patenting behaviour.

In summary, the patenting behaviour of firms is not only a function of their size, age or sector characteristics. These elements lie within a broader and coherent system of factors that influence a firm's propensity to develop a strong portfolio of patents. These factors relate to several dimensions of an innovation strategy, to an effective management of IP, and to the perceived barriers to the innovation process.

NOTES

1. The propensity to patent is defined (for example, Ernst, 2001) as the share of patentable inventions that are actually patented.
2. Given the survey selection criteria directed towards the largest firms in each sector of activity, no firm with less than 50 employees is included in the sample.
3. HT= aeronautic construction, desks and computing machines, pharmaceuticals products, radio, television and telecommunication machines; MH= professional equipment, motorcar vehicles, electric machines, chemical industries, other transport equipment, non-electric machines; ML= rubber and plastic materials, naval construction, other industrial sectors, non-iron metals, non-metallic mineral products, metallic works, petroleum and coal, steel industry; LT= paper, printing and editing, textile industry, clothing and leather, food, drinks and tobacco, wood and furniture.
4. See for instance, Brouwer and Kleinknecht (1999), Crépon et al. (1998), Duguet and Kabla (1998), Hall et al. (1986).
5. This is in line with the U-shaped relationship between size and research intensity found by Bound et al. (1984).
6. See, for example, Ritter and Gemünden (2003), Roberts and Berry (1985), Tether (2002), Tyler (2001).
7. See Levin et al. (1987), Brouwer and Kleinknecht (1999), Cohen et al. (2000) and Arundel (2001).
8. Authors like Crépon et al. (1996) and Brouwer and Kleinknecht (1999) have already adopted this dual approach. However, they used information about the number of yearly patent applications while the present data concern the active patents in the patent portfolio of the firms.
9. Owing to space limitation, details on the contribution of each variable to the axes as well as the percentage of variance explained are not reported in the present chapter. They are available upon request.

REFERENCES

Arundel, A. (2001), 'The relative effectiveness of patents and secrecy for appropriation', *Research Policy*, **30** (4), 611–24.

Arundel, A. and I. Kabla (1998), 'What percentage of innovations is patented?, *Research Policy*, **27** (2), 127–41.

Baldwin, J.R., P. Hanel and D. Sabourin (2002), 'Determinants of innovative activity in Canadian manufacturing firms', in A. Kleinknecht and P. Mohnen (eds), *Innovation and Firm Performance: Econometric Explorations of Survey Data*, New York: Palgrave.

Bound, J., C. Cummings, Z. Griliches, B. Hall and A. Jaffe (1984), 'Who does R&D and who patents?', in Z. Griliches (ed.), *R&D, Patents and Productivity*, Chicago, IL: National Bureau of Economic Research and University of Chicago Press, 21–54.

Brouwer, E. and A. Kleinknecht (1999), 'Innovative output and a firm propensity to patent: an exploration of CIS micro data', *Research Policy*, **28** (6), 615–24.

Cohen, W.M., R.R. Nelson and J.P. Walsh (2000), 'Protecting their intellectual assets: appropriability conditions and why US manufacturing firms patent (or not)', NBER working paper no. 7552.

Crépon, B., E. Duguet and I. Kabla (1996), 'Schumpeterian conjectures: a moderate support from various innovation measures', in A. Kleinknecht (ed.), *Determinants of Innovation – The Message from New Indicators*, New York: Palgrave.

Crépon, B., E. Duguet and J. Mairesse (1998), 'Research, innovation, and productivity: an econometric analysis at the firm level', *Economics of Innovation and New Technology*, **7** (2), 115–58.

Duguet, E. and I. Kabla (1998), 'Appropriation strategy and the motivations to use the patent system: an econometric analysis at the firm level in French manufacturing', *Annales d'Economie et de Statistique*, 49/50, 289–327.

Ernst, H. (2001), 'Patent application and subsequent changes of performance: evidence from time-series cross-section analyses on the firm level', *Research Policy*, **30** (1), 143–57.

Glazier, S.C. (2000), *Patent Strategies for Business*, Washington: LBI Law & Business Institute.

Hall, B.H., Z. Griliches and J.A. Hausman (1986), 'Patents and R and D: is there a lag?', *International Economic Review*, **27** (2), 265–83.

Levin, R.C., A.K. Klerovick, R.R. Nelson and S.G. Winter (1987), 'Appropriating the returns from industrial research and development', *Brookings Papers on Economic Activity*, (3), 783–831.

Parr, R.L. and P.H. Sullivan (1996), *Technology Licensing*, New York: John Wiley and Sons.

Peeters, C. and B. van Pottelsberghe (2003a), 'Measuring innovation competencies and performances – a survey of large firms in Belgium', IIR working paper no. 03-16.

Peeters, C. and B. van Pottelsberghe (2003b), 'Organizational competencies and innovation performances – the case of large firms in Belgium', IIR working paper no. 03-19.

Ritter, T. and H.G. Gemünden (2003), 'Network competence: its impact on innovation success and its antecedents', *Journal of Business Research*, **56** (9), 745–55.

Rivette, K.G. and D. Kline (2000), *Rembrandts in the Attic*, Boston, MA: Harvard Business School Press.

Roberts, E.B. and C.A. Berry (1985), 'Entering new businesses: selecting strategies for success', *Sloan Management Review*, **26** (3), 3–17.

Scotchmer, S. and J. Green (1990), 'Novelty and disclosure in patent law', *RAND Journal of Economics*, **21** (1), 131–46.

Sherry, E.F. and D.J. Teece (2004), 'Royalties, evolving patent rights, and the value of innovation', *Research Policy*, **33** (2), 179–91.

Teece, D.J. (1998), 'Capturing value from knowledge assets: the new economy, markets for know- how, and intangibles assets', *California Management Review*, **40** (3), 55–79.

Tether, B.S. (2002), 'Who co-operates for innovation, and why – an empirical analysis', *Research Policy*, **31** (6), 947–67.

Tyler, B.B. (2001), 'The complementarity of cooperative and technological competencies: a resource-based perspective', *Journal of Engineering and Technology Management*, **18** (1), 1–27.

Van Ophem, H., E. Brouwer, A. Kleinknecht and P. Mohnen (2001), 'The mutual relation between patents and R&D', in A. Kleinknecht and P. Mohnen (eds), *Innovation and Firm Performance: Econometric Explorations of Survey Data*, New York: Palgrave.

PART V

Intellectual property and strategic decision-making

13. IP-valuation as a tool to sustain innovation

Eric J. Iversen and Aris Kaloudis

1 INTRODUCTION

The creation of new knowledge, its commercialization and the ability to appropriate the economic benefits have increasingly become a competitive factor both for firms and, indeed, for economies. Therefore, initiatives that improve the conditions for the generation, diffusion and exploitation of new knowledge in the economy are increasingly sought after. In this light, this chapter considers how more efficient methods to value and capitalize intellectual assets might contribute to the main policy objectives of promoting and sustaining innovation in today's changing environment.

This chapter starts by exploring the role intangible assets (IAs) play in the emerging 'market for knowledge'. This theoretical discussion lays the foundations necessary to consider the need to improve conditions for valuation and capitalization of intellectual assets. The chapter then presents a brief survey of intangible valuation approaches. Finally, the discussion considers evidence of difficulties among smaller Norwegian actors in capitalizing on their intellectual assets, before deriving some implications about the need to improve conditions for the utilization of intellectual assets, especially through better valuation practices.

2 IAS IN THE EMERGING 'KNOWLEDGE MARKET'

We begin from the position that the valuation and capitalization of intellectual assets should be seen in terms of the growing need to improve the way economically important knowledge is generated and utilized in the economy. The argument is that the ultimate goal should be to promote and sustain innovation processes both at the firm and the aggregate level. The premise is that more reliable valuation techniques can lay the basis for better management of innovation processes within the firm, while at the same time providing for better co-ordination mechanisms between innovating firms and the wider economy (vis-à-vis collaborators, funding agencies, users, and so on).

In this light, we start by briefly exploring the role IAs, especially those protected by intellectual property rights (IPRs), play in the innovation process at the level of the economy. The role of this type of intangibles can be seen particularly in terms of an emerging 'market for knowledge' (Baumol 2002). The idea of a 'market for knowledge' goes beyond the generally accepted premise that new technological knowledge has become more important to the economy. It emphasizes, moreover, that the way economic activities are organized is also changing and, in doing so, new challenges are emerging.

2.1 Three Illustrative Scenarios

Three basic scenarios can be used to substantiate the increasing relevance of valuation techniques, while also illustrating the sort of challenges that are in question. The first involves the changing way innovation activities are organized. Here it has been pointed out that the innovation process increasingly implies joint ventures, R&D collaborations and other multi-actor arrangements in which different interests become involved in different capacities for different durations (Arora et al. 2001). The increasing currency of such constellations and the changing division of labour they imply, require new tools in order to work well. One prerequisite for such arrangements is an agreed way by which to value IAs prior to the collaboration as well as during and after it. Here trusted techniques for valuation are becoming essential.

New challenges also emerge from the changing environment for financing innovation, not least in life-science research. This second scenario is characterized by innovators who are faced by particularly high investment costs, by long horizons for development, testing, and so on, as well as by undeveloped or under-developed markets. Measuring intangibles becomes an important basis on which to attract investment as well as other funding for these types of innovators, who generally lack of traditional forms of collateral and who face evolving funding needs during the course of the innovation process. Innovators of this type also find themselves faced by a wider variety of financing instruments from a variety of sources (business angels, venture capital, public grants, and so on). In general, there is a need for standard methods for valuing intangibles where more than one funder is involved, where funding needs are subject to change at different stages and where traditional guidelines for funding do not apply.

A third scenario emerges at the firm level, in cases where the challenge of proactively organizing company activities substantially involves IAs.

In firms that are are built around 'knowledge' and the hopeful creation of IAs, there is a recognized need (especially in times of uncertainty) to develop a well-reasoned expectation of the value of what may be the bedrock of the company. This is true of single technology firms familiar from the dotcom era but it is also true, to varying degrees, of other companies, including diversified companies who need robust and reliable ways to gauge the relevant importance of their different in-house activities. In a range of settings, standardized valuation tools are thus also increasingly in demand at the firm level.

2.2 Contribution of Valuation Techniques

Such challenges imply an overall need to adapt the conditions for the sustainable and equitable functioning of the quasi-market on which the supply and demand of knowledge meet. In a well-working 'market for knowledge', we expect that new knowledge can find the right complementary resources (not least funding); that knowledge creators and users can be brought together under conditions that are favourable for developing new ideas; and that the same goes for promoting collaboration between different developers, in order to co-ordinate larger projects based on different pieces of knowledge. In this setting, there may be scope to improve interactions within knowledge markets or to improve the interaction between 'knowledge production' (generation and utilization of new knowledge) and other parts of the innovation system, specifically financial markets.

In this context, intangibles that have been codified in formal ways (such as in a patent, design right, trademark) or through contracts are seen as especially important. These intellectual assets[1] represent accumulated knowledge that is also quasi-transferable. They are less intangible, because of codification, and more of an asset because the firm has a basis on which to appropriate profits. The expectation that improved valuation methods for such assets can improve the market for knowledge is significantly based on the fact that information has a fundamental effect on the organization of markets, and on the perception of risks (Arrow 1999). In terms of improving the role of valuation reporting standards, it is necessary to focus on their potential effects on the micro as well as on the macro level.

At the level of the firm, valuation approaches based on intellectual capital models or business scorecard models are often broadened to include a large number of indicators encompassing all areas of business activity. This may cause information overload and reduce the efficiency of the new reporting standards. The OECD's International Symposium on Intellectual Capital (1999) suggests that there is a need to concentrate on firm's innovation processes and how these generate value. It is important to appreciate here, that understanding what determines the value of intellectual intangibles entails understanding the firm's place in the innovation system. Baum et al. (2000) found that the most important value-drivers in a company are (in rank order) innovation, the ability to attract talented employees, alliances, quality of processes, products or services, environmental performance, brand investment, technology and customer satisfaction. Hence, Baum et al. (2000) supports the argument that some firm-level aspects are more important than others. To be successful, a firm must know the potential value of its knowledge base, have a strategy for monetizing its intellectual assets and be effective in generating a return on these valuable assets.

In this light, improved accountancy practices for intellectual assets can have a variety of positive effects beyond immediate, actuarial tasks. For example, they can contribute to:

- making enterprises more aware of value-potential which might otherwise be overlooked (or under- or overvalued)
- sensitizing other actors in the innovation system to a more realistic understanding of the risks and rewards of through these values
- improving the working of different financial markets (including more accurate information) which are important to innovating small and medium-sized enterprises (SMEs)
- facilitate access to other markets (for example, the USA), including promoting different types of co-operation with foreign companies (mergers and acquisitions, also R&D collaboration)
- improve analysis of the workings of the economy in significant ways, which, for example, may lead to better economic and innovation policies.

At the level of the wider economy, the role of valuation reporting standards has implications for financial stability. The work of the Bank for International Settlements on financial risk measures and procyclicality (see Lowe 2002) notes, in particular, the possible effects of different methods and standards of intangible valuation on the aggregate economic conditions. The role valuation techniques of intangibles may play in this pursuit includes at least three general functions:

1. To enhance conditions for the generation of new knowledge. This entails the organization of markets for new knowledge, relative structures and appropriability mechanisms. The dissemination of knowledge and its spillover effects is also dependent on the existence of mechanisms for appropriability which can efficiently balance incentives to generate new knowledge against effective modes to spread it.

2. The (dynamically) efficient allocation of resources, such as financial, human and knowledge capital across economic activities. Given the importance of these factors to economic growth, their more effective utilization becomes a major policy issue;
3. The uncertainty generated in the economy when there are systematic and large gaps between the market value of companies and the book value of their tangible assets. New reporting techniques on firms' intangibles may reduce this gap and contribute to more stable economies. It is not our intention here to discuss the complex interactions between institutions, such as reporting standards, the financial system and macroeconomic trends. However, it is important to recognize that reporting techniques help determine how the market factors-in risk during the course of a business cycle. It raises the question of whether it is possible to reduce macroeconomic instability and avoid procyclical tendencies by means of well-designed and new reporting techniques. In short, what may be the macroeconomic effects of the new reporting initiatives on market perception and distribution of risks?

A final issue that is perhaps underestimated in the literature relates to the potential costs of a mandatory standardization of information disclosure of intellectual assets. In general, there is reason to suspect that poorly designed accountancy standards may be detrimental to the functioning of intangible markets. This raises the question of what the potential dangers of this exercise are. This is an issue that we leave to future discussion (see, however, Chapter 3 in this volume). However, some important issues here would involve reporting incentives, macroeconomic effects, costs – particularly, for the SMEs, arbitrariness of what is reported and what is not, and so on. In any case, a bad standard for reporting may prove to be significantly worse than no standard at all.

3   A BRIEF SURVEY OF INTANGIBLE VALUATION APPROACHES

In other markets, such as those for products, it can be relatively uncomplicated to arrive at a 'fair market price'. One often has the advantage of being able to look to the sale prices of equivalent goods in order to get to get an idea of the 'going price' and value the good on this basis. Market surveys are also applicable in such situations. Determining the fair market value of an intellectual asset, however, is much more complicated. One point is that there is no market to survey for a new and unproven idea. Another is that the novelty implied in these assets means that such equivalent benchmarks are not available, especially in the case of more radical ideas. Indeed, formal valuation of intellectual assets faces many challenges.

In view of the rising need for reliable valuation methods, a surprising diversity of approaches has developed in recent years (for example, Cañibano, et al. 1999). One investment-literature orientated survey (Sveiby 2002) identifies 21 approaches for measuring IAs. This section surveys several types of valuation methods for intangibles, especially those involving IPRs. The survey also takes into account that approaches also vary as to how they are designed to be used and by whom. We note that the applications for the different approaches range from designing econometric models, to improving accountancy standards for equity markets, to generating more specific tools for corporate management.

3.1 General Characteristics

There are basically two classes of approach: (1) the cost-based approaches which proceed from different methods to estimate the cost to develop the asset or an asset that accomplishes the same thing; (2) value-based approaches, which utilize discounted cash flow analysis or other approaches such as real option methods (familiar from financial theory) in order to predict market value. In addition there is a set of other tools that attempt more indirectly to estimate values not only prices. The individual approaches are characterized by different foci and different objectives. As a result they have different strengths in different contexts. In general, measuring 'intangibles' is done for a variety of different reasons. An accountancy/business management perspective wants to measure such assets in order to assist in decisions related to mergers and acquisitions or other investment decisions, to manage patent portfolios, to monitor the firm's performance/potential and report to shareholders, and so on. A financial analyst/investor perspective broadly wants to understand the same phenomena about companies, although their reasons for doing so are fundamentally different. In addition, theoreticians want to understand a wide range of phenomena, including more aggregate concerns, such as how such assets are allocated in the economy.

In addition to understanding why intangibles are being measured, there are differences in interpretation of what is considered to be an IA. As the motives for measurement suggest, there is a large range for what falls under the category. These vary in degree of 'intangibility' and the degree to which the company has control over it as an 'asset'. At the one end, we have 'IAs' that estimate human capital as a residual category of company value. At the other, we have intellectual assets as covered by patent, design right, trademarks or through contracts.

3.2   Distinguishing Patents and What is Patented

A first step to addressing the value of intellectual assets is to distinguish between the underlying invention – which might be called the underlying intellectual asset – and the IPR, which confers exclusive rights over that invention. This distinction implies that the direct financial value of a patent is the value of potential profits obtainable from fully exploiting the invention defined by the patent's claims that are in excess of those obtainable without patent protection.

On this basis, Pitkethly (2002; see also Chapter 14 in this volume) distinguishes the commercialization of inventions from the patents protecting such inventions on the basis that they hinge on one another, but are not co-dependent. In the one direction, the ability to commercialize an invention depends on many non-IPR factors, such as speed to market, control of complementary assets, and so on. In the other, IPRs may remain valuable even if the inventor no longer has any interest in direct commercialization. That is, a patent provides a right to protect anything falling within the scope of the claim, irrespective of whether the idea is commercialized and by whom. This gives the patent-holder the scope, for example, to use patents as a tool to measure internal technical staff, as a signalling mechanism in the market (for example, to potential collaborators), as a gate-opener in joint ventures or as strategic asset during standardization activities (see Chapter 10 in this volume).

In terms of valuation, the strength of the IP is nonetheless a critical factor in valuation approaches. The existence of a patent and its status provide important indications of the value of the asset as perceived by the applicant. Patenting can indicate that the applicant expects the invention's value to exceed the cost of filing for the right. The subsequent grant and the payment of maintenance fees provides further suggestion of the value even where there is no other indication of the invention's value reflected either directly on product or licence revenues or indirectly through value on the equity markets. The choices made at different points provide salient indicators of the asset's value environment. These information points have been picked upon especially by real option approaches, which we focus on in section 3.3. Another type of information that is developed by the process of patenting is patent citations. These have increasingly been used to identify important patents. We will feature approaches that use citations in section 3.4.

3.3   General Approaches to Valuation

Against the background above, we explore some different approaches to intangible valuation currently being used. These range from the more

IP and strategic decision-making

conceptual-based models that have emerged to address general management issues to the more technical approaches with roots in accountancy and actuarial work. We look first at the latter dominant tradition which can be divide into two sets of approaches:

- *Cost-based approaches*: these tend to proceed either from the costs related to the generation of the IA in question and/or cost estimates for a potential buyer to develop a solution which is the same or which accomplishes a similar result. Accordingly, this type is the more conservative approach and is favoured by some (especially in times of economic downturn) as providing relatively dependable valuation results at the lower end of what the asset may be worth. The issue is how they are used. They are arguably better at reflecting value to the asset-holder but less useful for financial markets, although they are rather limited in either case. One limitation in the latter case is that the market is interested in information about the value (not the cost) of internally generated intangibles.[2] In the former case, the approach can be useful to account for the accumulated development costs of a project or programme in cases in which these cannot be fully recouped for extraneous reasons.
- *Value-based approaches*: these tend to provide higher valuations than cost-based approaches. The basic approach attempts to establish what the market (especially the equity market) perceives the value contribution of intangibles to be when they assess company value. This set of methods is based on the strong assumption that capital markets are efficient, in other words that there are no imperfections in the market of IAs due to imperfect and asymmetric information. This is a serious limitation if the aim is to find the intrinsic value of the intangible. On the other hand, this approach provides tools to systematically investigate the shadow value (or marginal contribution) of each intangible relative to tangible assets (see Bosworth et al. 2000; Chapters 6–9 in this volume).

Two recent developments are noteworthy within these traditions. The first involves what the valuation is used for. The assessment of patents donated to charities – which qualify for tax deduction in the US – has recently provided a surprising scene in which to test acceptable norms for patent valuation. The perception that donations were being overvalued led in Autumn 2004 to the introduction in new legislation in the USA (HR 4825) of a provision to limit value setting either to a cost-based or a fair-market value estimation, whichever is smaller.[3] The bill has been signed into law.

A more analytical development has taken place within value-based approaches where option-based methods have gained currency. These methods represent a relatively new and promising approach to the valuation of IAs, which involves option-pricing techniques. Here, real option valuation methods are used to factor-in risk and other properties that may be captured in the option element of the intangible. One of the weaknesses of this approach is that the determination of the parameters necessary for estimating the real option value may become somewhat arbitrary (see below).

3.4 Conceptualizing Tools

Another line of approach involves conceptual models which can function as management tools. Approaches such as the intellectual capital model or the balance scorecard can be characterized as belonging to 'the new reporting paradigm' (see Upton 2001: 21). The balanced scorecard (Kaplan and Norton 1992) is one high-profile approach that addresses the limited applicability of financial reporting standards to firms with disproportionately high IAs. It tries to account for the aspirations of investors, customers, employees and suppliers in creating value, ultimately at the financial level. A further example is the Canadian Performance Reporting Initiative (CPRI). The fundamental premise behind CPRI is that the market and the firm need to acquire more insight into pre-transactional and forward-looking value-creation processes of the firm. The approach believes that traditional financial reporting is inherently limited in its ability to measure value creation. This suggests the need for a parallel reporting system to traditional cost-based financial reporting that enables measurement of value creation as it occurs.

3.5 Focus on Real- Option-based Approaches

Real- option-based approaches offer some of the most productive ways to address the valuation question, so they deserve more attention. Option-based valuation approaches provide a particularly apt framework in which to consider the management of companies' patent portfolios and other IPR assets. These approaches are based on option pricing in financial markets. Option pricing theory (OPT) understands an option to be a financial instrument that gives a right but not an obligation, at or before some specified time, to purchase or sell an underlying asset whose price is subject to some form of random variation.

This basic concept can be applied to situations other than financial options. Such non-financial options are known as real options. An example of a real option may be an R&D project. The cost of an R&D project

---

BOX 13.1   BASICS OF OPTION PRICING

A call option is an agreement often associated with stock options, which allows the contractor to buy a specified volume of a security (often a certain number of shares of the underlying stock) at a predetermined strike price within a given period. In contrast, a 'put option' allows but does not oblige the party to sell a security according to the same conditions. There are two types of option contracts; the American and European. Their difference lies in the exercise possibilities or when value can be realized.

- European options: European options can only be exercised on the expiry date of the contract.
- American options: American options can be exercised throughout the entire term.

Valuation of patents has been estimated on the basis of pricing methods of American options given the fact that patents can be exercised throughout the entire period in which the patent is valid, including the expiration date

---

may be identified as the price of a call option (see Box 13.2) on the future commercialization of the project and the future investment needed to capitalize on the R&D programme with the exercise price of the option. This approach is particularly apt where choices are involved – such as the choice to patent, to renew a patent, and so on – and where different outcomes can be envisaged. Taking account of such choices and such potential outcomes can lay the basis for a much more realistic valuation of assets than approaches that do not factor these in.

Patenting involves several, largely sequential, types of choices or options and, therefore, it is theoretically possible to divide up the various stages of the life of a patent into a series of options. First, there are the options comprising expansion, deferral and abandonment of the patent rights. Second, there is the option of licensing the patent. Patent royalty cash flows may be then considered as a perpetual American option. Third, one also has the option to sell the patent and the option not to license the patent. This gives two additional options. In principle, it should be possible to value each of these options using some of the concepts from real option theory. To explore these possibilities, various approaches have attempted to link value to individual stages in the life of a patent. The comprehensive study of Schankerman and Pakes (1986) is a notable example, which serves to establish the connection between the willingness of patent-holders to pay renewal- fees at regular intervals and patent value.

Real option theory predicts that early in a patent's or applications' life the option component is likely to comprise the major part of the patent value. This value is often considerable. The theory, in fact, supports the view that, early in their lives, one should usually renew patents even in the absence of any current returns. However, much work remains in developing the practical application of option pricing theory. On the other hand, pricing techniques of IPRs based on real option theories are already being used by market analysts in certain areas, and this approach deserves more attention. In fact, real option theories provide a new conceptual framework for a whole range of innovation policy issues (see Chapters 14 and 15 in this volume).

3.6   Focus on Citation-based Approaches

Another approach, which has increasingly been applied in theoretical analysis, relies on information found in individual patents. These approaches use the citations that patents make to antecedent patents. The expressed purpose of these citations is initially to distinguish the citing patent from the technological state of the art, as represented by the cited patent. This differentiation from other inventions provides trails of citations which then can be used at one level to establish the technological importance of the invention among its cohorts. At another level, the intensity of citations can be understood to indicate the commercial importance of the invention. In terms of 'valuation', this dynamic is thus indicative of the 'impact' of patented technology.

The association of citations with some 'impact' measure is based on different assumptions about what citation streams indicate. Sampat and Ziedonis (2003) indicate that, in general, citations can be interpreted to reflect entry into profitable areas of research and/or technological opportunities or market interest in a technological area. In this setting citing patents can be seen as reflecting knowledge spillovers from earlier inventions, thereby suggesting that some of the value spills over to subsequent inventions (that is, the citing patent: see Box 13.2). In the other direction, cited patents might also reflect a 'publicity effect' whereby economically successful patents are more widely known and therefore more often cited.

In different ways, the literature on this front has indicated that:

- citation counts are indicative of knowledge spillovers and, by implication, of the generation of higher levels of 'social value' (for example, Jaffe et al. 2000)

- citation-weighted patent stocks are indicative of the level of firm value (Hall et al. 2000)
- citations are a good indicator of whether a patent is licensed (Mogee 1997), but not of licence revenues (Sampat and Ziedonis 2003)

In addition, citations have been used as just one of a number of approaches to valuation, reflecting the complexity of the valuation question and the need for a range of different data. Harhoff et al. (1999) have combined citation analysis with interviews and surveys in the case of particularly important inventions. This combined approach is promising, and it confirms a relationship between citations and value. In addition, Lanjouw and Schankerman (1999) have analysed patent citations in the light of other information to construct composite measures of 'patent quality'. Adjusting for quality in this way improves the analysis both with regard to R&D expenditure and to economic significance.

BOX 13.2   THE CITATION-BASED APPROACH USES THE EXTENT OF CITATION STREAMS AS AN INDICATION OF THE VALUE OF THE PATENTED TECHNOLOGIES INVOLVED

- Citations made by a given patent (so-called 'backward citations') can imply something about both the quality of the citing patent and the degree of extra value that it derives in the form of a knowledge spillover from the cited patents. The number of citations made is thought to represent how much of the extra (social) value from previous inventions is being captured by the citing patent. By citing earlier patented technology, the citing patent is to a certain degree capturing excess value (a dividend on the social return) of the unappropriated value of the cited patents.
- Citations made to a given patent (so-called 'forward citations') can indicate how important the cited patent is, and therefore indicate something about its value. The citations streams can indicate an important new technology and/or market.
- Limitations: patent citations take years to develop, so they are best used retrospectively and not in real time. Nonetheless, they can contribute to more comprehensive analysis, for example, in association with interviews.

---

4 IMPORTANCE OF ACCURATE VALUES: EVIDENCE FROM NORWEGIAN PATENTING

The successful transformation from IAs to value in competitive markets is contingent on a multitude of factors, many of them external to the firm. How do IAs fare as firms attempt to navigate these contingencies? In light of the theoretical discussion above, this final section explores Norwegian patenting behaviour for indications as to how the knowledge market functions in Norway. It is based on a study sponsored by WIPO to understand how SMEs use the IPR system in Norway (Iversen 2003). This glance through a patent lens[4] suggests that some firms in particular have difficulties navigating the contingencies along the way from new knowledge (that is, the patent application) to IA (that is, a valid patent grant). In this exercise, we observe how different size classes of firms enjoy different levels of success in terms of grants – the smaller the firm, the higher the probability that it withdraws the application. Withdrawal rates reveal something about the way individual firms evaluate the worth of their IAs and their ability to realize that worth.

4.1 Patenting and Value

The premise for this exercise is that a patent application represents accumulated knowledge, as well as some economic return or other value. The fact that an economic agent applies for a patent indicates that the firm believes that it has accumulated novel knowledge, which it considers to be an asset with commercial possibility. We recognize, of course, that this mode of formalizing one's IA is neither equally attractive nor equally pertinent to all new economic knowledge in all firms in all industries. Nevertheless, those who do apply dedicate resources (both in time and money) in the quest to derive some value from new knowledge that they presumably have developed.[5]

In the light of this, we interpret withdrawal to mean that, in one way or another, the initial value expectations by the applicant are disappointed. The fact that an applicant withdraws their own application may be due to a number of reasons. There are two main types of interpretations. The first is that withdrawal indicates something about the quality of the invention and/or of the application. In other words, withdrawal can indicate that the application was poorly framed and the applicant had reason to believe that it would not be granted in an acceptable form. Alternately, withdrawal can be interpreted in line with a renewal approach, as an early indication of doubt about the invention's realistic potential value; indeed, many would assume that the quality of these patents is at the lower end of the scale.

The interpretation that immediately relates firm size with quality may well seem plausible on a case by case basis. However, since value is ultimately established on the market, such an interpretation ignores the fact that new technologies are inherently difficult to value in the face of comprehensive uncertainty. Furthermore, it tends to discard out of hand the role that other complementary factors may play in generating value from new technology. The second type of interpretation therefore involves accessing these complementary assets, or more to the point, the inability to do so. One likely reason for why an applicant does not follow up the application (following a fee schedule) is that the funding necessary to bring the idea to market is insufficient or has run out (see the discussion of the capitalization process above). Another scenario is that the small firm withdraws its application before publication due to uncertainty about its ability to defend itself against the threat of litigation by larger more powerful firms.

4.2   A Decade of Domestic Patenting in Norway

The WIPO study indicates several aspects about the Norwegian knowledge market. The first is largely anecdotal. In raw terms, innovative Norwegian firms tend to be less active in protecting their IP than firms in other European countries (Eurostat 2004). Whether this is due to their failure to recognize the value of their IAs or to some other reason[6] is not known. One can assume a problem (especially among some firms) in recognizing IAs and formalizing them. As indicated, one potential advantage of improved valuation exercises is that they might encourage firms to take stock of their IAs.

A second observation, however, is that Norwegian actors, not least SMEs, have used the patent and trademark systems more actively in the course of the 1990s. This suggests that the knowledge base is growing, the propensity to formalize intangibles is growing, the propensity to use the IPR system is growing, or a combination of these. In this situation, it is important to make sure that all actors have realistic expectations about the innovation process and that they have equal chances to derive value from it.

A final general observation is that the propensity to get as far as a patent application is strongly dependent on the size of the firm, for whatever reason. Smaller firms, on average, are much less likely to apply for patents than larger ones, even in the same industries. For example, large firms (over 100 employees) in the electrical equipment industry filed on average 1.6 applications in Norway, while medium-sized firms (50–99) on average filed 0.25 applications in the same period; the smallest are almost off the chart (0.03). This suggests that large enterprises tend to be more innovative, are better at recognizing the potential of IPRs to make the most of their new knowledge, are in a better position to capitalize on formalized IAs, or a combination these factors.

More generally, there are grounds to expect smaller firms to produce inventions more infrequently than larger ones. As a result, less experience and expertise accumulates in the smaller firms and this, in turn, puts them at a potential disadvantage when pitted against firms who are accomplished users of the patent system and who build up this competence in-house (see Bosworth and Wilson 1978).

4.3   Size-dependent Patent Withdrawal

A more specific point from the WIPO report is that SME patents are more often withdrawn than those of large entities. This raises the suspicion that smaller entities find it more difficult than larger ones to follow through on their attempts to capitalize on formalizing IAs. In this vein, Figure 13.1 shows that 'success' in Norwegian patenting is indeed dependent on firm size. There may be many factors behind the differences in success rates, where 'success' is measured as non-withdrawal. Part of the explanation is probably to be found at the firm level: larger firms have a better working understanding of the IPR system, they have internal resources (and, thus, staying power and fighting power in litigation), and they have a more conscious and better informed policy about IAs built into the enterprise's business strategy.

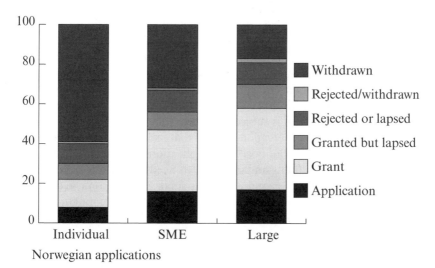

Source: Iversen (2003)

Figure 13.1   Norwegian applications by size-class and status (per cent, N = 12,277)[7]

The reason that a much larger proportion of SME applications have been withdrawn (one-third), compared with large enterprise applications (one-sixth), has to do both with such internal factors. However, it presumably also involves factors that are external to the firm, especially access to funding at critical stages in the development process. In general, the differences in withdrawal rates suggest several types of factors might be at play, including:

1. Smaller actors, especially independent inventors, tend to overestimate the value of their IAs going into a formalization process.
2. Smaller applicants are forced to cut losses during the long development process because of difficulties in accessing complementary assets – especially funding. This suggests that many, perhaps good, ideas are not developed because of the capitalization problem and the functioning of investment markets.
3. Smaller applicants have a poorer working understanding of the patent system and could use a greater degree of assistance when approaching it.

4.4 Some Implications

In terms of valuation and capitalization of IAs, this exercise indicates that there is potential to raise the efficiency of the utilization of IAs, not least in a country with a large population of small enterprises. Here, the domestic patenting record illustrates that the value of IAs is by no means predetermined or constant. The fact that smaller firms patent less often, on average, than larger enterprises indicates that something about the generation and/or utilization of new knowledge and/or the propensity to utilize the patent system is subject to scale.

If we interpret this observation to mean that scale can influence the degree of formalizing IAs, we can posit two implications for improved valuation methods. The first is that standard methods need to take into account this type of difference. The second is that, as small firms become acquainted with valuation methods, there is the possibility that they might become more aware of the potential value of their IAs. A positive side effect might be that they will more actively integrate a policy of formalizing IAs into their business strategy.

The size-related tendency to withdraw patent applications emphasizes the importance of improving firm-internal processes. The large proportion of SME withdrawals indicates that we face a need not only to increase awareness, but also to increase expertise about formalizing IAs. Here it is important that the smaller enterprises also have a realistic expectation of the potential value of IAs in the face of great uncertainty. The routinization of valuation exercises can promote this at the firm level.

Establishing accepted standards for IP valuation may have a more instrumental affect in terms of factors external to the firm. We need also to increase awareness and expertise not only in other companies, but in the institutional framework surrounding these companies. This wider recognition and more nuanced view of IAs, especially among banks and funding agencies, might improve the way financial markets work in relation to innovating firms.

5 CONCLUSION

Value creation in the economy is connected to knowledge creation, dissemination, and utilization in its constituent enterprises and institutions. Methods to improve the way intangibles are recognized and valuated via accountancy methods can improve the way the market for knowledge functions and, moreover, the way that emerging knowledge market interacts with established financial markets. The purpose of this chapter has been to explore the relationship between valuation of intangibles and innovation processes, which was done both in theoretical and empirical terms. The ultimate goal is further off. The goal facing us is to improve the way intellectual assets are generated and utilized in an environment in which IAs have become more important.

The discussion above suggests that, in order to improve the efficiency of the changing market for knowledge, it is first necessary to develop a finer-grained understanding of the problems different types of firms currently face in capitalizing on their intellectual assets. Better diagnosis is needed to assess the degree to which such problems tend to originate within the firm (for example, breakdown in their innovation management) and to understand this component within the context of problems that stem from outside the firm (for example, funding conditions, threat of litigation, uneven playing fields in collaboration, and so on). Improved modes of recognizing potential value, of attracting capital, of improving interfaces with collaborators and users, and of levelling playing fields between rivals can then lead to improvement in the overall conditions for the generation, diffusion and exploitation of new knowledge.

Given an improved understanding of the problems that SMEs in particular face, a next step would be to consider the applicability of the many instruments that already exist in different national and regional settings. These include measures designed to improve awareness and expertise in dealing with the IPR system, to improve the support structures, to differentiate the patent system to include 'petty patents' for lower-quality inventions, to develop insurance schemes against the threat of litigation, and so on (see Iversen 2003, for a set of recommendations). Such measures could be systematically assessed both in terms of their potential success to remedy the problem as well as in terms of consistency with the overall innovation system into which they are introduced.

NOTES

1. The term used by the UNECE High Level Task Force on Valuation.
2. Cost-based models may provide third parties with important information in certain cases, such as establishing the amount eligible for tax deduction for patent donations in the USA. See note 3.
3. See http://www.thomas.loc.gov/cgi-bin/bdquery/z?d108:h.r.04520. The donor can furthermore claim a percentage of the profits generated by the charity from the patent as a tax deduction. For a presentation, see www.independentsector.org/programs/gr/inkinddonations.htm#Patents.
4. Based on the WIPO study, the patent lens used here picks up 6,303 Norwegian entities who, together, were involved in 14319 'active' domestic patents during the 1990s. By 'Active', we mean any patent that was applied for and/or granted during the 1990s *and* any patent applied for before then but granted during the 1990s.
5. We recognize that the 'value' of patenting will differ among these actors and across time. Primarily, the value is seen in terms of aid the competitive position of the firm by affording it the room to cultivate its distinct qualities without threat of direct competition from imitations. In addition, there are other ways in which patenting can hold 'value' for the assignee which do not immediately involve the dollar sign: for example, signals to the market, strong-fences in R&D collaborations, and so on.
6. That is, related to the competitiveness of their markets, the relevance of patenting to their markets, and so on.
7. Two thousand and forty-two unknowns and unregistered applications have been removed.

REFERENCES

Arora, A., A. Fosfuri and A. Gambardella (2001), *Markets for Technology: Economics of Innovation and Corporate Strategy*, Cambridge, MA: MIT Press.
Arrow, J.K. (1999), 'Information and the organization of industry', in G. Chichilnisky (ed.), *Markets, Information and Uncertainty: Essays in Economic Theory in Honor of Kenneth J. Arrow*, Cambridge: Cambridge University Press.
Baum, G., C. Ittner, D. Larcker, J. Siesfeld, M.S. Malone (2000), 'Introducing the New Value Creation', Forbes ASAP, 4 April, www.forbes.com/asap/.
Baumol, William J. (2002) *The Free-Market Innovation Machine: Analyzing the Growth Miracle of Capitalism*, Princeton, NJ: Princeton University Press.
Bosworth, D.L. and R.A. Wilson (1978), 'Some evidence on the productivity of qualified manpower in Britain: a note', *Bulletin of Economic Research*, **30**, (1), 45–9.

Bosworth, D., A. Wharton and C. Greenhalgh (2000), 'IAs and the market valuation of UK companies: evidence from fixed effects models', working paper no. 2, Oxford Intellectual Property Research Centre.

Cañibano, Leandro, Manuel Garcia-Ayuso and Paloma Sánchez (1999), 'Accounting for intangibles: a literature review', project report, (Meritum Project, TSER.

Eurostat (2004), *Innovation in Europe: Results for the EU, Iceland and Norway*, Luxembourg: European Commission.

Hall, Bronwyn H., Adam Jaffe and Manuel Trajtenberg (2000), 'Market value and patent citations: a first look', NBER working paper W7741.

Harhoff, Dietmar, et al. (1999), 'Citation frequency and the value of patented inventions', *Review of Economics and Statistics*, **81**, 511–15.

Harhoff, Dietmar, Frederic Scherer and Katrin Vopel (1999), 'Citations, family size, and the value of patent rights', mimeo.

Iversen, E. (2003), *Norwegian Small and Medium-sized Enterprises and the Intellectual Property Rights System: Exploration and Analysis*, Geneva: World Intellectual Property Organization (WIPO).

Jaffe, A., M. Trajtenberg and M. Fogarty (2000), 'Knowledge Spillovers and Patent Citations: Evidence from a Survey of Investors', *American Economic Review Papers and Proceedings*, **(90)**, May, 215–18.

Kaplan, Robert and David Norton (1992), 'The balanced scorecard: measures that drive performance', *Harvard Business Review*, January–February, 71–9.

Lanjouw, Jean O. and Mark Schankerman (1999), 'The quality of ideas: measuring innovation with multiple indicators', NBER working paper W7345.

Lowe, P. (2002), 'Credit risk measurement and procyclicality', BIS working papers no. 116, Monetary and Economic Department.

Mogee, Mary Ellen (1997), 'Patent analysis methods in support of licensing', paper presented at the Technology Transfer Society Annual Conference, Denver, Colorado, 22 June.

Organisation for Economic Co-operation and Development (OECD) (1999), *The International Symposium on Intellectual Capital. Measuring and reporting intellectual capital: Experience, issues, and prospects*, Amsterdam, 9–11 June.

Organisation for Economic Co-operation and Development (OECD) (2001), www. oecd.org/EN/document/0,,EN-document-0-nodirectorate-no-20–16345–0,00. html.

Pitkethly, R. (2002), 'Options pricing rules in R&D and IP decisions', presentation at the Higher Level Taskforce on the Valuation and Captialization of Intellectual Assets, United Nations Commission for Europe, Geneva, 18–19 November.

Sampat, Bhaven N. and Arvids, A. Ziedonis (2003), 'Cite seeing: patent citations and the economic value of patents', presented at ZEW Workshop, Empirical Economics of Innovation and Patenting: Manheim: Germany, 14–15 March.

Schankerman, M. and A. Pakes (1986), 'Estimates of the value of patent rights in European countries during the post-1950 period', *The Economic Journal*, **96** (384), 1052–76.

Sveiby, Karl-Erik (2002), 'Methods for measuring IAs', www.sveiby.com/articles/ IntangibleMethods.htm.

Upton, S.W. Jr (2001), 'Business and financial reporting, challenges from the new economy', Financial Accounting Standards Board, special report no. 219-A, April.

14. Patent valuation and real options

Robert Pitkethly

1 INTRODUCTION

1.1 Why Value Patents?

Identifying the value of patent applications and patents[1] enables good patent management decisions to be made about them, including whether to apply for or renew a patent and whether to continue with a pre-existing application. All such judgements involve at least an implicit valuation quite apart from the valuations needed in sale or licensing decisions. This chapter discusses methods for making these judgements explicit and thereby more objective.

1.2 In What Circumstances Should Patents be Valued?

Early in an invention's life, information about the eventual value of any related patent will be scarce. Those most likely to have such information are the inventor, who should know the invention's technical significance, the patent agent, who should know the quality of patent protection obtainable, and marketing managers, who might predict the invention's sales and licensing revenue and any benefits derivable from patents.

Combining these people's expertise with an objective valuation method should improve the quality of managerial decision-making. However, there are problems, first, in selecting a valuation method and, second, in ensuring that decisions are unbiased. For many managers, the potential career costs of not applying for a patent are so much greater than the immediate costs that the advice 'When in doubt, file an application!' (Grubb 1982, p. 48) seems prudent. But can the doubt which makes it seem the correct course of action be accounted for?

Similar considerations apply to other decisions such as patent renewal decisions. Legal considerations may dictate choices and, if there is a reasonably predictable income stream, conventional valuation methods might be used but, in other cases, there are few commonly accepted valuation methods.

Thus, there is a strong possibility of a bias towards conservative patent management decisions wherever there is the slightest possibility of commercial success. Objective patent valuation is rarely considered and patents all too often are renewed and applications filed, not because they are valuable but because no one can or wants to prove that they are not.

2   INVENTIONS, PATENTS AND PATENT APPLICATIONS

A patent can be described as an exclusive right of limited duration over a new, non-obvious invention capable of industrial application, where the right to sue others for infringement is granted in return for publication of the invention. The underlying invention and the IPR conferring rights over the invention need to be distinguished. 'Patent' is sometimes used to mean the underlying invention alone, sometimes the patent right alone and often, the entire project of commercializing the patented invention comprising both the underlying invention and the patent together. Sometimes 'the invention' refers just to a particular embodiment, sometimes anything within the scope of a patent's claims.

However, the financial value of a patent per se must be the value of the potential extra profits from fully exploiting the invention defined by the patent's claims with the patent, compared with those obtainable without it. Projects comprising the commercialization of inventions and patents protecting such inventions are thus different, even if related, entities. The patent's value is of course dependent on, but distinct from, the underlying invention's value. One advantage of a patent system is that if the invention is worthless, so is the patent. Nonetheless, distinguishing between the patent, the underlying invention and commercialization of the patented invention is important since some decisions, such as whether to continue with an application or renew a patent, depend on the value of the patent per se.

Most patent systems have four major decision types confronting applicants and patentees: (1) whether to file a patent application; (2) whether to continue with it (at a number of decision points in the application procedure); (3) whether to keep any patent granted in force; (4) how to exploit the granted patent.

A simplified outline of the UK and European form of patent application procedure is shown in Figure 14.1. At each stage, the potential future benefits of continuing the application have to be balanced against the official and professional fees due for proceeding to the next stage. A patent, then, is not a simple investment project but a right with a complex series of possibilities which unfolds over time under conditions of considerable uncertainty and with a wide variety of courses of action open to patentees.

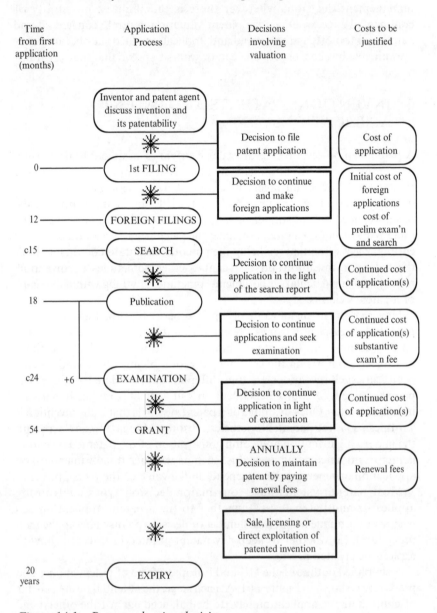

Figure 14.1   Patent valuation decisions

3 ACCOUNTING VALUATION METHODS

In valuing a patent the fundamental issue is by how much the returns from all possible modes of exploitation of the patented invention are greater than those that would be obtained without the patent.

A patent running from filing to expiry possibly 20 years later is complex. Technical and legal risk and managerial choice mean many outcomes are possible. There are many stages when the application may be abandoned or, after grant, when the patent may be allowed to lapse. Additionally, before the end of the first 'priority' year from the initial application, corresponding foreign applications may be filed expanding the 'application'. Any associated decision tree is thus going to be very complex.

Despite these problems a wide range of valuation methods has been described. The writers fall into four main categories: accountants, patent agents, licensing executives and economists. A distinction also needs to be drawn between top-down assessments of overall average patent values including values derived from information in patent specifications (for example, Reitzig 2003; Chapter 15 in this volume) and the bottom-up valuation of individual patents which this chapter is concerned with. It should also be noted that the present discussion concerns the present value and not the transaction structure concerned with individual patent valuations. It is thus how much to pay, not how, that matters.

Parr and Smith (1994) divide valuations of individual patents into cost-, market- and income-based methods, the latter of which includes simple discounted cash flow (DCF) methods. Arthur Andersen and Co. (1992) divide valuation methods into cost-, market-value and economic-value methods. However, it is better to classify individual patent valuation methods by the extra features they account for, over and above less sophisticated methods. These can be summarized in increasing order of sophistication as in Figure 14.2.

The categorization in Figure 14.2 is not of course comprehensive and the B-S equation has been adjusted in numerous ways to take account of extra features such as dividends, changing underlying asset volatility and changing interest rates. However, even the most sophisticated adjustments cannot account for everything. Any valuation method is thus just a step towards better decision-making.

3.1 Cost- and Market-based Methods – Accounting for Historical Costs and Market Conditions

Valuation methods based on the historical costs of obtaining patents ignore their future benefits and are thus an inaccurate guide to IPR value.

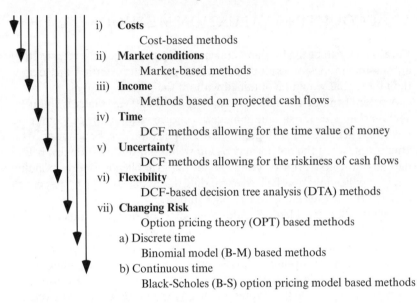

i) **Costs**
   Cost-based methods
ii) **Market conditions**
   Market-based methods
iii) **Income**
   Methods based on projected cash flows
iv) **Time**
   DCF methods allowing for the time value of money
v) **Uncertainty**
   DCF methods allowing for the riskiness of cash flows
vi) **Flexibility**
   DCF-based decision tree analysis (DTA) methods
vii) **Changing Risk**
   Option pricing theory (OPT) based methods
   a) Discrete time
      Binomial model (B-M) based methods
   b) Continuous time
      Black-Scholes (B-S) option pricing model based methods

Figure 14.2   Classification of patent valuation methods

Market-based methods make use of prices of comparable assets or licences which have recently been traded at arm's length in an active market. There are many such methods in common use including use, of 'market rates' for royalties. However, they involve basing valuations on other people's valuations, which may merely propagate suboptimal decisions. Cost- and market-based valuation methods are thus not rigorous objective ways of valuing patents.

3.2   Income-based Methods – Accounting for Future Value

Improvements on cost- or market-based methods include some forecast of future cash flows and thus appreciation of a patent's true value. However, it is only by accounting for time and uncertainty in future cash flows, as with conventional DCF methods, that one begins to find valuations with good theoretical foundations. The key issue in these methods is how the estimated cash flow is arrived at. It may be possible to forecast cash flows associated with a particular IPR through licensing or direct exploitation. However, methods which assume that the income due to a patent per se is an industry average royalty are merely a variant on market-based methods.

3.3   DCF-based Methods – Accounting for Time and Uncertainty

Discounted cash flow methods of valuation account for the time value of money and to some extent the riskiness of the forecast cash flows. Explanations of DCF valuations can be found in any corporate finance textbook (Brealey and Myers 1984) but it is worth discussing some of the peculiarities of using DCF techniques to value patents. One advantage of valuing patents with DCF methods is that since patents have limited lifetimes there is no problem with estimating residual values for cash flows beyond the edge of the forecasting horizon.

For any given project, though, a wide range of cash flows are possible. If the probabilities of these are known, a simple (but incorrect) DCF analysis would use all the cash flows and their probabilities to obtain a total expected cash flow and discount this using the company's current discount rate. Such an approach ignores several factors. First, the discount rate used should always reflect the risk of the cash flow concerned. If the project is not an average company project this will not be the same as the company's cost of capital. In practice, using the capital asset pricing model and finding quoted companies with cash flows of equivalent riskiness, potentially suitable discount rates can be obtained. Second, with a multi-stage cash flow such as with a patent the risk associated with the cash flow will vary considerably over the lifetime concerned. That for a newly granted patent about to be litigated for the first time will be much riskier than for a 15-year-old veteran which has survived many attempts at invalidation. Use of a single constant discount rate actually makes the opposite assumption that the risk adjustment increases as the patent ages, as later cash flows are assumed to be exposed to risk for longer.

The general idea of a discount rate's risk premium component varying over time is dealt with by Hodder and Riggs (1985) who advocate the use of sequences of distinct risk phases in evaluating high-risk projects whose risk varies from phase to phase. This should be standard practice and is covered in most basic corporate finance books (Brealey and Myers 1984). In practice, this would mean splitting the valuation of the patent into several distinct phases, for example, from application to receipt of search results, from the decision to continue to commencement of substantive examination, from acceptance to the end of the first year after grant, from grant to the first year of commercialization, and so on until the product becomes established and the patent eventually expires.

Those articles which do deal with the valuation of patents or R&D from a DCF point of view do not usually account for such considerations. Neil (1988), for example, writing on the valuation of IP, uses a single discount rate and takes the pragmatic view that small variations in the discount rate will have a smaller effect than any possible errors in the forecast cash flow. Parr (1988) also proposes the use of DCF method of valuation but also does not mention the possible variation in risk during the life of a particular piece of intellectual property.

A further approach to uncertainty which uses DCF involves simulation methods. The simplest type involves sensitivity analysis where variables are each adjusted in turn. Another example is that put forward by Stacey (1989), who advocates a probabilistic DCF approach. Since all the information involved in making IP-related decisions is highly uncertain, the costs and revenues are considered probabilistically, resulting in a frequency distribution of net present values (NPVs). In this and other 'Monte Carlo' simulations, all the variables in a model are adjusted at once, according to individual probability distributions, to produce an overall distribution of possible valuations. However, such methods, as Stacey says, involve time-consuming and costly calculations and are constrained by the difficulties in establishing the probability distributions needed. A further issue not raised by Stacey is what the NPV frequency distributions mean. If the probability distributions of NPVs are produced using a risk-free discount rate, not the opportunity cost of capital, the NPV distributions cannot represent actual NPVs since only time has been accounted for. If they do use an opportunity cost of capital the risk is double counted, first in the discount rate and second in the NPV frequency distribution (Brealey and Myers 1984). Problems with NPV distributions are also discussed by Trigeorgis (1996). Perhaps the real role of such simulations is to help understand the way in which the values vary with the parameters of the model constructed.

3.4   DTA-based Methods – Accounting for Flexibility

In addition to the problems of selecting discount rates appropriate to the risk associated with the various stages in a patent's life and those of calculating the possible cash flows which might occur, a third problem is that no account is taken of the various choices open to patent managers. For example, a patent could be allowed to lapse and there is the option to expand the patent family by making corresponding foreign applications. To a certain extent simulations such as those described above can be used to try and account for such outcomes. Where the number of such possibilities is limited though, and choices only occur at defined times, decision tree analysis (DTA) may be used. This is based on an underlying DCF analysis of each branch, starting with the final ones and working backwards in time to give a present value.

The big advantage of DTA over simple DCF analysis is that it builds in the value of flexibility encountered in a patent's life. This at least allows account to be taken of possibilities such as abandonment, though it does not solve the discount rate problem. The rates used ought to be appropriate to the risk involved at each stage and following each type of decision, though in practice a constant rate is usually used.

Decision tree analysis-based methods and the more sophisticated option pricing theory (OPT) based methods described below both take account of flexibility by recognizing opportunities to save unnecessary investment or exploit opportunities for extra investment. They will thus usually both produce higher valuations than the standard NPV valuations. The question is whether the extra refinement offered and extra value recognized by such methods justifies the extra cost and complexity involved.

3.5 OPT Methods – Accounting for Changing Risk

Option pricing theory was developed for use in pricing financial options. An option can be defined generally as a right but not an obligation, at or before some specified time, to purchase or sell an underlying asset whose price is subject to some form of random variation. For a financial option the underlying asset is usually a share whose price varies randomly over time (in a way usually assumed to be a Brownian motion type of Markov process).

Option pricing theory methods, in common with DTA analysis, have the possibility of different outcomes each with different cash flows, each having different risk which in each case evolves over time. However, each stage in the DTA method should use a discount rate appropriate to the risk involved in that stage, and the risk and thus the discount rate may well vary over time due to the differing nature of the pay-offs, and thus decisions, at each stage. In other words, for options more generally, changing risk needs accounting for since, in the limit of an infinite number of discrete DTA stages, each would need an appropriate discount rate.

The key point in accounting for this changing risk of future cash flows is to find some means of risk-neutral valuation. A certainty equivalent approach used in the context of basic DCF analysis is one possible approach, however, another and more powerful method is to use contingent claims analysis, the underlying idea of which is used in both discrete time and continuous time option valuation models.

3.5.1 Discrete time – binomial model (B-M) based methods
Contingent claim analysis (CCA) begins to solve the problem of changing discount rates. It assumes that the returns to a call option[2] on a share are equivalent to those of a portfolio or 'synthetic option' consisting of borrowing some money and buying some of the underlying shares. If it is

assumed that there are no arbitrage opportunities, the price of the option on an underlying share will be given by the price of this synthetic option. This allows the construction of equivalent risk-neutral decision tree probabilities so that the expected pay-outs can be discounted at the risk-free rate. This avoids the need to set an appropriate risk-adjusted discount rate for each branch in the tree.

Copeland and Weiner (1990) describe a number of situations in which non-financial 'real' options occur and in which a CCA valuation method can be used. Trigeorgis and Mason (1987) also discuss CCA analysis of options involved in a project. Contingent claim analysis applied to a decision tree in the absence of any flexibility provides the same answers as a conventional DCF analysis since the use of a single discount rate does not then matter. For simple decision trees involving flexibility, though, CCA is preferable to conventional DCF/DTA methods because it accounts for the value of the options.

3.5.2   Continuous time – Black–Scholes (B-S) option pricing models

Decision tree analysis methods can become inordinately complex resulting in what Trigeorgis (1996, p. 66) calls 'decision bush analysis'. Furthermore, while choices between a few discrete outcomes may occur, in most cases a range of outcomes is possible. In the case of share prices, for example, the range of values may be modelled as a lognormally distributed process. A further problem is that decisions about the underlying asset or project may have to be taken continuously or the price of the underlying share may evolve continuously. Once one involves continuous decisions, the discount rate changes continuously too. Unlike DCF-based DTA analysis using a single risk-adjusted discount rate, OPT methods accounting for continuous time, such as the Black and Scholes equation, solve these problems.

Before moving on to discuss the application of OPT to patent valuation, though, a brief overview of continuous time OPT valuation methods as developed for financial assets may be helpful.

3.5.2.1   Financial options   There has been a long history associated with option valuation methods dating back to at least around 1900 (Bachelier 1900), leading eventually to work by Boness (1964), Samuelson (1965) and Merton (1973). However, the key paper which described the valuation of options on financial assets was published by Black and Scholes in 1973. The B-S equation uses CCA and can be derived from a discrete time CCA analysis by letting the duration of each stage in the tree tend to zero (Cox et al. 1979). Assuming there are no arbitrage opportunities it gives the price C of a European call option on an underlying share as (Black and Scholes 1973):

$$C = SN\left(\left(\frac{\ln(S/E)+\left(r+\frac{1}{2}\sigma^2\right)t}{\sigma\sqrt{t}}\right)\right) - Ee^{-rt}N\left(\left(\frac{\ln(S/E)+\left(r+\frac{1}{2}\sigma^2\right)t}{\sigma\sqrt{t}}\right) - \sigma\sqrt{t}\right)$$

(14.1)

where:
  S = current underlying share price,
  σ = share price volatility,
  E = option exercise price,
  r = risk-free interest rate,
  t = time to expiry,
  $N(\ )$ = cumulative standard normal distribution.

The varying risk involved in an option over time is accounted for by the inclusion of the time remaining to expiry and the variance of the asset returns. The B-S equation is based on several key assumptions: (1) interest rates are constant; (2) share prices follow a random walk where the distribution of prices at the end of a given time period is lognormal with the variance assumed constant; (3) only European options allowing exercise only on expiry are considered; (4) markets are friction free with no transaction costs, no margin requirements or other penalties for short sales and with borrowing or buying any fraction of a share possible; (5) dividend payments are excluded.

These points are important when it comes to considering the application of OPT to patent valuation. However, the most important statement in Black and Scholes' original paper was that option pricing methods could be applied to other financial assets. Cox and Rubinstein (1985), for example, describe a wide range of financial OPT applications.

3.5.2.2 Real options The definition of an option and the OPT valuation methods mentioned above can also be applied to other underlying assets and such non-financial options are known as 'real options' around which a substantial literature has built up. For example Copeland et al. (1990) considered a pharmaceutical R&D project as a series of options. Mitchell and Hamilton (1988) identified the cost of an R&D project with the price of a call option on the commercialization of the project, the future investment needed, with the exercise price, and the present value of the returns from the investment with the value of the underlying share. The most recent and comprehensive overviews of real options can be found in the books by Trigeorgis (1996) and Dixit and Pindyck (1994, 1995). Less advanced outlines of these and OPT methods in general can be found in standard corporate finance textbooks such as Brealey and Myers (1984).

The field of real options has developed because conventional valuation methods do not or cannot cope with managerial flexibility. Kester (1984, p. 156) for example highlighted the existence of both shared and proprietary growth options in many capital budgeting decisions. Proprietary ones resulting from 'patents or the company's unique knowledge of a market or a technology that competitors cannot duplicate' being the more valuable. Kulatilaka and Marcus (1992) discuss an investment choice between gas- and oil-fired boilers and identify value due to many real options. An equivalence between the inputs required to value financial and real options can thus be identified:

Financial option on share	Real option
S Current price of the underlying share	= Present value of project cash flows
E Exercise price of the option	= Investment cost of project
t Time to expiry	= Time left to invest in
σ Standard deviation of underlying share returns	= Standard deviation of the project value
r Risk-free interest rate	= Risk-free interest rate

Trigeorgis (1986) has categorized real options, based on distinctions noted by Kester (1984) into options which are either proprietary or shared (as noted above), simple or compound (the latter involving a number of successive options) and expiring or deferrable (the latter being such as to allow an investment or decision to be deferred). On this basis one can identify most patent-related options as likely to be proprietary, compound, deferrable real options since they are by definition exclusive to the patentee (or exclusive licensee).[3] Patents also involve a number of successive stages and decisions which can often be postponed, at least until the next deadline in the application process, renewal fee deadline or when a sale or licensing decision is due.

3.6 Real Options – Patents, Problems and Solutions

The applicability of financial option valuation methods to non-financial assets has raised a number of questions which may also be relevant in applying OPT methods to patents.

An early example of such a debate occurs between Emery et al. (1978) and Rao and Martin (1981). The former concluded that using OPT for real investment decisions risked illogical decisions (Emery et al. 1978). The latter refuted those concerns but in arguing for the B-S approach raised concerns about the requirement for continuous trading in the underlying asset and the option, and the fact that interim cash flows were forbidden. Trigeorgis (1996) and Kester (1993) also identify three main points where real options may differ from conventional financial options.

First, with shared real options, the option holder also has to account for the effects of competition. Patents, however, are by definition proprietary, so this should be of minor concern save for the possible effects of non-infringing substitutes.

Second, there is the potential problem that the underlying asset may not be traded easily. The fact that an asset is not traded is not a general bar to using option pricing methods. However, the B-S equation depends for its derivation on a no-arbitrage equilibrium involving a traded security. Contingent claim analysis in general requires a traded asset or portfolio of assets whose stochastic change in value exactly matches that of the underlying asset on which an option is to be valued and from which the magnitude of the volatility can be obtained (termed a spanning traded asset). For most commodities and goods this should be possible. However, Dixit and Pindyck (1994, p. 148) have pointed out that: 'there may be cases in which this assumption will not hold; an example might be a project to develop a new product that is unrelated to any existing ones, or an R&D venture, the results of which may be hard to predict'. While Dixit and Pindyck go on to assume that CCA is possible in an example comprising investment in a project of uncertain outcome, the issue needs further discussion. Trigeorgis (1996) lists a large number of papers which deal with R&D-related options. A key question though must be whether the assumptions of CCA-based methods as used in OPT and the use of Brownian Motion type diffusion processes to model the price of the underlying asset are justified when considering patents.

As with predicting when earthquakes occur, we may not be able to predict whether a particular invention will be a success, but we should be able to show what the distribution of returns from inventions and IPRs are and from this deduce information about their current value. However, North (1996) has pointed to a distinction between risk and uncertainty, quoting Arrow (1951) and Lucas (1981). The latter of these said 'in cases of uncertainty, economic reasoning will be of little value'. North points out that Frank Knight (1921) made a fundamental distinction between risk and uncertainty,[4] for the former of which it was, given sufficient information, possible to derive probability distributions of outcomes, and for the latter of which, it was not. Of course, if the processes involved in the success of innovations and on which the value of IPRs depends are purely uncertain and not merely predictably risky, then deriving any forecastable value for IPRs may be impossible. However, this thought should not deter us since one can say that all IPRs have a value expressed in monetary terms and we have data showing that returns to inventions do form characteristic distributions, suggesting particular underlying stochastic processes which we can model. We need to be aware, though, of the potential strong influence of other factors such as the costs involved in commercializing an IPR-protected invention which the IPR's revenues might mirror more than they reflect any underlying stochastic process.

What remains debatable is what models should be used. Scherer (1997) shows that returns to patented inventions are highly skewed even within the sub-population of patents renewed to their full term. Common experience shows that the distribution of returns from patented inventions must be highly skewed at the end of their life with a few highly valuable patents and a lot of lapsed, and thus worthless, ones. Consequently, what type of diffusion process and distribution may best model the returns to patents needs careful consideration. Is a Brownian-type process or some jump diffusion process involving a mixture of Brownian-type process with Poisson jump processes[5] more appropriate? Should the distribution of returns be modelled as a form of paretian or lognormal distribution? This area needs further consideration. Dixit and Pindyck (1994, p. 85) also say: 'Likewise one might model the value of a patent as subject to unpredictable but sizeable drops in response to competitors' success in the market.'

Perhaps one needs to distinguish here between what happens after an invention is made and it becomes apparent whether it will be successful, and what happens after an inventor is employed and it becomes apparent whether they will invent anything. It is perhaps easier to study and model the former. Furthermore, mention of jump processes shows that it is possible to modify models of the stochastic processes involved to account for other factors.

One such factor concerns the volatility of returns to the underlying asset. The standard deviation which B-S assumed to be constant may not be so and the variance of the return on the underlying asset may vary over time. In the case of a patent this is very likely to be the case. The example of a staged pharmaceutical R&D project provided by Copeland (Copeland et al. 1990) illustrates this. As such a project survives longer, continuing with the project becomes less and less risky, the spread of potential outcomes narrower and more certain, and the variance less. Towards the end of a patent's life, as other worthless patents lapse, the distribution for a given cohort skews towards the upper end of the original distribution and only a few highly valuable patents are left in force. As Scherer (1997) says: 'That skew outcome distributions result with such striking regularity from innovation samples suggests that there must be some underlying stochastic process whose behavioural properties are well worth characterising.' If the volatility of the underlying asset is a known function of time, then adjusting the B-S formulae is not difficult with average values being taken over the options remaining life (Hull 1997). However, work has been done on pricing options on assets which even have stochastic volatilities (Hull and White 1987). As one might expect, the longer the life of the option the more significant stochastic volatility becomes.

The third point at which real options may differ from conventional financial call options on shares is that real options may consist of multiple or compound options in a chain with numerous interdependencies. Option values are not necessarily additive because of these interdependencies and so in general compound options will require more complex analysis.

The application of option pricing methods to real options involving innovation and by implication patents, is thus by no means a straightforward task. There is also the task of convincing management that considering OPT issues is worthwhile, a subject dealt with in the oil and gas industry by Kemna (1993). However, while there is a need to keep valuation methods simple, there seems a reasonable possibility that any fundamental reservations about the applicability of OPT methods to valuing patents can be overcome. That being the case, valuation is primarily a matter of identifying for a patent the variables needed for option valuation.

Despite the potential differences between financial and real options in the form of patents, there are several areas where there are definite similarities. Two areas in particular are the issue of limited liability and the establishment of optimal exercise strategies.

Limited liability or rather the ability to escape from financial commitments by going bankrupt and/or defaulting on interest payments is something which is a risk, or benefit, depending on one's view, of some financial arrangements. As Trigeorgis (1996) points out for some projects the combined value of default and abandonment options can be considerably larger than the project abandonment option value alone. Abandonment of a patent is similar to abandonment of a project except that being a pure real option with no obligations attached to abandonment there is no downside to abandonment, save the loss of the initial investment costs. There is also a possible upside in the value of the ability to exercise what amount to abandonment put options on the project. One might say that project abandonment options where abandonment involves no costs or penalties involve a form of limited liability.

Just as with analysis of a series of investment-project related options, there is usually an optimal exercise strategy for the options involved in a patent: for example, when to let a patent lapse, when to continue with an application, when to license or refuse licences, and in many other situations. The more one concentrates on the investment opportunities associated with a patent as opposed to the options inherent in the patent per se, the more the options concerned appear the same as any other investment option and the more ordinary investment option triggers become important. However, similar triggers might also be devised for decisions about the options involved in a patent per se.

I will now consider some of the issues which might be involved in attempting an option-based method of patent valuation and review some of the other difficulties involved. Before doing so it is worth considering some of the concepts raised by econometric studies of option and renewal fee-based patent valuation methods which also reveal the skewed distributions referred to above.

4   ECONOMETRIC VALUATION METHODS

Outside the field of academic economics the work done on the valuation of patents using econometric methods is probably little known. In general, the work only produces averaged values for particular types of patents based on the payment of renewal fees (for example, Pakes 1986; Pakes and Schankerman 1984; Sullivan 1994) or values based on attributes of particular patent specifications (for example, Retizig 2003). In both these cases, the patent values obtained are derived from information which reflects the judgment of patent attorneys when deciding to renew a patent or drafting the original patent specification. Renewal fee-based estimates may well overestimate the true value of patents for reasons of organizational bias mentioned above (which encourage conservative renewal policies). In any event, such measures are almost certainly based on ad hoc estimates made by patent attorneys of the worth of a patent on the underlying invention, rather than any novel and objective analysis, even if they may reflect some insider knowledge. Such methods do have a useful role to play, but not in enabling patent attorneys and managers to make better patent management decisions about the patents they draft and renew themselves.

Rather than discuss these methods at length here, therefore, it is just worth pointing out some features of Pakes's work which relate to viewing patents as real options.

Pakes (1985) found that the stock market did take account of unpredictable changes in R&D levels and levels of patenting by firms. Griliches (1981) also referred to this result, which supports the idea that patent values are to a certain extent reflected in stock market valuations (see Chapter 3 of this volume). Scherer (1997) has compared the distribution of values of high-tech start-up companies over time with the distribution of values of individual patented inventions, and found that they have similar highly skewed distributions which may also support such a view. There is some support therefore, for the view that stock market values are linked to values of the intellectual property rights held by the company. This supports the possibility of finding shares which reflect the volatility of patent values which may be helpful in option-based valuation methods.

In the later paper by Pakes (1986), the concept of viewing patents as options was expressed more explicitly. Pakes's view of the options represented by holding a patent is that payment of a renewal fee for a granted patent not only buys the monopoly profits over coming years but also buys (in all but the final year) an option on renewing the patent at the end of each year, the exercise price for which is the renewal fee then payable.

Pakes's work elucidated a number of other features of the options connected with the renewal fees. In common with financial options, the value of the options represented by holding a patent are positive and increase with increasing value of the current returns. Their value also decreases as the patent ages and the time to expiry decreases. This is not just because the time to expiry of the individual option considered is nearer its exercise date (for example, the patent's renewal date) but because each option's value has built into it the value of future options and the fewer they are, the less valuable the current option is.

Some features, however, differ from more normal financial options. One oddity is that for each option the exercise price increases year on year as the renewal fees usually increase with the age of the patent. A further feature shown by Pakes's work is that, as the patent ages, the distribution of the potential returns skews towards there being a few highly valuable patents and many relatively worthless ones. Options increase in value with increased variance of the potential returns, so this decrease in variability leads to a decrease in the value of the options which occur later in the life of a patent. Pakes also shows that deterministic (where no option values are included) and stochastic models (where they are) differ most at the beginning of the patent's life. Intuitively this is what one would expect. Also the actual data show that the decline in dropout rates slows towards the end of a patent's life, one explanation for which is that this will be the case if the option value of the patent drops to zero towards the end of the patent's life.

The previous discussion outlined how the valuation of a patent needs to be distinguished from the valuation of the underlying invention. The approach adopted by Pakes avoided this problem by working backwards from patent renewal data which do reflect patentees' valuations of the patents alone. However, as mentioned, Pakes's work only helps assess mean values for groups of patents in the past and not the present value of individual patents. Despite this, it is valuable in highlighting several useful concepts in considering individual patents as options.

5 OPTION PRICING AND PATENT VALUATIONS

It should be obvious by now that valuation methods for assets which involve choices and varied outcomes may seriously understate their true value if they do not take account of any options involved and also that patents are just such assets.

As noted earlier, Figure 14.1 shows a simplified version of the application process for a patent as well as the decisions and costs involved in acquiring and maintaining the patent. It is now possible to identify what options may be involved in valuing a patent. For example, Pakes treated the post-grant phase of a patent as a series of call options on the next year's benefits. Mitchell and Hamilton (1988) and Newton (1992) each treated R&D projects as call options on commercializing the R&D project results, while Copeland et al. (1990) viewed an R&D project as a series of abandonment put options. Eldor (1982) treated patent royalty cash flows as a perpetual American option, as does Norris (1996), who also pointed out that the choices to sell the patent and not to license the patent were two further options (that is, in addition to the more usual real options comprising expansion, deferral, abandonment and switching).

Norris (1996) views a patent's value as comprising the value of deferring investment in commercializing the invention. Lambrecht (1997) also treats a patent as part of a deferred investment problem. Takalo and Kanniainen (1997) investigate a series of research, patenting and development investment decisions concluding that the value of options to defer investment resulting from holding patents may result in delays in commercialization. They also distinguish between the value of the project with and without a patent by separating the research, patenting and commercialization decisions. Neither Norris nor Lambrecht distinguish the value of the patent per se; instead they distinguish between the patent race and the commercialization decision with the valuation concentrating on the value of the patentees' option to invest in commercialization of the invention under patent protection. Norris (1996), however, also models a cross-licensing deal using Margrabe's (1978) exchange option model.

These examples of the use of option-based thinking and valuation methods in situations involving patents, however, tend to concentrate on patents, on the one hand, as call options on the commercialization of the underlying invention and, on the other hand, as put options to abandon the patent, R&D project or invention in various ways. However, the options associated with patents can be viewed as call or put options since the two are linked. One of the basic equivalencies, which holds for European options at least, is that:

Call + (Present value of the exercise price) = Put + Underlying asset   (14.2)

This enables R&D projects to be considered in terms of both put and call options. It is arguably easier, though, to consider an application to be worth the value of a call option on future continuance of the patent application whose exercise price is the cost of moving to the next stage in the application. To value such a call option one would need to know the value of the underlying asset which is the option to continue the application to the next stage, and so on, the final link in the chain being the asset formed by the present value of the expected future monopoly profits from the patent. This is illustrated in Figure 14.3. However, this final asset can itself be expressed (as per Pakes) in similar terms as a chain of call options on the next year's benefits (including an option on the following year's benefits) exercisable by payment of the next renewal fee.

It is possible, therefore, to divide up the various stages of a patent's life into a series of options which it should be possible to value using some of the concepts described earlier. This may well be easier said than done and though a number of potential problems have been disposed of above, there remain some which need overcoming.

6   PROBLEMS IN APPLYING OPTION PRICING-BASED METHODS

6.1   Variance

As mentioned above, at each stage in the application process and life of a patent the variance of future returns will be different, as the fact that the patent has survived thus far makes it increasingly likely that it will be successful and profitable. As we have seen, single options or DCF valuations which ignore this and use the same discount rate and variance throughout the life of the patent are flawed. Some provision or estimate of the cost of the inaccuracy caused by ignoring this will have to be made.

Newton (1992), for example, outlined how one might begin to obtain volatilities for applying option pricing theory to R&D even if not to

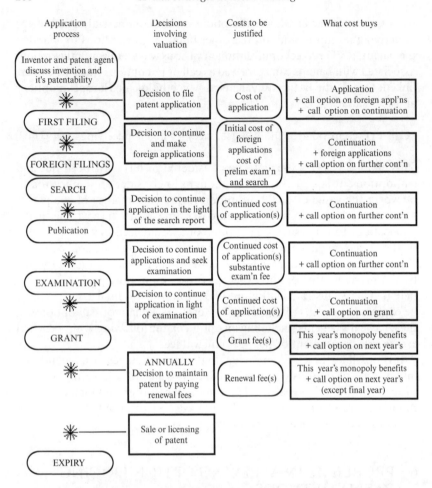

Figure 14.3   Patent option valuation decisions

patents. The overall approach adopted treats R&D as a call option on the development of the R&D results applying the B-S formula to R&D and discussing how the volatilities of R&D projects might be deduced. However, the paper did not take account of the fact that the variability of returns to an R&D project will probably vary throughout its life. The outcome of final clinical testing is likely to be less risky than early exploratory research.

6.2 Compoundedness

The B-S formula inherently cannot be used to value an option on an option (Black and Scholes 1973), since the variance of return on the option would keep changing and the formula assumes it to be constant. Several studies have addressed this problem. Trigeorgis (1996) discusses this area extensively. Option values are not necessarily additive because of interactions between them, but the interaction which can significantly affect values depends on several factors such as the option types, expiry date overlaps, and underlying asset value relative to the exercise prices. This is a complex area and the interactions may necessitate some solution using numerical analysis or Monte Carlo simulation methods.

6.3   Interim Payments

A further assumption of the B-S formula is that no interim dividends are payable. For a patent, cash flows may well occur while the options the patent involves are held. However, if the analyses outlined above are followed involving discrete steps, the cash inflows concerned will be for a different period than that covered by the option for a given step. For example, if a patent's value is the present value of the current year's cash flows plus an option on the present value of next year's cash flows and benefits, the current cash flows are separated from the option concerned. There are, in any event, means of adjusting the B-S equation to account for at least constant dividends (Merton 1973).

6.4   Cash Flows

It is possible to overcome many of the problems outlined above, but valuing patents using options, while attractive theoretically, is still complicated. In addition to the standard deviation of the patent's value, one will still need a predicted cash flow, from the patent per se, from its filing date until its lapse, together with a complete breakdown of all the costs involved in obtaining and maintaining it, including any legal costs incurred after grant in oppositions or litigation. Establishing this requires knowledge of the patent's effect on demand and on the cash flow that the underlying invention generates. The effects of competition from rival non-infringing inventions also need consideration. Quite apart from problems with revenue cash flows one will also need to decide how to treat the costs of the initial application as opposed to the costs of prosecuting any subsequent individual national applications. This will involve making decisions as to how to allocate the common application costs among the various national patents which might result.

7 PRACTICAL STEPS

Theoretically attractive analyses are sometimes of little practical use. In view of the difficulties of obtaining the data to carry out a thorough option-based analysis of a patent's value it is all the more important to ask what lessons can be learnt from the present analysis pending some conclusions from a more comprehensive study. It is reassuring that option-based patent valuation methods have already been used in a consultancy project as shown by Norris (1996). The key perhaps lies in trying to reduce the problem to its essentials and not be diverted from them by mathematical refinements. However, effort is required on two fronts. First, and most simply, is to construct general guidelines which are based on the insights of option-based patent valuation. Second, more work is required on the detailed issues involved in the application of option-based methods of patent valuation. In either case, one is in effect applying option pricing theory to establish optimal exercise strategies or simple rules for the management of the options inherent in a patent.

7.1 Options at Different Stages of a Patent's Life

Pakes's (1986) work has shown that the later years of a patent's life are dominated by the effects of technical obsolescence rather than the options on future monopoly profits. The implication is that managers need not be so concerned about option values late in a patent's life. Conversely, early in a patent's life most of the value lies in the option component and is non-negligible. Added to this, early renewal fees tend to be smaller than later ones and initial application fees are small. The view that one should always file an application on a prima facie patentable invention is thus supportable and accords with patent agents' experience and reluctance to decide against filing. Early in a patent's life the major part of the value is contained in the options associated with it and these are likely to be considerably more valuable than any initial renewal fees.

An option-based view of patent valuation therefore supports renewing patents very early in their lives, even in the absence of any returns which later in their life would be more likely to suggest lapsing is required. The valuable options which exist early in a patent's life in addition to the standard deviation of the patent's value, for which one will still need a predicted cash flow, from the patent per se, from its filing date until its lapse, together with a complete breakdown of all the costs involved in obtaining and maintaining it, are what justify Grubb's (1982) already mentioned exhortation 'When in doubt, file an application!'

7.2 Hurdle Years for Renewal Decisions

Pakes's method of analysis involves the concept of a hurdle rate, which the current returns to the patent must exceed for it to be renewed. The value of the option on the future returns may enable this value to be negative, as with an application. In practice, any patent on a product in production will probably be producing non-negligible returns compared with the renewal fee. However, if the returns and sales are zero later in a patent's life, then there will come a point when the option value is almost zero, and it should be abandoned. The critical decision is when the cut-off or hurdle year for non-renewal occurs, beyond which lack of any returns is unacceptable. This will very probably depend on the industry and product concerned. Considering the declining value of the options involved in a patent may thus, other things being equal, justify setting some form of hurdle year for renewal by which time they should be generating revenues.

7.3 Foreign Filing Decisions

Another critical decision comes about two-thirds of the way through the first year of a patent application's life when a decision must be made about foreign filings. It is quite likely that little further information on commercial prospects will be available, though early patent office search reports may give some idea of patentability. The driving consideration for such decisions may consequently be that, if the product is being developed further with the aim of marketing it, foreign applications should be made anyway in important markets since the cost of the options they provide will be negligible in relation to the development costs. While this may be the case where development costs are very high and there is an absolute requirement for patent protection, for example, in some cases in the pharmaceutical industry, this is not always the case. If the costs are not negligible relative to the development costs then more attention must be paid to the likely value of the options involved. At this early stage it is worth remembering that the application's option value is high and related to the potential future, not just current, market size that the patents will protect, and future and not just current levels of protection that are available. This is especially important when considering developing markets and legal systems in countries experiencing rapid growth.

7.4 Sale and Licensing Decisions

Option-based valuation methods can provide justifications for many existing decisions made about patents which depend on what might happen in the future and how the patent might be managed. Use of option-based valuation methods to calculate precise values is rather more complex. However, while more work is needed to show how these methods can be generally and regularly applied, the above discussion shows that all valuations, including those for the purposes of sale and licensing of patents, should ideally be carried out using option pricing-based methods.

8   CONCLUSION

Option-based valuation approaches are undoubtedly a useful framework in which to consider management of a company's IPRs even without applying such methods in detail. Despite the difficulties of a rigorous application of the method, the technique is already being used in some situations and should be developed further. Patent valuation is an exercise which is not optional but inherently about options.

NOTES

1. In the rest of this chapter the term 'patent' should be understood to include the preceding patent application unless otherwise stated.
2. An option is a right but not an obligation, at or before some specified expiry date to purchase (a call option) or sell (a put option) at a pre-specified (exercise) price, an underlying asset (such as a share but it may also be some other 'real' asset) whose price is subject to some form of random variation (European options can only be exercised at expiry; American options may be exercised before expiry).
3. This of course ignores the possible competitive effect of non-infringing substitute goods.
4. Which has not been drawn as distinctly so far in this chapter.
5. Where sudden random jumps in value occur randomly according to a Poisson distribution.

REFERENCES

Arrow, K.J. (1951), 'Alternative approaches to the theory of choice in risk-taking situations', *Econometrica*, **19** (4), 404–37.

Arthur Andersen & Co. (1992), *The Valuation of Intangible Assets – Special Report No. P254*, London: Economist Intelligence Unit.

Bachelier, L. (1900), 'Theorie de la speculation: annales de l'ecole normale superieure', in P.J. Cootner (ed.), *The Random Character of Stock Market Prices*, Cambridge, MA: MIT Press.

Black, F. and M. Scholes (1973), 'The pricing of options and corporate liabilities', *Journal of Political Economy*, May–June, 637–54.

Boness, A.J. (1964), 'Elements of a theory of stock option value', *Journal of Political Economy*, **72** (2), 163–75.

Brealey, R. and S. Myers (1984), *Principles of Corporate Finance*, Singapore: McGraw-Hill.

Copeland, T. and J. Weiner (1990), 'Proactive management of uncertainty', *McKinsey Quarterly*, **4**, 133–52.

Copeland, T., T. Koller and J. Murrin (1990), *Valuation – Measuring and Managing the Value of Companies*, New York: John Wiley & Sons.

Cox, J., S. Ross and M. Rubinstein (1979), 'Option pricing: a simplified approach', *Journal of Financial Economics*, **3** (1/2), 145–66.

Cox, J.C. and M. Rubinstein (1985), *Options Markets*, Englewood Cliffs, NJ: Prentice Hall.

Dixit, A.K. and R.S. Pindyck (1994), *Investment under Uncertainty*, Princeton, NJ: Princeton University Press.

Dixit, A.K. and R.S. Pindyck (1995), 'The options approach to capital investment', *Harvard Business Review*, May–June, 105–15.

Eldor, R. (1982), 'On the valuation of patents as real options', Foerder Institute for Economic Research, Tel-Aviv University, working paper 41–82, September.

Emery, D.R., et al. (1978), 'An investigation of real investment decision-making with the options pricing model', *Journal of Business Finance and Accounting*, **5** (4), 363–9.

Griliches, Z. (1981), 'Market value, R&D, and patents', *Economic Letters*, **7** (2), 183–7.

Grubb, P.W. (1982), *Patents for Chemists*, Oxford: Oxford University Press.

Hodder, J.E. and H.E. Riggs (1985), 'Pitfalls in evaluating risky projects', *Harvard Business Review*, January–February, 128–35.

Hull, J.C. (1997), *Options, Futures, and other Derivatives*, New York: Prentice Hall International.

Hull, J. and A. White (1987), 'The pricing of options on assets with stochastic volatilities', *Journal of Finance*, **42** (2), 281–300.

Kemna, A.G.Z. (1993), 'Case studies on real options', *Financial Management*, Autumn, 259–70.

Kester, W.C. (1984), 'Today's options for tomorrow's growth', *Harvard Business Review*, March–April, 153–60.

Kester, W.C. (1993), 'Turning growth options into real assets', in R. Aggarwal (ed.), *Capital Budgeting under Uncertaint*, New York: Prentice Hall.

Knight, F. (1921), *Risk, Uncertainty and Profit*, Boston, MA: Houghton Mifflin.

Kulatilaka, N. and A.J. Marcus (1992), 'Project valuation under uncertainty: when does DCF fail?', *Journal of Applied Corporate Finance*, **5** (3), 92–100.

Lambrecht, L.B. (1997), 'Strategic sequential investments and sleeping patents', Judge Institute working paper series WP 22/96.

Lucas, R.E.J. (1981), *Understanding Business Cycles. Studies in Business-Cycle Theory*, Cambridge, MA: MIT Press.

Margrabe, W. (1978), 'The value of an option to exchange one asset for another', *Journal of Finance*, **33**, March, 177–98.

Merton, R.C. (1973), 'Theory of rational option pricing', *Bell Journal of Economics and Management Science*, **4** (1), 141–83.

Mitchell, G.R. and W.F. Hamilton (1988), 'Managing R&D as a strategic option', *Research Technology Management*, May–July, 15–22.

Neil, D.J. (1988), 'The valuation of intellectual property', *International Journal of Technology Management*, **3** (1/2), 31–42.

Newton, D.P. (1992), 'Application of option pricing theory to R&D', Manchester Business School working paper no. 237.

292

IP and strategic decision-making

Norris, M. (1996), 'Option valuation of patents in the telecommunications industry', Cambridge MBA dissertation thesis, Cambridge University.

North, D. (1996), Public lecture entitled 'Reflections on economics and cognitive science – some provisional thoughts', 28 May, Judge Institute of Management Studies, Cambridge.

Pakes, A. (1985), 'On patents, R&D and the stock market rate of return', *Journal of Political Economy*, **93** (2), 390–409.

Pakes, A. (1986), 'Patents as options: some estimates of the value of holding European patent stocks', *Econometrica*, **54**, 755–84.

Pakes, A. and M. Schankerman (1984), *The Rate of Obsolescence of Patents, Research Gestation Lags, and the Private Rate of Return to Research Resources*, Chicago, IL: University of Chicago Press.

Parr, R.L. (1988), 'Fair rates of return', *Patent World*, (July), 36–41.

Parr, R.L. and G.V. Smith (1994), 'Quantitative methods of valuing intellectual property', in M. Simensky and L.G. Bryer (eds), *The New Role of Intellectual Property in Commercial Transactions*, New York: John Wiley and Sons, pp. 39–68.

Pitkethly, R. (1997), 'The valuation of individual IPRs: a review and consideration of patents', World Conference, New Developments in Intellectual Property: Law and Economics, St Peter's College, Oxford, 17–18 March.

Rao, R.K.S. and J.D. Martin (1981), 'Another look at the use of options pricing theory to evaluate real asset investment opportunities', *Journal of Business Finance and Accounting*, **8** (3), 421–29.

Reitzig, M. (2003), 'What determines patent value? Insights from the semiconductor industry', *Research Policy*, **32**, 13–26.

Samuelson, P.A. (1965), 'Rational theory of warrant pricing', *Industrial Management Review*, **6** (2), 13–32.

Scherer, F.M. (1997), 'The distribution of profits from invention', final report on Sloan Foundation Grant B1995-60, Harvard University, January.

Stacey, S.G. (1989), 'Valuing intellectual property', *Technology Strategies*, December, pp. 22–5.

Sullivan, R.J. (1994), 'Estimates of the value of patent rights in Great Britain and Ireland, 1852–1876', *Economica*, **61**, 37–58.

Takalo, T. and V. Kanniainen (1997), 'Do patents slow down technological progress?', World Conference, New Developments in Intellectual Property: Law and Economics, St Peter's College, Oxford, 17–18 March.

Trigeorgis, L. (1996), *Real Options: Managerial Flexibility and Strategy in Resource Allocation*, Cambridge, MA: MIT Press.

Trigeorgis, L. and S.P. Mason (1987), 'Valuing managerial flexibility', *Midland Corporate Finance Journal*, 5, Spring, 14–21.

15. Valuing patents and patent portfolios from a corporate perspective: theoretical considerations, applied needs and future challenges[1]

Markus Reitzig

1 INTRODUCTION

Patent laws (or their legal predecessors) have existed in France since 1790, in the USA since 1791 and in Germany since 1877. Despite their longevity, however, patent valuations are not yet routine procedures for practitioners in the corporate world.

Some of the oldest uses for evaluations have been for damage payments arising from litigation, and accordingly, most of the corresponding literature in this field stems from lawyers.[2] Since the 1960s patents have also attracted the interest of theoretical[3] and empirical economists[4] accountants[5] and, most recently, management scholars.[6] However, the different disciplines have substantially different understandings of what the value of a patent is and how it can be assessed (see Reitzig 2002).[7] This finding very much corresponds to the understanding of Pitkethly (1999, p. 3) who says '[t]he first questions to be asked of any valuation are: who is doing the valuation?, for whom? and for what purpose?'

This chapter takes a strategic management perspective. Valuation considerations are not bound by any formal legal constraints or accounting standards. Patents are regarded as an asset for a corporation whose value is determined by the value of its underlying technology; its technical, legal and market uncertainty; and the competition scenario as perceived by the patent holder. In this sense, it views patents akin to real options.[8]

This chapter takes the discussion one step further than Pitkethly (see Chapter 14 in this volume) by asking:

- how can we actually assess the input parameters (for example, expected cash flows, volatilities, and so on) when valuing patents as real options?
- And, more specifically, how can this task actually be carried out at reasonable costs for large portfolios of patents when a few hundred patents or even more must be evaluated quickly?

From the experience of this author, the last question still causes most problems for analysts and R&D managers. To address the issue concerned with how to value patent portfolios, the discussion first considers issues that arise in operationalizing the real options measures. In particular, section 1 explores the use of market benchmarking. It argues that market benchmarking may not always be a practical method and that the methodology should rely on more widely available measures that are likely to be correlated with value. It then sets out the magnitude of this problem as one of the more acceptable definitions of value requires not only information about the company's own patents, but also counterfactual information about other companies (section 2.1). Section 2.2 first outlines the various cash flow drivers, and then summarizes the various indicators likely to be closely associated with the cash flows generated by the patent, many of which are obtained from patent data – such as the scope of the patent, the life of the patent, the size of the patent family, and so on. The discussion of various proxies adopts a perspective focused on expected cash flows from patents and valuation rather than the use of IP indictors to inform management awareness *per se*. Section 2.2.2 then provides empirical evidence as to the extent to which such drivers are correlated with underlying value, drawing on a wide range of existing studies. The discussion also provides an indication of the accessibility, cost and timeliness of such indicators for use in carrying out patent valuations. Section 2.2.3 explores how such value drivers might be used in the valuation process. Ideally, these drivers might be combined in some way and then used in a real options calculation. However, given the present state of the art, this ideal outcome seems some considerable way away. Finally, Section 3 draws the main conclusions of this chapter.

1.1   Real Option Valuation of Patents – Existing Practice

According to Pitkethly (1999; Chapter 14 in this volume), the three most difficult valuation issues are,

1. determining the present value of cash flows from the patent,
2. determining the volatility of these cash flows, and
3. allowing for an evaluation that views patents as compound options.

In addition to these three problems, the assessment of investment costs and the investment time also pose difficulties. These estimates are required for the Black and Scholes formula (Black and Scholes 1973) and other more complicated models.[9]

Market benchmarking studies (using spanning–traded intellectual property assets) may be used to estimate the parameters that are needed to calculate the value of the patent as an option. If these studies are used, one is implicitly assuming that a spanning–traded intellectual property (IP) asset or portfolio of assets is observable that shows characteristics that are similar to the object of valuation. A spanning asset should, in principle, exhibit stochastic fluctuations that are perfectly correlated with the IP asset and is often called a 'twin security'. The traded, observable twin security can be valued using standard options theory and this method is termed a contingent claims approach to the valuation of the non-traded IP asset. There exists substantial empirical evidence that the market value of corporations is correlated with their IP stock.[10] Hence, in general, these findings render it plausible to believe that at times suitable spanning conditions for IP assets can be defined and, consequently, to apply market benchmarking to patent valuation.

However, even though cases may exist in which this approach yields scientifically valid results,[11] there are likely to be a substantial number of scenarios in which spanning–traded IP assets are hard to find: patents protecting radical inventions, patents protecting inventions that are exploited by multi-product companies, bargaining patents protecting inventions in highly cumulative technologies, and so on. In these cases, it may be difficult to find valid proxies for the present value of the cash flows and their volatility by searching traded–spanning assets.

Validity, however, is only one criterion that affects the suitability of a patent valuation from a corporate perspective. Other criteria are information availability (time constraints) and evaluation costs for assessments. These are briefly discussed in the next section.

1.2 Suitability Criteria for Patent Valuation Methods from a Corporate Perspective

Typically, a strategic manager would ask:

- What is the value of our own IP stock within each technology sector?
- What licence fee should we charge for the use of a specific group of patents?

- What is the maximum price we should pay for the IP portfolio of a competitor that is for sale?

When these assessments are needed for groups of patents rather than individual patents, certain caveats apply. In many of these cases it might be difficult to find a coherent spanning bundle of IP assets to apply real-option models in the aforementioned way and validity becomes a problem (that is, finding proxies that speak to the patent's value). Even if the bundle of patents was coherent enough so that the real option model would be feasible, there might still remain problems due to the novelty of the technology. The benchmarking application fails if equivalent stocks of IP assets are not yet traded, that is, information availability may become a problem. Most importantly, it appears to be costly to apply a detailed real option-based evaluation to each individual IP asset or each subdividable bundle of IP assets. Evaluation costs become non-trivial.

Ideally, information for an evaluation should satisfy the following criteria:

1. The assessment needs to be based on determinants or indicators that unambiguously reflect the value of the valuation object, that is, evaluation validity must be guaranteed.
2. Evaluation costs per patent should be rather low.
3. Information should be available as early as possible in the lifetime of the patents that are to be valued.
4. Information should be publicly available so that it can be accessed by third parties.

Since there are many examples in which market benchmarking evaluations of patents prove inconvenient or fall short, this chapter considers different approaches than have hitherto been taken by the majority of the practitioners to date. To do this, the remaining sections of the chapter consider the basic questions: what is the value of a patent from a management perspective? And which potential ways exist to estimate its value?

2 PATENT VALUATION FROM A MANAGEMENT PERSPECTIVE

2.1 A Definition of Patent Value

What is the value of a patent from a management perspective? A patent's value is not observable but is a theoretical term (as will become clearer in the following). Thus, strictly speaking, patent values can not be 'measured' at all. They must be assessed or calculated according to their definition.

What is a suitable definition for patent value? An options framework defines patent value as the value of the opportunity to invest or not to invest in a given technology for a given market. In particular, the value of an invention and the patent protecting it are not identical from a theoretical standpoint. However, while this definition may be useful in some cases, in others (for example, if the volatility can not be assessed by observing spanning assets) it may be more convenient to tackle the assessment problem from a different side. Harhoff et al. (2003) argue that for a majority of empirically relevant scenarios, a patent's value is defined as the difference in discounted-future profits the patent holder makes during the remaining lifetime of the patent compared with the profits he or she would realize if his/her strongest competitor in the field held the patent.[12] This value is often referred to as the 'asset value' of a patent.

Equation (15.1) formalizes this definition in a very general fashion.

$$Patent\ Value_{anticipated} = \hat{E}\left(\Pi_I^I - \Pi_I^C\right) = \hat{E}(p_I, q_I, c_I, p_C, q_C, c_C - p_I{}^*, q_I{}^*, c_I{}^*, p_C{}^*, q_C{}^*, c_C{}^*)$$

$$(15.1)$$

where:

Π_I^I:	profits of the patent holder if he/she holds the technology
Π_I^C:	profits of the patent holder if the strongest competitor held the patent
p_I, q_I, c_I:	prices charged, quantities sold, and costs incurred by the patent holder
p_C, q_C, c_C:	prices charged, quantities sold, and costs incurred by the competitor
$p_I{}^*, q_I{}^*, c_I{}^*$:	counterfactual prices charged, quantities sold, and costs incurred by the patent holder if the competitor held the patent
$p_C{}^*, q_C{}^*, c_C{}^*$:	counterfactual prices charged, quantities sold, and costs incurred by the competitor if he/she held the patent.

The assessment of a patent's value according to this definition also imposes obvious problems. According to the chosen definition, we should not limit the calculation to the (expected) present value of cash flows for the patent holder if he/she holds the patent. We also need to assess the scenario in which the strongest competitor held the patent. The expected cash flow in the second scenario are, however, counterfactual, that is, they can never be observed (and this is why 'patent value' is, strictly speaking, a theoretical term).

The question, therefore, is how can the different (and partly counterfactual) profits constituting the patent's value be proxied? Alternatives to spanning assets need to be found for estimating future and partly counterfactual cash flows and their volatility. One alternative is to identify their 'value drivers' or operationalizations of those value drivers. Despite its obvious limitations,[13] this methodology has been widely accepted in the field of company valuation where the practical assessment of 'real options' is as difficult as valuing patents.[14] Section 2.2.1 follows such an approach of an alternative real option valuation using value drivers instead of market benchmarking.

2.2 Assessing Patent Value without Market Benchmarking

2.2.1 A different 'real option' framework for patents

Reitzig (2002) argues that value drivers (or value determinants) of patents can be sub-summarized under a real option framework. According to Table 15.1, there are three analogous parameters between financial and real options: the time to invest in the project, the present value of project cash flows and the standard deviation of the project value.

- The patent's duration (or lifetime) corresponds to the maximum time to invest in the project.
- The present value of project cash flows should be determined by the patent's and the underlying invention's value drivers;[15] namely, these are novelty, its inventive step (non-obviousness), disclosure, breadth, difficulty in (technically) inventing around, its position within a portfolio of other patents, and the complementary assets of the patent holder.
- The standard deviation of the patent's value (volatility) should be determined by technical, legal and market uncertainty.

Table 15.1   Financial options and real options

Financial option on share	Real option
Time to expiry	Time left to invest in
Exercise price of the option	Investment cost of project
Current price of the underlying share	Present value of project cash flows
Standard deviation of underlying share returns	Standard deviation of the project value (volatility)
Risk-free interest rate	Risk-free interest rate

Source: Adapted from Pitkethly (1999).

Patent duration   Various microeconomic models used to help designing patent systems optimally start from the premise that the economic value of a patent for its holder increases with the patent's duration. More recent models (see, for example, Matutes et al. 1996) differ from their predecessors (see Nordhaus 1967) as they make more realistic assumptions as to the distribution of returns-per-period over time.[16] While, on balance, longer-lived patents are more valuable than shorter-lived ones; from an options perspective what is important is the length of time remaining to expiry (that is, the length of time the patent is likely to survive, conditional on how long it has survived to date). The longer the potential life of the patent that remains, the more time the company has to invest in a project embodying the underlying technology and the more years in which revenues are improved by patent protection.

Novelty and inventive step (non-obviousness)   Green and Scotchmer (1995) were the first to introduce 'novelty' and 'inventive step' (non-obviousness) into an economic model of patent value. As a legal term, novelty is a well-known characteristic and applies when the proposed invention is mutually exclusive from the state of the art (existing technology). Inventive step (or non-obviousness) refers to the technical distance of the proposed invention from the state of the art. While novelty and inventive step characterize a patent, they also characterize the underlying technological invention. The general idea is that 'inventions' differ in the degree to which they deviate from the existing state of the art. Other things being equal, it is expected that more radical inventions will be more valuable than incremental improvements. This was demonstrated by some of the earliest models of the economics of invention.

Patent breadth   Klemperer (1990) and Gilbert and Shapiro (1990) have assumed that the scope of the claims and technology area covered by a patent, namely, the patent's breadth, affects the patent's value. These authors assume that the patent breadth has a positive impact on the patent value.

Disclosure   As a quid pro quo for the grant of a right allowing for the exclusion of competitors from a technology, governments generally require that the patent owners publicly disclose the details of their invention so broader society can benefit from the new knowledge once the patent has expired. Green and Scotchmer (1995) assume that disclosing technical information confers a positive externality on the patent holder's competitors, which the patenting firm might want to avoid. Accordingly, disclosure should reduce a patent's value for the owner. However, while patent disclosure may give away technically sensitive information that competitors can use as inputs to their own inventive activity, disclosure also acts as a shop window for inventions and attracts potential customers or licensees (see Chapter 10 of this book).

Difficulty in inventing around   If patents block the ability of competitors to invent and produce in certain technological terrains, it becomes difficult for competitors to circumnavigate the protected invention with a new technology. Gallini (1992) introduced this idea into a formal model for the first time.

Complementary assets   While patents protect products or processes from basic imitation, complementary technology and other complementary assets are often needed to commercialize the patent protected invention. Teece (1986) analyses in more detail the way in which the commercial success of an invention depends on the availability of complementary assets.

Technical, legal and market uncertainty   The value of patent-based cash flows is subject to three kinds of uncertainty. Technological uncertainty, which was first acknowledged in economics by Gilbert and Newberry (1982), assumes that patenting usually takes place at a point where the commercial success of the final product still depends on overcoming future technical obstacles. Next to technical uncertainties, market uncertainties matter significantly. Again Gilbert and Newberry (1982) were the first to explicitly model this aspect in the theoretical economic literature on patents.[17] Finally, legal uncertainty enters the 'volatility' of the present cash flows from a patent. Legal uncertainty differs from the technical and market uncertainty in two ways. First, it is partly determined by the patent owner. This imposes an additional problem to a real option evaluation of patents in that the volatility becomes endogenous. Lanjouw (1998) was the first to introduce this issue to the economic literature. Expanding on the model by Pakes (1986), she introduces legal uncertainty that is created by the risk of entering and winning infringement suits. Later studies, such as the one by Harhoff and Reitzig (2001), have taken up the idea in a somewhat different fashion. Second, legal uncertainty may hardly enhance but rather reduce the value of the underlying patent value. Thus, it is questionable to what extent legal uncertainty affects the value of the option after all.

2.2.2   Empirical evidence – the importance of value drivers
A distinction needs to be made between the existing forms of empirical evidence – studies using expert ratings – and studies using alternative measures both to proxy patent value and value drivers as defined above. A study by Reitzig (2003a) has linked expert ratings of various value

determinants to patent values. This study, which regressed the estimated values of 127 semiconductor patents on expert ratings of several value drivers, found that novelty and the inventive step were highly correlated with the patents' values. While difficulties in inventing around, and the extent of, disclosure were found to be of minor importance, the latter had a positive, not negative, impact on values. This particular finding emphasizes how important it is to distinguish between different 'uses' or modes of exploitation for patents when referring to value drivers for assessments.

Patents may serve various purposes. Until about 20 years ago, it was assumed that patents would be predominantly used to exclude competitors from the use of their technology. While recent surveys reported in Harabi (1995) and Cohen et al. (2000) still find empirical evidence for this traditional assumption, other recent studies suggest that patents serve other purposes (see Chapter 10 in this volume). Rahn (1994), for example, underlines the importance of patents as a means to 'exchange technology' with competitors. In a survey of the American semiconductor industry, Hall and Ham Ziedonis (2001) argue that the main motives for patenting in the field are triggered by negotiation considerations. Thus, the findings by Reitzig (2003a) have to be put into perspective. Disclosure may exert positive externalities for a semiconductor company participating in a patent pool with major players in the field in that disclosing technical know-how conveys the impression of competence to potential negotiation partners. On the other hand, it may have negative externalities for chemical corporations that do not participate in patent pools and are rather interested in hiding as much of their technology from competitors as they can.[18]

Indirect empirical evidence showing that the validity of patent age or duration is a value driver has been provided in two large-scale empirical studies by Schankerman and Pakes (1986) and Lanjouw et al. (1996). Schankerman and Pakes (1986) use the observable renewal decision by patent holders from Germany, the UK and France between 1955 and 1978 as the dependent variable within a structural estimation model that regards the renewal decision as an investment decision. Their data set comprises 1.7 million renewal decisions. The findings show that the overall value of a patent (from grant to lapse) increases non-linearly with its age.[19] Comparable to the work of Schankerman and Pakes (1986) is the study by Lanjouw et al. (1996). The authors analyse renewal decisions for German patent cohorts between 1953 and 1988. The data set consists of more than 20 000 observable renewal decisions. The results by Lanjouw et al. (1996) are comparable to the ones by Schankerman and Pakes (1986).[20]

Indirect empirical evidence on the relevance of novelty as a value driver is provided by a study carried out by Carpenter et al. (1980). They show that patent references to the scientific literature made during the examination procedure (see below for more details) are correlated with patent value.

Some very preliminary empirical evidence exists on the importance of the inventive step as a value driver for patents. In a study of 613 European chemical patents Reitzig (2004) has shown that indicators which portray the size of the inventive step of the invention are correlated with the patent's value. Similar results are found through structural equation modelling in Reitzig (2003b).

Some preliminary empirical evidence also exists on the validity of patent breadth as a value driver of patents. Lerner (1994) found that the value of American biotechnology firms increases with the 'scope' of the patents they hold. Lerner measured 'scope' by the number of four-digit international patent classifications (IPCs) assigned to the patents in his sample. Arguing that the number of four-digit IPCs proxies for the breadth of the patent he sustains the theoretical assumption that patent breadth is positively correlated with patent value. Moreover, patent claims (see also below) should theoretically reflect a patent's breadth as well. By showing that patents weighted by their claims correlate with macroeconomic measures of national performance, Tong and Frame (1992) yielded the very first empirical evidence that patent breadth is another patent value driver. Lanjouw and Schankerman (2001) find that the likelihood of a patent being litigated increases with its number of claims, again suggesting that patent breadth may be an important value determinant of the patent.[21] The attractiveness of claims as an indicator of value in Europe has recently been enhanced as is now available electronically.

Finally, some empirical evidence exists for the relative importance of market uncertainty vis-à-vis technological uncertainty. In a study published by the European Patent Office (EPO) in 1994, European patent applicants mention that in 7 per cent of the cases they decide against filing for a patent because of technical uncertainty.[22] For Japanese applicants this is true in 14 per cent of the cases.[23] The study also reveals that in 20 per cent of the cases when European applicants decide against a filing, market uncertainty affects their decision-making (for Japanese applicants this figure goes up to 31 per cent).

2.2.3 An interim conclusion

Patent value is a theoretical term that is difficult to calculate in practice. The appeal of real option assessments lies in the account they take of the limited lifetime of a patent and the uncertainty about expected cash flows. Practical problems are imposed by the need to estimate cash flows and their volatility. Since most of the value determinants are latent constructs they must be transformed into an appropriate 'measurement'. One way to do this is to use value indicators. The alternative, market benchmarking, is not feasible in all cases.

2.3 Indicators of Patent Value

Recalling the criteria for selecting a valuation method, valuations need to be scientifically valid, they should be executable at any time and for any type of patent portfolio (in-house and competitors), and they should not be costly to construct.

One approach is to use indicators of patent value that are generated by the patent system itself. According to the framework developed in section 2.2.1 such indicators are valid if either they operationalize (that is, reflect) one (or more) of the value drivers or if they refer directly to the present value of cash flows from the patent (expected prizes, quantities, costs). Figure 15.1 illustrates the different types of validity for value indicators according to this method.

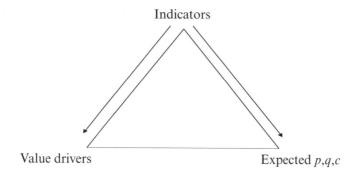

Figure 15.1   Ways to use indicators for patent valuations

Reitzig (2002; 2003b) presents a tabulated survey of the existing scientific empirical studies examining the correlation between a patent's value and patent information indicators. Studies are characterized by the underlying sample size, the underlying statistical/econometric model, the latent variable used as a correlate for the patent's value, and the resulting type of validity.[24] The studies are briefly recapitulated below.

Backward patent references (backward citations)   Backward citations refer to relevant state-of-the-art documents that are quoted by the inventor and/or patent examiners on the patent application. Several econometric studies have used the number of backward citations as an indicator of patent value including Carpenter et al. 1980; Narin et al. 1987; Lanjouw and Schankerman 1999, 2001; Harhoff et al. 2003.

Forward citations   The term 'forward citation' refers to the number of times a granted patent is quoted as relevant state of the art during the examination of subsequently examined patents. Forward citations as value indicators were tested in the following studies: Narin et al. 1987; Trajtenberg 1990; Lanjouw and Schankerman 1999; Albert et al. 1991; Hall et al. 2000, Harhoff et al. 2003.

Family size   Family size reflects the number of jurisdictions either the same patent application, or applications based on the same prior application, were submitted to. Family size was tested as a value correlate in the following studies: Lanjouw et al. 1996; Lanjouw and Schankerman 1999; Guellec and van Pottelsberghe de la Potterie 2000; Harhoff and Reitzig 2004.

Scope   The scope variable is supposed to capture a patent's breadth, traditionally with respect to the number technology sub-classes embraced by the invention. The scope variable was tested in the following studies: Lerner 1994; Harhoff et al. 2003; Harhoff and Reitzig 2004; Lanjouw and Schankerman 2001.

Patent ownership   The patent ownership variable describes who holds the property right. In many studies, the variable was used to distinguish between individual and corporate ownership. Ownership was tested in the following studies: Lanjouw and Schankerman 2001; Harhoff and Reitzig 2004; Guellec and van Pottelsberghe de la Potterie 2000.

The number of claims   The number of claims is supposed to capture the breadth of the patent. Either as an absolute number or as a weighting factor it was tested in the following studies: Tong and Frame 1992; Lanjouw and Schankerman 1999, 2001; Harhoff and Reitzig 2004.

The patenting strategy (mode of filing)   Patents can be filed in different ways. On an international level, an application via the so-called Patent Co-operation Treaty (PCT) route is an alternative mechanism to applying separately in various jurisdictions. Different strategic rationales are associated with the different modes of filing.[25] The mode of filing/patenting strategy variable was tested in the following studies: Guellec and van Pottelsberghe de la Potterie 2000; Reitzig 2002, 2004.

The number of applicants   Patents can be filed by more than one applicant. The variable was tested in the study by Guellec and van Pottelsberghe de la Potterie (2000).

The number of trans-border research co-operations   Applications can be filed by multiple applicants from different nations. This information can indicate that the patent application is the product of a trans-border research co-operation. This variable was tested in the study by Guellec and van Pottelsberghe de la Potterie (2000).

Key inventors   According to Lotka (1926) a small 'elite' of (key) inventors accounts disproportionately much for the scientific output of a corporation. A variable referring to key inventors was tested in a study by Ernst et al. (2000).

Legal disputes (oppositions against patents)   EP patents can be legally 'attacked' in an opposition procedure up until nine months after their date of grant. This variable was tested in the study by Harhoff et al. (2003).

A review of these studies finds on balance the following conclusions.[26]

Backward references (backward citations) have been tested as indicators for patent value in the past. The main distinction needs to be made between patent and non-patent citations. Based on theoretical considerations and results from various empirical studies in the field, it seems as though backward citations to the patent and non-patent literature operationalize novelty and they should therefore be valid correlates of a patent's value. Besides, the attractiveness of a technological field should also be reflected in the number of citations to the patent literature. Nonetheless, the studies also show that correlations between a patent's value and backward citations are not always straightforward, which somehow limits their applicability. In particular, it seems as though the marginal effects for non-patent and patent citations on patent value could substantially differ, and non-patent publications were themselves optimally sub-categorized along a series of dimensions (see Sorenson and Fleming 2004, for an analysis in a related context). Backward citations can be compiled for in-house patent portfolios and competitors' portfolios alike. They are available early in the lifetime of a patent (after the publication) and are available at low cost (electronically stored in data banks).

Forward citations have been examined most extensively in the literature. Both theoretical considerations and empirical results suggest that forward citations are better indicators of patent value than backward citations. Patents that are cited more often in subsequent examinations than others should – on average – have a higher technical and, therefore, economic value. The number of forward citations is positively related to the extent of inventive activity. Forward citations can be calculated from publicly available sources and are therefore applicable to in-house evaluations as well as to evaluations of competitor patents. The downside of forward citations is that they are not available until a substantial time after grant and usually a time window of at least four to five years is required. Thus, they are not suited for the valuation of patents at a very early stage in their lifetime. Computation costs for this type of indicator are low.

Both theoretical considerations and the results from various empirical studies find that *family size* is a valid correlate of patent value. From a theoretical standpoint it makes sense to assume that patent applicants are only willing to incur multiple application costs (that are associated with the number of jurisdictions in which protection is sought) if they expect corresponding high returns from the patent. Unfortunately, the lack of variation in this measure, owing to the custom within certain corporations that file patents to routinely select standard countries, has meant that this variable may have little explanatory power. However, the indicator is publicly available at an early stage of the lifetime of a patent and is available at low cost.

Scope has been tested as an indicator for patent value in a series of studies, however, its theoretical foundation is questionable since the number of four-digit IPCs may well reflect the multi-functionality of a patent instead of its breadth. It has been found to be a significant correlate of patent value in about half the studies mentioned above. Regarding its availability, the indicator appears attractive because it can be computed directly after the publication of the granted patent and, since it is electronically available, compilations costs are low.

From a theoretical perspective it is plausible to assume that *patent ownership* is a valuable gauge, with corporate patents being more valuable than patents filed by individuals (especially in research-intensive industries). However, the theoretical rationale is less convincing than for other indicators (for example, forward citations). Since the ownership information is available early in the lifetime of the patent and computable at low costs, the indicator may be interesting where it shows variation (it might not show enough variation when looking at the portfolio of just one corporation).

The number of claims is interesting as an indicator of patent value for various reasons. From a theoretical standpoint there is reason to believe that they reflect the present value of the cash flows from the patent by operationalizing its breadth. At the same time the pure number of claims as a measure is not convincing. Claims are also difficult to assign to only one input parameter of a Black-and-Scholes based real option valuation of a patent (see below). Preliminary empirical evidence for their role as a value indicator, however, exists. Nonetheless, the attractiveness of claims as an indicator of value in Europe has recently been enhanced as it is now available electronically.

From a theoretical standpoint, *the patenting strategy (PCT or non-PCT)* will reflect the anticipated value of cash flows from the invention.[27] Until now, however, there exist only two empirical studies testing whether patenting strategy variables indicate patent value. Depending on the type of variable computed, data may not be available until 29 months after grant (PCT II). However, the information necessary to compute the indicator is electronically available.

Very little empirical evidence exists on the validity of the *number of applicants, the number of trans-border research co-operations,* and *key inventors* as patent value indicators. Thus, we will refrain from discussing these indicators but consider instead the suitability of *oppositions* as indicators of patent value. Even though they have not been validated in more than one study, either, they appear to have great potential as indicators of patent value. Expanding on a model by Lanjouw and Lerner (1998), Harhoff and Reitzig (2004) have shown that from a theoretical standpoint, oppositions should clearly be correlated with the anticipated cash flows. The major drawback with this indicator is that it is not available until nine months after grant, and it may reflect the legal uncertainty of the patent option rather than its value.

2.4   Assessing the Value of Patents with Indicators

So far, the purpose of this chapter has been to show that alternative valuation measures to a market benchmarking exist that might satisfy a company's needs. This section considers how indicators can be used for patent assessments and the evaluation of portfolios.

Theoretically, a sophisticated patent evaluation technique should:

1. identify relevant indicators for the patent(s) to be valued,
2. assign the different indicators to the calculation of the present value of cash flows and their volatility respectively,
3. choose an algorithm for the calculation of the present value of cash flows and their volatility through indicators (functional form, weights),
4. calculate the value of the individual patents using option algorithms, a simplistic example being Black and Scholes's (1973) formula,[28]

and, in the case of a portfolio evaluation,

5. calculate the portfolio value based on the information about the individual patents.[29]

Unfortunately, in practice we are still far away from this and the following section considers where the obstacles to carrying out a scientifically sophisticated valuation using indicators lie and what the existing practice is.

2.4.1 Obstacles to indicator valuations from a theoretical perspective

Even though there is substantial empirical evidence that supports the hypotheses that backward citations, forward citations, family size and other indicators are correlated with a patent's value, it is easy to find particular portfolios of patents where this is not the case.[30] Companies usually take a representative (historical) test portfolio whose value has been known to validate the significance of certain indicators for their own purposes, but this imposes various additional problems, the most dominant of which may be to assess the value of the test portfolio and to find a representative sample.

Very little is still known about the multitude of effects that are reflected by certain indicators. None of the studies mentioned above validates indicators of patent value within a structural model that can distinguish the correlations between indicators and the present value of patent cash flows from correlations between indicators and the volatility of the underlying value. Nevertheless there is good reason to believe that there is a substantial amount of overlap between cash flows and volatility.[31] Thus it appears scientifically questionable to assign indicators to the different input parameters of a real option valuation algorithm (for example, the Black and Scholes formula) without further empirical investigation.

Furthermore, little is known about whether indicators add up linearly in their explanatory power to predict the present value of the cash flows or not. Most of the studies described above estimate indicators in a reduced form. This does not mean, however, that a simple addition of the indicators will be the most convenient way to assess the input parameters for the real option assessment. Furthermore, weights of indicators may vary substantially across industries and companies. Little is known on what one forward citation, backward citation or opposition may reveal about the value of a patent in hard financial terms. One exception is the study by Harhoff et al. (2003). Using a 1977 cohort of German patents renewed to full term, the authors show that, on average, patents are 11.2 times more valuable when successfully surviving an opposition.

Finally, it is difficult to model interrelations between the values of individual patents within the same (company) portfolio. Little is known about the impact of the average number of backward citations of the patents in one sample on the value of an additional forward citation of one individual patent in the same sample.

2.4.2   Existing practice

So far, the purpose of this chapter has been to show that alternative valuation measures to market benchmarking exist that might satisfy a company's needs. Ideally, such measures would reflect the likely level of returns and degree of risk attached to those returns, so the measures could be used in a real options formula. However, the current state of play, with regard to the strength of the correlations with patent value and the absence of measures of risk (let alone uncertainty), means that the likely outcome of using such indicators is going to be more modest (not to say theoretically more simple). Patent indicator assessments in practice are carried out in the following way:

- Indicators are compiled for each patent within the portfolio that is subject to valuation.
- A weight is assigned to each indicator.
- The values of the individual patents are calculated by adding up linearly the weighted size of each indicator.

In the case of a portfolio evaluation:

- The portfolio value is calculated as the sum of the individual patents' values.

Hence, strictly speaking, the 'option value' of the patents is not structurally determined, but correlates of future cash flows are added up in a more simplified fashion. In practice, indicator assessments differ with respect to the number and types of indicators chosen for the assessment and with respect to the assignment of the weights. In some cases, the weight of certain indicators is determined by calibrating them as a test portfolio of patents whose value is known from other sources. In other cases, a factor analysis of indicators yields the weights of each proxy.

Assessments of this type show tremendous shortcomings from a scientific standpoint. The obstacles to a proper application of a real option framework as mentioned before made this point very transparent. The existing obstacles do in fact define various future research tasks (see below for a summary). Nonetheless, there are several scenarios in which even the existing indicator valuation approaches offer an interesting alternative to other methods from a corporate perspective.

Even though indicators of patent value have not yet been tested in structural models that would assign them to option valuation algorithms, their usefulness as indicators of patent value can hardly be doubted. Many indicators are suitable for the assessments of portfolios comprising property rights which are granted only shortly before the evaluation). Finally, the indicators can be compiled at low costs.

Thus, existing indicator assessments can preferably be considered an interesting alternative in cases when:

- Large portfolios of patents need to be valued. Here, the cost advantage of an indicator assessment over other types of valuations increases; besides, the relative evaluation error for the entire portfolio decreases compared to the relative error of each individual patent.
- The evaluated portfolios are not subject to high legal or market uncertainty.
- The evaluated portfolios consist of rather interrelated patents.
- It is difficult to find comparable traded IP portfolios.

3   SUMMARY AND FUTURE CHALLENGES

From a strategic management perspective, valuations of patents using the real options approach should yield optimal results. However, in practice, real option valuations of patents impose problems because of the difficulty of assessing the present value of cash flows and the volatility of the cash flows (see also, Pitkethly 1999).

This chapter has argued that market benchmarking exercises may be problematic, mainly because it can be either impossible or too costly to find spanning–traded IP assets. This commonly occurs when several different spanning IP assets need to be found for the individual patents within the portfolio. This chapter presents alternative approaches to the assessment of the present value of the cash flows and the volatility of the cash flows. It was shown that a patent's present value of cash flows is driven by the patent's novelty, its inventive step (non-obviousness), breadth, disclosure, difficulty in inventing around, and the availability of complementary assets. Equally, it was argued that the volatility is determined by technical, market and legal uncertainty. Reviewing the empirical literature on patent indicators, the chapter then presented existing knowledge on how the present value of cash flows may become subject to an assessment by indicators (that correlate directly with expected cash flows or operationalize latent value drivers).

The chapter has also presented existing shortcomings of current practice, such as the problem of assigning weights to indicators or assigning indicators correctly to the input parameters of a real option valuation. Despite their shortcomings, however, simplistic indicator evaluations are still worthwhile. They are especially appealing in scenarios where large portfolios of patents need to be evaluated quickly on a regular basis.

NOTES

1. An earlier version of this chapter was presented at the High Level Taskforce on the Valuation and Captialization of Intellectual Assets, Geneva, 18–19 November 2002.
2. For Germany see for example Vollrath (1983), Assmann (1985), Lehmann (1988), Heil and Roos (1994) and Karnell (1996).
3. See for example Nordhaus (1967), Gilbert and Shapiro (1990), Klemperer (1990), Scotchmer and Green (1990), Gallini (1992) and Green and Scotchmer (1995).
4. See for example Scherer (1965), Griliches (1981) and Pakes (1986).
5. See for example Löcke (1998), KPMG (1999) and Schildbach (2000).
6. See for example Rivette and Kline (2000).
7. See Reitzig (2002), chapter 4.
8. Note that *strictly speaking* this chapter must not claim to view patents as *real options* because the management perspective of the patent holder introduces a *subjective* dimension to the value. At least in theory, however, a 'real option' should have an *objective value* which does not depend on the perspective of the patent holder. Yet, for the purpose of this chapter I will stick to the term 'real option' to express that the value of the patent protected invention is subject to a risk and that the patent holder may decide whether he/she exercises his/her exclusivity right or not. I will elaborate on the problem of the objectiveness of the underlying's value in more detail at a later point.
9. See Geske (1979) for a model that takes account of the compoundedness of options. As a matter of fact, the compound option character of a patent is striking. One example of the compound character is mentioned in Pakes (1986). The owner of the patent (option) receives an additional option of renewing his patent after a certain period of time. For the purpose of this chapter, I will not go into the details of the problems that are associated with the application of the Black and Scholes (1973) formula to patents because of the compound option character of patents. No formalizations will be presented. It should be kept in mind, however, that the real option valuation of patents might even require more complex models than the one presented by Black and Scholes (1973).
10. See for example Griliches (1981), Conolly et al. (1986), Conolly and Hirschey (1988), Cockburn and Griliches (1988), Megna and Klock (1993), Hall et al. (2000) and Chapters 6–9 of the present book.
11. Such cases may be valuations of patents in discrete product technologies held by one-product corporations (for example, biotech patents held by start-ups).
12. See Harhoff et al. (2003). The authors compare asset and renewal values for patents in three different empirically relevant scenarios, namely, (a) in a standard scenario where inventions do not build upon each other in a cumulative way and no blocking power can be exerted by the use of patents, (b) a scenario in which inventions build upon each other in a cumulative manner and where blocking power can be exerted, and (c) a scenario in which a patent protects a substitution technology.
13. From a theoretical standpoint, the value of the underlying of a real option is objective (see, for example, Laux 1993). If the real option was traded, the objective value could be calculated from arbitrage considerations. From a theoretical point, assessing the value of the underlying of a real option using value drivers breaks with real option theory. From a practical standpoint, there is often no other way to pursue the valuation of a 'real option'.
14. See Copeland et al. (1994, pp. 42–4).
15. *Note*: as Pitkethly (1999) correctly mentions, in practice the distinction between a value driver of a patent and its underlying invention is not always feasible (though theoretically desirable of course).
16. Consistent with the literature on technology cycles the more recent models do not assume that returns-per-period are constant but that returns-per-period are subject to the life stage of the underlying technology.
17. See Gilbert and Newberry (1982, p. 521).
18. See Reitzig (2002), ch. 7 for some preliminary empirical evidence that disclosure may also have negative effects on a patent's value in the chemical industry.

IP and strategic decision-making

19. See Schankerman and Pakes (1986, p. 1073).
20. See Lanjouw (1998, p. 697).
21. As Lanjouw and Schankerman (2001) point out, claims also mark potential points of disputes; thus, their theoretical interpretation is more difficult than suggested above. Claims may refer to both the *legal robustness* and the *breadth* of a patent simultaneously. Therefore, they may operationalize opposing effects at the same time. Thus, their suitability to empirically buttress breadth as a value determining parameter is limited.
22. See EPO (1994, p. 109).
23. See EPO (1994, p. 110).
24. The survey shows that many of the studies do not validate indicators of patent value directly. This is due to the fact that in many of the studies the dependent variable of the analysis is not the patent value itself but a value correlate. As a matter of fact, this renders the discussion of the empirical results difficult at times when trying to interpret the correlation between an observable indicator and the patent's value. To a certain extent it appears possible to draw some general conclusions about the validity of the variables tested as indicators of patent value.
25. See Reitzig (2002) for more details.
26. See Reitzig (2002, ch. 4) for a comprehensive discussion.
27. For a detailed discussion see Reitzig (2004).
28. Note that the term 'simplistic' here is only meant to insinuate that the buyer's option model might require simplifying assumptions that render the patent valuation unrealistic (for example, lacking interrelatedness between patents within one portfolio, no compoundedness). The actual estimation of the model using patent indicators is all but trivial from an econometric standpoint.
29. Note that this can be a tricky exercise because option values are not always purely additive. Thus, the option value of the portfolio will not necessarily be the aggregate option value of the individual patents. Consider two patent portfolios in which the individual patents have equal absolute option values. In one portfolio, however, the options are interrelated, in the other they are not. Then, the portfolio values of the two different portfolios will differ. The simple addition of the option values of the individual patents would lead to a useless result for the portfolio value in the case of interrelated options.
30. Reitzig (2003a) describes that for the evaluation of a corporate patent portfolio of 90 semiconductor patents various 'established' indicators did not turn out to be significantly correlated with the patents' values. Forward citations were significant, family size and backward citations were not.
31. Take the following as an example: family size may operationalize the breadth of a patent and it may therefore be positively correlated with the present value of the cash flows. At the same time patent breadth may be positively correlated with a patent's probability to be invalidated or amended (legal volatility). In a first attempt to disentangle these structural effects, Reitzig (2003b) encounters problems of the aforementioned kind.

REFERENCES

Albert, M.B., D. Avery, F. Narin and P. McAllister (1991), 'Direct validation of citation counts as indicators of industrially important patents', *Research Policy*, **20**, 251–9.
Assmann, H.-D. (1985), 'Schadensersatz in mehrfacher Höhe des Schadens', *Betriebs-Berater*, **1985**, 15–25.
Black, F. and M. Scholes (1973), 'The pricing of options and corporate liabilities', *Journal of Political Economy*, May–June, 637–54.
Carpenter, M., M. Cooper and F. Narin (1980), 'Linkage between basic research literature and patents', *Research Management*, March, 30–35.

Cockburn, I. and Z. Griliches (1988), 'Industry effects and appropriability measures in the stock market's valuation of R&D and patents', *American Economic Review*, **78** (2), 419–32.

Cohen, W.M., R.R. Nelson and J.P. Walsh (2000), *Protecting Their Intellectual Assets: Appropriability Conditions and Why U.S. Manufacturing Firms Patent (or not)*, Cambridge, MA: NBER (National Bureau of Economic Research), working paper series.

Conolly, R. and M. Hirschey (1988), 'Market value and patents: a Bayesian approach', *Economics Letters*, **27** (1), 83–7.

Conolly, R., B. Hirsch and M. Hirschey (1986), 'Union Rent Seeking, Intangible Capital, and Market Value of the Firm', *Review of Economics and Statistics*, **68** (4).

Copeland, T., T. Koller and J. Murrin (1994), *Valuation – Measuring and Managing the Value of Companies*, New York, John Wiley & Sons.

Ernst, H., C. Leptien and J. Vitt (2000), 'Inventors are not alike: the distribution of patenting output among industrial R&D personnel', *IEEE Transactions of Engineering Management*, **47** (2), 184–99.

Gallini, N.T. (1992), 'Patent policy and costly imitation', *Rand Journal of Economics*, **23** (1), 52–63.

Geske, R. (1979), 'The valuation of compound options', *Journal of Financial Economics*, **7** (1), 63–81.

Gilbert, R. and D. Newberry (1982), 'Preemptive patenting and the persistence of monopoly', *American Economic Review*, **72** (3), 514–26.

Gilbert, R. and C. Shapiro (1990), 'Optimal patent length and breadth', *Rand Journal of Economics*, **21** (1), 106–12.

Green, J.R. and S. Scotchmer (1995), 'On the division of profit in sequential innovation', *Rand Journal of Economics*, **26** (1), 20–33.

Griliches, Z. (1981), 'Market value, R&D, and patents', *Economic Letters,* **7**, 183–7.

Guellec, D. and B. van Pottelsberghe de la Potterie (2000), *Analysing Patent Grants*, Brussels: Free University.

Hall, B. and R. Ham Ziedonis (2001), 'The patent paradox revisited: an empirical study of patenting in the U.S. semiconductor industry, 1979–1995', *Rand Journal of Economics*, **32**, 101–28.

Hall, B.H., A. Jaffe and M. Trajtenberg (2000), *Market Value and Patent Citations: A First Look*, Cambridge, MA: NBER (National Bureau of Economic Research).

Harabi, N. (1995). 'Appropriability of technical innovations: an empirical analysis', *Research Policy*, **24**, 981–92.

Harhoff, D. and M. Reitzig (2001), 'Strategien zur Gewinnmaximierung bei der Anmeldung von Patenten: Wirtschaftliche und rechtliche Entscheidungsgrößen beim Schutz von Erfindungen', *Zeitschrift für Betriebswirtschaft*, **5**, 509–30.

Harhoff, D. and M. Reitzig (2004), 'Determinants of opposition against EPO patent grants – the case of biotechnology and pharmaceuticals', *International Journal of Industrial Organization*, (22/4), 443–80.

Harhoff, D., F. Scherer and K. Vopel (2003), 'Citations, family size, opposition and the value of patent rights', *Research Policy*, **32** (8), 1343–63.

Heil, U. and M. Roos (1994), 'Zur dreifachen Schadensberechnung bei Übernahme sonderrechtlich nicht geschützer Leistungen', *Gewerblicher Rechtsschutz und Urheberrecht*, **1994**, 26–31.

314   *IP and strategic decision-making*

Karnell, G. (1996), 'Gedanken zur Bemessung von Schadensersatzansprüchen bei Patentverletzungen', *Gerwerblicher Rechtsschutz und Urheberrecht*, **1996**, 335–45.

Klemperer, P. (1990), 'How broad should the scope of patent protection be?', *Rand Journal of Economics*, **21**(1), 113–30.

KPMG (1999), *International Accounting Standards*, Stuttgart: Schäffer-Poeschel.

Lanjouw, J.O. (1998), 'Patent protection in the shadow of infringement: simulation estimations of patent value', *Review of Economic Studies*, **65**, 671–710.

Lanjouw, J.O. and J. Lerner (1998), 'The enforcement of intellectual property rights', *Annales d'Economie et de Statistique*, (49/50), July, 223–46.

Lanjouw, J.O. and M. Schankerman (1999), *The Quality of Ideas: Measuring Innovation with Multiple Indicators*, Cambridge, MA: NBER (National Bureau of Economic Research), reprinted in Lanjouw, J.O. and M. Schankerman (2004), 'Patent quality and research productivity: measuring innovation with multiple indicators', *Economic Journal*, **114** (495), pp. 441–65.

Lanjouw, J.O. and M. Schankerman (2001), 'Characteristics of patent litigation: a window on competition', *Rand Journal of Economics*, **32** (1), 129–51.

Lanjouw, J.O., A. Pakes and J. Putnam (1996), *How to Count Patents and Value Intellectual Property: Uses of Patent Renewal and Application Data*, Boston: NBER.

Laux, C. (1993), 'Handlungsspielräume im Leistungsbereich der Unternehmes: Eine Anwendung der Optionstheorie', *Zeitschrift für betriebswirtschaftliche Forschung*, **45** (11), 933–58.

Lehmann, M. (1988), 'Juristisch-ökonomische Kriterien zur Berechnung des Verletzergewinns bzw. des entgangenen Gewinns', *Betriebs-Berater*, **25**, 1680–87.

Lerner, J. (1994), 'The importance of patent scope: an empirical analysis', *Rand Journal of Economics*, **25** (2), 319–33.

Löcke, J. (1998), 'Erstmalige Aufstellung befreiender IAS-Konzernabschlüsse nach Interpretation SIC-8', *Der Betrieb*, **36**, 1777–80.

Lotka, A.J. (1926), 'The frequency distribution of scientific productivity', *Journal of the Washington Academy of Sciences*, **16** (6), 317–23.

Matutes, C., P. Regibeau and K. Rocket (1996), 'Optimal patent design and the diffusion of innovations', *Rand Journal of Economics*, **27** (1), 60–83.

Megna, P. and M. Klock (1993), 'The impact of intangible capital on Tobin's Q in the semiconductor industry', *American Economic Review*, **83**, 265–9.

Narin, F., E. Noma and R. Perry (1987), 'Patents as indicators of corporate technological strength', *Research Policy*, **16**, 143–55.

Nordhaus, W.D. (1967), *The Optimal Life of a Patent*, Cowes Foundation Discussion Paper, New Haven, CT.

Pakes, A. (1986), 'Patents as options: some estimates of the value of holding European patent stocks', *Econometrica*, **54** (4), 755–84.

Pitkethly, R. (1999), 'The valuation of patents: a review of patent valuation methods with consideration of option based methods and the potential for further research', Judge Institute working paper WP 21/97, Cambridge.

Rahn, G. (1994), 'Patenstrategien japanischer Unternehmen', *Gewerblicher Rechtsschutz und Urheberrecht* (International), **5**, 377–82.

Reitzig, M. (2002), *Die Bewertung von Patentrechten – eine theoretische und empirische Analyse aus Unternehmenssicht*, Wiesbaden: Deutscher Universitaetsverlag.

Reitzig, M. (2003a), 'What determines patent value – insights from the semiconductor industry', *Research Policy*, 32/1, 13–26.

Reitzig, M. (2003b), 'What do patent indicators really measure? A structural test of "novelty" and "inventive step" as determinants of patent profitability', Copenhagen, LEFIC working paper 2003-1.

Reitzig, M. (2004), 'Improving patent valuation methods for management – validating new indicators by analyzing application rationales', *Research Policy*, 33/6/7, 939–57

Rivette, K. and D. Kline (2000), 'Discovering new value in intellectual property', *Harvard Business Review*, January–February, 54–66.

Schankerman, M. and A. Pakes (1986), 'Estimates of the value of patent rights in European countries during the post 1950 period', *Economic Journal*, **96** (384), 1052–76.

Scherer, F.M. (1965), 'Firm size, market structure, opportunity and the output of patented inventions', *American Economic Review*, December (55), 1097–125.

Schildbach, T. (2000), 'Ansatz und Bewertung immaterieller Anlagewerte in W. Ballwieser (ed.), US-amerikanische Rechnungslegung, Stuttgart: Schäffer-Pöschel, pp. 99–138.

Scotchmer, S. and J. Green (1990), 'Novelty and disclosure in patent law', *RAND Journal of Economics*, **21** (1), pp. 131–46.

Sorenson, O. and L. Fleming (2004), 'Science and diffusion of knowledge', *Research Policy*, December, **33** (10), pp. 1615–34.

Teece, D. (1986), 'Profiting from technological innovation: implications for integrating, collaboration, licencing and public policy', *Research Policy*, **15**, 285–305.

Tong, X. and J.D. Frame (1992), 'Measuring national technological performance with patent claims data', *Research Policy*, **23**, 133–41.

Trajtenberg, M. (1990), 'A penny for your quotes: patent citations and the value of innovations', *Rand Journal of Economics*, **21** (1), 172–87.

Vollrath, U. (1983), 'Zur Berücksichtigung der Entwicklungs- and Schutzrechtskosten bei der Bemessung der Schadenersatz-Lizenzgebühr für Patentverletzung', *Gerwerblicher Rechtsschutz and Urheberrecht*, **1983**, 52–6.

Index

Barclays PLC 207, 208, 215
basic research 224, 225, 236, 237, 238, 240, 243
Baum, G. 252
Belgium *see* patenting behaviour of Belgium-based firms study
benchmarking 79, 166, 173, 295, 296, 309
Berne Convention 30, 31
best practice 192–4
Bishop Steering 188–9, 194
Black-Scholes (B-S) option pricing models 276–8, 279, 281, 286–7, 295, 306–7, 308
Bloom, N. 113, 116, 122
blueprints 89, 90
Blundell, R. 115, 118, 122, 148
Bond, S. 120–21
book value of assets 69, 112, 136, 137, 147, 165, 253
Bosworth, D.L. 93, 96, 99, 100, 101, 102, 119, 146, 148, 181–2, 194, 197, 263
brands 51, 133, 152, 155, 194, 196, 197
breach of confidence 29, 36–7
Brealey, R. 273, 274, 278
Brooking, A. 86, 179
Brouwer, E. 224, 226, 228, 229
Buchan, E. 5, 192, 193
Burrone, Esteban 183, 185, 191
Business Council of Australia 168
business models 69–70, 72

call options 258, 275, 277, 284, 285, 286
Cambridge Antibody Technology 183, 191–2
Canadian Performance Reporting Initiative (CPRI) 257
capacity transfer 94–5
capital asset pricing model 273
capitalization 50, 51, 52, 53, 54, 57, 59, 60, 78
see also market valuation
cash flows 41, 50, 273, 275, 287, 288, 294, 295, 308
see also DCF (discounted cash flow); future cash flows; present value of cash flows
Chambré, Peter 192

Ch'ang, Sharyn 194
change 168, 170, 175, 232, 233, 234, 242
see also technological change
Chauvin, K.W. 99, 147
China 5, 8, 197
Choi, J.P. 195–6
citations, patent *see* patent citations
Cochlear 166, 168, 169, 170, 171, 172, 173
Cockburn, I. 113, 115, 116, 118, 122, 148
collaboration *see* alliances; networks; production cartels; R&D collaboration; research consortia; vertical partners
collateral for borrowing 186–7, 250
commercialization
and complementary assets 75–6, 192, 255
and first-mover advantage 76, 154
innovation 132, 184, 188
inventions 255, 269, 284, 285, 300
and patents 119, 151, 261, 284, 300
R&D projects 258, 284
and risk 194
and trademarks 155–6
Committee for Economic Development of Australia 168
communications 31, 232, 233, 239
competences 6, 232, 233, 239, 241, 242, 301
competition 7, 102, 154, 279, 298, 299, 300, 301, 310
competitive advantage 66, 67, 70, 74, 75, 76, 127, 179
competitive strategy 70–72
competitor analysis 166, 173
competitors
IPR monitoring 182–3, 230, 231, 242
and patent disclosures 181
R&D collaboration 226, 227, 228, 237, 238, 240, 241, 243
complementary assets 75–6, 192, 255, 262, 264, 300, 310
complementary resources 251
compositions 30, 182
computers 4–5, 30, 52, 59, 60, 101, 162, 200, 201
concentration, industrial 92–3